DRUMMOYNE'S
GREAT WAR

Drummoyne War Memorial First World War Biographies

Volume 3 1917-1918

BRENDAN BATEMAN

Copyright © 2025 by **Brendan Bateman**

All rights reserved. Apart from fair dealing for the purposes of study, research, criticism or review as permitted under the Copyright Act, no part of this publication may be reproduced, distributed or transmitted in any form or by any means without prior written permission.

Please be aware that this work has been written in Australian English and uses Australian language, spelling, grammar and punctuation conventions. These are notably different to American, Canadian and British language conventions.

The author commenced writing these biographies in 2009, utilising an older citation and referencing system from Trove, consistent with the APA style recommended by the National Archives of Australia (NAA). Variations in newspaper reference formatting, such as italicising *The* in some titles while omitting it in others, reflect the conventions of that period.

Every effort has been made to contact copyright holders to obtain permissions for images and sourced material. The writer will be pleased to amend in future editions any errors or omissions brought to his attention. Extensive references to Red Cross and War Service records are included throughout the text in footnotes. To streamline the presentation and reduce the number of footnotes, the author has occasionally provided a single reference per section.

Please note that URLs in footnotes and the reference list remain live and underlined to ensure accessibility. This allows readers to easily access external resources in the eBook version, coded from the paperback. However, due to the ever-changing nature of websites, some links may become inactive over time. We recommend verifying sources independently if any links appear broken.

The bibliography is included in Volume 3, as the original manuscript, totalling 250,000 + words and 355 images, was divided into three volumes for commercial viability.

The author has adopted the RSL's preferred capitalisation of ANZAC, instead of Anzac.

Please note that some images are very old, which may affect their clarity.

Cover design by Judith San Nicolas
Memorial vector and water colour illustrations by Ann-Marie Bateman
Typeset in Garamond 12 pt/Avenir Pro Light 26 pt
Printed and bound in Australia
Prepared for publication by The Erudite Pen

 A catalogue record for this book is available from the National Library of Australia

Drummoyne's Great War: Drummoyne War Memorial First World War Biographies Volume 3 1917–1918 First Edition

ISBN 9780994335142 black and white; ISBN 9780994335173 colour; eISBN 9781763876804

To Ann-Marie, always.

Contents

Messines 1917 9
Ernest Shannon 17
Sidney Harold Colley 33
George Columbus Ryng 41
Arthur James Vincent 49
Alfred William Potiphar 63
Third Ypres 1917 73
John Kilgour 85
Thomas Charles Price 93
Charles Leslie Thornton 99
Herbert John Wilder 105
Jack Hammond Fitzgerald 113
Stephen John Harrison 123
Russell Thompson Sydney Jarvis MM 131
Frederick Miller 145
Clive Townsend Thompson 153
George Brown 159
Bert Arthur Simpson 167
Joseph Marcus Harwood 177
William Ruffley 187
Joseph Ignatius Connell 203
Hugh McQuat 219
Palestine 1916-1918 229
George Campbell Gear 237
Spring Offensive 1918 247
Gainsford Wilton Evans 257

Robert Alexander Smith	265
Claude Edward Pierpoint	279
John Stephen Coolahan MC	289
Robert James Henderson MC and Bar	301
Bertie George Englert	343
Arvan James Prichard	357
Colin Godfrey Wilson	375
The 100 Days 1918	385
John Michael Joseph Wills	393
John Donald Edwards	405
Albert Bates	413
Harold Kingsley Percival	429
John Walker	443
Mervyn Willoughby Thornton	451
Harold Yabbicom Mortimore	463
Frederick Jordan	473
Commemoration and Rememberance	483
Bibliography	501
Index	507

List of Abbreviations

AAMC	Australian Army Medical Corp
ADBD	Australian Division Base Depot
ADS	Advanced Dressing Station
AFA	Australian Field Artillery
AIF	Australian Imperial Force
ALH	Australian Light Horse
ASC	Army Service Corp
AWM	Australian War Memorial
BDM	Births, Deaths and Marriages Registry
BEF	British Expeditionary Force
Capt.	Captain
CCS	Casualty Clearing Station
CMF	Citizens Military Forces (Militia)
CO	Commanding officer
Cpl	Corporal
CWGC/IWGC	Commonwealth War Graves Commission (also referred to as Imperial War Graves Commission)
FAB	Field Artillery Brigade
GSU	Graves Services Unit
HQ	Headquarters
L/Cpl	Lance Corporal
Lt or Lieut.	Lieutenant
Lt Col.	Lieutenant Colonel
MEF	Mediterranean Expeditionary Force
MDS	Main Dressing Station
NCO	Non-Commissioned Officer
OIC	Officer in Charge, Base Records
Pte	Private
RAMC	Royal Army Medical Corp
RAP	Regimental Aid Post
SB or S/B	Stretcher bearer(s)
Sig.	Signaller

Messines 1917

The main British offensive around Arras came to an end in mid-May 1917. Heightened concerns in relation to the state of the French Army,[1] not to mention the ongoing uncertainty caused by the Russian revolution in March 1917 that had installed a provisional government in place of the Tsarist regime, required the British to assume the lead in future offensive action. The BEF Commander and now Field Marshall, Douglas Haig, had always favoured an attack in Belgian Flanders near Ypres. This was supported by the British Admiralty as way of expelling the Germans from the Channel ports and their submarine bases. Although the planning for an attack focused around Ypres had been considered for some time, the need for the British to take the lead at this stage of the war led to what would be known as the Third Battle of Ypres or simply 'Passchendaele'.

---

[1] Mutinies in the French Army had broken out in early May 1917, resulting in the cancellation of any further attacks as part of the Nivelle offensive, and the replacement of General Nivelle with General Petain on 15 May 1917 as commander of the French Army. Although the fact of the mutinies was largely kept secret until after the war, Haig makes a number of references to private advice received from General Petain and other senior French officers during 1917 regarding French units refusing to go to the front lines and with some soldiers being shot – see for example, *Haig Diaries*, p. 298 (June 7), p. 302 (June 28), p. 329 (September 19) and p. 339 (November 9).

A new tactic was to be deployed as part of the forthcoming offensive – rather than one big offensive like the Somme the year before, this would comprise a number of smaller step-by step-actions, each with limited objectives. The tactic involved the artillery providing a creeping barrage for the advancing infantry, which would not advance beyond the protection of their own artillery. The troops would seize the German positions, and the artillery would then set down a 'box barrage', which would provide protection from anticipated German counter-attacks on the newly captured positions. The artillery would then be brought forward to repeat the process, gradually driving the Germans back through this 'bite and hold' tactic. It was hoped that this strategy would wear the Germans down sufficiently to pose a threat to the German coastal bases of being cut off, forcing a withdrawal.

Before Haig could launch the new offensive, it was decided necessary to make safe the right flank south of Ypres by eliminating a German salient. This would be achieved by capturing the Messines–Wytschaete Ridge and thereby depriving the Germans of the high ground with its commanding views in the area including to Ypres itself. The attack on Messines Ridge would involve the first deployment of the 'bite and hold' strategy.

Preparations for an attack on the Messines section of the front had been in train for several months with numerous underground mines, having been started in July 1916, now complete and packed with enormous quantities of explosives. In all, 19 mines would be exploded under the German positions at the start of the attack, including a number constructed by the 1st Australian Tunnelling Company under the infamous Hill 60. Before the mines were exploded, British General Charles Harington is credited with saying[2]:

---

[2] *Hill 60, Ypres: The Peak of Military Mining* - https://sjmc.gov.au/hill-60-the-peak-of-mine-warfare/ (accessed 18 April 2023).

'Gentlemen, we may not make history tomorrow, but we shall certainly change the geography.'

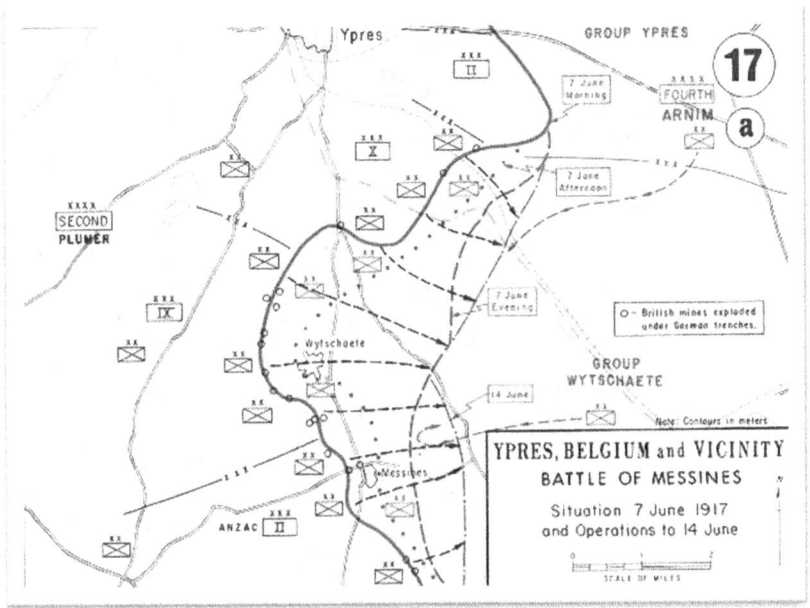

Map of the Battle of Messines, June 1917 (Wikipedia, public domain, accessed 22 April 2023).

The attack would involve nine divisions from the British Second Army under General Sir Herbert Plumer. II ANZAC Corp comprising the 3rd Australian Division, the New Zealand Division and British 25th Division, reinforced by 4th Australian Division, was allocated for the attack on the southern section around Messines itself.

Whereas the other Australian divisions based in Egypt had been reformed and eventually transferred directly to France from March 1916, the 3rd Australian Division had been formed from new recruits in Australia and was sent to England to undertake further training where it was placed under the command of Major-General John Monash. Monash would become one of Australia's most distinguished soldiers during the First World War, having commanded the 4th Infantry Brigade at Gallipoli, promoted to command the 3rd

Australian Division in France (1916–1918) and would eventually be promoted to command the Australian Army Corps in 1918.

Having only arrived on the Western Front in December 1916, the Battle of Messines would mark the 3rd Australian Division's first major engagement. By this stage the other Australian divisions had seen active service both in the Middle East and in France. This would lead to the 3rd Division to be referred to derisorily as the 'Lark Hill Lancers', the 'Neutrals' or the 'Deep Thinkers' on account of it being full of volunteers who had waited until late 1915 or early 1916 before enlisting in the AIF and finally committed to the fighting in France.[3]

Portrait of Lieutenant General Sir John Monash circa 1918. AWM AO2697.

---

[3] Bean, *Official History*, Vol. 4, p. 561.

The 3rd Australian Division's objective was to capture the southern shoulder of Messines Ridge and was the southern most of the nine attacking divisions. The plan for the 3rd Division's role in the attack on Messines was code named 'Magnum Opus' with training and conferences going over the particulars of the plan occupying the attention of many of the battalions engaged.

The attack was planned in detail including the construction of huge models built behind the lines, which was to be studied by the troops. Large quantities of munitions and artillery were packed into the rear areas with seven days of bombardment commencing on 31 May 1917. With preparations for the coming attack in full swing, the artillery increased its rate and frequency of fire on the Germans' strong points. The Germans, anticipating the attack, bombarded the approaches that would be taken by the attacking troops with phosgene gas, necessitating respirators to be worn during the approach march[4] and which made the task one of nightmarish difficulty. Some 500 men of the 3rd Australian Division would succumb to gas on the approach as they moved through Ploegsteert Wood.[5]

At 3:10 a.m. on 7 June 1917, the 19 powerful mines exploded under the German trenches along the Messines–Wytschaete Ridge.[6] Supported by great volumes of artillery fire[7] the attacking troops surged forward to capture the enemy positions. The creeping box barrage provided cover to the attacking infantry. German concrete 'pillboxes' presented a new and difficult obstacle, which had to be overcome often by individual acts of bravery. Anxious to prove itself worthy of the reputation of the other veteran Australian divisions, the 3rd Australian Division made a very successful attack alongside the New Zealand Division just south of the Messines village. Within two hours of the opening of the attack, the 3rd Division and those adjacent

---

[4] 37th Battalion Unit Diary June 1917 - https://www.awm.gov.au/collection/C1345112?image=15
[5] Bean, *Official History*, Vol. 4, p. 353.
[6] Haig estimated some one million pounds of explosives was used – *Haig Diaries*, p. 298 (June 7).
[7] Some 2,500 guns opened fire on the enemy's positions – *Haig Diaries*, p. 298 (June 7).

to it had secured their objectives including capturing Messines itself. Although the attacking units secured their objectives, the well-positioned and established German machine guns took their toll, temporarily forcing back the lines of men looking at extending the gains.[8]

Troops quickly entrenched to secure the captured positions, protected by artillery that broke up the emerging German counter-attacks. The 4th Australian Division under Major-General William Holmes moved up to launch the afternoon attack, which commenced at 3 p.m. to secure the German Oosttaverne Line along the ridge, to all but eliminate the German salient south of Ypres, and opening the way for the main offensive at Ypres planned for July. Although some fighting continued, the result was virtually decided by the end of the first evening with the ridge being taken and enemy counter-attacks repulsed.

The Battle for Messines was considered one of the more successful offensives of the war, attributed to its extensive planning and preparation. The objective was largely secured within several hours of the attack commencing, and successfully defended against German counter-attacks. Haig noted in his diary that the operation was the most successful he had yet undertaken.[9] Charles Bean wryly commented on the success of the Battle of Messines[10]:

> The working out of the 2nd Army's plan was as smooth as that of previous British offensives had been confused.

> Despite the comparative success of the attack, Australian casualties were still significant with the 3rd and 4th Australian Divisions suffering 4,122 and 2,677 casualties respectively.[11]

---

[8] 37th Battalion Unit Diary June 1917 - https://www.awm.gov.au/collection/C1345112?image=16
[9] *Haig Diaries*, p. 298 (June 7).
[10] Bean, *Official History*, Vol. 4, p. 353.
[11] Bean, *Official History*, Vol. 4, p. 682.

Ernest Shannon

Lieutenant

34th Battalion, 9th Infantry Brigade, 3rd Australian Division

Killed in action 1 June 1917, Ploegsteert, Belgium

Buried Strand Military Cemetery, Ploegsteert, Belgium

Dearest Ernest our beloved son and brother gave his life for us

Studio portrait of Ernest Shannon. Source - https://harrowercollection.com.au/category/pre-world-war-one-new-south-wales/26th-infantry-regiment/ (accessed 22 April 2023).

Ernest Shannon was born on 14 September 1890 in Wagga Wagga to James and Mary Shannon.[12] Ernest attended Wagga Wagga High School and while there is reported by his mother Mary[13] to have received first prizes at the Wagga Show and School for essays entitled 'The Commonwealth in relation to the Empire' and 'Why I am Proud to be an Australian'. In 1908 Ernest gained a scholarship to attend Teachers Training College, Sydney, where he was reported to be a keen sportsman, travelling to Melbourne to compete against the Victorian Teachers College. He eventually took up a teaching position at Drummoyne Public School.

Photograph of Ernest Shannon. Source - https://canadabayheritage.asn.au/a-last-goodbye/ (accessed 22 April 2023).

In 1912, Ernest is said to have matriculated and entered the University of Sydney where he enrolled in a Bachelor of Arts. Ernest had also served as a lieutenant in the senior cadets and in 1915 was a temporary lieutenant in the 26th Infantry CMF,[14] having passed courses in military science, field engineering, military typography, tactics and imperial defence & history.

---

[12] NSW BDM Registration No. 35001/1890.
[13] http://beyond1914.sydney.edu.au/profile/4008/ernest-shannon (accessed 12 July 2018).
[14] MILITARY FORCES OF THE COMMONWEALTH. (1915, July 10). *Commonwealth of Australia Gazette* (National: 1901-1973), p. 1308. Retrieved April 20, 2023, from http://nla.gov.au/nla.news-article232465143

While teaching at Drummoyne Public School and having just completed his second year of a Bachelor of Arts, Ernest applied for a commission in the AIF on 26 November 1915 at the age of 25 years and two months.[15] At the time, his family was living at *Dalswinton*, Tavistock Street, Drummoyne.[16]

No.6 School of Instruction for Officers at Sydney. Lieutenant Ernest Shannon is in the fifth row, seventh from the left. Source - *Australian Town and Country Journal* (1915, November 24), http://nla.gov.au/nla.news-article263751966

Ernest was commissioned as a second lieutenant in the 34th Battalion, which was gazetted on 3 February 1916.[17] The 34th Battalion had been formed earlier in the year at a camp established at the Maitland Showground in New South Wales. It was planned that the bulk of the battalion's recruits would be drawn from the Maitland area and thus it was dubbed 'Maitland's Own'.[18] The battalion embarked from Sydney on HMAT A20 *Hororata* on 2 May 1916 as part of the new units that were to form the 3rd Australian Division. Ernest disembarked at

---

[15] War service records accessible at https://recordsearch.naa.gov.au/SearchNRetrieve/Interface/ViewImage.aspx?B=8077996
[16] In 1919, his parents moved to *Simla*, Marmion Road, Abbotsford.
[17] AUSTRALIAN IMPERIAL FORCE. (1916, February 3). *Commonwealth of Australia Gazette* (National: 1901-1973), p. 217. Retrieved April 20, 2023, from http://nla.gov.au/nla.news-article232467793
[18] https://www.awm.gov.au/collection/U51474 The first recruits for the 34th Battalion in fact hailed from the far north-west of the state and arrived at Maitland after joining a recruiting march that began at Walgett. These men were known as the 'Wallabies'.

Plymouth in England on 23 June 1916 and proceeded to the Australian training base at Salisbury, Wiltshire, where he would remain for the next five months training. During that time, he joined the Lyndhurst Bombing School where he was commended by the commander of the 11th Brigade for his enthusiasm and efficiency as an instructor involved in training some 1,200 men in bombing. On 7 August 1916, Ernest returned from the Bombing School having been recently promoted to lieutenant.[19]

The 34th Battalion, along with other elements of the 3rd Division, embarked for France from Southampton on 21 November 1916, arriving in Le Harve the next day.[20] Companies of the battalion then entrained for Outtersteene, where they went into billets. Within a week, the 33rd and 34th Battalions were the first to move straight into the front lines and begin to experience fighting on the Western Front.[21] Based in the relatively quiet sector of Armentieres for the next several months, the battalion fell into a routine of rotating in and out of the lines, during which time it experienced spasmodic shelling from artillery and trench mortars as winter descended on the front.

In late December 1916, Ernest marched out to 2nd ANZAC School of Training where he is likely to have undertaken advanced training, which would have come as a welcome relief from the cold and wintery conditions in the front lines. He returned to his battalion on 23 January 1917 as it continued its routine, alternating between time in the trenches and performing fatigue duties in reserve positions and billets.

The intensity of activity increased during May as the weather improved, and with it the anticipation of a German trench raid[22], which

---

[19] AUSTRALIAN IMPERIAL FORCE. (1917, January 4). *Commonwealth of Australia Gazette* (National: 1901-1973), p. 9. Retrieved April 20, 2023, from http://nla.gov.au/nla.news-article232452578
[20] 34th Battalion Unit Diary November 1916 - https://www.awm.gov.au/collection/C1344212?image=2
[21] 34th Battalion Unit Diary November 1916 - https://www.awm.gov.au/collection/C1344212?image=6
[22] 34th Battalion Unit Diary May 1917 - https://www.awm.gov.au/collection/C1344236?image=6

eventually occurred on 17 May but was successfully repulsed.[23] The Germans made another attempted raid the next evening with a raiding party of about 200 men, and this too was broken up by artillery, machine gun and rifle fire, with the enemy withdrawing after 'being completely demoralised' leaving many dead and wounded in no man's land.[24] Ernest missed both actions as on 12 May 1917 he had been granted 'indulgence leave' to Paris and did not return until 22 May 1917.

On 20 May, the battalion moved to the Belgian Flanders sector of the front where it took up positions at Ploegsteert Wood, just south of Messines on the night of 23–24 May.[25] This was a prelude to the 3rd Australian Division's first major engagement of the war, the attack on Messines–Wytschaete Ridge, which was planned to commence on 7 June 1917. The 34th Battalion entered the front-line trenches on the night of 26–27 May when it relieved the 33rd Battalion. Ordered to send out patrols and undertake trench raids in preparation for the forthcoming attack, Ernest furnished a report of a patrol that he led on the night of 28–29 May,[26] with him and five other men successfully entering a German trench undetected. His report stated:

> Having travelled about 75 yards, I heard a slight tapping around the corner where I saw what I took to be a single Hun standing on the parapet fire step. I cried 'Hands Up' which he promptly did at the same time yelling in a terrified manner at the same time another Hun who was crouched behind the first brought his rifle to the ready and started backing down the trench.

---

[23] 34th Battalion Unit Diary May 1917 - https://www.awm.gov.au/collection/C1344236?image=7
[24] 34th Battalion Unit Diary May 1917 - https://www.awm.gov.au/collection/C1344236?image=9
[25] 34th Battalion Unit Diary May 1917 - https://www.awm.gov.au/collection/C1344236?image=24
[26] 34th Battalion Unit Diary May 1917 - https://www.awm.gov.au/collection/C1344236?image=26

I immediately fired and he returned a shot, after which I got 3 more in and he fell backwards. ... Hearing running along the trench from each direction and to avoid being trapped, we hopped over the parapet. We lay amongst the wire for some time, being fired at from the trench but got clear.

To his disappointment, Ernest did not get the chance to 'bag' a prisoner.[27]

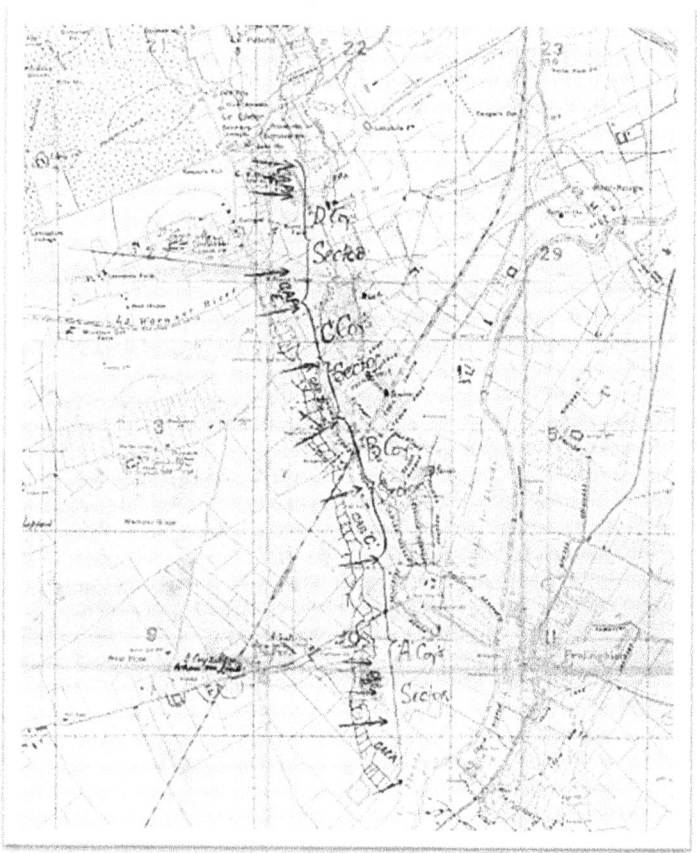

Map of 34th Battalion's dispositions near Le Touquet and Ploegsteert Wood May 1917. Source - 34th Battalion Unit Diary May 1917 - https://www.awm.gov.au/collection/C1344236?image=36

---

[27] Statement of Sam Scott Taylor (563) dated 4 August 1917 - https://www.awm.gov.au/collection/R1501273

On the next raid in the early hours of 1 June 1917, Ernest was not so lucky. Ernest penned a brief letter to his mother in the early hours of 1 June[28]:

My Darling Mother,   1/6/17

This is just a last line in case I do not come back tonight. In 20 minutes I am going on a most dangerous enterprise into the enemy trenches. One never knows one's luck and this, my dearest one on earth, is to say good-bye, in case I go to the Great Beyond. With last love and kisses,

Ernest   12:40 am

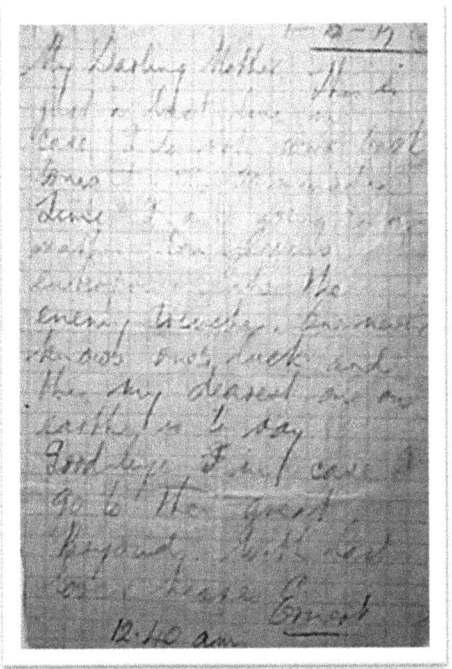

Letter written by Ernest Shannon to his mother just before the attack in which he would be killed. Source - https://canadabayheritage.asn.au/a-last-goodbye/ (accessed 22 April 2023).

---

[28] https://canadabayheritage.asn.au/a-last-goodbye/ (accessed 22 April 2023)

The 34th Battalion Unit Diary describes the events of the trench raid in which Ernest was involved[29]:

PLOEGSTEERT WOOD 2:30 am. Small silent Raid with a strength of 2 Officers, 2 NCO's and 22 men was put over from 'B' Coy's Sector against the enemy's front line. Object to gain identification Kill Bosches and destroy dugouts. The Raiders were divided into two parties. Lieut. Shannon with 12 men to enter the enemy trench from the right. Lieut. Brodie and 12 men to enter from the left. Both parties to work towards the centre.

The enterprise was entirely successful and was only marred by the death of Lieut. Shannon, a very gallant and efficient officer.

The right party entered enemy's trench without opposition but after bombing the first dugout, were attacked by a number of the enemy who issued from the rear exit of a second dugout. Lt. Shannon was killed by a bomb thrown by one of this party. Our men immediately attacked the enemy and forced them back to the dugout, where they destroyed them by throwing in bombs.

The left party (Lieut. Brodie's) met considerable opposition in passing through the enemy wire, but succeeded in entering the trench and destroying two dugouts and the enemy who occupied them.

As it was now broad daylight and the enemy's opposition increased, the parties withdrew to our own front line. The men of Lt. Shannon's party displayed great determination and bravery in bringing back his body in broad daylight under heavy fire from the enemy's trenches.

---

[29] 34th Battalion Unit Diary June 1917 - https://www.awm.gov.au/collection/C1356843?image=2

The original time set down for this enterprise was 1-30 am but by order of higher authority it was postponed to 2-30 am to coincide with other enterprises which were supported by artillery fire on our right flank.

As our own enterprise was a silent one, and it was broad daylight at 3 am, this only allowed 30 minutes for the crossing of 'No Mans Land', the negotiation of the enemy's wire and the cleaning up of his trenches. This restriction of time was a great handicap to the enterprise.

… Lieut. Shannon buried in military cemetery in rear of the wood.

A transcription of the same report that appears in the University of Sydney Book of Remembrance[30] states that Ernest was killed by a bomb 'thrown by one of <u>his</u> party'. This amendment may have been influenced by some of the accounts obtained by the Red Cross, but the report in the unit diary, although not entirely clear, appears to use the word 'this' to convey that the bomb was thrown by the Germans who emerged from the dug-out.

Ernest's name appeared in the 313th casualty list published in late June 1917 as having been killed in action.[31] The following notice appeared in the *Albury Banner and Wodonga Express* on 29 June 1917[32]:

---

[30] http://beyond1914.sydney.edu.au/profile/4008/ernest-shannon
[31] AUSTRALIA'S ROLL OF HONOR. (1917, June 22). *The Age* (Melbourne, Vic.: 1854-1954), p. 8. Retrieved April 20, 2023, from http://nla.gov.au/nla.news-article154974334n ; FALLEN HEROES. (1917, June 22). *The Daily Telegraph* (Sydney, NSW: 1883-1930), p. 6. Retrieved April 20, 2023, from http://nla.gov.au/nla.news-article239390217
[32] AT THE FRONT AND AT HOME. (1917, June 29). The *Albury Banner and Wodonga Express* (NSW: 1860-1938), p. 19. Retrieved April 20, 2023, from http://nla.gov.au/nla.news-article99862748

> Lieutenant Ernest Shannon has been killed in France. He was the second son of Mr. and Mrs. James Shannon, Drummoyne, and was in his 27th year. He received his early education at Wagga, where his parents lived some years ago, and later joined the teaching staff of the Drummoyne Public School, which position he gave up on securing his commission.

In circumstances where there was a contemporaneous record in the unit diary of the events surrounding Ernest's death and the location of his grave, the Red Cross surprisingly interviewed no fewer than 44 individuals concerning his fate.[33] Some of the men interviewed were present on the raid whereas some others reported what they had been told by others. There are a number of discrepancies among the accounts as to whether Ernest was killed by one of his party's own bombs or that thrown by the Germans,[34] or even by machine gun fire.[35]

One account reported that a man in Ernest's party threw a bomb, which a German picked up before it exploded and threw it back, killing him,[36] while another stated that one of the bombs Ernest had thrown bounced back and killed him.[37] Based on the statements of those who were clearly with Ernest in the trench during the raid, it is clear that he was killed by a bomb thrown by the Germans that exploded, badly wounding him in the upper right leg, with some

---

[33] Australian Red Cross Wounded and Missing Files - https://www.awm.gov.au/collection/R1501273
[34] The accounts that he was killed by one of the party's own bombs appears to be based on the report dated 16 August 1917 of Sergeant Frederick Seth (178) who does not appear to have witnessed the incident as he states, 'it is believed he was killed by one of his own bombs' - Australian Red Cross Wounded and Missing Files - https://www.awm.gov.au/collection/R1501273
[35] Statement of Private McCannon (2365) dated 6 December 1917 - Australian Red Cross Wounded and Missing Files - https://www.awm.gov.au/collection/R1501273. There is no record of a Private McCannon with this regimental number. It may be James Joseph McCannon (2626) who was in the 36th Battalion.
[36] Statement of Private Patrick L Jordan (2340) dated 1 August 1917 - Australian Red Cross Wounded and Missing Files - https://www.awm.gov.au/collection/R1501273
[37] Statement of Private Alexander Wells (912) dated 20 July 1917 - Australian Red Cross Wounded and Missing Files - https://www.awm.gov.au/collection/R1501273

accounts stating that his leg was blown off or almost severed.[38] Private Ferdinand J Walsh (2691) reported being told by a Private M Morring that he had carried Ernest over his shoulder back to the battalion's lines, but he died while being carried back.[39]

What is not in dispute, however, was Ernest's bravery. Many of the informants volunteered comments that Ernest was notorious for his bravery, who was always up for a dangerous job, with the men 'well content when he was in charge of a hazardous undertaking'.[40] One simply said, 'Shannon will do me'.[41] Another stated that he was one 'of our best officers – he was frightened of nothing'[42] and others described him as very game,[43] perhaps a bit too game.[44] Ernest was buried later in the day, presided over by Chaplain McCook with all officers of the battalion present.[45]

A brief family notice was published on 16 June 1917[46]:

---

[38] Statement of Private George Colchin (387) dated 15 August 1917; Statement of Captain Walter W Matthews dated 17 August 1917; Statement of Sergeant Major Richie M McCormack (1190) dated 14 August 1917 - Australian Red Cross Wounded and Missing Files - https://www.awm.gov.au/collection/R1501273

[39] Statement of Private Ferdinand J Walsh (2691) dated 8 August 1917 - Australian Red Cross Wounded and Missing Files - https://www.awm.gov.au/collection/R1501273. There is no record of a Private M Morring having enlisted in the AIF and a subsequent note on the Red Cross files records the name of Michael Moran, a private in 1st Platoon, A Company in the 34th Battalion. There is no record of a Pte Michael Moran as being in 34th Battalion.

[40] Statement of Quartermaster Sergeant Alfred McGrath (852) dated 4 August 1917; Private Roger B Whelan (2015) in a statement dated 6 December 1917 reported that Ernest used to go on all the 'suicide missions' - Australian Red Cross Wounded and Missing Files - https://www.awm.gov.au/collection/R1501273

[41] Statement of Quartermaster Sergeant Alfred McGrath (852) dated 4 August 1917 - Australian Red Cross Wounded and Missing Files - https://www.awm.gov.au/collection/R1501273

[42] Statement of George H Lyndon (2610) dated 2 August 1918 - Australian Red Cross Wounded and Missing Files - https://www.awm.gov.au/collection/R1501273

[43] Statement of Corporal Hearty dated 27 December 1917; Statement of Private Roger B Whelan (2015) dated 6 December 1917 - Australian Red Cross Wounded and Missing Files - https://www.awm.gov.au/collection/R1501273

[44] Statement of Private McCannon (2365) dated 6 December 1917 - Australian Red Cross Wounded and Missing Files - https://www.awm.gov.au/collection/R1501273

[45] Statement of Lt Frederick M Waugh (4559) dated 4 August 1917 - Australian Red Cross Wounded and Missing Files - https://www.awm.gov.au/collection/R1501273

[46] Family Notices (1917, June 16). *The Daily Telegraph* (Sydney, NSW: 1883-1930), p. 10. Retrieved April 20, 2023, from http://nla.gov.au/nla.news-article239386645 ; Family Notices (1917, June 16). *The Sydney Morning Herald* (NSW: 1842-1954), p. 12. Retrieved April 20, 2023, from http://nla.gov.au/nla.news-article15709060

SHANNON — Killed In action, 1st June, 1917, Lieutenant Ernest Shannon, aged 26 years 9 months, son of Mr. and Mrs. James Shannon, Tavistock Street, Drummoyne. To know him was to love him.

A more detailed personal notice was published on 22 June 1917 reporting on Ernest's death[47]:

The friends of the late Lieutenant Ernest Shannon have received word that he was killed in action in France on June 1. This promising young officer was the second son of Mr. and Mrs James Shannon, Tavistock Street, Drummoyne, and was in his 27th year. He received his early education in Wagga Wagga, and later joined the teaching staff of the Drummoyne Public School, which position he gave up on securing his commission. He sailed for England about 12 months ago, and, after a probationary period at Salisbury, left for the western front early in the year. He was most successful as a teacher, his school squad winning the Challenge Shield in 1914 and 1915. On the news of his death reaching them, all his late scholars stood up with bared and bowed heads, as a token of respect to the memory of their late loved master. He had a promising career before him at the Sydney University, where he did fine work in his various classes. Lieutenant Shannon is a nephew of Major W. T. Charley, now with his regiment in Egypt, and of Major Philip Charley, of Belmont Park, Richmond, New South Wales.

On 25 July 1917, Ernest's photograph was published in *The Sydney Morning Herald* with a brief tribute to him, but which averted to Ernest having been awarded the Croix de Guerre.[48]

---

[47] PERSONAL. (1917, June 22). *The Daily Telegraph* (Sydney, NSW: 1883-1930), p. 6. Retrieved April 20, 2023, from http://nla.gov.au/nla.news-article239390203
[48] A SYDNEY HERO. (1917, July 25). *The Sydney Morning Herald* (NSW: 1842-1954), p. 14. Retrieved April 20, 2023, from http://nla.gov.au/nla.news-article15760644

Clipping from *The Sydney Morning Herald*, 25 July 1917, page 14. Source - https://canadabayheritage.asn.au/a-last-goodbye/

Ernest's mother Mary wrote to Sydney University in September 1917 to provide information to the President of the Sydney University Union for the War Memorial Section, which included a clipping of a personal notice published on 22 June 1917.[49] Personal and family notices were also published on the anniversary of Ernest's death in 1918[50]:

---

[49] http://beyond1914.sydney.edu.au/profile/4008/ernest-shannon (accessed 12 July 2018).
[50] Family Notices (1918, June 1). *The Sydney Morning Herald* (NSW: 1842-1954), p. 11. Retrieved April 20, 2023, from http://nla.gov.au/nla.news-article15772316 . The Latin phrase *aut vincere aut mori* translates as 'either to conquer or to die'. Further family notices were published in Ernest's anniversary in 1919 – see Family Notices (1919, June 2). *The Sydney*

SHANNON - In fond remembrance of our gallant teacher, Lieut Ernest Shannon, of Drummoyne School, killed in action France June 1, 1917. Inserted by L Simpson, W Wyatt, and L Tillett.

SHANNON - A sad token of everlasting love to the memory of our dear son Lieut. Ernest Shannon, 34th Batt, killed in action, June 1, 1917. Sadly missed and deeply mourned by his loving mother and father, M and J Shannon Drummoyne.

SHANNON - In sad and loving memory of our dear and only brother, Lieut Ernest Shannon, killed in action in France, June 1, 1917. Inserted by his loving brother and sister in law, Phil and Mysie Shannon, Cootamundra.

SHANNON - In ever loving memory of our darling brother, Lieut, Ernest Shannon, killed in action in France, 1st June 1917. Aut vincere aut mori. Inserted by his loving sisters Ethel, Jean, Eva.

Apart from the reference in the notice published on 25 July 1917, there is a suggestion in correspondence from Mary Shannon and recorded on the Sydney University Book of Remembrance that Ernest had been awarded the Croix de Guerre. In a letter dated 3 May 1917 to Mary Shannon, the OIC advised that it had received no official advice that he had been awarded the honour, and there is no record that this was in fact the case.

Ernest is buried at Strand Military Cemetery, Ploegsteert, Belgium. He is also commemorated on the Parramatta NSW Public School Teachers Honour Roll[51] and the Presbyterian Church Drummoyne Roll of Honour.[52]

Morning Herald (NSW: 1842-1954), p. 8. Retrieved April 20, 2023, from http://nla.gov.au/nla.news-article15841480
[51] https://vwma.org.au/explore/people/113142 (accessed 22 April 2023).
[52] https://www.warmemorialsregister.nsw.gov.au/content/presbyterian-church-drummoyne-roll-honour

Photograph of the wooden cross erected over the grave of Ernest Shannon.
Source - https://canadabayheritage.asn.au/a-last-goodbye/

Photograph of the grave of Ernest Shannon at Strand Military Cemetery, Ploegsteert, Belgium (author, 2018).

Sidney Harold Colley

Private No. 38

34th Battalion, 9th Infantry Brigade, 3rd Australian Division

Killed in action 7 June 1917, Messines, Belgium

No known grave. Commemorated the Ypres (Menin Gate) Memorial

Sidney Harold Colley was born at Inverell in about 1896,[53] one of five children of Charles and Sarah Anne Colley.[54] His enlistment papers[55] record his age at the time of enlistment as 21 years and 2 months, which would mean he would have been born around September 1894. Sidney may have intentionally lied about his age in order to enlist without parental consent since according to the Honour Roll Circular completed by his wife Maude, she gave his age at the time of his death as 19 years and 7 months, which would make it about November 1896.

Sidney was born and had attended school at the town of Elsmore near Inverell, and was a blacksmith by profession, although his wife noted that he had also worked in mines.

Sidney joined the AIF on 29 November 1915 at Narrabri[56] and appears to have enlisted as part of the 'Wallabies' recruitment march, which arrived in Newcastle on 8 January 1916. Plans to continue the march onto Sydney were cancelled by military authorities who wished to use the marchers as the basis of a new locally-raised battalion.[57] On his enlistment application, Sidney stated that he was not married and gave his mother Sarah as his next of kin who was then living at Ross Hill, Inverell. She subsequently moved to 7 College Street, Drummoyne.

In a letter dated 17 October 1918, Maude Colley advised the OIC that she had married Sidney on the day before he embarked for overseas with registration records showing that Sidney married Martha S M Robinson in Drummoyne in 1916.[58] Sidney's service records have

---

[53] NSW BDM Registration No. 32095/1897. Based on the information available it is more likely that Sidney was born at the end of 1896 but his birth not registered until 1897. It is noted that according to the official birth registration details, his first name was spelt Sydney.
[54] Sidney's siblings were Louis R (16799/1894), Ernest A (33163/1895), Lillian R (4020/1900) and Vetress I (32353/1902).
[55] War service records accessible at https://recordsearch.naa.gov.au/SearchNRetrieve/Interface/ViewImage.aspx?B=3270869
[56] War service records accessible at https://recordsearch.naa.gov.au/SearchNRetrieve/Interface/ViewImage.aspx?B=3270869&S=1
[57] https://www.awm.gov.au/articles/encyclopedia/recruiting_march/wallabies (accessed 22 April 2023).
[58] NSW BDM Registration No. 5655/1916.

an entry recording that a marriage certificate had been produced and Mrs Maude Colley of *Daphne*, 74 Belgrave Street, Neutral Bay, was accordingly recorded as his wife on the service records. On the war pension records, in addition to a Martha Sylvia Maud Colley being noted as his wife, there is also noted a child, Rita Alice Colley, as being entitled to receive a war pension on account of her father's service. Registration records show that Rita was born in 1916[59] and may have been the reason for the hasty marriage before Sidney's embarkation for overseas.

Sidney was assigned to the 34th Battalion, which was in the process of being established at the Maitland Showground.[60] It was planned that the bulk of the battalion's recruits would be drawn from the Maitland district; however, the first recruits hailed from the far north-west and arrived in Maitland after joining a recruitment march that began in Walgett. The 34th Battalion became part of the 9th Brigade of the 3rd Australian Division.

The day after Sidney's marriage to Maude, the 34th Battalion embarked from Sydney on HMAT A20 *Hororata* on 2 May 1916, bound for England. Sidney and the rest of the battalion disembarked at Plymouth on 23 June 1916. The 34th Battalion undertook further training in England before it embarked at Southampton for northern France in November 1916. The battalion served mainly in the nursery sector around Armentieres acclimatising to the Western Front during the winter of 1916–1917.

It may have been in frustration to the lack of action that resulted in Sidney showing some ill-discipline. In March 1917, Private Colley was charged with failing to report at a place of rendezvous when instructed by a senior officer. He was awarded 14 days' Field Punishment No. 2 by the commanding officer of the 34th Battalion, Lt Col Malcolm St John Lamb, on 27 March 1917, serving time in detention barracks in Armentieres.

---

[59] NSW BDM Registration No. 44217/1916.
[60] 34th Battalion Unit History - https://www.awm.gov.au/collection/U51474

The 34th Battalion saw its first major action in the Ypres sector in Belgium in June 1917 when the 3rd Australian Division was committed as part of the initial attacking force during the Battle of Messines. The attack, which commenced on 7 June, would be Sidney's first and last day in action. Sidney's name would appear among those killed in action in the casualty lists published in July 1917.[61] On 6 July 1917, a personal notice was published in The *Inverell Times*[62]:

PRIVATE SID COLLEY.

Mr. Ernest Colley, of Inverell, was informed of the sad news yesterday that his brother, Private Sid Colley, had been killed in action on June 7th. Deceased who was just 19 years of age, is survived by a wife and young child, having been married just prior to enlisting. The late Private Colley joined the 'Wallabies', taking part in that contingent's well known route march from Narrabri. He had been in France since November, and had seen a good deal of fighting. Another brother, Private Louis Colley, is still in the firing line. Deceased's mother resides in Sydney.

There is little information regarding the circumstances on Sidney's death, just a brief cryptic note in the Red Cross records - 'Buried old No Man's Land in our wire in front of Anton's Farm 1 ½ mile W.S.W. of Messines'.[63] This was based on a certificate provided by AIF Headquarters on 12 July 1918.

---

[61] 323rd LIST. (1917, July 20). *The Land* (Sydney, NSW: 1911-1954), p. 13. Retrieved April 22, 2023, from http://nla.gov.au/nla.news-article102889419 ; New South Wales. (1917, July 18). *Australian Town and Country Journal* (Sydney, NSW: 1870-1919), p. 15. Retrieved April 22, 2023, from http://nla.gov.au/nla.news-article263768173

[62] PRIVATE SID COLLEY. (1917, July 6). The *Inverell Times* (NSW: 1899-1907, 1909-1954), p. 4. Retrieved April 22, 2023, from http://nla.gov.au/nla.news-article183592005. Similar notices appeared in Inverell's "Black Thursday." (1917, July 7). *Daily Observer* (Tamworth, NSW: 1917-1920), p. 8. Retrieved April 22, 2023, from http://nla.gov.au/nla.news-article103738088 , THE KURRAJONGS (1917, July 10). *The Farmer and Settler* (Sydney, NSW: 1906-1955), p. 2. Retrieved April 22, 2023, from http://nla.gov.au/nla.news-article116639622 and INVERELL MOURNS. (1917, July 7). *The Daily Telegraph* (Sydney, NSW: 1883-1930), p. 10. Retrieved April 22, 2023, from http://nla.gov.au/nla.news-article239370336

[63] Australian Red Cross Wounded and Missing Files - https://www.awm.gov.au/collection/R1481316

In about September 1918, Maude Colley wrote to the OIC noting that she had not received any of Sidney's personal belongings, even though she had received notice from the Red Cross confirming his death and place of burial. In its reply dated 11 October 1918, in addition to noting that it was very unlikely that any personal effects would be recovered, the OIC advised Maude that on his enlistment, Sidney was a single man and had nominated his mother as his next of kin. The OIC advised that if she wanted to be noted on the records as 'Stated to be Wife' it would be necessary for her to forward their marriage certificate 'together with evidence that you were not divorced or legally separated'.[64]

On 17 October 1918, Maude responded to the OIC's letter furnishing her original marriage certificate. In its letter dated 23 October 1918, the OIC confirmed that Maude had been noted on Sidney's records as his wife.[65]

Even though there was a record of the location of Sidney's burial during the battle, his grave was not located after the war and Sidney's name was added to an addenda panel to the Ypres (Menin Gate) Memorial commemorating those killed in Belgian Flanders with no known grave. In August 1923 a piece of district news was published in The *Inverell Times*[66]:

DISTRICT NEWS

LONG PLAIN.

HONORING SOLDIERS.

---

[64] War service records accessible at https://recordsearch.naa.gov.au/SearchNRetrieve/Interface/ViewImage.aspx?B=3270869&S=1
[65] War service records accessible at https://recordsearch.naa.gov.au/SearchNRetrieve/Interface/ViewImage.aspx?B=3270869&S=1
[66] DISTRICT NEWS (1923, August 24). The *Inverell Times* (NSW: 1899-1907, 1909-1954), p. 7. Retrieved April 22, 2023, from http://nla.gov.au/nla.news-article183547954

About fifty of the residents of Long Plain gathered on Saturday afternoon at the Long Plain Memorial Hall to witness the planting of kurrajong trees in commemoration of the six Long Plain boys who lost their lives in the Great War.

Their names are: — Robert Worgan, Thomas McKenzie, Sydney Colley, Walter Winkworth, Harold Dix, William Kent.

Mrs. Prince planted the first tree in memory of her son, Robert Worgan; Mrs. T. Mitchell for her nephew, Thomas McKenzie; Mrs. Leach for her brother, Walter Winkworth; Mr. Lowrey Bell for his cousin, Sydney Colley; Mrs. Marquhardt for her nephew, Harold Dix; Mr. T. G. A. Mitchell for his old friend, William Kent.

At the close of the function afternoon tea was provided by the ladies.

Sidney's brother Louis had enlisted in August 1915 and was originally assigned as a reinforcement to the 1st Battalion but eventually served with the 5th Pioneer Battalion, returning to Australia in April 1919.[67]

Sidney is one of the most commemorated soldiers on the Drummoyne War Memorial as he is also commemorated on the Inverell Methodist Church Honour Roll,[68] the Sinclair Public School and Long Plain First World War Roll of Honour,[69] the Inverell War Memorial and Cenotaph,[70] the Inverell District Great War Honour Roll,[71]

---

[67] https://www.aif.adfa.edu.au/showPerson?pid=58068 (accessed 22 April 2023). Note the spelling of Louis' name on both the AIF Project Database and the on his service records held at the National Archives of Australia is Lewis Rowland.
[68] https://www.warmemorialsregister.nsw.gov.au/memorials/inverell-methodist-church-first-world-war-honour-roll
[69] https://www.warmemorialsregister.nsw.gov.au/memorials/sinclair-public-school-and-long-plain-first-world-war-roll-honour-inverell
[70] http://www.inverellremembers.org.au/soldier-profile.php?sid=328
[71] https://www.warmemorialsregister.nsw.gov.au/memorials/inverell-district-great-war-honour-roll

the Long Plain Soldier's Memorial Hall Memorial Trees at Inverell[72] and the Presbyterian Church Drummoyne Roll of Honour.[73]

Photograph of the addendum panel with Sidney Colley's name inscribed at the Ypres (Menin Gate) Memorial (author, 2018).

---

[72] https://www.warmemorialsregister.nsw.gov.au/memorials/long-plain-soldiers-memorial-hall-memorial-trees
[73] https://www.warmemorialsregister.nsw.gov.au/content/presbyterian-church-drummoyne-roll-honour

George Columbus Ryng

Gunner, No. 1222
10th Field Artillery Brigade, 4th Australian Division
Killed in action 8 June 1917, Messines, Belgium
No known grave. Commemorated Ypres (Menin Gate)
Memorial, Ypres, Belgium

George Columbus (Col) Ryng[74] was born in 1893 to James and Susannah Ryng in the parish of Hunters Hill, Sydney. He was one of seven children born to James and Susannah between 1881 and 1895 comprising five brothers and two sisters, with George being the second youngest.[75] James Ryng was a stonemason and built the family home, which was at 5 Ernest Street, Hunters Hill.[76]

We know little of George's early life apart from that both his parents had died while he was still young – his father in 1901 and his mother in 1906,[77] and at the time of his enlistment he was employed as a carter.[78]

George applied to join the AIF on 27 October 1914[79] at the age of 21 and nominated his brother Joseph Michael Ryng living at Sisters Crescent, Drummoyne, as his next of kin. George was enlisted as a private and assigned to E Company in the 13th Battalion. At some point during his service, George made a will in which he left all his money and personal belongings to Miss Vera Kirby of Lyons Road, Drummoyne.[80]

The 13th Battalion was raised from late September 1914 and was recruited in New South Wales, and with the 14th, 15th and 16th Battalions formed the 4th Brigade, commanded by Colonel John Monash.[81] George, along with the remainder of the battalion, travelled by train

---

[74] The family is said to have referred to him as 'Col' according to a post by his great niece, Madeleine Gross, on 15 Feb 2017 - https://rslvirtualwarmemorial.org.au/explore/people/326924 (accessed 28 June 2018).
[75] NSW BDM Registration No. 31967/1893. His mother's name is in some entries spelt Susannah.
[76] https://rslvirtualwarmemorial.org.au/explore/people/326924 (accessed 28 June 2018).
[77] NSW BDM Registration No. 8984/1906. In a response to a letter dated 20 August 1920 from the OIC to Joseph Ryng, Joseph then living at *Glentworth*, Ady Street, Hunters Hill, advised that George's parents were dead and that he was the eldest brother.
[78] A person who carries or conveys goods by cart, typically involving a light two wheeled vehicle.
[79] War service records accessible at https://recordsearch.naa.gov.au/SearchNRetrieve/Interface/ViewImage.aspx?B=8074447
[80] A reference to a Vera Kirby can be found in the *Freeman's Journal*, 8 August 1912 in a report on the St Brigid's Orphanage Ball, Ryde - RYDE ORPHANAGE BALL. (1912, August 8). *Freeman's Journal* (Sydney, NSW: 1850-1932), p. 29. Retrieved April 22, 2023, from http://nla.gov.au/nla.news-article108036039. Vera was born in 1893 – NSW BDM Registration No. 29956/1894 and http://www.thefrasers.com/dianef/dat1.htm#39
[81] https://www.awm.gov.au/collection/U51453 (accessed 28 June 2018).

to Broadmeadow in Victoria in late November where it undertook further training. After a ceremonial march through Melbourne on 17 December,[82] the battalion embarked from Melbourne on HMAT A38 *Ulysses* on 22 December 1914,[83] and after a brief stop in Albany, Western Australia, it proceeded to Egypt, arriving at Alexandria on 31 January 1915.[84] When the 4th Brigade arrived in Egypt it became part of the New Zealand and Australian Division, which undertook training at its camp at Heliopolis.

On 12 April 1915, George joined the MEF as the Australian and New Zealand forces in Egypt prepared for the landings on the Gallipoli peninsula. The battalion embarked on HMAT A33 *Ascot* on 12 April, sailing at noon the next day.[85] The troopship arrived at Mudros Harbour on the island of Lemnos on 17 April and commenced boat drills and disembarking.[86] The battalion sailed as part of the landing forces on 24 April, arriving off ANZAC Cove at 4:30 p.m., with A, B and most of C Company disembarking under fire at 9:30 p.m. on 25 April, with D Company and one platoon of C Company disembarking during the early hours of 26 April, taking up positions at the head of Monash Valley.[87]

The companies of the battalion manned the front-line trenches on Pope's Hill and Quinn's Post and took part in repulsing Turkish attacks as well as the unsuccessful attack on Baby 700 hill at the head of Monash Valley on 2–3 May. The battalion remained in the vicinity of Pope's Hill and Quinn's Post until 13 May when relieved by the 1st

---

[82] 13th Battalion Unit Diary December 1914 - https://www.awm.gov.au/collection/C1342722?image=4
[83] 13th Battalion Unit Diary December 1914 - https://www.awm.gov.au/collection/C1342722?image=4
[84] 13th Battalion Unit Diary January 1915 - https://www.awm.gov.au/collection/C1342731?image=6
[85] 13th Battalion Unit Diary April 1915 - https://www.awm.gov.au/collection/C1343250?image=3
[86] 13th Battalion Unit Diary April 1915 - https://www.awm.gov.au/collection/C1343250?image=3
[87] 13th Battalion Unit Diary April 1915 - https://www.awm.gov.au/collection/C1343250?image=4

Australian Light Horse.[88] It was during this period in the line that George was one of a number other ranks wounded in the fighting. He was said to have suffered a bullet wound to the foot and leg and was evacuated on the *Gloucester Castle* to Cairo hospital. George's name appeared in the casualty lists published in June 1915.[89] Although George's service records note that on 4 July 1915 he embarked on HMT *Scotian* for Gallipoli, it is unclear if George returned to ANZAC Cove as on 16 July he was evacuated to a convalescent camp on Malta, said to be suffering from severe rheumatic fever.[90]

George remained on Malta until mid-November and for a brief period while unfit for service was employed by the Camp Police. He embarked on HT *Bornu*, returning to Cairo where he was discharged to his unit on 28 December 1915. By this time the 13th Battalion had been withdrawn following the evacuation from Gallipoli. George was one of 39 other ranks that rejoined the 13th Battalion at Ismailia on 3 January 1916.[91] His time with the battalion was again short lived as on 20 January he was evacuated to hospital at Moascar sick with tonsillitis.

While in Egypt the AIF was expanded and reorganised. The 13th Battalion was split and provided experienced soldiers for the 45th Battalion. The 4th Brigade was combined with the 12th and 13th Brigades to form the 4th Australian Division. George was one of those soldiers who on 3 March 1916 was transferred to the newly established 45th Battalion, but his new unit did not appear to have agreed with him. On 5 March he was charged with being absent without leave, for which he was awarded 7 days' confinement to barracks and forfeited two days' pay. On 7 March 1916 he was again admitted to hospital,

---

[88] 13th Battalion Unit Diary May 1915 - https://www.awm.gov.au/collection/C1343251?image=3
[89] NEW SOUTH WALES. (1915, June 5). *Observer* (Adelaide, SA: 1905-1931), p. 39. Retrieved April 22, 2023, from http://nla.gov.au/nla.news-article164191360
[90] According to a letter from the OIC to George's brother dated 10 September 1915 - war service records - https://recordsearch.naa.gov.au/SearchNRetrieve/Interface/ViewImage.aspx?B=8074447.
[91] 13th Battalion Unit Diary January 1916 - https://www.awm.gov.au/collection/C1342717?image=2

this time suffering from 'skin eruptions'. George returned to the unit on 11 March 1916 but within a week had volunteered to be transferred to the 10th Field Artillery Brigade (FAB) of 4th Division Artillery and assigned to the 39th Battery. He was among the 101 other ranks transferred to the 4th Division Artillery on 17 March 1916.[92] Each battalion had been ordered to supply 100 men to the divisional artillery, with a further 100 to be furnished from the Light Horse.

The 4th Divisional Artillery embarked from Alexandria to join the BEF in France in early June 1916, and after arriving in Marseilles, moved north eventually taking up positions in French Flanders. On arrival, the 4th Divisional Artillery was partnered with the 2nd Divisional Artillery to be 'practised' in the science of artillery before assuming responsibility for the sector as the 2nd Divisional Artillery withdrew.

By mid-July, the 4th Divisional Artillery including George's 10th FAB was in the Fromelles Salient, temporarily attached to the 5th Australian Division[93], and did not follow the 4th Division when it was transferred to the Somme sector on account of the inexperience of the artillery. Extensive preparations were undertaken in order to support the attack by the 5th Division on the Fromelles sector, which commenced on 19 July. The brigade began firing early in the morning and did not cease until 10 p.m. The next day, owing to the large number of wounded men lying in no man's land after the failed attack, battery fire was withheld.[94]

The brigade was withdrawn from Fromelles on 1 August 1916 and by the end of the month had moved to Reninghelst where it provided support to the 4th Canadian Division,[95] before moving to the Ypres sector in October 1916 to rejoin its division. The brigade was involved

---

[92] 45th Battalion Unit Diary March 1916 - https://www.awm.gov.au/collection/C1346075?image=2
[93] 10th Field Artillery Brigade Unit Diary July 1916 - https://www.awm.gov.au/collection/C1355603?image=3
[94] 10th Field Artillery Brigade Unit Diary July 1916 - https://www.awm.gov.au/collection/C1355603?image=4
[95] 10th Field Artillery Brigade Unit Diary August 1916 - https://www.awm.gov.au/collection/C1355919?image=2

in counter-battery work with German artillery, as well as shelling specific targets identified through observation. On 11 November, the brigade began to hand over its positions to British artillery units.[96]

The brigade moved to the Somme sector near Flers, relieving the 2nd Divisional Artillery. During December 1916, the brigade's diary noted that on the whole the sector was quieter with the weather alternating between cold with sharp frosts, and raining, with few days being favourable for observation.[97] The activity of the brigade's batteries was limited to 'routine' firing.

Early in the new year while still based near Flers, George was evacuated to the 38th Casualty Clearing Station (CCS) said to be suffering from venereal disease. He was transferred by ambulance train to Rouen and ultimately would be absent for 66 days, not being discharged to the Australian main depot at Etaples until 10 March 1917. His return was short lived as on 19 March 1917, George was again evacuated with an undisclosed illness, this time to the 51st General Hospital. He would be absent for a further 55 days before being discharged to Etaples on 12 May 1917.

During George's absence, the brigade was involved in following up the German withdrawal to the Hindenburg Line, including action in the Noreuil valley. It provided support to the attacks on Bullecourt in April and May 1917, with the brigade itself coming under heavy artillery and machine gun fire[98] suffering 20 killed and 50 wounded.[99] The accuracy of the German fire was explained when a map was taken from a captured German prisoner, which showed the location of the brigade's batteries.[100] George rejoined just before the brigade withdrew and returned to the Ypres sector of the front.

---

[96] 10th Field Artillery Brigade Unit Diary November 1916 - https://www.awm.gov.au/collection/C1356138?image=9
[97] 10th Field Artillery Brigade Unit Diary December 1916 - https://www.awm.gov.au/collection/C1356139?image=8
[98] 10th Field Artillery Brigade Unit Diary May 1917 - https://www.awm.gov.au/collection/C1355604?image=2
[99] 10th Field Artillery Brigade Unit Diary May 1917 - https://www.awm.gov.au/collection/C1355604?image=4
[100] 10th Field Artillery Brigade Unit Diary May 1917 - https://www.awm.gov.au/collection/C1355604?image=4

From 21 May 1917, the brigade was in action along the Ypres front in preparation for and the carrying out of the Battle of Messines, a preliminary action to the opening of the Third Battle of Ypres. The attack on Messines Ridge commenced on 7 June and continued until 14 June 1917.

It was on 8 June 1917, during the first days of the attack on Messines Ridge, that George was killed in action. George's name appeared in the 323rd casualty list as killed in action published in July 1917.[101] There is no information regarding the circumstances of George's death with even the unit diary dealing with its involvement in the battle with a single limited entry.[102] No investigation appears to have been undertaken by the Red Cross. It is possible that George's battery suffered a direct hit, and during the initial stages of the attack, his remains either quickly buried and lost, or not able to be identified.

18-pounder gun of the 38th Battery of the Australian Field Artillery dug in among the ruins of an old factory near Zonnebeke, in the Ypres Sector. Frank Hurley, 24 October 1917 AWM ID No. E01209.

---

[101] 323rd LIST. (1917, July 20). *The Land* (Sydney, NSW: 1911-1954), p. 13. Retrieved April 22, 2023, from http://nla.gov.au/nla.news-article102889419
[102] 10th Field Artillery Brigade Unit Diary June 1917 - https://www.awm.gov.au/collection/C1355155?image=2

A solitary personal notice was published in *The Sydney Morning Herald* on 14 July 1917[103]:

RYNG. - Killed in action June 4, 1917, Private George Columbus Ryng, previously wounded at the Dardanelles, dearly beloved friend of Vera K. Sadly missed.

His memory is as dear to-day
As on the day he sailed away.

Inserted by his loving friend, Vera.

George has no known grave and is commemorated on the Menin Gate Memorial in Ypres, Belgium.

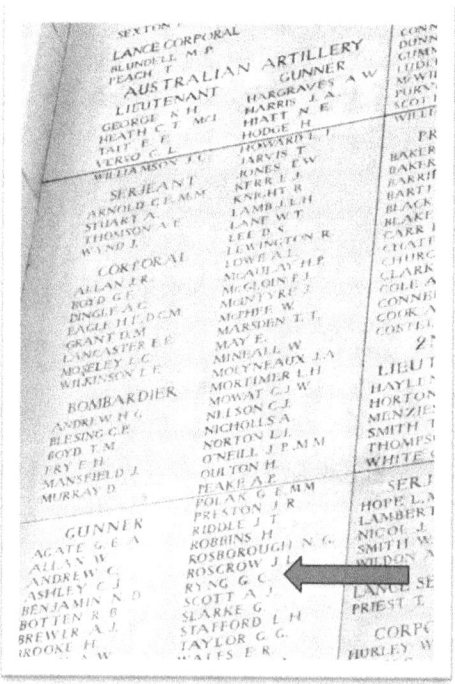

Photograph of the panel on which is inscribed the name of George Ryng on the Ypres (Menin Gate) Memorial (author, 2018).

---

[103] Family Notices (1917, July 14). *The Sydney Morning Herald* (NSW: 1842-1954), p. 12. Retrieved April 22, 2023, from http://nla.gov.au/nla.news-article15739855

Arthur James Vincent

Corporal, No. 2163A
37th Battalion, 10th Infantry Brigade, 3rd Australian Division
Killed in action 8 June 1917, Messines, Belgium
No known grave. Commemorated Ypres (Menin Gate)
Memorial, Ypres, Belgium

Arthur James Vincent was born in Wangaratta, Victoria in 1879,[104] one of 15 children of Reuben Brett Vincent and Mary Vincent (nee White).[105] Arthur attended the Oxley School in Wangaratta and spent two years serving with the Victorian Mounted Rifles.

While working as a farmer, on 26 April 1902 at the age of 23, Arthur enlisted in the 6th Battalion Australian Commonwealth Horse in Melbourne for service in South Africa in the Boer War. During his service towards the end of the war, Arthur attained the rank of sergeant. After returning from South Africa, Arthur spent seven years in New Zealand, and time in his home State of Victoria before moving to New South Wales. During this period, he undertook general labouring jobs including as a lorry driver. It is reported that Arthur had been employed at the Cooperative Store in Wangaratta in the delivery of goods, and was regarded as 'a trustworthy and highly valued employee', while his personal qualities are said to have gained him the 'esteem of all his acquaintances'.[106]

While in New South Wales, Arthur married Alice Matilda Dewsbury[107] on 8 January 1914 at St Bede's Anglican Church, Drummoyne, with the ceremony presided over by Rev. T D Reynolds.[108] Alice had been born in 1874 in Goulburn[109] so was five years Arthur's senior. The couple is reported to have honeymooned in nearby Abbotsford.

Arthur and his wife must have returned to Wangaratta sometime after their wedding as in 1915, Alice gave birth to their only child, Jean Isabel Mary.[110] The next year, Arthur enlisted in the AIF at the

---

[104] Victorian BDM Registration No. 1879/12684.
[105] The eldest was Walter (1862) followed by Emily (1863), Albert (1865), Ernest (1867), Alice (1868), Henry (1871), Reuben Jacob (1873), Henry (1875), Maud (1877), Arthur (1879), William (1883), George (1884), William (1884), Daisy (1885) and Amy (1887). When Arthur was killed in 1917, there were eleven surviving children.
[106] Pte. Arthur J. Vincent, (1917, July 2). *Shepparton Advertiser* (Vic.: 1887-1953), p. 2 (EVENINGS.). Retrieved April 23, 2023, from http://nla.gov.au/nla.news-article92108084
[107] NSW BDM Registration No. 864/1914.
[108] MARRIAGE. (1914, January 17). *Goulburn Evening Penny Post* (NSW: 1881-1940), p. 6 (EVENING). Retrieved April 23, 2023, from http://nla.gov.au/nla.news-article98822438
[109] NSW BDM Registration No. 11099/1874.
[110] Victorian BDM Registration No. 1915/ 26189. Jean died in NSW in 1935 at the age of 20 – NSW BDM Registration No. 131/1935.

Wangaratta Training Centre on 3 April 1916[111] where he gave his occupation as labourer and specified his wife Alice as his next of kin, who was living with Mrs D Austin at Wangaratta.[112] It is reported that at the time of his enlistment he was a member of the Oddfellows Lodge.[113]

Arthur remained at Wangaratta for a month where he was nominally assigned to the 10th Reinforcements to the 22nd Battalion before being transferred to the NCO Training School at Geelong where he remained until late June. Said to have qualified for appointment to the rank of sergeant, and with his service records indicating that he was nominally appointed to the rank of corporal on 24 June 1916, Arthur requested to revert to the ranks so that he could be with his brother George, who had enlisted in February 1916, and had been assigned to the 37th Battalion, which formed part of the newly established 3rd Division.[114] Arthur was duly reassigned to the 3rd Reinforcements of that battalion and followed his brother when he embarked from Melbourne on HMAT A9 *Shropshire* on 25 September 1916.[115]

Arthur arrived in Plymouth, England, on 11 November 1916 and moved to Lark Hill at Salisbury to undertake further training at the Australian base. Not long after his arrival, the 3rd Division departed England for France[116] but Arthur would remain behind with the other reinforcements. In late November, Arthur had been appointed acting corporal before being formally appointed to that rank on 24 January

---

[111] War service records accessible at https://recordsearch.naa.gov.au/SearchNRetrieve/Interface/ViewImage.aspx?B=8398260
[112] According to the Nominal Roll. Mrs D Austin was Alice's sister-in-law and her husband gave Alice away at the wedding in Drummoyne in 1914 according to the report of the wedding in the *Goulburn Evening Penny Post* of 17 January 1914 - MARRIAGE. (1914, January 17). *Goulburn Evening Penny Post* (NSW: 1881-1940), p. 6 (EVENING). Retrieved April 23, 2023, from http://nla.gov.au/nla.news-article98822438 .
[113] PTE. ART. VINCENT. (1917, June 30). *Wangaratta Chronicle* (Vic.: 1914-1918), p. 3 (Mornings). Retrieved April 23, 2023, from http://nla.gov.au/nla.news-article92125801
[114] George Vincent (1335) served in D Company of the 37th Battalion and returned to Australia in December 1918 - https://www.aif.adfa.edu.au/showPerson?pid=309141
[115] George Vincent (1335) had embarked from Melbourne on HMAT A3 *Persic* on 3 June 1916.
[116] 37th Battalion Unit Diary November 1916 - https://www.awm.gov.au/collection/C1345133?image=3

1917. In early February 1917, Arthur proceeded overseas for service in France via Folkestone, arriving at the 3rd ADBD at Etaples on 4 February. Two days later, he marched out of the base to join his battalion on 7 February 1917.

Arthur was one of 46 reinforcements to join the battalion, with it having only recently been relieved after a failed raid on the German trenches near Armentieres.[117] Within a week of joining his battalion, however, Arthur was evacuated to hospital suffering from scabies where he remained until 22 February 1917.

The battalion undertook training through March and early April in new methods of attack before returning to the lines at Armentieres. Its stay in French Flanders would end on 28 April when the battalion moved to Ploegsteert in Belgium.[118] May 1917 saw the preparations for the forthcoming attack on Messines Ridge, with Allied artillery increasing its attention on Messines village, Schnitzel Farm and other strong points in the enemy lines.[119] The 3rd Australian Division's objective was to capture the southern shoulder of Messines Ridge.

The battalion's unit diary recorded the training and conferences to go over the particulars of the plan occupying all its attention[120] as part of the 3rd Division's operation codenamed 'Magnum Opus'. As the time for the attack drew near, the battalion began to move to its jumping-off positions, with the approach march by the battalion affected by heavy gas shelling, necessitating the wearing of respirators.[121]

The offensive opened at 3:10 a.m. on 7 June with the 10th Brigade, of which the 37th Battalion formed part, advancing flanked by the 9th

---

[117] 37th Battalion Unit Diary February 1917 - https://www.awm.gov.au/collection/C1345135?image=2
[118] 37th Battalion Unit Diary April 1917 - https://www.awm.gov.au/collection/C1357320?image=2
[119] 37th Battalion Unit Diary May 1917 - https://www.awm.gov.au/collection/C1345010?image=2
[120] 37th Battalion Unit Diary May 1917 - https://www.awm.gov.au/collection/C1345010?image=2 ; Bean, *Official History*, Vol. 4, p. 576.
[121] 37th Battalion Unit Diary June 1917 - https://www.awm.gov.au/collection/C1345112?image=15

and 12th Brigades on the right and left respectively.[122] The creeping box barrage provided cover to the attacking infantry. The C and D Companies formed the first wave with A Company from the 37th Battalion and D Company of the 40th Battalion forming the second wave.[123] Although the attacking units secured their objectives, the well-positioned and established German machine guns took their toll, including from the numerous pillboxes. Attempts to extend the gains beyond the initial objectives of the first stage of the attack were meet with strong resistance from machine gun fire temporarily forcing back the lines of men.[124]

Early on the morning of 8 June, the attack resumed with the 44th Battalion passing through the 37th Battalion to take the objective called the 'Green Line'.[125] The battalion was finally relieved late in the morning of 9 June suffering casualties of one officer and 66 other ranks killed and 10 officers and 321 other ranks wounded, with another four other ranks missing.[126] Arthur was counted among the dead from the fighting.

Alice relayed in her subsequent correspondence to the OIC that she had received letters from Arthur's soldier friends reporting that he was killed whilst leading his platoon into action. Initially reported as killed in action between 7–9 June 1916, on 25 July 1917, Arthur was confirmed to have been killed in action on 8 June 1917. He was reported as having been buried by Chaplain Alfred Avery Mills CJ of the 41st Battalion near Bethleem Farm.

---

[122] 37th Battalion Unit Diary June 1917 - https://www.awm.gov.au/collection/C1345112?image=5
[123] 37th Battalion Unit Diary June 1917 - https://www.awm.gov.au/collection/C1345112?image=6
[124] 37th Battalion Unit Diary June 1917 - https://www.awm.gov.au/collection/C1345112?image=16
[125] 37th Battalion Unit Diary June 117 - https://www.awm.gov.au/collection/C1345112?image=17
[126] 37th Battalion Unit Diary June 1917 - https://www.awm.gov.au/collection/C1345112?image=18

Photograph of the Bethleem Farm Commonwealth War Grave Cemetery, Messines, Belgium (author, 2018).

Alice, then residing in Randwick, received a telegram from the Defence Department advising of Arthur's death, and she immediately telegrammed Arthur's parents in Wangaratta to convey the sad news. The first notice of Arthur's death appeared in *The Age* on 29 June 1917[127] followed by a more detailed account in the *Wangaratta Chronicle* on 30 June 1917[128]:

---

[127] Family Notices (1917, June 29). *The Age* (Melbourne, Vic.: 1854-1954), p. 1. Retrieved April 23, 2023, from http://nla.gov.au/nla.news-article154978826 . See also Family Notices (1917, June 30). *The Argus* (Melbourne, Vic.: 1848-1957), p. 13. Retrieved April 23, 2023, from http://nla.gov.au/nla.news-article1629593

[128] PTE. ART. VINCENT. (1917, June 30). *Wangaratta Chronicle* (Vic.: 1914-1918), p. 3 (Mornings). Retrieved April 23, 2023, from http://nla.gov.au/nla.news-article92125801 . A notice was also published in the *Shepparton Advertiser* on 2 July 1917 - Pte. Arthur J. Vincent, (1917, July 2). *Shepparton Advertiser* (Vic.: 1887-1953), p. 2 (EVENINGS.). Retrieved April 23, 2023, from http://nla.gov.au/nla.news-article92108084 .

PTE. ART. VINCENT.

Mr. and Mrs R. B. Vincent, of 'Mundarlo,' Wangaratta, received the sad intelligence on Wednesday evening that their son, Pte. Arthur James Vincent had been killed in action on 7th June in France. The Defence Department sent the official word to Pte. Vincent's wife, who with her little daughter, aged 22 months, resides at Randwick, Sydney, with her parents, and she telegraphed the news to Wangaratta. It was only on Monday that Mr. and Mrs Vincent had a cheery letter from their son, in which he said he hoped to return home again shortly. Fate, however, decreed otherwise, and the news received on Wednesday came as a great shock. Pte. Vincent was the fifth son and 38 years of age. He was a native of Wangaratta. At the time of enlisting he was employed at the N.E. Co-operative Store, and went into camp on 2nd April, 1916. He trained at Wangaratta with the third platoon under Lieut. Brading, and also went through an N.C.O.'s school at Geelong prior to sailing on 25th September in the Shropshire as an Acting-Sergeant. In England he was attending a special school for bombers, when he heard that his brother Pte. Geo. Vincent was going to France, so he left the school and forfeited all chance of gaining a Commission in order that he might be with him. He left England on 5th February, and was in action on 7th February, and since then participated in much of the heavy fighting at different points.

This was not Pte. Vincent's first experience of soldiering, for he served in the latter part of the Boer War as a Sergeant, and afterwards returned to Australia on the ill-fated Drayton Grange, when many of the men died from sickness. On arrival he went to New Zealand where he remained for seven years.

Then he went to N.S.W., and was married at Sydney. Pte. and Mrs Vincent came to Wangaratta to live a few years back. All who knew the late Pte. Vincent held him in the highest esteem, his happy, genial and manly manner winning for him their respect and affection. Pte. Vincent belongs to one of Wangaratta's pioneer families, and the large circle of friends will sympathise with Mr. and Mrs. Vincent in their loss of a dutiful son, and condole with the wife in her sorrowful bereavement. Pte. Vincent's brother George was with him in France, also his brother-in-law, Gunner R. Gadd, as well as the following seven cousins and three nephews:— Bombardier Les Vincent, Far.-Sgt. Bert Vincent, Ptes. Victor and Louis Vincent, Driver Ernie White, Sgt. Ralph Cecil, Pte Wm. Dobbie, and Ptes. Woodberry, and Roy Kennedy, and Stretcher-bearer Percy Vincent. Brothers and sisters of deceased are — Messrs Walter Vincent, Shepparton; Ernest, Oxley; Reuben, Kentucky, N.S.W.; Henry, Laceby; Pte. George, on service; Mrs James Kennedy, Oxley; Mrs G. Woodberry, Milawa; Mrs R. H. Jones, Mrs H. S. White, Mrs R. B. Gadd and Miss Daisy Vincent, of Wangaratta. Pte. Vincent was a member of the Oddfellows' Lodge, and is the seventh member of the Loyal Junction branch to fall in action.

A similarly detailed account of Arthur's family and personal connection to the Wangaratta district appeared in a notice published in the *Shepparton Advertiser* on 5 July 1917.[129]

Personal notices were also published in early July 1917 by Arthur's family reporting on his death[130]:

---

[129] PTE. ARTHUR JAMES VINCENT. (1917, July 5). *Shepparton Advertiser* (Vic.: 1887-1953), p. 4 (EVENINGS.). Retrieved April 23, 2023, from http://nla.gov.au/nla.news-article92110905

[130] Family Notices (1917, July 7). *Goulburn Evening Penny Post* (NSW: 1881-1940), p. 2 (EVENING). Retrieved April 23, 2023, from http://nla.gov.au/nla.news-article98884038

Vincent — Killed in action in France, June 7th, Cpl. A. J. Vincent, the beloved husband of Alice M. Vincent, late of Goulburn.

Just when his life was brightest,
Just when his hopes were best,
His country called, he answered.
In God's hand he rests.

Inserted by his loving wife and child, Alice M. and Jean Vincent. 'Lyn,' Hooper-street, Randwick.

Vincent — A tribute to the memory of Cpl. A. J. Vincent, killed in action in France, June 7th. Inserted by his brother-in-law, A. Dewsbury.

Alice Vincent published another family notice in the *Wangaratta Chronicle* on 21 July 1917, which noted at that time the uncertainty of the precise date on which Arthur was killed[131]:

KILLED IN ACTION.

VINCENT - Killed in Action in France, between June 7th and 9th, 1917, Cpl. A. J. Vincent, dearly beloved husband of Alice M. Vincent, and loved father of Baby Jean, 'Lyn,' Hooper Street, Randwick, Sydney,

In a hero's grave he is lying,
Somewhere in France he fell;
Little we thought, when we parted,
It was our last farewell.

---

[131] Advertising (1917, July 21). *Wangaratta Chronicle* (Vic.: 1914-1918), p. 2 (Mornings). Retrieved April 23, 2023, from http://nla.gov.au/nla.news-article92125699. An equivalent notice was published in *The Sydney Morning Herald* on 4 July 1917 - Family Notices (1917, July 4). *The Sydney Morning Herald* (NSW: 1842-1954), p. 10. Retrieved April 23, 2023, from http://nla.gov.au/nla.news-article15757028

Some details of Arthur's death were conveyed by letters received by Alice Vincent, including from the chaplain, Alfred Mills, who assisted in burying Arthur's remains, which details were subsequently published in the *Wangaratta Chronicle* in October 1917[132]:

> Mrs A. M. Vincent, Drummoyne, N.S.W., has received a letter from Chaplain A. A. Mills, France, in which he says:-'I desire to express my deep sympathy with you in the very great loss you have sustained by the death of your husband, Cpl. Art. J. Vincent, who was killed in action on June 7th. As Chaplain working on the portion of the battlefield where your husband fell it was my sad duty to lay the body to rest, side by side with fallen comrades, in a flat that has been marked and Registered. Your husband was in the forefront of one of the greatest struggles of the war when death met him. He bravely made the supreme sacrifice, but we already know that the sacrifice was not in vain. May this knowledge give you some measure of comfort in what must be the dark hour of loss and sorrow.'-

> Chaplain A. I. Davidson also writes to Mrs Vincent to say:- 'Your husband, Cpl,. A. J. Vincent, was killed in the great battle of Messines -a splendid victory but only won at great sacrifice, and the pity is your's was one. Our men did magnificently and were real heroes. The sad thing is that so often it is the best fellows who really do such fine work that brings them into such danger - but in the battle everyone was in danger. I found our men ready in every way for their great effort.

---

[132] NEWS OF SOLDIERS. (1917, October 24). *Wangaratta Chronicle* (Vic.: 1914-1918), p. 4 (Mornings). Retrieved April 23, 2023, from http://nla.gov.au/nla.news-article92127397

Their interest in religious things was splendid, and they were prepared to meet their death. God gave them strength in their hour of need, as He will also give you for your great sorrow. Your husband died a hero's death in one of the greatest battles ever fought, and we can only trust that his sacrifice will have a share in bringing nearer to an end this awful struggle. God help you to bear your loss.'

In memoriam notices were published on the anniversary of Arthur's death in June 1918 by his parents and wife[133]:

IN MEMORIAM

VINCENT — In loving memory of our dear Son, Arthur J. Vincent, 37th Battalion, killed in action at Messines, on June 7th, 1917, aged 38 years,

It was on that fatal day in June,
Our brave son's life was ended;
A link was broken in our chain,
That never can be mended.
He answered to his country's call,
For sons to guard her shore;

---

[133] Family Notices (1918, June 8). *Wangaratta Chronicle* (Vic.: 1914-1918), p. 2 (Mornings). Retrieved April 23, 2023, from http://nla.gov.au/nla.news-article92115378. Alice published a further notice in *The Daily Telegraph* in Sydney a week later on 15 June 1918 - Family Notices (1918, June 15). *The Daily Telegraph* (Sydney, NSW: 1883-1930), p. 10. Retrieved April 23, 2023, from http://nla.gov.au/nla.news-article239260654. Additional notices were published by family and friends in *The Age* - Family Notices (1918, June 7). *The Age* (Melbourne, Vic.: 1854-1954), p. 1. Retrieved April 23, 2023, from http://nla.gov.au/nla.news-article155098010 and *The Argus* - Family Notices (1918, June 7). *The Argus* (Melbourne, Vic.: 1848-1957), p. 1. Retrieved April 23, 2023, from http://nla.gov.au/nla.news-article1664327

In honour's cause he gave his all,
And men can do no more.
Our brave Hero.
He died that shirkers might live.

—Inserted by his loving parents, R. B. and M. Vincent.

IN MEMORIAM,

VINCENT — In loving memory of my beloved husband, Cpl. A. J. Vincent, killed in action at Battle of Messines, France, June 7, 1917.

We still can see his smiling face,
Although one year has passed;
And in our memory, still he lives,
And will until the last.

—Inserted by his loving Wife, Alice M., and infant daughter, Jean Vincent.

Although there was a record of the location of Arthur's grave, and confirmation given by Chaplain Alfred Mills that it had been registered, the grave could not be located by the GSU after the war. In 1923, the OIC finally advised Alice that the attempts to locate Arthur's grave had been unsuccessful. The OIC commented[134]:

> I might add that the vicinity in which this casualty occurred was repeatedly the scene of very heavy fighting, and it is possible all traces of his burial place were obliterated by shell-fire.

Up until this time, the OIC had been corresponding with Alice regarding the epitaph that she would like inscribed on Arthur's headstone. On the first two attempts, the OIC had to reject Alice's epitaph

---

[134] War service records accessible at https://recordsearch.naa.gov.au/SearchNRetrieve/Interface/ViewImage.aspx?B=8398260

for exceeding the maximum number of 66 characters. Alice finally settled on[135]:

> In memory of the loved husband of A. M. Vincent and father of Jean

As Arthur's grave was not located, the epitaph was never engraved, and Arthur's name was recorded as one of the many thousands of missing in the fighting in Belgian Flanders on the Ypres (Menin Gate) Memorial at Ypres.

Photograph of the 37th Battalion panel on which is inscribed the name of Arthur Vincent, the Ypres (Menin Gate) Memorial, Ypres (author, 2018).

---

[135] During the course of her correspondence with the OIC, Alice lived at '*Springfield*', Melody Street, Coogee, '*Lyn*', Hooper Street, Randwick and c/o Mrs D Austin of Bridge Street, Drummoyne.

Alfred William Potiphar

Driver, No. 154

36th Battalion, 9th Infantry Brigade, 3rd Australian Division

Killed in action 22 July 1917, Messines, Belgium

Buried Kandahar Farm Cemetery, Neuve-Eglise, Belgium

Photograph of Alfred Potiphar. Source - Sunday Times (Sydney), Sun 10 Jun 1917 Page 3 https://trove.nla.gov.au/newspaper/page/13214734

Alfred William Potiphar was born in London, England, on 14 August 1884,[136] and was the son of Frederick and Elizabeth Potiphar. Educated in London, and a fitter by trade, Alfred served with the Royal Field Artillery for 10 years. He emigrated to Australia before the outbreak of the war and married Ellinor (Ella) Else Jane Spring[137] in Newtown in 1915.[138] At the time of his enlistment in the AIF on 10 January 1916,[139] he and his wife were living at *Hazeldene*, 103 Renwick

---

[136] It is uncertain if this date taken from the AIF Project database is correct. According to his attestation paper, Alfred was 35 years and five months at the time of his enlistment on 10 January 1916. This would mean that he was born in 1880. According to https://www.wikitree.com/wiki/Potiphar-2 he was born in 1881.

[137] Ella was born in 1895. Alfred's brother-in-law and Ellinor's brother, William Spring, also enlisted in the AIF and was assigned to the 13th Battalion. He was killed in action on 11 April 1917.

[138] NSW BDM Registration No. 16313/1915; https://www.wikitree.com/wiki/Spring-1024

[139] War service records accessible at https://recordsearch.naa.gov.au/SearchNRetrieve/Interface/ViewImage.aspx?B=8019608

Street, Drummoyne.[140] Although married only for a short time before his enlistment, Alfred would have known that Ella was pregnant prior to his departure for overseas as she gave birth to Ellinor May Elva Potiphar on 5 July 1916.[141]

Alfred qualified to enlist due to changes in the enlistment standards in June 1915, which reduced the minimum height requirement to 5 feet 2 inches. His medical records indicate that he was just half an inch above the amended minimum standard. Initially assigned as a driver in the Army Service Corps, in March 1916, Alfred was reassigned as a driver to the regimental transport for the 36th Infantry Battalion sometimes known as 'Carmichael's Thousand'.[142]

Alfred embarked with the 36th Battalion from Sydney on HMAT A72 *Beltana* on 13 May 1916, arriving in Devonport, England, on 9 July 1916. Prior to his departure, he is reported to have been presented with a fountain pen, wallet, and other useful gifts from his friends.[143] Alfred's brother-in-law, William Spring, is also commemorated on the Drummoyne War Memorial, and Alfred's picture appeared alongside that of William and other members of the Spring family in the *Sunday*

---

[140] The AIF Project records the address as 103 Renwick Street, Leichhardt. This was the home of Ella's parents, Elizabeth and Arthur Spring.

[141] NSW BDM Registration No. 26551/1916; Family Notices (1916, July 8). *The Daily Telegraph* (Sydney, NSW: 1883-1930), p. 8. Retrieved April 23, 2023, from http://nla.gov.au/nla.news-article239215704

[142] The 36th Battalion was granted the title 'Carmichael's Thousand' as it was largely due to the efforts of Ambrose Carmichael that the battalion was formed. Ambrose Carmichael was a member of parliament in the State Government of NSW when he decided to initiate the formation of a battalion largely from amongst rifle clubs throughout the state. He was successful in his goal and enlisted himself with the battalion, rising to the rank of captain and winning the Military Cross for his bravery and for his ability to inspire the men under his command - see https://www.leichhardt5000.com.au/carmichaels-1000-their-triumphs-and-their-trials-by-margaret-clarke/ and https://monumentaustralia.org.au/themes/conflict/ww1/display/21642-carmichael%60s-thousand. The battalion was disbanded after April 1918 due to a fall in the number of recruits – see https://www.awm.gov.au/collection/LIB100045442 and Carmichael's Thousand. (1918, September 30). *The Argus* (Melbourne, Vic.: 1848-1957), p. 6. Retrieved April 23, 2023, from http://nla.gov.au/nla.news-article1420387

[143] RECRUITING. (1916, May 19). *The Sydney Morning Herald* (NSW: 1842-1954), p. 9. Retrieved April 23, 2023, from http://nla.gov.au/nla.news-article15644458 .
COMPLIMENTARY MESSAGES. (1916, June 11). *Sunday Times* (Sydney, NSW: 1895 - 1930), p. 2. Retrieved April 23, 2023, from http://nla.gov.au/nla.news-article121340544

Times on 10 June 1917.[144] In January 1917, Alfred's name and that of William Spring, among others, were added to the Drummoyne Meth-

Group portrait of AASC (Australian Army Service Corps) Regimental Transport to the 36th Battalion. Alfred Potiphar is on the far left of the second row. AWM ID No. P04957.001.

odist Church Roll of Honour for having left on active service in the war.[145]

After further training in England, in November 1916, the 3rd Division including the 36th Battalion received orders to proceed to France via Southampton. Boarding the *Caesarea* and the *African Prince*, they disembarked at Le Harve at 7:25 a.m. on 23 November 1916.[146] Arriving in Bailleul, the battalion commenced instruction in the use of box respirators and gas masks before moving to Armentieres where it undertook visits to the front lines at the end of the month. The battalion had a total complement of 35 officers and 976 other ranks.[147]

---

[144] ANOTHER FIGHTING FAMILY (1917, June 10). *Sunday Times* (Sydney, NSW: 1895-1930), p. 3. Retrieved April 23, 2023, from http://nla.gov.au/nla.news-article122799927. See the account of William Spring who was killed in action at Bullecourt in April 1917.

[145] MEMORIAL AND ROLL OF HONOUR. (1917, January 20). *The Methodist* (Sydney, NSW: 1892-1954), p. 9. Retrieved April 23, 2023, from http://nla.gov.au/nla.news-article155432160

[146] 36th Battalion Unit Diary November 1916 - https://www.awm.gov.au/collection/C1342692?image=2

[147] 36th Battalion Unit Diary November 1916 - https://www.awm.gov.au/collection/C1342692?image=5

On 4 December, the battalion began to relieve the 34th Battalion in the front lines, and although in the 'nursery sector', the battalion soon began to take casualties. By mid-January 1917, the battalion had graduated to a new sector of the front lines, and on 22 January suffered losses of 11 killed, 36 wounded and four missing.[148] The battalion rotated in and out of the lines through February and March 1917 experiencing periodic intense cold and snow. During this time, Alfred was admitted to the 9th Australian Field Ambulance suffering from a septic infection to his thumb that kept him out of action for about three weeks. Alfred rejoined his battalion on 6 March 1917.

In mid-April, the battalion received orders to proceed to the Flanders sector of the front in preparation for the forthcoming Battle of Messines. On 6 and 7 June, the battalion began its approach march, with much gas being encountered, causing delays in the brigades of the 3rd Division reaching their jumping-off points. The 36th Battalion was, however, to be held in reserve as the 33rd, 34th and 35th Battalions of the 9th Brigade led the assault.

In what was the first deployment of the 'bite and hold' strategy, the attack on Messines Ridge in Belgium involved using creeping barrages to allow the attacking infantry to move forward and occupy the German trenches, before the artillery 'boxed' or provided a protective curtain of shell-fire around the occupied area to prevent the Germans reforming to launch a counter-attack. The battalion reported that the barrage was perfect, with the men being able to shelter under it as close as 50 yards.[149] Although the attack was successful, the losses were still significant with four officers killed and five wounded, and casualties among the other ranks being 66 killed, 318 wounded and 16 missing.[150]

---

[148] 36th Battalion Unit Diary January 1917 - https://www.awm.gov.au/collection/C1342700?image=3
[149] 36th Battalion Unit Diary June 1917 - https://www.awm.gov.au/collection/C1342704?image=14
[150] 36th Battalion Unit Diary June 1917 - https://www.awm.gov.au/collection/C1342704?image=15

The battalion was relieved on 13 June by the New Zealand Otago Battalion and had a brief rest before returning on the night of 2 and 3 July 1917. The battalion experienced heavy shelling from the enemy, with considerable damage to their position but fortunately few casualties. At 12:30 a.m. on 22 July, the battalion began its attack on enemy positions in the area designated Warneton Road.

There is no record of the circumstances in which Alfred met his death but owing to his assignment as a driver to battalion transport, it is more likely that he was killed not in the attack on Warneton Road but on the approaches to the front line from enemy shelling. Alfred was killed in action 22 July 1917, at Messines, Belgium.

Telegrams were received by Ella Potiphar advising the news of Alfred's death, which in turn was reported in *The Daily Telegraph* on 14 August 1917[151]:

> Driver A. W. POTIPHAR. - Mrs. E. Potiphar, of 'Hazeldene,' Renwick Street, Drummoyne, has received a private cable, also an official cable, that her husband, Driver A. W. Potiphar, was killed in action in France on July 22. He enlisted in January, 1916 and left Sydney with the regimental transport to 'Carmichael's Thousand.' He leaves a widow and one child. His brother-in-law Private William Spring, is also missing.

On 10 August 1917, Ella Potiphar wrote to the OIC[152]:

> Will you please give me some information regarding my husband's death in France. I had a private cable on August 1st notifying me of my husband being killed. I am very anxious to know. It is a very trying time for me as we were married only a few months when he left here. Hoping you will not lose any time in giving me the required information.

---

[151] MEN WHO FELL. (1917, August 14). *The Daily Telegraph* (Sydney, NSW: 1883-1930), p. 2. Retrieved April 23, 2023, from http://nla.gov.au/nla.news-article239379600
[152] War service records accessible at https://recordsearch.naa.gov.au/SearchNRetrieve/Interface/ViewImage.aspx?B=8019608

Ella's letter was acknowledged by the OIC on 16 August but it advised that no further information was available other than that communicated in the cable advising her that he had been killed in action on 22 July.

Notices were included in the Roll of Honour published in *The Sydney Morning Herald* on 25 August 1917 marking the news of Alfred's death[153]:

ROLL OF HONOUR.

POTIPHAR. — Killed in action in France, July 22, 1917, my dearly loved husband, Driver Alfred W. Potiphar, of Drummoyne.

When alone in my sorrow the bitter tears flow
There stealeth a dream of the dear long ago,
And, unknown to the world he stands by my side,
And whispers the words: 'Death cannot divide.'

Inserted by his sorrowing wife (nee Ella Spring), and daughter, Baby Elva. Home papers please copy.

POTIPHAR. — Killed in action in France, July 22, 1917, Driver A. W. Potiphar, Drummoyne.

One of the best Australia could send.

Inserted by loving mother-in-law, Mrs. Spring, sister, brothers-in-law, Gwen, Sid., and Will (on active service).

POTIPHAR. — Killed in action in France, July 22, 1917, Driver Alfred W. Potiphar, Drummoyne.

---

[153] Family Notices (1917, August 25). *The Sydney Morning Herald* (NSW: 1842-1954), p. 10. Retrieved April 23, 2023, from http://nla.gov.au/nla.news-article15756462. Further memorial notices were published by family and friends on the anniversary of Alfred's death in 1918 – see Family Notices (1918, July 22). *The Sydney Morning Herald* (NSW: 1842-1954), p. 6. Retrieved April 23, 2023, from http://nla.gov.au/nla.news-article15794583

He fought for those he loved so dear. That we may all live free. And on the battlefield of France. He gave his life for you and me.

Inserted by his loving grandma and aunt, Mrs. Edgar, and A. Williams and uncle, William Edgar.

POTIPHAR. — Killed in action in France, July 22, 1917, Driver Alfred Potiphar, Drummoyne, dearly loved brother of Nurse Spring, Royal Hospital, Paddington.

Far away on the field of battle, there, 'midst the shot and shell, In defence of those he loved so dearly, My brother and hero fell.

The few personal effects that Alfred had at the time that he was killed were eventually transmitted to Ella in April 1918. In August 1919, Ella made a request for a photograph of Alfred's grave, which was not provided until July 1920.

Alfred is buried in Kandahar Farm Cemetery at Neuve-Eglise (now Nieuwkerke), Belgium.[154] Alfred is also commemorated on the Leichhardt War Memorial.[155]

---

[154] https://www.cwgc.org/find-records/find-war-dead/casualty-details/444032/alfred-william-potiphar/ (accessed 23 April 2023).
[155] https://vwma.org.au/explore/memorials/4665/people?page=2 (accessed 23 April 2023).

Photograph of the grave of Alfred Potiphar, Kandahar Farm Cemetery at Neuve-Eglise, Belgium (author, 2018).

Third Ypres 1917

The Battle for Messines was a prelude to the Third Battle of Ypres,[156] which began at the end of July 1917. Intense preparations followed Messines for the forthcoming major offensive out of the Ypres salient. Unofficially referred to as the Passchendaele offensive, it comprised a number of set piece attacks as part of the continuation of the 'bite and hold' strategy. The offensive commenced on 15 July with the preliminary artillery bombardment before the infantry went over the top on 31 July.

The attack involved the British Second Army (Plumer) in the south, the British Fifth Army (Gough) in the centre, and the French First Army (Anthoine) in the north, with the main effort spearheaded by the British Fifth Army and the French First Army. The first day of the offensive, 31 July 1917, witnessed some initial success until the afternoon when the rain began to fall. The rain would continue for several days and turn the battlefield into a quagmire, disrupting the

---

[156] The First Battle of Ypres occurred in October–November 1914 shortly after the outbreak of hostilities when the Germans attempted to breakthrough Allied lines to seize the Belgian channel ports as part of the 'race to the sea.' British and French forces managed to stop the German attacks resulting in the creation of a defensive salient around the town of Ypres. The Second Battle of Ypres took place in April–May 1915 with a German assault to take the salient and marked the first use by the Germans of poison gas. Although initially successful, the Germans failed to exploit the gaps that were created in the Allied lines, with British forces reinforcing and eventually stabilising the front.

'bite and hold' tactic as the guns and ammunition could not be moved forward, and the infantry unable to keep pace with the creeping artillery barrage across the sodden and upturned ground. Even if the infantry managed to reach their objectives, they were often isolated and could not be effectively resupplied, resulting in heavy losses with few successes. It would not be until late August that BEF commander Haig ordered a pause to the offensive to wait for fine weather and fresh troops.

Although Australian artillery units participated in the early stages of the offensive and were often exposed to serious German counter-battery fire including poison gas, the Australian infantry were mercifully spared the fighting of July and August. This would change in September. Plumer's British Second Army would take over the main offensive effort in the centre from Gough's British Fifth Army, which was exhausted by the efforts of July and August. Included in Plumer's forces to be committed to the coming assault were the three divisions of I ANZAC Corps, the 1st, 2nd and 5th, to which was added the 4th Division in order to keep Australian units paired.

The Australian infantry involvement in the Passchendaele offensive commenced with the attack by the 1st and 2nd Divisions on the Menin Road Ridge on 20 September. Although overnight rain had caused some anxiety, it had cleared by the morning. The 1st and 2nd Divisions left their jumping-off lines at 5:40 a.m., the first time two Australian divisions had attacked side by side, which Charles Bean recorded as adding much to the enthusiasm of the attackers.[157] Advancing behind a creeping barrage, the German artillery began falling on the Australian trenches forcing many of the rear waves to press forward rather than maintain staggered columns, resulting in the whole attacking force pressing forward as one line.

---

[157] Bean, *ANZAC to Amiens*, p. 365.

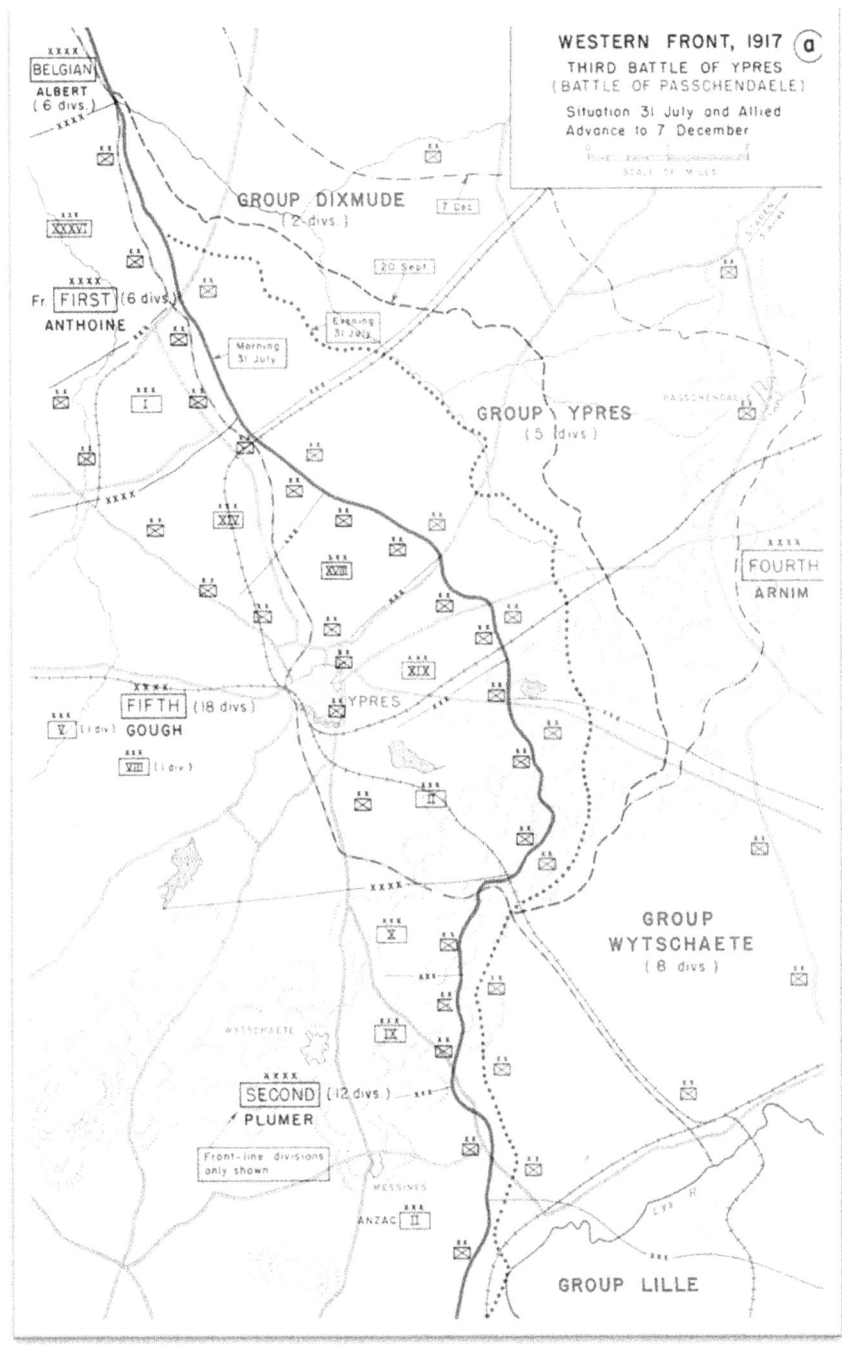

Map of Third Battle of Ypres (Wikipedia, public domain).

Like the attack on Messines Ridge in June, the attack on Menin Road went almost precisely according to plan with the objective secured by 21 September. It had featured the densest barrage that had yet covered the Australians troops, with Bean observing 'the advancing barrage won the ground; the infantry merely occupied it, pouncing on any points at which resistance survived'.[158] The feared German concrete pillboxes were set upon by the infantry as the barrage cloud cleared, giving the defenders little time to react. The attack had advanced the line to the shattered remnants of a forest called Polygon Wood just outside Zonnebeke. Despite the success, the fighting had cost some 5,000 casualties in the Australian divisions.[159]

After a brief pause to allow time for the pioneers and engineers to repair roads and construct light rail systems to enable guns and ammunition to be brought forward, the second step in the attack occurred at 5:50 a.m. on 26 September with the attack by the 4th and 5th Divisions on Polygon Wood. Again, the creeping barrage provided assuring cover, and the troops kept pace with its advance. Most of the initial objectives were quickly captured including the area known as the Butte, a raised earthen embankment that once served as a rifle range. The Butte is now the location of the 5th Australian Division's memorial. Fierce German counter-attacks were successfully beaten off by concentrated artillery and machine gun fire. Casualties across the two divisions were again not inconsequential, with some 5,500 suffered.[160]

The capture of Polygon Wood had advanced the Allied front to a position from which it could attack the main ridgeline known as Broodseinde Ridge. After another pause during which feverish work was undertaken to build roads and railways to support the forthcoming attack, preparations were completed to enable the third step of the attack on Broodseinde Ridge to commence on 4 October 1917.

---

[158] Bean, *Official History*, Vol. 4, p. 761.
[159] Bean, *ANZAC to Amiens*, p. 367.
[160] Bean, *ANZAC to Amiens*, p. 369.

Photograph of the 5th Australian Division memorial erected on the Butte at Polygon Wood (author, 2009).

This would involve the 1st and 2nd Australian Divisions to which would be added 3rd Australian Division and the New Zealand Division from II ANZAC Corp who would attack side by side for the first time, adding again to the high spirits of the troops according to Bean.[161] The ANZAC commanders had decided to assemble the whole of their attacking battalions well forward so that when the attack commenced, they might quickly advance clear of the answering German barrage.

---

[161] Bean, *ANZAC to Amiens*, p. 369.

With zero hour set at 6:00 a.m. on 4 October, rain began to fall the day before, dampening the prospects of success. Forty minutes before the attack was scheduled to commence, spirits were further dampened when a German bombardment began to land on the Australian forward lines, hitting the waiting units of the 1st and 2nd Divisions the hardest. Some 20 officers were killed and it is estimated about a seventh of the attacking units of I ANZAC Corp were killed or wounded by the preliminary German bombardment.[162] Contrary to initial suspicions, the Australian attack had not been detected but rather the Germans were launching their own attack. The opposing forces met in no man's land with the Australians quickly gaining the ascendency in the confusion, driving the Germans back or capturing many. Like the previous attacks on the Messines and Menin Road Ridges, the attack on Broodseinde Ridge was almost completely successful. It had, however, come at a significant cost to the Australian forces with total losses among the three Australian divisions of 6,432 killed, wounded or missing.[163]

German pillbox within Tyne Cot Cemetery, Broodseinde Ridge (author, 2009).

---

[162] Bean, *Official History*, Vol. 4, p. 844.
[163] Bean, *Official History*, Vol. 4, p. 876.

Photograph of the plaque denoting the 3rd Australian Division's capture of a German pillbox on which is now erected the Cross of Sacrifice within the Tyne Cot Commonwealth War Cemetery (author, 2009).

Further attacks were made after 4 October as the next set piece was to capture the village of Passchendaele itself and beyond. Notwithstanding that rain had commenced to fall from 5 October at an increasing heaviness, turning roads and the front lines into a quagmire, the BEF Commander Haig made what Bean described as the most questioned decision of his career to press on with the next stage of the Ypres offensive.[164] A preliminary attack by the 2nd Australian Division commenced on 9 October, with a second stage scheduled to commence at 5:30 a.m. on 12 October after a brief preliminary barrage.

The preparations for the attack were poor – only a preliminary barrage was possible as the artillery could not be moved forward quickly enough over the muddy and shell-scarred landscape. Despite the efforts of the gunners, most batteries did not reach their intended

---

[164] Bean, *Official History*, Vol. 4, p. 883.

positions by the 9th or even the 12th of October. Some guns were simply temporarily abandoned in the mud, and what guns did get in place often had insufficient ammunition due to problems in transporting shells along the crowded and often impassable roads. The replacement infantry, travelling along the same routes, were already exhausted by the time they reached the forward trenches. Further, the objective set for the attacking troops was also double the previous 'bite and hold' operations. Charles Bean concluded[165]:

> Had Godley [Commander ANZAC II Corps] really known the conditions of October 9th – the thinness of the barrage, the complete absence of smoke screen, the ineffectiveness of the bombardment, the exhaustion of the troops – how could he have hoped for success with deeper objectives than any since July 31st, shorter preparation, and with the infantry asked to advance at a pace unattempted in the dry weather of September?

The attack commenced on 12 October with less preparation than had been previously undertaken. On this occasion, the 3rd Australian Division and New Zealand Division were committed to the attack, with the 4th Australian Division in support on their right.[166] Heavy rain continued to fall, causing the attacking infantry to become bogged down in the mud below the village of Passchendaele. While some units managed to reach the outskirts of the town, by evening they were forced to retire with heavy losses. The 3rd and 4th Divisions suffered some 3,000 and 1,000 casualties respectively.[167] The Australian divisions were replaced by the Canadian Corps who eventually succeeded in capturing Passchendaele heights on 10 November 1917, by which time the offensive came to an end, having failed to achieve the hoped for breakthrough.

---

[165] Bean, *Official History*, Vol. 4, pp. 907-908.
[166] Bean, *ANZAC to Amiens*, p. 374.
[167] Bean, *ANZAC to Amiens*, p. 374.

Ypres, Belgium. Australian troops making their way to the trenches, along a track to Westhoek, which is strewn with wreckage. 28 October 1917. AWM ID No. E01222.

Broodseinde Ridge is now the location of the largest Commonwealth War Grave Cemetery in the world, Tyne Cot Cemetery. The land on which the cemetery is located was captured by the 3rd Australian Division on 4 October 1917 as part of its attack on the ridge. The cemetery is littered with the remains of a number of German concrete pillboxes, one of which forms the base of the Cross of Sacrifice erected in the cemetery. Some 11,961 Commonwealth servicemen of the First World War are buried or commemorated in Tyne Cot Cemetery, of which 8,373 of the burials are unidentified.

Brendan Bateman

Passchendaele, Belgium. A section of the Tyne Cot Cemetery which contained 11848 service graves including 609 of members of the AIF. AWM ID No. H12653.

John Kilgour

Private, No. 2372A

1st Pioneer Battalion, 1st Australian Division

Died of Wounds, 18 September 1917, Ypres, Belgium

Buried Lijssenthoek Military Cemetery, Belgium

John Kilgour was born in Oban, Argyllshire, Scotland, in or about 1882.[168] His parents, George and Alison Kilgour (nee Forrester),[169] lived at *Rockmount*, in Oban. John was second eldest of four children, and one of three sons. The eldest son, James, was born in 1880, the only daughter, Elizabeth, was born in 1896, and the youngest child, Alexander, was born in 1896.[170]

According to the Honour Roll Circular completed by his mother after the war,[171] John attended high school in Oban and took on the trade of a house painter. While in Scotland, John had served three years with the Garrison Artillery. At the age of 28, he decided for one reason or another to emigrate to Australia. His older brother, James, also emigrated to Australia some time prior to the outbreak of the war, it being possible that they travelled together to Australia. James was also a painter by profession and had similarly served three years with the Garrison Artillery.

After being in Australia for about six years, John enlisted in the AIF at the Drummoyne recruitment office on 28 April 1916.[172] His brother James also joined on the same date and his service number immediately precedes that of John (2371). John was 34 years and nine months and James was 36 years and nine months on enlistment.[173]

---

[168] War service records accessible at - https://recordsearch.naa.gov.au/SearchNRetrieve/Interface/ViewImage.aspx?B=7371874 (accessed 24 April 2023).

[169] https://www.cwgc.org/find-records/find-war-dead/casualty-details/431374/john-kilgour/#&gid=1&pid=2 (accessed 24 April 2023).

[170] A notice published in *The Mercury* in June 1917, reported the wedding of Charles Kilgour to Elizabeth Palmer at St Stephen's Church, Phillip Street, Sydney. Charles is described as the fourth son of the late George Kilgour of Oban, Scotland. See Family Notices (1917, July 30). *The Mercury* (Hobart, Tas.: 1860-1954), p. 1. Retrieved February 17, 2024, from http://nla.gov.au/nla.news-article1082253 . Charles is reported to have died on 5 July 1943 at the age of 58. He was at the time living at 9 Sunnyside Street, Gladesville – see Family Notices (1943, July 7). *The Sydney Morning Herald* (NSW: 1842-1954), p. 12. Retrieved February 17, 2024, from http://nla.gov.au/nla.news-article17855682 . If Charles was another brother, he would have been born in about 1885.

[171] Accessible at https://www.awm.gov.au/collection/R1641589

[172] War service records accessible at https://recordsearch.naa.gov.au/SearchNRetrieve/Interface/ViewImage.aspx?B=7371874

[173] James Forrester Kilgour served with the 1st Pioneer Battalion until the end of the war when he was transferred to the 1st Australian Mechanical Transport Company in December 1918. James returned to Australia in August 1919. James appears to have become engaged In England prior to his return to Australia, but did not marry his wife, Emily, until 1922 at Gladesville. James died in the same year of his marriage. By 1933, Emily was living with

Both John and James specified 28 Polding Street, Drummoyne, as their address on their respective applications. According to the General Index, Michael J Ahern is recorded as the occupant of this property. Correspondence from the OIC after the war on John's service records is addressed to a Mrs J F Kilgour, care of Mrs Sumner at *Caringa*, Duncan Street, Drummoyne. Mrs JF Kilgour would be James' future wife, Emily Kilgour.

John and James embarked with the 4th Reinforcements to the 1st Pioneer Battalion from Sydney on 22 August 1916 on board HMAT A18 *Wiltshire*. In the same month, both John and James had their names included on an honour board unveiled at the Drummoyne School of Arts to honour members who had enlisted.[174] While on board the *Wiltshire*, the brothers were charged with smoking between decks, and awarded 24 hours' detention. John and James arrived at Plymouth, England on 13 October 1916. After a period of training at the main Australian base near Salisbury, the men marched into the Pioneer Training Battalion on 9 November 1916 at Perham Downs Base Depot. The brothers eventually proceeded overseas for France from Folkestone on board the SS *Golden Eagle* on 28 February 1917 and arrived at the 1st ADBD at Etaples on 1 March 1917. John and James proceeded to join their unit on 5 March and were taken on strength with the 1st Pioneer Battalion six days later.

The 1st Pioneer Battalion had been established in March 1916 in Egypt and had arrived in France on 1 April 1916.[175] In March 1917, the battalion was at Mametz Camp on the Somme sector of the front, where its units were variously engaged in the construction of dugouts,

---

Mrs E Roberts at 119 Majors Bay Road, Concord. As Emily was not married to James during the period of his war service, her application for a 'Nearest Female Relative' badge was refused.

[174] Drummoyne Honor Roll. (1916, August 9). *Australian Town and Country Journal* (Sydney, NSW: 1870-1919), p. 15. Retrieved February 17, 2024, from http://nla.gov.au/nla.news-article263606094 . Other men commemorated on the honour board include Jack Connell, Downie Dodd, Albert Erickson, Hugh Breckenridge, Stuart Weir, Russell Barton and R Walker.

[175] 1st Pioneer Battalion Unit Diary April 1916 - https://www.awm.gov.au/collection/C1355099

observation posts, light railways and second-line defences.[176] The battalion continued its construction and repair works throughout April and May until relieved when in June 1917 it moved to Dernancourt.[177]

By August, the battalion had moved to Lumbres in France, but in proximity to the Ypres front in Belgium. Companies from the battalion were sent to Ypres to carry out works including the construction of gun pits and dugouts. On 1 September, the battalion moved to Vieux in Belgium, before moving closer to the Ypres front on 7 September 1917. The casualties suffered by the battalion began to grow as work in close proximity to the frontlines exposed the pioneers to shell-fire and gas attacks.

Between 15 and 19 September, the battalion was engaged in road and railway construction, burying signalling cable and construction of the Hooge tunnel near Zillebeke.[178] The works being undertaken by the pioneers were preparatory for the opening of the attack on the Menin Road Ridge by the 1st and 2nd Australian Divisions, which would commence on 20 September 1917. However, the works also included preparations for the second stage of the attack, scheduled to commence on 25 September, which required works to enable the massed supporting artillery to be quickly moved forward to new emplacements, and fresh troops to be brought forward to initiate the second stage.

As Charles Bean recorded, almost the entire engineering force of I ANZAC Corps, which included the 1st Pioneer Battalion, concentrated on the work of providing new forward and lateral tracks using timber planks for the troops to reach their jumping-off points for the attack over heavily churned-up ground.[179] Bean further noted that the circuit roads under construction by the pioneers came at a heavy cost with the forward ground always heavily shelled, frequently with

---

[176] 1st Pioneer Battalion Unit Diary March 1917 - https://www.awm.gov.au/collection/C1347348
[177] 1st Pioneer Battalion Unit Diary June 1917 - https://www.awm.gov.au/collection/C1347350
[178] 1st Pioneer Battalion Unit Diary September 1917 - https://www.awm.gov.au/collection/C1347353
[179] Bean, *Official History*, Vol. 4 pp. 747 and 794.

mustard gas, which shelling increased once the roads under construction were observed by German aircraft.[180] The main bombardment for the attack commenced on 15 September, inviting German retaliatory barrages on Westhoek and in the rear areas while the preparatory works were proceeding.

Engineers supply dump near Birr Cross-Road, which is stocked with piles of duckboards and timber. Along the timber plank road in the background more soldiers can be seen approaching the area. AWM ID No. E04613.

It was during these preparatory works, on 17 September 1917, that John was reported to have been wounded in action. John was initially admitted to the 6th Australian Field Ambulance on the same day suffering from shell wounds to both legs with compound fractures. He was transferred to the 17th CCS where he died on 18 September 1917 from his wounds. He was 35 years old and would be one of 50 other

---

[180] Bean, *Official History*, Vol. 4 p. 794.

ranks in the battalion that would become casualties during the Menin Road attack.[181]

John's personal effects were returned to his mother in March 1918, with his medals issued on account of his war service following several years later.

John is buried in the Lijssenthoek Military Cemetery, the second largest Commonwealth cemetery in Belgium.[182] He is also commemorated on the Oban War Memorial in Oban, Scotland.[183]

Plaque on the Oban War Memorial inscribed with the name of John Kilgour. Source - https://vwma.org.au/explore/people/170725.

---

[181] Bean, *Official History*, Vol. 4, p. 789.
[182] Commonwealth War Graves Commission - http://www.cwgc.org/find-a-cemetery/cemetery/14900/LIJSSENTHOEK%20MILITARY%20CEMETERY
[183] https://canmore.org.uk/site/93215/oban-war-memorial

Photograph of the grave of John Kilgour, Lijssenthoek Military Cemetery (author, 2018).

Thomas Charles Price

Private, No. 5464

18th Battalion, 5th Infantry Brigade, 2nd Australian Division

Killed in action, Menin Road, Belgium, 20 September 1917

Buried, Hooge Crater Cemetery, Zillebeke, Belgium

Thomas Charles Price was born in London England in about 1886 and emigrated to Australia with his parents Thomas Plant[184] and Ophelia Lydia Price at the age of 18 months.[185] Thomas was educated at Drummoyne Public School and his parents resided at *Avoca*, 8 Westbourne Street, Drummoyne at the time of his enlistment in February 1916.[186] A barber by profession and just over 29 years' old, he enlisted in Grenfell and was taken to the Cootamundra Recruiting Office where he was accepted into the AIF.

Thomas was assigned to the 14th Reinforcements to the 18th Infantry Battalion, embarking from Sydney on 22 August 1916 on HMAT A18 *Wiltshire*. Shortly before departing, Thomas made his will in which he bequeathed his entire estate to his mother, Ophelia Price. He arrived in Plymouth, England, on 13 October 1916 and marched into the 5th Training Battalion at Rollestone where he undertook training at the Australian base. Thomas embarked on *Princess Henrietta* on 13 December 1916 from Folkestone for service in France. Thomas finally joined his battalion on 26 January 1917 and was one of 136 reinforcements to arrive that day.[187]

On 9 February 1917, the battalion went into the front-line trenches near Flers to replace the 26th Battalion, experiencing the mud and cold conditions of winter in the trenches. Apart from improving the condition of the saps, the battalion was also engaged in undertaking salvage work, uncovering many unburied dead in the vicinity.[188] Thomas was briefly admitted to the 38th CCS suffering from

---

[184] The middle name, Charles, appears on the nominal roll and was inserted by hand on Thomas' attestation paper sometime later. According to the Commonwealth War Graves records, the middle name was Plant, and this appears on the Honour Roll Circular completed by his father after the war.
[185] https://www.awm.gov.au/collection/C2097478 (accessed 24 April 2023)
[186] War service records accessible at https://recordsearch.naa.gov.au/SearchNRetrieve/Interface/ViewImage.aspx?B=8022245
[187] 18th Battalion Unit Diary February 1917 - https://www.awm.gov.au/collection/C1342396?image=2
[188] 18th Battalion Unit Diary February 1917 - https://www.awm.gov.au/collection/C1342396?image=6

diphtheria but rejoined his unit in time for it to follow up the German withdrawal to the Hindenburg Line.[189]

Thomas was again taken sick in April 1917, and was this time admitted to the 18th General Hospital at Camiers where he remained until 7 May 1917. Said to be suffering from pyrexia, or fever of unknown origin, he was taken to the Divisional Rest Station before being admitted to hospital. Consequently, Thomas missed the battalion's involvement in the Second Battle of Bullecourt in May 1917.

After periods at convalescent hospitals and depots at Etaples and Cayeux, Thomas did not finally rejoin his battalion until 1 August 1917. By mid-August, the battalion was moving towards Flanders in Belgium where it undertook various training exercises including lectures on new form of German gas. On 29 August the battalion, along with all the 2nd Division, was inspected by the British Commander in Chief, Field Marshall Sir Douglas Haig.[190]

Early September saw further training with the battalion participating in a practice of the brigade's attack scheme.[191] On 11 September orders were received for the battalion to take up positions near Westhoek. While the 5th Brigade was initially held in reserve, it provided working parties to carry supplies to the forward lines. On 19 September, the time came for the 18th Battalion to join in the attack, which was to take place on Menin Road Ridge as part of the continuation of the Third Battle of Ypres that had commenced on 31 July 1917.

Drawing trench stores, the battalion moved forward at 6:30 p.m. to assembly points at Bellewaarde Ridge, before moving out at 1:40 a.m. the next day to the jumping-off tape at Westhoek Ridge.[192] It was during the night of 19–20 September that the weather began to turn

---

[189] 18th Battalion Unit Diary February 1917 - https://www.awm.gov.au/collection/C1342396?image=7
[190] 18th Battalion Unit Diary August 1917 - https://www.awm.gov.au/collection/C1342403?image=9
[191] 18th Battalion Unit Diary September 1917 - https://www.awm.gov.au/collection/C1355880?image=4
[192] 18th Battalion Unit Diary September 1917 - https://www.awm.gov.au/collection/C1355880?image=7

with steady rain beginning to fall as the troops made their way along their access tracks to their jumping-off positions. As the tracks turned to mud, Charles Bean reported that consideration was given to postponing the attack, but with the promise of improving conditions, the decision was made to proceed.[193]

The 2nd Division held the left side of the Australian section of the line, with the 1st Division on its right. The 5th Brigade was aligned to the left side of the 2nd Division front, with the 20th Battalion in front and the 18th Battalion behind it.

At 5:40 a.m., the British barrage opened up and the battalion moved out in attack formation.[194] The German artillery had already begun to fall on the Australian lines before the attack had commenced, but the 20th Battalion was already waiting in no man's land in order to avoid any German bombardment. However, the shell-fire put pressure on the 18th Battalion, catching its tail, which was only relieved when the British bombardment commenced allowing the attackers to begin to move forward.[195]

The 18th Battalion moved through the first objective, which had been captured by the 20th Battalion and attacked the defensive positions called ANZAC Spur and Iron Cross Redoubt. Encountering little resistance, the battalion captured the second objective designated as the Blue Line by 7:41 a.m., before moving further forward to the Green Line and consolidating its position.[196] Although the battalion observed the Germans mustering for a counterattack, it was broken up by artillery fire, as was another attempt later that evening. The battalion diary records that its losses in the fighting included four officers killed and five wounded, with the other ranks suffering an estimated

---

[193] Bean, *Official History*, Vol. 4, pp. 753-4.
[194] 18th Battalion Unit Diary September 1917 - https://www.awm.gov.au/collection/C1355880?image=7
[195] Bean, *Official History*, Vol. 4, p. 757.
[196] 18th Battalion Unit Diary September 1917 - https://www.awm.gov.au/collection/C1355880?image=8

200 casualties.[197] Thomas Price would be one of the other ranks who was killed in the attack on Menin Road on 20 September 1917. Thomas' name was among those listed as killed in action in the 344th casualty list published in October 1917.[198]

A brief family notice appeared in *The Sydney Morning Herald* on the anniversary of Thomas' death in 1918 from his brother Harry and sister-in-law Maggie Price,[199] with additional notices being published in 1920 by family and friends[200]:

PRICE. — In loving memory of our dear son and brother, Thomas Charles Price, killed in action, September 20, 1917.

We loved him in life,
Let us not forget him in death.

Inserted by his sorrowing father, mother, sisters, and brothers, Drummoyne.

PRICE. — In loving memory of Tom Price, late of Drummoyne, killed in action, France. September 20, 1917.

He died that we might live.

Inserted by Mr. and Mrs. Briggs, Drummoyne.

---

[197] 18th Battalion Unit Diary September 1917 - https://www.awm.gov.au/collection/C1355880?image=9 . Bean records the battalion's casualties as 12 officers and 263 other ranks (Bean, *Official History*, Vol. 4, p.789).
[198] 1917 '344th LIST.', *The Land* (Sydney, NSW: 1911-1954), 26 October, p. 13., viewed 24 Apr 2023, http://nla.gov.au/nla.news-article102892258 ; FOR AUSTRALIA (1917, October 22). *The Sun* (Sydney, NSW: 1910-1954), p. 2. Retrieved April 24, 2023, from http://nla.gov.au/nla.news-article221390634 ; NEW SOUTH WALES. (1917, October 23). *The Daily Telegraph* (Sydney, NSW: 1883-1930), p. 7. Retrieved April 24, 2023, from http://nla.gov.au/nla.news-article239242203 ; KILLED. (1917, October 23). *The Sydney Morning Herald* (NSW: 1842-1954), p. 8. Retrieved April 24, 2023, from http://nla.gov.au/nla.news-article15755871
[199] Family Notices (1918, September 30). *The Sydney Morning Herald* (NSW: 1842-1954), p. 6. Retrieved April 24, 2023, from http://nla.gov.au/nla.news-article15804759
[200] Family Notices (1920, September 20). *The Sydney Morning Herald* (NSW: 1842-1954), p. 6. Retrieved April 24, 2023, from http://nla.gov.au/nla.news-article16866852

We do not know the circumstances of Thomas' death, but it appears that his remains were buried by his comrades, as according to the records of the GSU,[201] Thomas' grave was marked with a cross marked simply as 'In Memory 5464 T. C. Price 18/A.I.F. Bn.' Thomas' remains were exhumed and reburied in the Hooge Crater Cemetery, Zillebeke in 1920.[202]

Photograph of the grave of Thomas Price, Hooge Crater Cemetery, Zillebeke (author, 2018).

---

[201] Commonwealth War Graves Commission https://www.cwgc.org/find-war-dead/casualty/459100/price,-thomas-charles/#&gid=null&pid=1

[202] By that time, Thomas' parents were living on Undine Street, Five Dock.

Charles Leslie Thornton

Private, No 10089

14th Australian Field Ambulance, 5th Australian Division

Killed in action, 21 September 1917, Polygon Wood, Belgium

Buried Hooge Crater Cemetery, Zillebeke, Belgium

He Died the Noblest Death Man May Die for God, Right and Liberty

Charles Leslie Thornton was the son of Sydney James and Sarah Ellen Thornton. Charles was born in 1895[203] and he had one older brother, Mervyn, who was born in 1894,[204] and a younger brother, Alan, born in 1898.[205] Sydney and Sarah lived for a period at *Uki*, Bridge Road, Drummoyne[206] with Mervyn attending Drummoyne Public School and Charles Cleveland Street Public School. Both had been members of the senior cadets, but Charles was also a member of the 18th Infantry CMF at the date of his enlistment.

Charles applied to enlist in the AIF a month after his older brother on 13 August 1915[207] at the age of 20 years and three months while employed as a clerk.[208] On Charles' attestation form it is recorded that he had previously been rejected to join the AIF on account of suffering from varicocele,[209] and among his distinctive marks is recorded a scar from varicocele on the left side and also a scar on the right inguinal region. The fact that Mervyn and Charles have sequential regimental numbers might suggest that they applied to enlist on the same date but that Charles was initially rejected as unfit until he had his medical matters attended to.

The brothers were both assigned to the 5th Reinforcements to the 8th Field Ambulance as part of the Australian Army Medical Corps (AAMC) and embarked from Sydney on HMAT A71 *Nestor* on 9 April 1916. The brothers travelled to Egypt before embarking again this

---

[203] NSW BDM Registration No. 16448/1895. According to one source, his actual date of birth was 5 May 1895 - https://rslvirtualwarmemorial.org.au/explore/people/249307 (accessed 11 September 2018).
[204] NSW BDM Registration No. 28876/1894. The record for Mervyn's birth misspells his father's name as Sidney. According to one source, his actual date of birth was 27 March 1894 - https://rslvirtualwarmemorial.org.au/explore/people/288753 (accessed 11 September 2018).
[205] NSW BDM Registration No. 34031/1898. Alan died in 1899 although his forename in the records is spelt Allen – see NSW BDM Registration No. 3080/1899.
[206] Renamed Victoria Road and Sydney Thornton is noted as living in the house located between Seymour Street and Drummoyne Avenue according to the Sands General Index Directory.
[207] War service records accessible at https://recordsearch.naa.gov.au/SearchNRetrieve/Interface/ViewImage.aspx?B=8390374
[208] See account for Mervyn Thornton who died of illness in October 1918.
[209] An enlargement of the veins within the loose bag of skin that holds your testicles (scrotum).

time from Alexandria on 28 May 1916 on the *Corsican*. After a period of training in England, they embarked for France on 16 July 1916, marching in to the 5th ADBD at Etaples on 19 July 1916.

On 31 July 1916, the brothers marched out from the base camp, having been transferred to the 14th Field Ambulance. They were among 14 reinforcements to join the unit from Rouen.[210] At the end of July 1916, the 14th Field Ambulance was stationed near Sailly in French Flanders serving with the 5th Australian Division, which division had been severely depleted following the failed attack on Fromelles. Charles' service record after this date contains no further entries.

The 14th Field Ambulance served in the lines around Outtersteene in French Flanders before being withdrawn to Bellancourt in mid-October 1916 where it participated in the first conscription referendum and received word that it was to proceed to the Somme sector.[211] On arrival near Albert in late October, the unit found its positions in poor condition due to recent rains, making the work of the stretcher bearers difficult. This resulted in a number of bearers breaking down from the strain and stress of the work and weather[212] including Charles' brother.

The conditions through November 1916 continued to deteriorate, as did the state of the men in the unit with cases of influenza, diarrhoea and trench foot becoming prevalent.[213] The 14th Field Ambulance endured the harsh winter of 1916–17 in and out of the line, and by March 1917 was based at the 1st ANZAC Collection Station at Becordel, just east of Albert on the Somme.[214]

---

[210] 14th Field Ambulance Unit Diary July 1916 - https://www.awm.gov.au/collection/C1353548?image=8
[211] 14th Field Ambulance Unit Diary October 1916 - https://www.awm.gov.au/collection/C1353551?image=4
[212] 14th Field Ambulance Unit Diary October 1916 - https://www.awm.gov.au/collection/C1353551?image=6
[213] 14th Field Ambulance Unit Diary November 1916 - https://www.awm.gov.au/collection/C1352965?image=2
[214] 14th Field Ambulance Unit Diary March 1917 - https://www.awm.gov.au/collection/C1354680?image=2

The 14th Field Ambulance provided support to the Second Battle of Bullecourt in May 1917, where it processed a large number of casualties over the course of the fighting, and its stretcher bearers were placed under significant strain as well as suffering extensive losses. According to Charles Bean, on no one were the conditions more severely experienced than by the bearers of the Field Ambulances who were required to carry wounded for over a mile and a half entirely in the open.[215] By June, the unit moved to the Divisional Rest Station near Warloy where it took stock of its losses from the fighting at Bullecourt and refitted.[216]

At the end of July 1917, the unit began moving north to Flanders[217] to support the forthcoming Third Battle of Ypres. On 17 September 1917, the 14th Field Ambulance moved to Steenvorde with the 14th Brigade of the 5th Division. Sections of the unit were then attached to the 1st and 2nd Australian Divisions on 20 September for duty in the Ypres salient, which divisions were engaged in the attack on the Menin Road Ridge. The move would be a fateful one for Charles as on 21 September, he was reported as being killed in action. We have no information regarding the circumstances on Charles' death other than he is likely to have been killed during the fighting near Polygon Wood[218] while acting as a stretcher bearer.[219] Charles was one of 14 other ranks from the 14th Field Ambulance killed during the fighting between 18 September and 1 October 1917.[220]

---

[215] Bean, *Official History*, Vol 4, p. 474.
[216] 14th Field Ambulance Unit Diary June 1917 - https://www.awm.gov.au/collection/C1352971?image=3
[217] 14th Field Ambulance Unit Diary July 1917 - https://www.awm.gov.au/collection/C1354681?image=5
[218] As noted in the Honour Roll Circular completed by Charles' father after the war - https://s3-ap-southeast-2.amazonaws.com/awm-media/collection/RCDIG1068841/document/5541236.PDF
[219] The Memorial Notice published in *The Sydney Morning Herald* on the anniversary of Charles' death on 21 September 1918 by his brother noted that he had been killed while stretcher bearing.
[220] 14th Field Ambulance Unit Diary September 1917 - https://www.awm.gov.au/collection/C1352974?image=10

On the first anniversary of Charles' death, Mervyn along with his parents posted memorial notices in *The Sydney Morning Herald*[221]:

THORNTON. — In loving memory of our dear son, Pte. C. Leslie Thornton, late 14th Field Amb., killed in action Sept. 21st, 1917.

Oh, brave and gentle heart,
Well have you done your part,
For God, King, and country.

Inserted by his loving mother, father, and Fred.

THORNTON. — In fond memory of my dearly loved and only brother. Private C. Leslie Thornton, killed in action, stretcher bearing, September 21st, 1917.

Greater love hath no man than this.

Inserted by his loving brother, Mervyn, on active service, A.I.F.

Charles is buried in Hooge Crater Cemetery, Zillebeke, Belgium.

---

[221] Family Notices (1918, September 21). *The Daily Telegraph* (Sydney, NSW: 1883 1930), p. 8. Retrieved April 24, 2023, from http://nla.gov.au/nla.news-article239359457

Photograph of the grave of Charles Thornton at Hooge Crater Cemetery, Zillebeke, Belgium (author, 2018).

Herbert John Wilder

Private, No.3003

58th Battalion, 15th Infantry Brigade, 5th Australian Division

Killed in action 25 September 1917, Polygon Wood, Belgium

No known grave. Commemorated Ypres (Menin Gate) Memorial, Ypres, Belgium

Herbert (Bert) John Wilder was born in Scone, NSW, on 28 December 1882, the son of Charles William and Cecilia (nee Taylor) Wilder.[222] Herbert was one of 10 children and attended school at Belltrees near Scone. He married Annie Mulligan in Scone in about 1909[223] and they had three children: Herbert Charles,[224] Eleanor Annie[225] and Adolphus Theodore.[226]

Herbert applied to enlist in the AIF on 21 August 1916[227] at Victoria Barracks at the stated age of 32 years and eight months.[228] He gave his occupation as a labourer[229] and named his wife Annie as his next of kin. At the time, they were living at 25 Cometrowe Street, Drummoyne. Transferred initially to the Royal Agricultural Showgrounds at Moore Park, Herbert was moved to B Company in the Bathurst Depot Battalion before being assigned to the 7th Reinforcements to the 58th Battalion at Liverpool in October 1916.

Embarking from Sydney on HMAT A19 *Afric* on 3 November 1916, Herbert sailed for England where he disembarked at Plymouth on 9 January 1917. During the voyage to England, Herbert was admitted to the ship's hospital for a month suffering from measles. He joined the 15th Training Battalion at Lark Hill on the Salisbury Plain[230] where he undertook further training. In March 1917, Herbert was posted for service in France and proceeded to the 5th ADBD at

---

[222] NSW BDM Registration No. 20610/1883. According to the NSW BDM database, Herbert's father was Christian William whereas according to the AIF Project database and CWGC, his father was Charles William. Birth records for the other children confirm his name as Charles.
[223] NSW BDM Registration No. 9180/1909.
[224] NSW BDM Registration No. 11254/1910 in Sydney.
[225] NSW BDM Registration No. 35568/1912 in Tingha.
[226] NSW BDM Registration No. 27524/1914 in Redfern.
[227] War service records accessible at https://recordsearch.naa.gov.au/SearchNRetrieve/Interface/ViewImage.aspx?B=8388560
[228] If Herbert's date of birth is correct, then he would have been 33 years and eight months at the time of his enlistment.
[229] This is confirmed by the Honour Roll Circular completed by Annie Wilder after the war - https://www.awm.gov.au/collection/R1667992 . In a statement obtained by the Red Cross in March 1918, Private A Pascall (3282) stated that Herbert was a miner - https://www.awm.gov.au/collection/C1408295
[230] https://www.aif.adfa.edu.au/OrderOfBattle/Training.html (accessed 7 January 2019).

Etaples and was taken on strength by the 58th Battalion on 26 March. He was assigned to the Lewis Gun Section of XV Platoon in D Company.

The 58th Battalion had been raised in Egypt in February 1916 as part of the expansion of the AIF, with half of its recruits coming from the 6th Battalion, which had served at Gallipoli, and the other half comprised of fresh reinforcements from Australia. The 58th Battalion was predominantly composed of men from Victoria and became part of the 15th Brigade of the 5th Australian Division.[231] The battalion's initiation to fighting in France was a disastrous one, with it almost wiped out in the attack on German lines at Fromelles in July 1916.

At the time that Herbert joined the 58th Battalion, it had been involved in following up the Germans after their withdrawal to the prepared defensive line called the Hindenburg Line, and on 26 March was at Morchies providing support as the 2nd Division was commencing its ultimately successful an attack on the village of Lagnicourt.[232] The battalion also launched a successful silent attack on 27 March to advance its line to the Lagnicourt–Doignies Road.[233] Relieved, the battalion was held in reserve in early to mid-April 1917 to support further attacks to advance the front line, including the first attack on the Hindenburg Line at Bullecourt. On 20 April, the battalion was replaced and moved to Mametz where it underwent training and re-equipping. To commemorate the landing at ANZAC Cove two years earlier, a holiday was given to the men with brigade sports held and a very good dinner provided on 25 April.[234]

The battalion remained at Mametz Camp until 8 May when it received orders to move forward in readiness to support the capture of Bullecourt, where it observed many Australian dead that remained unburied in the communication trenches and first and second lines on

---

[231] https://www.awm.gov.au/collection/U51498 (accessed 7 January 2019).
[232] 58th Battalion Unit Diary March 1917 - https://www.awm.gov.au/collection/C1346195?image=11
[233] 58th Battalion Unit Diary March 1917 - https://www.awm.gov.au/collection/C1346195?image=12 and https://www.awm.gov.au/collection/C1346195?image=46
[234] 58th Battalion Unit Diary April 1917 - https://www.awm.gov.au/collection/C1356022?image=8

the way to the front[235] The battalion moved into the front lines on 10 May, entering the salient, which was the only part of the Hindenburg Line that had been captured. It found the trenches, such as they were, badly knocked about and many places in an untenable condition. Almost immediately, the battalion came under German artillery fire and bombing attacks.[236]

It was during the battalion's defence of the captured Hindenburg salient that Herbert is reported as being wounded in action on 12 May 1917 with his service record containing the word 'buried', which suggests that he may have been buried after an explosion from shelling. The battalion's diary records that heavy German shelling between midnight and 4 a.m. on 12 May knocked out two Lewis Gun teams with numerous casualties suffered by those teams, and with whole lengths of trenches being filled in by the shelling.[237]

Herbert was admitted to the 3rd AFA and reported to be suffering from an injury to his right knee. Transferred to the 5th Divisional Rest Station, he rejoined his unit on 18 May, well before Annie was formally notified in mid-June that he had been wounded and news had reached his brother[238] or his name appeared in the casualty lists.[239] By the time Herbert had rejoined his unit, it had been relieved and eventually moved into training and rest camps, where it remained until 17 September 1917 when it received orders to prepare to move to the Ypres sector in Belgium.

The 58th Battalion's next major engagement would be in the Third Battle of Ypres, which had commenced on 31 July 1917. The 1st and 2nd Australian Divisions had been engaged in the attack on Menin Road Ridge on 20 September 1917, which advanced the line to the

---

[235] 58th Battalion Unit Diary May 1917 - https://www.awm.gov.au/collection/C1346196?image=6
[236] 58th Battalion Unit Diary May 1917 - https://www.awm.gov.au/collection/C1346196?image=7
[237] 58th Battalion Unit Diary May 1917 - https://www.awm.gov.au/collection/C1346196?image=10 and https://www.awm.gov.au/collection/C1346196?image=13
[238] WEST WYALONG. (1917, July 6). The *Albury Banner and Wodonga Express* (NSW: 1860-1938), p. 2. Retrieved April 24, 2023, from http://nla.gov.au/nla.news-article101116341
[239] NEW SOUTH WALES. (1917, June 28). *The Sydney Morning Herald* (NSW: 1842-1954), p. 8. Retrieved April 24, 2023, from http://nla.gov.au/nla.news-article15757382

shattered remnants of a forest called Polygon Wood just outside Zonnebeke. The 4th and 5th Divisions were called up for the next stage of the attack, which would involve the 58th Battalion in seizing Polygon Wood with the attack to commence on 26 September.

While still in the rear areas, the battalion along with other elements of the 5th Division received training on the proposed assault on Polygon Wood, which included a model of the wood and surrounding areas in order that the troops could familiarise themselves with the terrain.[240] Finally, orders arrived to relieve the 56th Battalion in the front lines on the night of 23–24 September. The relief was successfully completed with 24 September being relatively quiet.

Circumstances changed in the early hours of 25 September 1917 with increasing ferocity in the German artillery bombardment and reports of the enemy massing for an attack. At 6 a.m., the unit diary notes that two platoons of D Company were sent forward to reinforce A Company in the line. At 6:40 a.m., the enemy attempted to storm the battalion's sector, but were successfully repulsed.[241] It was during this fighting and while serving in the Lewis Gun Section of XV Platoon in D Company that Herbert was killed in action on 25 September 1917.

Herbert's name appeared in the 345th casualty list as having been killed in action[242] with reports beginning to circulate in local papers of Herbert's death including *The Wyalong Advocate and Mining, Agricultural and Pastoral Gazette*[243]:

---

[240] 58th Battalion Unit Diary September 1917 - https://www.awm.gov.au/collection/C1357072?image=19
[241] 58th Battalion Unit Diary September 1917 - https://www.awm.gov.au/collection/C1357072?image=26
[242] AUSTRALIAN CASUALTIES. (1917, October 25). *The Sydney Morning Herald* (NSW: 1842-1954), p. 8. Retrieved April 24, 2023, from http://nla.gov.au/nla.news-article15754165
[243] Private H. J. Wilder. (1917, October 20). *The Wyalong Advocate and Mining, Agricultural and Pastoral Gazette* (NSW: 1900-1928), p. 4. Retrieved April 24, 2023, from http://nla.gov.au/nla.news-article108605397 . Other reports appeared in PTE. H. J. WILDER KILLED. (1917, October 23). *Young Witness* (NSW: 1915-1923), p. 2. Retrieved April 24, 2023, from http://nla.gov.au/nla.news-article113644758 and WEST WYALONG. (1917, October 26). The *Albury Banner and Wodonga Express* (NSW: 1860-1938), p. 6. Retrieved April 24, 2023, from http://nla.gov.au/nla.news-article101119127

Private H. J. Wilder.

The death has occurred in action on September 25th of Private H. J. (Bert) Wilder, of the 58th Battalion, brother of Mr. E. A. Wilder, of West Wyalong. The deceased soldier hero enlisted from Drummoyne, and has been on service for six months. In addition to his aged parents (who reside near Scone), and five brothers and sisters, he leaves a wife and three children to mourn their very sad loss. We extend our deep sympathy to the relatives.

A number of statements were obtained by the Red Cross during its investigations into the circumstances of Herbert's death.[244] Overall the statements are remarkably consistent in recording that Herbert's platoon was moving forward from support lines to reinforce the line under German attack near Polygon Wood. While moving forward across open ground, Herbert was hit in the neck by a machine gun bullet and died almost instantly. His close friend, Lance Corporal Edward R Ward, (3238) in a letter dated 13 February 1918 advised the Red Cross:

> [Herbert] was killed on the morning of the 25.9.17. He was shot through the neck and died almost immediately. He never spoke, he was in the same platoon as me and was in the Machine Lewis Gun Section.
>
> He was just behind Pte. N.E. Smith, who was carrying the Gun and when Pte. Wilder fell he took off his equipment and undid his clothes, and he saw that he was shot through the neck with a bullet and was quite dead. ... He was no doubt buried on the field as he was killed going over to the front line.

---

[244] https://www.awm.gov.au/collection/C1408295 and https://s3-ap-southeast-2.amazonaws.com/awm-media/collection/RCDIG1057876/document/5645605.PDF

Private Arthur Pascall (3282), Private Norman E Smith (1970) and Lance Corporal Frederick Coustley (1644) all advised the Red Cross that they had seen Herbert shot through the neck and killed outright while going across open space between the support and front lines at Polygon Wood. Although neither Pte Pascall nor Pte Smith could advise the Red Cross if Herbert had been buried, L/Cpl Coustley stated that Herbert had been buried where he fell by mates from his company.

More detail regarding the events was given in a statement by Private Charles Higgins (1921) to the Red Cross in February 1918[245]:

> He was in my platoon and he was killed by a M.G. bullet as we were going into the front line at about 7 o'clock in the morning near Polygon Wood. ... There was an attack on at the time by the Germans and we were rushing up in support. The Germans came over eight times during the day following but we continued to hold the ground. He came from NSW, and I have known him for about 6 months. He was rather short and we always called him Bert.

Although a note was made on Herbert's service record that he was buried in vicinity of Polygon Wood, his remains were not located after the war, and Herbert joins the more than 6,000 Australians commemorated on the Menin Gate Memorial who died in the fighting in Belgium but who have no known grave.

---

[245] Pte Higgins stated that Herbert was shot in the leg, but all the other statements confirm that Herbert was hit in the neck. This would also explain his almost instantaneous death.

Photograph of the 58th Battalion panel on which is inscribed the name of Herbert Wilder at the Ypres (Menin Gate) Memorial, Ypres (author, 2018).

Jack Hammond Fitzgerald

Driver, No. 22189
8th Field Artillery Brigade, 3rd Australian Division
Killed in action 26 September 1917, Menin Road, Ypres
Buried The Huts Cemetery, Dickebusch, Belgium

Jack Hammond Fitzgerald was born in Carlton North in Melbourne, Victoria, in 1898.[246] He was one of five children of Robert and Louisa Jane Fitzgerald (nee Raines) and appears to have been the youngest of the five children. He had an older brother, Robert, and three sisters: Lilian, Rita and Joy Fitzgerald.[247] Jack attended Princes Hill State School in North Carlton, Victoria, and served four years as a senior cadet with the 60th (Brunswick-Carlton) Infantry immediately before he joined the AIF.

A plumber by occupation, Jack gave his postal address on his application to enlist as C/- Mrs Stephens, Johnstone Street, Balmain, at the time of his enlistment on 1 February 1916 in Melbourne.[248] As he was only 18, he required parental consent but both his parents were deceased. In a letter dated 1 February 1916, his sister Lilian Fitzgerald stated that she was Jack's guardian and consented to him proceeding to active service abroad. There may be some doubt regarding the authenticity of this letter as it is dated the same date as Jack's enlistment but is on the letterhead of Gibson's Grand Central Hotel in Adelaide. Further, the handwriting on the consent letter does not readily match Lilian's handwriting in her letter to the OIC in June 1922 advising of her change of address to 5 Cuba Street, Petone, New Zealand.

Jack nominated as his next of kin his brother, Robert Edwin Fitzgerald, who was residing at Herbert Street, North Carlton. Robert would also join the AIF and eventually serve in the same unit as Jack, and die of wounds suffered in May 1918.[249]

Jack was assigned as a reinforcement to the Field Artillery and proceeded to the artillery training base at Maribyrnong, Victoria. On 1 April 1916, he was initially allocated to the 108th Battery of the 23rd

---

[246] Victoria BDM Registration No. 1908/1898.
[247] According to a letter written by Joy to the OIC in June 1920, she advised that the eldest was Mrs W S Lockhead nee Lilian Fitzgerald, Mrs G D Lockhead nee Rita Fitzgerald and herself, Mrs W H Durning. At the time, Joy was living at *Scarbro*, 62 St Georges Crescent, Drummoyne.
[248] War service record accessible at https://recordsearch.naa.gov.au/SearchNRetrieve/Interface/ViewImage.aspx?B=3901859
[249] Robert's attestation paper and service record give his middle name as Edward; however, in 1922, his sister Lilian Lockhead (nee Fitzgerald) made a statutory declaration that his middle name was Edwin.

Howitzer Brigade, but subsequently transferred to the 32nd Battery of that brigade. He was given the rank of driver and embarked from Melbourne on 20 May 1916 on board HMAT A7 *Medic*. The day before his departure, Jack made his will by which he appointed his sister Lilian Fitzgerald of The Dandies Company, Sydney, NSW, as his sole executrix and beneficiary. Jack disembarked along with the other reinforcements at Plymouth on 18 July 1916 and proceeded to the artillery school at Larkhill Camp on the Salisbury Plain in England.

Larkhill, England. 25 December 1916. AIF soldiers training at Camp 14 as artillery officers probably for 3rd Division Artillery. Jack Fitzgerald was training at Larkhill at the time prior to his departure for France at the end of December 1916. AWM ID No H13935.

After completing his training, Jack proceeded to France on 31 December 1916 when he sailed from Southampton. It was shortly after his arrival in France that Jack was transferred from the 23rd FAB to the 30th Battery of the 8th FAB. At the time, the 3rd Australian Division's artillery was being reorganised, with each brigade to consist of three batteries – each comprising six 18 pounder guns, and one battery comprising six 4.5 inch howitzers. The 29th, 30th, 31st and 108th

Batteries made up the 8th FAB, and was placed under the command of Lt. Col. William G Allsop.[250]

In January 1917, the brigade was serving at Strazale in France and throughout the month, provided support to the infantry brigades of the division in the line. This involved responding to requests for artillery support to prevent German threats and troop concentrations, providing support to Australian incursions, and also in counter-battery work when the Germans fired their own artillery on the Australian trenches. Detailed operational orders were issued to the brigade regularly throughout February and March, prescribing the time and extent of artillery support to be provided in aid of infantry operations. Relieved at the end of March, the brigade returned to the Tilques training areas where it remained until 10 April 1917.[251]

The 8th FAB along with the 3rd Australian Division transferred to the Ypres sector of the Western Front in April 1917, where in addition to acclimatising to the conditions in Belgian Flanders, also received its first operational order dealing with enemy tanks. The routine of providing support to the front-line infantry continued until the 3rd Division issued Operational Order no. 4 on 13 May 1917 entitled 'Magnum Opus'. The order required a gradual increase in artillery fire on enemy positions, concentrating on cutting barbed wire entanglements, and targeting of roads behind German lines, until the end of the month.[252] Further operational orders were issued during the month to implement operation Magnum Opus, specifying targets for additional attention, including the use of poison gas. All this activity was in aid of the preparations for the Battle of Messines, which commenced on 7 June 1917.

For its part in the coming offensive, the 8th FAB was given detailed orders as to the advancing barrage that it would provide in support of the attacking troops, including how the barrage would pivot and move

---

[250] 8th FAB Unit Diary January 1917 - https://www.awm.gov.au/collection/C1355154?image=2
[251] 8th AFB Unit Diary April 1917 - https://www.awm.gov.au/collection/C1357120
[252] 8th FAB Unit Diary May 1917- https://www.awm.gov.au/collection/C1357121?image=10

onto other targets when certain points were reached, and the rate of fire it was to maintain. In addition to providing a protective barrage to prevent German troops concentrating to counter-attack, in all the brigade would continuously fire its guns for a precise 10 hours and 35 minutes.[253] As mentioned previously, the Battle for Messines Ridge was considered one of the more successful offensives of the war, due to its extensive planning and preparation. The objective was largely secured within several hours of the attack commencing, and successfully defended from German counter-attacks.

The Battle for Messines was a prelude to the Third Battle of Ypres, which began at the end of July 1917. During July and August, operational orders would be issued almost daily to the 8th FAB regarding the support it was to provide to the offensive by Allied units. The brigade was withdrawn from the line on 29 August for rest in the reserve area.[254]

The brigade returned to the front lines outside of Ypres on 9 September 1917,[255] whereupon it returned to action with a procession of operational orders to support the preparation of the renewal of the Third Battle of Ypres with the attack on the Menin Road. The brigade was placed under overall command of the I ANZAC Corps providing support for the 1st Australian Division in its attack, with a full five days of preliminary bombardment. Like the attack on Messines Ridge in June, the attack on Menin Road that commenced on 20 September 1917 went almost precisely according to plan with a dense barrage covering the Australians troops.

The first step in the Third Battle of Ypres, the taking on the Menin Road, was completed on 21 September 1917. On the same day, Jack made a written request to his commanding officer to be reassigned as a gunner in his battery, which was approved. Preparations

---

[253] 8th FAB Unit Diary June 1917, Appendix 1 Operational Order No. 22 - https://www.awm.gov.au/collection/C1357122?image=5
[254] 8th FAB Unit Diary August 1917 - https://www.awm.gov.au/collection/C1355466?image=3
[255] 8th FAB Unit Diary September 1917 - https://www.awm.gov.au/collection/C1357365?image=2

commenced for the next step of the offensive, which included the attack on Polygon Wood by I ANZAC Corps. This required moving forward the whole massed artillery over a battlefield so churned up by artillery from both sides. The field artillery moved into positions near Bellewaarde and Hooge, and the preparations for the next step of the battle followed the same approach of the first which had been considered successful.

The attack commenced on 26 September 1917 but this time, the massed artillery of the I ANZAC Corps (of which the 8th FAB was just one unit), would be supporting the 4th and 5th Australian Divisions.

Men of the Australian Field Artillery getting their guns into position on Bellewaarde Ridge, on 21 September, following the advance of the infantry the day before. AWM ID No. E00791.

A dump of 18 pounder shell cases at Birr Cross Roads, in the Ypres Sector, where positions were occupied by the 2nd Divisional Artillery, during the battle of Zonnebeke, 20 September 1917, when these shells were used. AWM ID No. E00810.

On 26 September 1917, Jack was serving with his battery in the gun pits at Clapham Junction on Menin Road, just outside Ypres. According to a statement given by Gunner Peter N Smart (15992) to the Red Cross,[256] Jack was killed outright by a piece of shell striking him through the forehead. Gunner Smart reported that Jack was brought down to the wagon lines and was buried at Dickebusch, next to the grave of Bombardier Bert Hodgson. He went onto state:

> Jack Fitzgerald was a very fine fellow and one of my best friends ... He had a fine funeral. Capt. Owens – O.C. wagon line went to the funeral. I was not able to go myself as I was on the guns until knocked (12th Oct). ...

---

[256] Australian Red Cross Wounded and Missing Files - https://www.awm.gov.au/collection/R1488311

Jack Fitzgerald had no parents but had an aunt in North Carlton as he told me but did not say his aunt's name. We slept beside one another in dug-out and wagon line. He was a Driver, but was about to be transferred to "Gunner".

Bombardier Limbert Frederick (22127) advised the Red Cross in January 1918 that Jack was killed instantly by a shell at Sanctuary Wood, Hooge, but on 30 September. He stated[257]:

We had just received an S.O.S. and were to start action when a shell landed behind our dump. He was at the Gun Pits and was killed.

Jack was buried in the cemetery that became known as The Huts, which takes its name from a line of huts strung along the road from Dickebusch (now Dikkebus) to Brandhoek, used by field ambulances during the 1917 Allied offensive on this front. Nearly two-thirds of the burials are of gunners as many artillery positions existed nearby.[258]

Jack's name was included among those killed in action in the 345th casualty list published in late October 1917.[259] A month after Jack's death, his brother Robert joined the 8th FAB. Robert had enlisted in Melbourne on 20 October 1916 at the age of 21 years and six months with service number 32395. Robert served with the brigade until he suffered gunshot wounds on 13 May 1918 and died the same day at the 5th Australian Field Ambulance. Robert is buried at Querrieu British Cemetery, northeast of Amiens.

Although there is no evidence that either Jack or Robert had lived in Drummoyne, their sisters had lived for a period of time in the suburb, and the youngest sibling, Joy Durning, continued to live in Drummoyne well into the 1920s. It is therefore somewhat puzzling

---

[257] Australian Red Cross Wounded and Missing Files - https://www.awm.gov.au/collection/R1488311
[258] The Commonwealth War Graves Commission - http://www.cwgc.org/find-a-cemetery/cemetery/15500/THE%20HUTS%20CEMETERY
[259] THE 345th CASUALTY LIST. (1917, October 27). *The Mildura Cultivator* (Vic.: 1888-1920), p. 2. Retrieved April 25, 2023, from http://nla.gov.au/nla.news-article74806695

that only one brother, Jack, is commemorated on the Drummoyne War Memorial.

Photograph of the grave of Jack Fitzgerald at The Huts Cemetery, Belgium. The War Graves Project, CWGC. Reproduced with permission.

Photograph of The Huts Cemetery, Belgium. The War Graves Project, CWGC. Reproduced with permission.

Stephen John Harrison

Private No. 6746

1st Battalion, 1st Infantry Brigade, 1st Australian Division

Killed in action 3 October 1917, Passchendaele, Belgium

Buried Tyne Cot Cemetery, Passchendaele, Belgium

Stephen John Harrison was the youngest of three brothers, and was born in about 1897[260] in Woollahra, Sydney. A farm hand by occupation at the time of his enlistment, Stephen applied to join the AIF on 17 July 1916 at the age of 18 years and 9 months, having served for two and a half years in senior cadets with the 22nd Battalion.[261] On enlistment, Stephen gave his postal address as c/- Mrs Rogerson, Terry Street, Blakehurst. As both his parents were deceased, he did not require parental consent to enlist.

One of Stephen's brothers, Richard Seth Harrison, had already served with the ANMEF from August 1914, which saw action in German New Guinea where he contracted malaria, and after discharge from that unit, applied to join the AIF in January 1916.[262] On his re-enlistment, Richard gave Stephen (who had not applied to enlist at the time) as his next of kin and his address as C/- Mrs Thornton at Spring Creek, Muswellbrook.

Stephen named his eldest brother, William, was his next of kin, and gave his address as C/- Mrs Thompson, Lyons Road, Drummoyne.[263] Stephen was assigned to C Company in the 1st Battalion and formed part of the 22nd Reinforcements to that unit. The 22nd Reinforcements embarked from Sydney on SS *Port Nicholson* on 8 November 1916, arriving in Devonport in England on 10 January 1917. While undertaking further training with the 1st Training Battalion at the Australian base at Larkhill on the Salisbury Plain, Stephen was charged with two offences including being absent without leave from 11 February 1917 until arrested by Military Police in Salisbury City at 7:30 a.m. on 12

---

[260] NSW BDM Registration No. 34574/1897.
[261] War service records accessible at https://recordsearch.naa.gov.au/SearchNRetrieve/Interface/ViewImage.aspx?B=4734474
[262] Richard Seth Harrison (4690) service records accessible at https://recordsearch.naa.gov.au/SearchNRetrieve/Interface/ViewImage.aspx?B=4734414 . Richard was assigned to the 12th Reinforcements to the 18th Battalion. Richard received a gunshot wound to his right arm with severe fractures to his forearm and nerve damage during the Second Battle of Bullecourt on 3 May 1917. He was medically discharged from the AIF and returned to Australia in February 1918.
[263] Richard's last known address after discharge in February 1918 was *Ngahere*, Lyons Road, Drummoyne.

February 1917. He was awarded one day's Field Punishment No. 2 and forfeited 2 days' pay by Captain H C Pearce.

Stephen embarked for service in France on 19 April 1917 from Folkestone, arriving at the main Australian base at Etaples on 20 April where he joined the 1st ADBD. Stephen left the depot on 11 May and was taken on strength by the 1st Battalion on 14 May 1917. The battalion had just come out of the fighting at Bullecourt, where as part of the 1st Australian Division, it had been fed into the second attempt to take the fortified village as the attack by the 2nd Australian Division floundered. We do not know if at the time of his posting that he became aware that his older brother, Richard, had been severely wounded in action at Bullecourt while serving with the 18th Battalion in the 2nd Australian Division.

In May 1917, the 1st Battalion was moved from Bullecourt to Bazentin le Petit to receive reinforcements and undertake 'specialist' training.[264] Throughout June–July 1917, the battalion continued training around Lavieville, with officers and men being granted periods of leave or being assigned to specialist training schools.[265] It was during this time that on 18 July 1917, Stephen made his will, by which he bequeathed his estate to his brother William who he stated was living at *Mahuta*, College Street, Gladesville.

After experiencing its longest rest during the war, on 26 July 1917, the 1st Australian Division commenced its move north to the Ypres sector of the front in Belgian Flanders. The 3rd and 4th Australian Divisions, which formed the II ANZAC Corps, had already been involved in a preliminary attack at Messines Ridge in June 1917 in the lead-up to the Third Battle of Ypres. The three divisions of I ANZAC Corps were now to be committed to reinvigorate the Ypres offensive with an attack on the Menin Road Ridge, which commenced on 20 September 1917.

---

[264] 1st Battalion Unit Diary May 1917 - https://www.awm.gov.au/collection/C1347455?image=4
[265] 1st Battalion Unit Diary June 1917 - https://www.awm.gov.au/collection/C1347457?image=2

Stephen's unit, the 1st Battalion, was spared most of the heavy fighting, with the battalion having been moved back into reserve on 20 September, and then into support lines until relieved on the night of 21–22 September by the 55th Battalion.[266] It had been intended that the reserve brigades, the 1st and 6th Brigades, would be brought up on the afternoon of 20 September, but this was countermanded when it was realised that the front was already crowded. Although the reserve brigades did ultimately relieve the attacking battalions, the 1st Battalion was spared the expected German counterattack. Nevertheless, the battalion suffered some 147 casualties in the short period that it was in the line and in support trenches.[267]

The second step in the attack occurred on 26 September with the attack by the 4th and 5th Divisions on Polygon Wood, which was captured despite fierce German counter-attacks. The third step was the attack on Broodseinde Ridge by the 1st, 2nd and 3rd Australian Divisions, and the New Zealand Division, which commenced on 4 October 1917. This time, the 1st Battalion along the remainder of the 1st Brigade would be leading the attack on the right side of the line. On 2 October 1917, the battalion was moved back into the line, this time at Westhoek Ridge, with reconnoitring of the front occurring on 3 October.[268] After dusk on 3 October, the attacking units began marching out to the jumping-off tapes.

Before zero hour, a German bombardment began to land on the Australian forward lines, hitting the waiting units of the 1st and 2nd Australian Divisions. The German bombardment was in fact a prelude to the Germans launching their own attack, with the opposing forces meeting in no man's land. The Germans were driven back and Broodseinde Ridge captured. It had, however, come at a significant cost to the Australian forces with total losses among the three

---

[266] 1st Battalion Unit Diary September 1917 - https://www.awm.gov.au/collection/C1347460?image=4 .
[267] 1st Battalion Unit Diary September 1917 - https://www.awm.gov.au/collection/C1347460?image=4 . Charles Bean records the battalion's total casualties as eight officers and 144 other ranks – Bean, *Official History*, Vol. 4 p. 789.
[268] 1st Battalion Unit Diary October 1917 - https://www.awm.gov.au/collection/C1347461?image=2

Australian divisions of 6,432 killed, wounded or missing. The 1st Battalion's losses comprised 13 officers and 267 other ranks.[269]

Among the battalion's losses was Stephen Harrison. Initially reported as killed in action on 8 October 1917, the Field Service Report completed in December 1917 specifies his date of death as 3 October 1917 based on a report by the commanding officer of Stephen's battalion dated 6 October. Stephen's name was included among those reported as killed in action in casualty lists published in November 1917 with the date of death specified as 3 October.[270] While 8 October appears to be a clear error given the report of his death was made on 6 October, the date of 3 October neither reconciles with the date of the attack on Broodseinde Ridge, or a statement given by one of his comrades to the Red Cross.[271]

In a statement made on 6 February 1918, Private Lindsay J Selmes (6083) of the 1st Battalion described how in a charge at Ypres, Stephen was wounded by the same shell that had wounded him. Pte Selmes saw Stephen's face and neck swell up and apart from commenting that he did not think that Stephen would live, he never heard of him afterwards. A more comprehensive account of the circumstances of Stephen's death was given by Private Isaac Settle (6846) in May 1918[272]:

---

[269] Bean, *Official History*, Vol. 4 p. 876.
[270] KILLED. (1917, November 16). *The Sydney Morning Herald* (NSW: 1842-1954), p. 9. Retrieved April 25, 2023, from http://nla.gov.au/nla.news-article15751339 and Australian Casualties. (1917, November 21). *Australian Town and Country Journal* (Sydney, NSW: 1870-1919), p. 16. Retrieved April 25, 2023, from http://nla.gov.au/nla.news-article263771653 . Other casualty lists which did not specify the date of death included NEW SOUTH WALES (1917, November 15). *The Sun* (Sydney, NSW: 1910-1954), p. 2. Retrieved April 25, 2023, from http://nla.gov.au/nla.news-article221390407 and 218 DEAD. (1917, November 16). *The Daily Telegraph* (Sydney, NSW: 1883-1930), p. 8. Retrieved April 25, 2023, from http://nla.gov.au/nla.news-article239244699 .
[271] Australian Red Cross Wounded and Missing Files - https://www.awm.gov.au/collection/R1485846
[272] Australian Red Cross Wounded and Missing Files - https://www.awm.gov.au/collection/R1485846

I am very pleased to give all the information I can as he, Jack, was my best pal, since I enlisted. I am sorry to inform you he was shot through the head by a machine gun bullet on 4th October at Passchendaele. I can vouch for the fact as he and I hopped over the parapet together as we had previously made it up that we would stick together during the advance. I had several remarks made to me about the natural smile he had on his face after death. I could not tell you as to whether he was buried in a grave or not but I think he would be buried in a grave by himself as there was intense shellfire on that particular sector for several weeks. ....

It is more likely, therefore, that Stephen was killed during the advance on 4 October, which succeeded in seizing Broodseinde Ridge. The uncertainty surrounding Stephen's burial remained until 1922 when it was determined by the IWGC that the details recorded against the remains interred at Grave 3, Plot 34, Row A at Tyne Cot Cemetery incorrectly specified them as the remains of Private Joseph R Harrison (4140) of the 26th Battalion who had been killed on 8 October 1917. The IWGC corrected the records and advised the OIC accordingly. Stephen Harrison is buried in the Tyne Cot Cemetery, Belgium.

Photograph of the grave of Stephen Harrison, Tyne Cot Cemetery, Belgium (author, 2018).

Russell Thompson Sydney Jarvis MM

Lance Corporal, No. 11994

9th Field Ambulance, Australian Army Medical Corps

Killed in action 4 October 1917, Ypres, Belgium

Buried Ypres Reservoir Cemetery, Ypres, Belgium

Greater Love Hath No Man Than To Lay Down His Life For His Friends

Photograph of Russell Jarvis. Source - DISTINGUISHED SOLDIERS. (1917, October 10). *Sydney Mail* (NSW: 1912–1938), p. 6. Retrieved April 25, 2023, from http://nla.gov.au/nla.news-article160629284

Russell (Russ) Thompson Sydney Jarvis was born on 1 January 1884 in Sydney to Charles and Margaret Jarvis.[273] According to his future wife, Russell was most closely associated with Drummoyne[274] and his mother Margaret is recorded as living at *Strathmore*, 70 Thompson Street, Drummoyne.[275]

Russell attended Fort Street School in Sydney along with his future work colleague, George Whitney. He was employed as a proofreader with *The Sydney Morning Herald*, and George was employed as a journalist with the paper after he had graduated from the University of

---

[273] https://www.aif.adfa.edu.au/showPerson?pid=152666 (accessed 11 June 2017); http://www.cwgc.org/find-war-dead/casualty/99130/JARVIS,%20RUSSELL%20THOMPSON%20SYDNEY; NSW BDM Registration No. 576/1884.

[274] Honour Roll Circular completed by Alice Jarvis https://d2uipk7udysvkd.cloudfront.net/collection/RCDIG1068875/document/5573603.PDF

[275] http://cdn.cityofsydney.nsw.gov.au/learn/history/archives/sands/1910-1919/1914-part4.pdf page 36

Sydney. Russell married Alice Redden in about 1913[276] and they lived at *'Soissons'*, 44 Birchgrove Road, Balmain[277] where they had a son, Maurice Russell Jarvis.[278]

At the age of 31 years and eight months, Russell enlisted in the AIF on 10 August 1915[279] at Holsworthy and was initially assigned to the 12th Reinforcements to the 3rd Battalion. Two months later, he had been transferred to the AAMC and the Field Hospital based at Liverpool. On 8 March 1916, Russell was assigned to section A of the 9th Field Ambulance. The 9th Field Ambulance was raised in February 1916 in connection with the 3rd Australian Division in Melbourne before moving to Sydney to be raised and organised. The unit moved to Liverpool on 7 March 1916[280] so Russell was transferred the next day. During April, men from the unit attended general hospitals in Sydney to be trained in practical nursing.

The 9th Field Ambulance began to embark for overseas from 1 May 1916, with sections being allocated to different troop ships. Russell embarked with the last section of the unit under command of Lt Col Frederick A Maguire (said to be a personal friend of Russell[281]) from Sydney on HMAT A8 *Argyllshire* on 11 May 1916, calling in at Durban, Cape Town, Dakkar, before arriving in England. Prior to embarking for overseas, Russell made his will in which he appointed his wife and mother as his executrices.

The *Argyllshire* arrived in Plymouth, England, where Russell along with the rest of the 9th Field Ambulance disembarked on 10 July 1916. Most of the unit moved to the Australian training base at Lark Hill camp on the Salisbury Plain, where it was officially placed under the

---

[276] NSW BDM Registration No. 13616/1913.
[277] http://cdn.cityofsydney.nsw.gov.au/learn/history/archives/sands/1910-1919/1916-part3.pdf page 32
[278] NSW BDM Registration No. 27123/1914.
[279] War service record accessible at https://recordsearch.naa.gov.au/SearchNRetrieve/Interface/ViewImage.aspx?B=7362520
[280] 9th Field Ambulance Unit Diary, February 1916-April 1917 - https://www.awm.gov.au/collection/C1352926?image=3
[281] Statement of Lance Corporal GE Jackson (11990) made 8 January 1918 - https://s3-ap-southeast-2.amazonaws.com/awm-media/collection/RCDIG1049522/document/5637193.PDF https://www.awm.gov.au/collection/R1491937

authority of the 3rd Australian Division. While at Lark Hill, on 8 November 1916, Russell was charged with disobedience of Standing Order 11 in that he used a latrine reserved for NCOs. His punishment was one day confinement to barracks imposed by the unit commander Lt Col Maguire.

Panorama group portrait of members of the 9th Field Ambulance at camp in England prior to service on the Western Front, October 1916. Russell is in the second row, sixth from the right. AWM Item No. P08861.001.

The unit moved by train to Southampton on 23 November 1916, embarking at 7 p.m. that evening for Le Harve, France. The unit arrived at Armentieres on 1 December 1916 where it took over from the 103rd RAMC, establishing a Regimental Aid Post (RAP), Advanced Dressing Station (ADS) and Main Dressing Station (MDS). The RAP would be located closest to the front line. Wounded would then be carried by stretcher from the RAP to the ADS some 800 yards behind, and then by car to the MDS. During the month of December 1916, the unit had 708 admissions, an average of 23 a day, the vast majority of whom were cases of sickness rather than injury. The trend continued through January 1917 as an intense cold snap gripped the front during that winter.

Russell was fortunate to avoid the worst of the winter conditions in the front lines as on 23 December 1916, he was himself admitted to the 11th Field Ambulance suffering from mumps. He was eventually transferred to the 7th General Hospital at St Omer where he remained until 17 January 1917.

February 1917 saw an increase in fighting activity with both sides initiating raids, resulting in increasing numbers of casualties being received by the 9th Field Ambulance, along with a similar number of sick. During February, the unit had 948 admissions of whom 719 were sick and 328 wounded.[282]

In early March, the 9th Field Ambulance received orders to hand over its MDS and ADS to the 11th Field Ambulance and 3/2 West Lancashire Field Ambulance, as it moved to the MDS at Pont de Nieppe closer to Belgian Flanders, where it arrived on 15 March 1917. It then took over the posts (RAPs, bearer posts and ADSs) established by the New Zealand Field Ambulance in the Ypres salient. On 19 March 1917, Russell was promoted to the rank of lance corporal.

In April 1917, the unit was again moved, this time to an MDS at Pont d' Achelles on the French/Belgian border. During April, the ratio of sick to wounded admitted into the Field Ambulance reduced as fighting around the Ypres salient intensified with the onset of spring. On 25 May, a Corps MDS was established at Pont d' Achelles to service the II ANZAC Corps, with Lt Col Maguire appointed its commander. Russell's section in the 9th Field Ambulance was one of those attached for duty with the new Corps MDS to deal with the increasing number of casualties coming in from the front.

At the start of June 1917, advance parties from the unit moved forward to a divisional collection post established at a place called Hyde Park Corner in anticipation of the imminent attack on Messines Ridge to be undertaken by the 3rd Australian Division. Zero hour was at 3:00 a.m. on 7 June with the unit diary noting the admission of a great number of gassed cases, about 200 in all, with the attacking units being caught by a German artillery and gas attack near Ploegsteert Wood and Hill 63 as they were moving forward to the jumping-off lines. A total of 970 wounded were admitted during the day,[283] with more than 2,000 the day after.[284]

---

[282] 9th Field Ambulance Unit Diary, February 1916-April 1917 - https://www.awm.gov.au/collection/C1352926?image=37
[283] 9th Field Ambulance Unit Diary, June 1917 - https://www.awm.gov.au/collection/C1352940?image=5
[284] 9th Field Ambulance Unit Diary, June 1917 - https://www.awm.gov.au/collection/C1352940?image=6

It was during the fighting at Messines that Russell was commended for his bravery, which ultimately resulted in him being awarded the Military Medal on 24 June 1917.[285] The citation was in the following terms:

> On 10th June, 1917, at PLOEGSTEERT WOOD, this N.C.O. was on duty evacuating casualties from a temporary R.A.P. in a shell hole in No Man's Land. There was a heavy hostile bombardment on the area at the time. A 5.9 inch shell fell into a neighbouring shell hole in which a party of Divisional Signal Engineers were working, killing many, wounding and burying four others. Lance Corporal JARVIS led his party to this shell hole regardless of hostile barrage, succeeded in digging out the wounded men and then in conveying them to the nearest R.A.P. for attention. By his utter disregard for personal safety and by his bravery and example to his men this N.C.O. undoubtedly saved the lives of these wounded men.

News of Russell's decoration appeared in *The Sydney Morning Herald* on 10 September 1917.[286]

After the battle, the 9th Field Ambulance was relieved, its first time out of the line since 1 December 1916.[287] It returned to front lines duties the following month and was eventually moved to Ypres itself at the end of September 1917 to take over responsibility for the forward area east of the town. The unit proceeded to the town's prison where its walls and basements provided the ideal location to set up an ADS, before sections moved out to relieve the RAMC bearers at all the forward posts, including at a place called Bavaria House. The unit

---

[285] Published in the Fourth Supplement No. 30234 to the *London Gazette* on 14 August 1917 and published in the *Commonwealth Gazette* No. 219 on 20 December 1917 - https://www.awm.gov.au/collection/R1519694 . See also https://www.awm.gov.au/collection/R1626928

[286] AUSTRALIANS HONOURED. (1917, September 10). *The Sydney Morning Herald* (NSW: 1842-1954), p. 8. Retrieved April 25, 2023, from http://nla.gov.au/nla.news-article15753119

[287] 9th Field Ambulance Unit Diary, June 1917 - https://www.awm.gov.au/collection/C1352940?image=8

diary remarked on the condition of the countryside as bare and one mass of shell holes, and with most of it in full view of the enemy.[288] These conditions meant that the carrying of casualties was very heavy and almost impossible at night. The diary contains a drawing of the unit's dispositions prior to the forthcoming attack on Broodseinde Ridge.

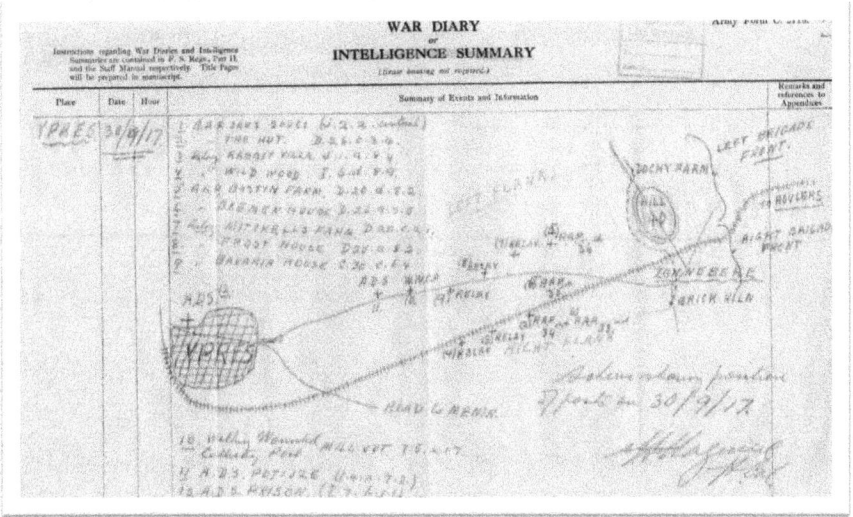

Extract from 9th Field Ambulance Unit Diary 30 September 1917 showing dispositions of the various RAPs, relay posts and ADSs - https://www.awm.gov.au/collection/C1353329?image=9

A sergeant and 16 men from the 9th Field Ambulance were stationed at Bavaria House. This post was to act as a relay post, as wounded from the front would be relayed back through the posts towards an ADS, with stretcher bearers moving the wounded between the posts.

On 2 October, as a result of a divisional 'side step', responsibility for all the posts south of the Ypres–Roulers railway line was handed over the medical units with I ANZAC Corps (shown as numbers 1–4

---

[288] 9th Field Ambulance Unit Diary September 1917 - https://www.awm.gov.au/collection/C1353329?image=7

on the map). The post at Bostin Farm was also evacuated due to heavy shelling and several direct hits. At 'zero hour', 5:25 a.m. on 4 October, the bearers moved forward to begin the task of bringing the wounded through the relay posts. The conditions presented a severe test for the bearers, with no paths and the countryside a continuous chain of muddy shell holes. In the space of six hours from 6 a.m. to 12 noon, a total of 670 casualties had been brought in and admitted to an ADS at either the Prison or Potijze.[289] Heavy rain during the day, and the cold, compounded the difficulty of evacuating wounded from the front lines. The unit diary noted that there were no gas or bayonet cases, and only a small percentage of bullet and shrapnel wounds. Instead, practically every case was caused by high explosives.[290]

One of those who would become a casualty of a high explosive shell was Russell Jarvis. Russell was killed in action 4 October 1917 at the age of 33 near Bavaria House[291] from a shell burst right on top of him and another stretcher bearer, Private Charles Culley (8896), as they were carrying a wounded soldier to an ADS.

Red Cross statements[292] obtained after the event confirmed that 'Russ' Jarvis was killed with Private Culley by a shell when carrying a patient to an ADS. Both were killed outright and their bodies brought down and buried together the next day in a military cemetery behind Ypres prison. According to Private Geoffrey Weberging (12556), a Church of England clergyman officiated in the presence of Lt Col Maguire and 20 men from the unit. Private Thomas F Hodge (11985)

---

[289] 9th Field Ambulance Unit Diary October 1917 - https://www.awm.gov.au/collection/C1353330?image=8
[290] 9th Field Ambulance Unit Diary October 1917 - https://www.awm.gov.au/collection/C1353330?image=8
[291] Statement of L/Cpl GE Jackson - https://s3-ap-southeast-2.amazonaws.com/awm-media/collection/RCDIG1049522/document/5637193.PDF
https://www.awm.gov.au/collection/R1491937 and unit diary entry 9 October 1917 - https://www.awm.gov.au/collection/C1353330?image=15
[292] Australian Red Cross Wounded and Missing Files - https://www.awm.gov.au/collection/R1491937

stated that the wounded soldier they were carrying on the stretcher was a German.²⁹³

Bavaria House on the Zonnebeke Road, used as an ADS by the 9th Australian Field Ambulance from 1–21 October 1917, when Australians were taking part in the Third Battle of Ypres. Russell Jarvis would be killed by a high explosive shell near this location while carrying a wounded soldier on a stretcher. AWM ID No. C04572.

A photograph of Russell was published on 10 October 1917, before news of his death was officially received, as one of a number of distinguished soldiers who had received awards for gallantry as a way to appeal for recruits.²⁹⁴ An announcement would be placed in *The Sydney Morning Herald* two days later that Alice had received a telegram reporting that her husband had been killed in action²⁹⁵:

---

²⁹³ Statement of Pte FF Hodge (11985) - https://s3-ap-southeast-2.amazonaws.com/awm-media/collection/RCDIG1049522/document/5637193.PDF
https://www.awm.gov.au/collection/R1491937
²⁹⁴ DISTINGUISHED SOLDIERS. (1917, October 10). *Sydney Mail* (NSW: 1912-1938), p. 6. Retrieved April 25, 2023, from http://nla.gov.au/nla.news-article160629284
²⁹⁵ http://www.balmainrowingclub.com/lest-we-forget (accessed 11 June 2017). Rothwell Oliver Barder is also commemorated on the same website. See also WAR CASUALTIES. (1917, October 12). *The Sydney Morning Herald* (NSW: 1842-1954), p. 8. Retrieved April 25, 2023, from http://nla.gov.au/nla.news-article15740215

A private cable message has been received by Mrs. Russell Jarvis, of Longnose Point, Balmain, announcing that her husband, Lance-corporal Russell Jarvis, aged 33 years, has been killed in France. He was previously employed on the staff of the "Sydney Morning Herald," and his mother, Mrs. M. Jarvis, resides at Strathmore, Thompson-avenue. Drummoyne. He was recently awarded the Military Medal.

A notice was published on 17 October 1917 in *The Sydney Morning Herald* by members of the Drummoyne Tennis Club in tribute to Russell[296]:

JARVIS. - Lance-corporal Russell Jarvis, A.M.C. (awarded the Military Medal for conspicuous bravery at the Battle of Messines), killed in action, October 2, 1917. A tribute from his former comrades of the Drummoyne Tennis Club.

A brief family notice appeared in the same paper later that month[297]:

JARVIS-Killed in action, France, October 4, 1917, Lance-corporal Russell Jarvis, M.M., husband of Alice Jarvis, Soissons, 44 Birchgrove-road Balmain, and youngest son of Mrs. M. Jarvis, Strathmore, Thompson-street, Drummoyne.

In the Honour Roll Circular completed by Alice Jarvis sometime after the war,[298] she named George Whitney as a person who could provide the official historian with further information in connection with Russell. George Whitney was a poet and a journalist with *The Sydney Morning Herald*, and lived on Collingwood Street,

---

[296] Family Notices (1917, October 17). *The Sydney Morning Herald* (NSW: 1842-1954), p. 10. Retrieved April 25, 2023, from http://nla.gov.au/nla.news-article15737411
[297] Family Notices (1917, October 27). *The Sydney Morning Herald* (NSW: 1842-1954), p. 16. Retrieved April 25, 2023, from http://nla.gov.au/nla.news-article15761000
[298] Honour Roll Circular accessible at https://www.awm.gov.au/collection/R1643387

Drummoyne.[299] George wrote an obituary to Russell in the Sydney *Arrow* on 19 October 1917[300]:

Drummoyne Player Killed in Action

Mr. George C. Whitney writes: "Lance-Corporal Russell Jarvis, A.M.C., of the Drummoyne Club was killed in action in France on October 2. He left here in May, 1916, with the 9th Field Ambulance. We all know the heroic work our stretcher-bearers have done — exposed without a chance of protecting themselves to a shell or the bullet of some sniper; and the fact that Jarvis was awarded the Military Medal for conspicuous bravery at Messines in June shows he was made of the same stuff as thousands of our gallant lads. It came as no surprise to his old club-mates and friends, who were familiar with his fearlessness, and who were saddened by the news of his death so soon after this distinction. He was 33 years of age, and leaves a widow and little boy.

A number of the B Grade players of 1914 and 1915 will doubtless remember Rus Jarvis. In the former season he was the strongest player in the Drummoyne four, who were runners-up in B V.; and he played with great coolness and resource in the semi-final and final engagements. I have repeatedly heard opponents remark what a good sport he was, and though one expects a high standard of sportsmanship in tennis, such tributes sound none the less pleasing. He is the second member of the club to lose his life in the way, Pte. E. J. Cummings having died of wounds at Lemnos, August, 1915.

---

[299] https://canadabayconnections.wordpress.com/2013/04/09/face-to-face-with-the-past/ (accessed 11 June 2017). Charles was also born in 1884 and like Russ, attended Fort Street Public School. https://allpoetry.com/George-Charles-Whitney (accessed 11 June 2017).
[300] Drummoyne Player Killed in Action (1917, October 19). *Arrow* (Sydney, NSW: 1916-1933), p. 8. Retrieved April 25, 2023, from http://nla.gov.au/nla.news-article103528950. News also appeared in the *Referee* - BOWLS (1917, October 24). *Referee* (Sydney, NSW: 1886-1939), p. 16. Retrieved April 25, 2023, from http://nla.gov.au/nla.news-article120294131

Some of Russell's personal effects were consigned on HMAT *Barunga*, which was lost to enemy action on 20 June 1918. On 11 November 1918, the Recruiting Officer at Armidale wrote to the OIC on behalf of Alice Jarvis asking for inquiries to be made regarding his Military Medal ribbon 'which she would prize above all other things'. Alice Jarvis was advised of the loss of Russell's personal effects in letter from the OIC dated 9 May 1919 when she was then living c/- Mrs Coventry, Tulloch West, Rockdale.

Russell Jarvis is buried at Ypres Reservoir Cemetery located to the northwest of Ypres.[301] He is also commemorated on the Fort Street High School Great War Honour Roll,[302] the Townsville 9th Field Ambulance Honour Roll[303] and in the *Record of Service: members of the staff of The Sydney Morning Herald and the Sydney Mail who served in the Great War.*[304]

Extract from Record of Service: members of the staff of *The Sydney Morning Herald* and the *Sydney Mail* who served in the Great War - https://www.awm.gov.au/collection/C2615468?image=12 .

---

[301] http://www.cwgc.org/find-a-cemetery/cemetery/9500/YPRES%20RESERVOIR%20CEMETERY
[302] https://www.warmemorialsregister.nsw.gov.au/memorials/fort-street-high-school-great-war-honour-roll
[303] https://vwma.org.au/explore/memorials/8299
[304] https://www.awm.gov.au/collection/C2615468 and page 12 - https://www.awm.gov.au/collection/C2615468?image=12

Photograph of the grave of Russell Jarvis at Ypres Reservoir Cemetery (author, 2018).

Frederick Miller

Private, No. 758

18th Battalion, 5th Infantry Brigade, 2nd Australian Division

Killed in action 5 October 1917, Zonnebeke, Belgium

Buried Railway Dugouts Burial Ground, Zillebeke, Belgium

Transplanted human worth will bloom to profit otherwhere

Frederick Miller was born in about 1895[305] in Marrickville, NSW, and was the only son of Henry and Jessie Malvenia Miller[306] who at the time of Frederick's enlistment were living at *Canberra*, Tranmere Street, Drummoyne.[307] Frederick had three sisters: Emily Florence Miller,[308] Alma Miller[309] and Muriel Miller.[310]

Frederick attended Gladstone Park Public School in Balmain and was living at '*Fenella*', Thames Street, Balmain, when he enlisted on 11 August 1916 at Victoria Barracks having just turned 21.[311] He was at the time serving with the 29th Infantry CMF at Rozelle. Frederick specified his occupation as horse driver[312] and in a display of military intelligence was initially assigned to the 7th Reinforcements to the 1st Cyclist Battalion.

Prior to embarking for overseas, Frederick underwent some dental treatment on 27 September 1916 involving a number of teeth extractions and six amalgam fillings. On 7 November 1916, he made his last will and testament by which he appointed his sisters, Alma and Muriel Miller, as joint executrices and beneficiaries. Frederick embarked from Sydney on HMAT A24 *Benalla* on 9 November 1916, arriving in Devonport, England, on 9 January 1917.

Frederick joined the 5th Training Battalion before proceeding for service overseas in France on 25 April 1917 via Folkestone. Frederick, however, was reassigned as a reinforcement to the 18th Infantry

---

[305] NSW BDM Registration No. 24146/1895.
[306] Other information suggests that his mother's name was Jessie Malvina Miller (nee Peek) – and the spelling of her name changed on the official records with the birth of each child.
[307] The name of the house provided on the original attestation paper signed by Frederick is not clearly legible as either *Canberra* or *Canbarra*, but the certified copy specifies it as *Canbarra*. Subsequent correspondence between the OIC and Henry Miller indicates the correct spelling is *Canberra*.
[308] Born 1889 at Marrickville – NSW BDM Registration No. 7489/1889. Note her mother's name is spelt Malviena.
[309] Born 1898 at St Leonards – NSW BDM Registration No. 7126/1898. Note spelling of mother's name Malvena.
[310] Born 1891 at Marrickville - NSW BDM Registration No. 21273/1891. Note spelling of mother's name Malvina.
[311] War service records accessible at https://recordsearch.naa.gov.au/SearchNRetrieve/Interface/ViewImage.aspx?B=1907128
[312] On the Honour Roll Circular completed by his father after the war, he gave Frederick's occupation simply as 'commerce' – see https://www.awm.gov.au/collection/R1648011

Battalion, which he joined on 13 May 1917 when it was billeted in Fricourt. The battalion had just been engaged in the Second Battle of Bullecourt and had been relieved on 5 May 1917. Frederick's arrival coincided with a church parade followed by an inspection and presentation of decorations by the commander of I ANZAC Corps, General Sir William Birdwood.[313] The battalion remained in Contay where it undertook further training and reorganisation for the next month, before moving back to the reserve lines near Bapaume as part of the 2nd Division's relief of the 3rd Australian Division.[314]

In June 1917, Frederick's sister, Emily, enlisted in the Australian Army Nursing Service as a staff nurse at the age of 27. She embarked on HMAT *Runic* from Melbourne on 19 September 1917 for Egypt.

The battalion struck camp at the end of July 1917 and moved eventually to billets near Arques in the Pas de Calais region southwest of the Flanders sector by the end of August 1917[315] where it undertook further training in new attack formations.

On 10 September 1917, the battalion looked over ground on which it was to participate in the forthcoming attack on the Menin Road Ridge as part of the Third Battle of Ypres. At 1:40 a.m. on 20 September 1917, the battalion moved forward to the jumping-off tape on Westhoek Ridge in preparation for the attack. The artillery barrage opened at 5:40 a.m. The 18th Battalion passed through the 20th Battalion which had already seized the first objective, with the 18th Battalion taking the second objective by 7:41 a.m., before occupying the next line by 8:00 a.m.[316] Attempted German counter-attacks were successfully smashed by Allied artillery fire. The battalion was relieved by 22 September 1917 after having suffered casualties of six officers and 54 other ranks killed, and six officers and 218 other ranks wounded.

---

[313] 18th Battalion Unit Diary May 1917 - https://www.awm.gov.au/collection/C1342400?image=3
[314] 18th Battalion Unit Diary June 1917 - https://www.awm.gov.au/collection/C1342401?image=9
[315] 18th Battalion Unit Diary August 1917 - https://www.awm.gov.au/collection/C1342403?image=6
[316] 18th Battalion Unit Diary September 1917 - https://www.awm.gov.au/collection/C1355880?image=8

In early October 1917, the battalion made preparations for the next stage of the Ypres offensive, with working parties engaged with engineers in preparations for the attack.[317] The men involved in these works were exposed to sporadic artillery fire, with the battalion taking casualties. The 2nd Division was to attack on the front near Zonnebeke with the 5th Infantry Brigade in reserve. On 4 October 1917, the battalion moved through Westhoek Ridge where it continued to provide working parties and take casualties. Included among the duties of one of the working details was to collect and bury dead near the jumping-off tape at Zonnebeke, with about 45 dead being buried.[318]

On the evening of 5 October, the battalion relieved the 24th Battalion in the front lines. During this relief, one officer and 11 other ranks were killed. It was during this relief that Frederick is likely to have been killed in action. A handwritten note of Frederick's service records from the commanding officer of the 18th Battalion states that[319]:

> Pte Miller was a Btn [Battalion] observer and was standing by in a trench near Btn HQ on Broodseinde Ridge, 100 yrds to the right of Broodseinde Road – a shell landed in trench killing him instantly [and] was buried by members of Btn, where he fell.

Private George A McLeod (6369) provided a statement to the Red Cross[320] a year after Frederick had been killed. Pte McLeod was next to Frederick when he was killed and helped bury him with another man on the morning of 6 October in the field as it was impossible to get his body back to the nearest military cemetery.

---

[317] 18th Battalion Unit Diary October 1917 - https://www.awm.gov.au/collection/C1342404?image=3
[318] 18th Battalion Unit Diary October 1917 - https://www.awm.gov.au/collection/C1342404?image=5
[319] War service records accessible at https://recordsearch.naa.gov.au/SearchNRetrieve/Interface/ViewImage.aspx?B=1907128
[320] Australian Red Cross Wounded and Missing Files - https://www.awm.gov.au/collection/R1495940

In another statement, Private Oscar Moritz Selig (3917)[321] advised the Red Cross in August 1918 that Frederick was a mate of his, and that based on information given to him by Pte McLeod he understood that the location of his grave had been badly smashed up after 'the Huns came through'.

Frederick's family published *in memoriam* notices as did Pte Selig and his family in early November[322]:

MILLER - Killed in action in France, October 5, 1917, Pte. Fred. Miller, dearly loved and only brother of Muriel, Lucy, Alma, and Nurse F. Miller (on active service), aged 22 years. He died as he lived—nobly.

MILLER - Killed in action in France, October 5, 1917, Pte. Fred. Miller, lifelong devoted chum of Private Oscar Selig (on active service), aged 22 years.

He sacrificed his life for his country's cause.

MILLER - Killed in action in France, October 5, 1917, Pte. Fred. Miller, dearly beloved friend of Mr. and Mrs. H. Selig and family, Balmain, aged 22 years.

A young life nobly ended.

The official telegram advising of Frederick's death was received by his father Henry on 28 October 1917. On 20 November 1917, Henry Miller wrote to Senator George Foster Pearce, the Minister for Defence, asking for assistance to get information of Frederick's death to his eldest daughter, Emily Miller, then serving overseas with the Australian Army Nursing Service.[323]

---

[321] https://www.aif.adfa.edu.au/showPerson?pid=270302 . Oscar's parents lived at 348 Darling Street, Balmain, New South Wales and he returned to Australia 18 November 1918 having been awarded the Military Medal during the fighting at Pozières in August 1916.
[322] Family Notices (1917, November 3). *The Sydney Morning Herald* (NSW: 1842-1954), p. 12. Retrieved April 25, 2023, from http://nla.gov.au/nla.news-article15761608
[323] https://www.aif.adfa.edu.au/showPerson?pid=208417

Group portrait of the matron and members of Australian Army Nursing Service, No. 1 Australian General Hospital. Identified back row first on left Staff Nurse (SN) Emily Florence Miller. AWM ID No. D00781.

Further family notices were published on the anniversary of Frederick's death in 1918 by family and friends[324]:

---

[324] Family Notices (1918, October 5). *The Daily Telegraph* (Sydney, NSW: 1883-1930), p. 8. Retrieved April 20, 2024, from http://nla.gov.au/nla.news-article239571890 ; Family Notices (1918, October 5). *The Sydney Morning Herald* (NSW: 1842-1954), p. 11. Retrieved April 20, 2024, from http://nla.gov.au/nla.news-article15805293

MILLER - In affectionate remembrance of my beloved only
son. Private Fred Miller, 18th Battalion, killed in action, Ypres,
October 5, 1917, aged 22 years.
'I know transplanted human worth will bloom to
profit otherwhere.'
His sorrowing father, Henry Miller. Tranmere-street,
Drummoyne.

MILLER - In loving memory of Fred, our dear and only
brother, killed in action in France, October 5, 1917.
Just when life was brightest:
Just when his hopes were best;
His country called, and he answered;
Now somewhere in France he rests.
Inserted by his loving sisters, Florrie (Australian Nursing Staff,
abroad), Muriel, Lucy, and Alma.

MILLER - In loving memory of our dear friend, Pte Fred.
Miller, 18th Batt., killed in action, October 5, 1917.
God grant us victory.
That his life be not given in vain.
Inserted by Mr. and Mrs. H. Selig, Bert, Doris, Etta, and his
devoted comrade, Pte. Oscar Selig, M.M. (on active service).

In late 1924, Frederick's remains were located by a Graves Registration Unit and were exhumed and reburied at Railway Dugouts Burial Ground (Transport Farm) at Zillebeke, two kilometres southeast of Ypres, Belgium. Frederick's remains were identified by the clothing disc. On 28 February 1925, Frederick's father then living at *Neilslie*, Mobbs Street, Eastwood,[325] was advised by the OIC that Frederick's remains had been successfully recovered and reburied.

---

[325] https://www.cwgc.org/find-records/find-war-dead/casualty-details/490255/frederick-miller/

Frederick Miller is also commemorated at St John's Church of England, Balmain.[326]

Photograph of the grave of Frederick Miller at Railway Dugouts Burial Ground (Transport Farm) at Zillebeke (author, 2018).

---

[326] http://www.leichhardt5000.com.au/wp-content/uploads/2015/02/MILLER-Frederick-.pdf

Clive Townsend Thompson

Driver, No. 30183

10th Field Artillery Brigade, 4th Australian Division

Killed in action 8 October 1917, Passchendaele, Belgium

Buried Ypres Town Cemetery Extension, Menin Gate, Belgium

Studio portrait of 30183 Driver Clive Townsend Thompson, 10th Australian Field Artillery Brigade from Drummoyne, NSW. AWM ID No. H06533.

Clive Townsend Thompson was born in Strathfield in 1897,[327] the son of Joseph Peebles Thompson and Mary Ann Thompson (nee Warren), who had been married in about 1892.[328] Clive attended Sydney Grammar School and Bathurst Government Farm where he trained in agriculture.[329] With three months compulsory service and three years of voluntary service with the 31st Infantry CMF, Clive enlisted

---

[327] NSW BDM Registration No. 20556/1897. The Honour Roll Circular completed by his father after the war noted that his birthplace was Strathfield and NSW BDM records his birth district as Burwood.

[328] NSW BDM Registration No. 6226/1892. Clive had at least one sibling, Freda M Thompson, BDM Registration No. 21326/1895.

[329] https://www.awm.gov.au/collection/R1673440 and https://s3-ap-southeast-2.amazonaws.com/awm-media/collection/RCDIG1068841/document/5540964.PDF

in the AIF on 5 September 1916 at the age of 19 years and three months.[330] He enlisted with the consent of his parents and gave their home at 17 Collingwood Street, Drummoyne, as his postal address.

Clive was initially based at the Royal Agricultural Showgrounds at Moore Park, during which time he was assigned to the 22nd Reinforcements to the 1st Field Artillery Brigade (FAB). He embarked from Sydney on 9 November 1916 on HMAT A24 *Benalla* disembarking in Devonport, England, early in the new year before travelling to the Reserve Brigade Australian Artillery training camp at Lark Hill in Wiltshire on 12 January 1917. Clive undertook several months of training after which he was promoted to the position of gunner before proceeding to France via Southampton on 14 June 1917, marching into the Australian General Base Depot at Rouelles the next day.

At the end of July 1917, Clive marched out to join the 4th Divisional Artillery where he was taken on strength on 2 August 1917. On arrival, he was transferred to the 10th Field Artillery Brigade and posted to the 38th Battery. A week later he was appointed to the position of driver to complete the establishment strength of the battery.

In July 1917, the 10th FAB was serving in the Ypres sector, in proximity to Ploegsteert, where it had been active in supporting the preparatory bombardment for the Third Battle of Ypres, which would open on 31 July 1917. The brigade itself would be subjected to counter-battery bombardment including the use of a new 'mustard oil' gas in late July.[331] The 10th FAB participated in the commencement of the general attack on 31 July that signalled the opening of the offensive.

On the day that Clive joined the brigade, it was enduring what the unit diary described as trying conditions on account of the mud, and wet dugouts and blankets.[332] The roads were in an indescribable state, dugouts were falling in and the men's clothes and blankets wet from

---

[330] War service records accessible at https://recordsearch.naa.gov.au/SearchNRetrieve/Interface/ViewImage.aspx?B=1832798
[331] 10th FAB Unit Diary July 1017 - https://www.awm.gov.au/collection/C1355832?image=3 ; https://www.awm.gov.au/collection/C1355832?image=7
[332] 10th FAB Unit Diary August 1917 - https://www.awm.gov.au/collection/C1355833?image=3

rain, all the time exposed to counter-battery work by German guns. In these circumstances, the unit diary recorded '[i]t is wonderful how the men stick it and yet carry on hard work especially as so many of their mates have been killed, wounded or gassed. It is the usual example of the Australian grit and spirit.'[333]

The 10th FAB was relieved on 5 and 6 August and retired to the wagon lines, during which time two men and five horses were killed, and one wagon destroyed from Clive's 38th Battery during the relief.[334] The brigade rotated in and out of the fighting over the next month until in mid-September when it began preparing for the next stage of the offensive, the attack on the Menin Road Ridge. Throughout the time, the brigade's positions were heavily shelled, with it suffering 57 casualties before the attack commenced.[335] The brigade principally supported the 7th Infantry Brigade in its attack and suffered relatively few casualties[336] with the infantry expressing great satisfaction with the artillery support provided to it.[337]

Ultimately, Clive's active service in the 10th FAB was a brief one as he was killed in action two months after joining his unit. As the brigade was involved in preparations for the next stage of the Passchendaele offensive, the attack on Broodseinde Ridge, the brigade's positions came under regular shelling by German artillery and bombing from enemy airplanes. The attack commenced on 4 October 1917, and the 10th FAB was engaged in its 'usual routine' of providing support to the attacking forces. It was during this period of fighting that Clive is reported to have been killed in action 8 October 1917.

---

[333] 10th FAB Unit Diary August 1917 - https://www.awm.gov.au/collection/C1355833?image=4
[334] 10th FAB Unit Diary August 1917 - https://www.awm.gov.au/collection/C1355833?image=5
[335] 10th FAB Unit Diary September 1917 - https://www.awm.gov.au/collection/C1355834?image=7
[336] 10th FAB Unit Diary September 1917 - https://www.awm.gov.au/collection/C1355834?image=8
[337] 10th FAB Unit Diary September 1917 - https://www.awm.gov.au/collection/C1355834?image=9

A very brief notice appeared in *The Sydney Morning Herald* on 17 November 1917 presumably published by Clive's parents[338]:

THOMPSON. - Killed in action in France on October 8, 1917, Driver Clive T. Thompson, youngest son of Mr. and Mrs. J. P. Thompson, of Collingwood-street, Drummoyne, aged 20 years.

Clive's name would appear in casualty lists in early December 1917[339] and his photograph would be published in *The Daily Telegraph* on 10 December 1917 as having been killed in action.[340] Clive's father made an application in June 1918 to the Supreme Court for an order for administration of his estate.[341]

There is no information in connection with the circumstances of Clive's death, with no investigation by the Red Cross or any other statements on Clive's service records. Such records as do exist and held by the CWGC indicate that Clive was originally buried in a grave with two other men, Driver A M Whyte (1051)[342] and Driver E Poole (2067),[343] with one cross bearing their three names. All three were members of the 10th FAB and were killed on the same day, 8 October 1917.[344] Their bodies were exhumed in 1919 and reburied in the Ypres Town Cemetery Extension near the Menin Gate, Ypres.[345]

---

[338] Family Notices (1917, November 17). *The Sydney Morning Herald* (NSW: 1842-1954), p. 11. Retrieved April 25, 2023, from http://nla.gov.au/nla.news-article15738475
[339] CASUALTY LIST. (1917, December 6). *The Sydney Morning Herald* (NSW: 1842-1954), p. 8. Retrieved April 25, 2023, from http://nla.gov.au/nla.news-article15756797
[340] MORE CASUALTIES. (1917, December 10). *The Daily Telegraph* (Sydney, NSW: 1883-1930), p. 8. Retrieved April 25, 2023, from http://nla.gov.au/nla.news-article239234986
[341] Advertising (1918, June 7). *The Sydney Morning Herald* (NSW: 1842-1954), p. 1. Retrieved April 25, 2023, from http://nla.gov.au/nla.news-article15781530
[342] Alexander McGregor Whyte - https://www.cwgc.org/find-war-dead/casualty/446762/whyte,-alexander-mcgregor/
[343] Edward Poole - https://www.cwgc.org/find-war-dead/casualty/446670/poole,-edward/
[344] AM Whyte - https://www.aif.adfa.edu.au/showPerson?pid=322691; E Poole - https://www.aif.adfa.edu.au/showPerson?pid=243298
[345] CWGC - https://www.cwgc.org/find-war-dead/casualty/446738/thompson,-clive-townsend/#&gid=null&pid=1

Photograph of the grave of Clive Thompson, Ypres Town Cemetery Extension, Ypres (author, 2018).

George Brown

Lance Corporal, No. 1892

35th Battalion, 9th Infantry Brigade, 3rd Australian Division

Killed in action 12 October 1917, Passchendaele, Belgium

No known grave. Commemorated Ypres (Menin Gate) Memorial, Ypres, Belgium

George Brown was born in the Lancashire village of Bolton in about June 1888[346] and was baptised at St Matthews in Little Bolton in June 1889 when his parents William and Alice Brown were living at 10 Nottingham Street, Bolton.[347] It is unclear when George immigrated to Australia but from the war pension documents on George's service records,[348] it appears that he had already been married to Eva Elizabeth Brown by the time they had emigrated from Bolton. Based on family notices published in 1918, George also had an uncle already in Australia.

George enlisted in the AIF on 30 March 1916 and gave his postal address as Blackwall Point Road, Five Dock, and described his occupation on his enlistment form as a labourer.[349] At the time of George's enlistment, he was 27 years and 9 months old, and he and Eva had four children: Emily, George, Doris, Annie and Frank.[350] George was initially allocated to the 55th Battalion at a depot camp in Goulburn. However, in early May 1916, he was transferred to the 2nd Reinforcements to the 35th Battalion at the Rutherford Depot Camp.

The 35th Battalion had been formed in December 1915 in Newcastle, New South Wales. The bulk of the battalion's recruits were drawn from the Newcastle region and thus it was dubbed 'Newcastle's Own'. Reflecting the demographics of the area, there were a high proportion of miners among the battalion's original members.[351] The 35th Battalion became part of the 9th Brigade of the 3rd Australian Division.

George embarked from Sydney on 4 September 1916 on board HMAT A16 *Port Sydney,* arriving in Plymouth, England, on 29

---

[346] https://www.freebmd.org.uk/cgi/districts.pl?r=80737855:9888&d=bmd_1680086578
[347] https://www.lan-opc.org.uk/Bolton-le-Moors/Little-Bolton/stmatthew/baptisms_1888-1889.html - Register: Baptisms 1888 - 1894, Page 30, Entry 236.
[348] War service records accessible at https://recordsearch.naa.gov.au/SearchNRetrieve/Interface/ViewImage.aspx?B=1796619
[349] War service records accessible at https://recordsearch.naa.gov.au/SearchNRetrieve/Interface/ViewImage.aspx?B=1796619
[350] The war pension records on George's service file give each of the children's address as Bolton, England, which might suggest that they had been born in England. However, there are birth records in NSW that appear to match possibly three of the children – Emily (26976/1912), George (41986/1913) and Doris Annie (30536/1915).
[351] https://www.awm.gov.au/unit/U51475/

October 1916. After initial training at the Australian training base on the Salisbury Plain, George proceeded to France from Folkestone on 20 December 1916 on board the *Princess Victoria* and taken on strength with the 35th Battalion on 26 January 1917. By that time, the battalion had been in the Somme front since November 1916 and had endured the harsh winter of 1916–17.

Between January and April 1917, the battalion was serving along with the rest of the 9th Brigade around Armentieres sector of the Somme front, exposed to intermittent periods of intense shelling, and with it, casualties. In late April the brigade moved to Pont de Nieppe, north of Armentieres, where the pattern continued.[352] It was while in this sector that on 18 May 1917, George was taken sick with a septic foot and initially admitted to the 2nd Australian CCS, before being admitted to hospital.

George eventually rejoined his battalion on 14 June 1917. During George's absence, the battalion had been transferred to the Flanders sector of the front in Belgium and had been involved in the 3rd Australian Division's first major engagement, the Battle of Messines, which had commenced on 1 June. George rejoined the day after the battalion had been relieved by the 2nd NZ Infantry Brigade in the front lines, but the relief was short lived as the battalion moved into support lines to assist in consolidating the ground gained at Messines. The time in the lines was spent patrolling and fighting off German patrols, periods of intense shelling and also mustard gas attacks.[353]

The diary of the battalion in July summed up its time in action at Messines as follows[354]:

---

[352] 9th Brigade Unit Diaries January – April 1917 - https://www.awm.gov.au/collection/C1347567?image=4
[353] 9th Brigade Unit Diary July 1917 - https://www.awm.gov.au/collection/C1347570?image=3
[354] 35th Battalion Unit Diary July 1917 - https://www.awm.gov.au/collection/C1344238?image=3 . There are no Battalion diaries for the period before July 1917.

The month was one of the most strenuous in the history of the Battalion (not including the big offensive in June) as the new ground in front of Messines was in a very wet and muddy state, and hastily constructed trenches combined with long tours in the line, and the natural desire of the enemy to prevent us settling down – made conditions very trying for all ranks.

The battalion was withdrawn from the line and set about resting and recuperating in August around the town of Wismes, southeast of the port of Calais.[355] While enroute to its rest area, George was promoted to lance corporal on 5 August 1917. September saw the battalion continue to be rested, with its time punctuated by sports days and competitions, swimming excursions to Terdinqhem, and concluding with an inspection of the division by Field Marshall Sir Douglas Haig on 22 September. By the end of September, the battalion was heading back to the Ypres front, this time to the Zonnebeke sector.[356]

The next major action of the battalion was the attack on the ridge of Passchendaele in October 1917 as the next stage of the Third Battle of Ypres. It was at the start of this battle that George would meet his end. The battle was characterised by heavy rain, which turned the battlefield into a quagmire, as thick mud tugged at the advancing troops and fouled their weapons.[357] The battalion's attack commenced at 5:25 a.m. on 12 October with the unit diary recording heavy casualties from machine gun fire and difficulty in consolidating the limited gains of the day. The battalion was forced to withdraw initially to the vicinity of Augustus Wood, some 300 yards from the jumping-off point,

---

[355] 35th Battalion Unit Diary August 1917 - https://www.awm.gov.au/collection/C1342682?image=2
[356] 35th Battalion Unit Diary September 1917 - https://www.awm.gov.au/collection/C1342685?image=2
[357] https://www.awm.gov.au/unit/U51475/

before finally consolidating its front some 200 yards from the original tape line from which the attack had commenced.[358]

There is no record of how or when precisely George was killed during the first day of the attack, but there is an entry on George's service record in January 1918 that he had been reportedly buried some 200 yards north-northeast of Augustus Wood.

The fact that George's death is not recorded in any detail, while unfortunate, is understandable given the significance of the battalion's losses in little more than 48 hours. The battle was a disaster for the 35th Battalion. The unit diary recorded that after the conclusion of operations at Passchendaele, the battalion suffered casualties of eight officers and 45 other ranks killed, eight officers and 208 other ranks wounded, one officer and 55 other ranks missing, and one rank gassed – a total of 326 casualties.[359] The battalion history recorded that of the 508 men that crossed the start line, only 90 remained unwounded at the end.[360]

After being advised of George's death by telegram on 19 November 1917, Eva wrote to the OIC requesting a certificate of death. Eva was at the time living at *Ashton,* 38 Plunkett Street, Drummoyne. The OIC replied in its letter dated 11 December 1917[361]:

> I have to acknowledge receipt of your communication of 19th ultimo, and to inform you that the necessary formal official confirming documents covering the report of the death of your husband, the late No. 1892, Private G. Brown, 35th Battalion, have not yet been received from abroad.

---

[358] 35th Battalion Unit Diary October 1917 - https://www.awm.gov.au/collection/C1342686?image=2
[359] 35th Battalion Unit Diary October 1917 - https://www.awm.gov.au/collection/C1342686?image=3 .
[360] 35th Battalion Unit History - https://www.awm.gov.au/unit/U51475/
[361] War service records accessible at https://recordsearch.naa.gov.au/SearchNRetrieve/Interface/ViewImage.aspx?B=1796619

Your request, however, has been noted for compliance at the earliest possible date.

It is confidently anticipated that later advice coming to hand by mail will furnish further particulars re death and burial, and these, on receipt, will be promptly transmitted to you.

In December 1917, George's name appeared in the official casualty list as having been killed in action.[362] In January 1918, Eva moved to *Stanhope*, 52 The Avenue, Drummoyne, and wrote to the OIC advising of her change of address,[363] and again sought details of George's death. In February 1918, the OIC responded to advise Eva that no further information had been received. Ultimately, the OIC's confidence expressed in its December 1917 letter would not be realised, since details regarding neither George's death nor final resting place would be provided to Eva. It was not until May 1918 that formal confirmation of George's death was provided to Eva but without any details of the circumstances of it.

Eva's disappointment continued as in June 1918, she again wrote to the OIC noting that she had received a letter from Chaplain G E Norman dated 20 November 1917. The chaplain had advised Eva that he had packed a few personal effects belonging to George, which he had given to the military authorities for forwarding to her, which she had not yet received. A letter dated 2 July 1918 from the OIC reported that it had received no such parcel and there was in any event considerable delay in the return of personal effects to Australia owing to a lack of shipping accommodation. Eva would eventually receive the parcel in September 1918.

On the anniversary of George's death in October 1918, a memorial notice was published by George's uncle in *The Daily Telegraph*[364]:

---

[362] NEW SOUTH WALES (1917, December 3). *The Sun* (Sydney, NSW: 1910-1954), p. 2. Retrieved April 25, 2023, from http://nla.gov.au/nla.news-article221411758
[363] In 1921, she again moved this time to *Foleyville*, York Street, Five Dock
[364] Family Notices (1918, October 12). *The Daily Telegraph* (Sydney, NSW: 1883-1930), p. 8. Retrieved April 25, 2023, from http://nla.gov.au/nla.news-article239573851

BROWN. — In loving memory of our dear nephew, Pte. George Brown, killed in action, in France, October 12th, 1917.

He answered to his country's call,
He gave his best, his life, his all.

Inserted by George and Harriet Bennett, Mortlake.

Photograph of the panel inscribed with the name of George Brown at the Ypres (Menin Gate) Memorial, Ypres (author, 2018).

George is commemorated on the Ypres (Menin Gate) Memorial as one of the 6,178 Australians who were killed in the Ypres sector in Belgium but who have no known grave.

Bert Arthur Simpson

Private, No. 170
36th Battalion, 9th Infantry Brigade, 3rd Australian Division
Killed in action 12 October 1917, Passchendaele, Belgium
Buried Tyne Cot Cemetery, Passchendaele, Belgium

In the Garden of Sleep Where the Poppies Bloom

Photograph of Bert Simpson. Source - ANOTHER AUSTRALIAN WINS THE VICTORIA CROSS (1917, July 15). *Sunday Times* (Sydney, NSW: 1895-1930), p. 22. Retrieved April 29, 2023, from http://nla.gov.au/nla.news-article122792111

Born in Darlinghurst in 1889 and registered as Bertie Arthur Simpson[365], Bert was the son of Henry Arthur and Louise Marion Simpson. Bert attended West Marrickville Public School and was a travelling salesman at the time of his enlistment in late 1915. He named his father as his next of kin and his residential address 25 Havelock Street, Drummoyne.

Bert's application to enlist in the AIF is dated 14 December 1915 when he was 26 years and one month old.[366] Passed fit by the preliminary medical examination for active service at the Board of Health recruiting depot, he was provisionally accepted for enlistment. Bert completed his attestation to join the AIF on 6 January 1916 in Liverpool and was subsequently assigned to A Company in the newly established 36th Battalion.

The 36th Battalion was raised at Broadmeadow Camp in Newcastle, NSW, in February 1916. The bulk of the battalion's recruits had been enlisted as a result of a recruiting drive conducted amongst the rifle clubs of NSW by the Minister for Public Information in the NSW government, Ambrose Carmichael. Thus, the battalion became known as 'Carmichael's Thousand'. Carmichael led by example and enlisted as well, serving in the battalion as a captain.[367] Although we have no way of knowing for certain, it may be that Bert was a member of a rifle club and determined to join following Carmichael's campaign.

---

[365] NSW BDM Registration No. 3545/1889.
[366] War service records accessible at https://recordsearch.naa.gov.au/SearchNRetrieve/Interface/ViewImage.aspx?B=8085164
[367] 36th Australian Infantry Battalion https://www.awm.gov.au/collection/U51476 accessed 25 July 2018.

The 36th Battalion became part of the 9th Brigade of the newly established 3rd Australian Division. Unlike the other Australian divisions in the AIF, the 3rd Division proceeded directly to England from Australia to undertake further training rather than proceed to Egypt where those other divisions were being reformed. Bert sailed from Sydney with the battalion on 13 May 1916 on HMAT A72 *Beltana*, arriving in Devonport in the United Kingdom on 9 July 1916.

Although there is no entry on Bert's service records, the battalion spent the next four months training at the Lark Hill Australian base on the Salisbury Plain. The 36th Battalion proceeded overseas from Southampton to France on 22 November 1916, boarding the transports *Caesarea* and *African Prince*, and disembarking at Le Harve the next day.[368] Arriving in Bailleul on 25 November, the battalion moved into billets where it was visited by General Godley, the commander of II ANZAC Corps, and General Monash, the commander of the 3rd Division, before moving to billets near Armentieres.[369] The battalion visited the front lines near Armentieres to gain experience in the trenches before taking up positions in the trenches for the first time on 4 December when it relieved the 34th Battalion,[370] just in time for the onset of the terrible winter of 1916–17.[371]

The routine over winter involved time in the front-line trenches, providing working parties in the rear areas and additional training. Even though the conditions did not lend itself to operations, raids both by the battalion and the enemy broke the routine but also caused casualties. One brief German raid on 22 January 1917 resulted in 11 killed, 36 wounded and four missing.[372] The pattern continued into February 1917, and it was when the battalion was in billets near

---

[368] 36th Battalion Unit Diary November 1916 - https://www.awm.gov.au/collection/C1342692?image=2
[369] 36th Battalion Unit Diary November 1916 - https://www.awm.gov.au/collection/C1342692?image=2
[370] 36th Battalion Unit Diary December 1916 - https://www.awm.gov.au/collection/C1356084?image=2
[371] 36th Australian Infantry Battalion https://www.awm.gov.au/collection/U51476 accessed 25 July 2018
[372] 36th Battalion Unit Diary January 1917 - https://www.awm.gov.au/collection/C1342700?image=3

Armentieres providing working parties and undertaking training that on 23 February 1917, Bert was evacuated sick. Initially admitted to the 9th Australian Field Ambulance, Bert was transferred to the 2nd CCS where he was diagnosed with severe synovitis of the right knee.[373]

Admitted to the 2nd Australian General Hospital at Wimereux on 25 February, the commanding officer of the battalion was required to provide a report into the circumstances of Bert's injury, certifying that the injury was the result of an accident in the trenches when he was acting as an observer, and not the result of any conduct by Bert. A note on Bert's medical history form reports that the injury was suffered from a fall in a trench, and his name appeared among those reported ill in casualty lists published in March 1917, with the illness noted as serious.[374]

Bert's injury was sufficiently serious that he was invalided to England on 1 March 1917 and boarded the Hospital Ship *St David* at Boulogne on 3 March. Admitted to the 1st Southern General Hospital, Bert remained in hospital for over four months until 16 July 1917. The day before he was discharged, Bert's photograph was published in the *Sunday Times* in Sydney, noting that he was in hospital in England.[375] On his discharge from hospital, he was granted leave with orders to report to the Training Depot at Codford on 30 July 1917. During his absence, the battalion and the 3rd Division was involved in its first major offensive operation, the Battle of Messines, in June 1917.

Bert's parents were advised that he had been admitted to hospital with severe knee synovitis, and his mother requested any additional information as 'naturally both his father and I are very anxious to hear something of him, by so doing you would receive our grateful

---

[373] Soft tissue inflammation of the knee.
[374] NEW SOUTH WALES. (1917, March 23). *The Sydney Morning Herald* (NSW: 1842-1954), p. 9. Retrieved April 29, 2023, from http://nla.gov.au/nla.news-article15726120 ; ILL (1917, March 22). *The Sun* (Sydney, NSW: 1910-1954), p. 7 (FINAL EXTRA). Retrieved April 29, 2023, from http://nla.gov.au/nla.news-article221959606
[375] ANOTHER AUSTRALIAN WINS THE VICTORIA CROSS (1917, July 15). *Sunday Times* (Sydney, NSW: 1895-1930), p. 22. Retrieved April 29, 2023, from http://nla.gov.au/nla.news-article122792111

thanks'.[376] On 7 August 1917, the OIC notified Bert's parents that Bert was convalescing but was unable to provide any additional information in response to a request from Henry Simpson when he wrote[377]:

> Could you kindly let me know if you have any further information concerning him. Naturally am anxious and would be greatly relieved by you giving me any information as to his welfare.

It would appear that Bert spent some more time at Codford, as he did not join the overseas training battalion until 28 August 1917 and then did not embark from Southampton until 17 September 1917.

Bert finally rejoined the battalion on 30 September 1917, just as it was going back into the front lines[378] and before the 3rd Division's next major action, this time the attack on Broodseinde Ridge. Perhaps fortunately for Bert, the 9th Brigade was held in reserve during this battle, which commenced on 4 October 1917. Following the successful attack on Broodseinde Ridge, the battalion began preparations for its role in the next stage of the Ypres offensive, this time on the village of Passchendaele itself. It began its approach march through Ypres on 10 and 11 October, with the offensive to start the next day.[379] The battalion's narrative describes the experience of the battle as the battalion struggled to make its way to the jumping-off tapes, enduring rain, boggy conditions, German shelling and gas attacks. The battalion suffered over 100 casualties just during the approach march.[380]

---

[376] War service records accessible at https://recordsearch.naa.gov.au/SearchNRetrieve/Interface/ViewImage.aspx?B=8085164
[377] War service records accessible at https://recordsearch.naa.gov.au/SearchNRetrieve/Interface/ViewImage.aspx?B=8085164
[378] 36th Battalion Unit Diary September 1917 - https://www.awm.gov.au/collection/C1342693?image=3
[379] 36th Battalion Unit Diary October 1917 - https://www.awm.gov.au/collection/C1342694?image=2
[380] 36th Battalion Unit Diary October 1917 - https://www.awm.gov.au/collection/C1342694?image=5

As the ground became impassable closer to the front, the conditions forced the whole brigade to approach in single file, dangerously exposed to the German barrage.[381] At zero hour the leading companies of the battalion began their assault as the German barrage increased in intensity. While the soft ground conditions absorbed much of the effect of each shell burst, the number of casualties from direct hits was described as 'remarkable'.[382] While the 34th Battalion was able to make progress, the 35th and Bert's 36th Battalion had 'their hands full' mopping up German dugouts, which delayed their progress and caused many casualties. Having secured the first objective, the Red Line, the barrage lifted onto the next objective, the Blue Line. Heavy machine gun fire from Crest Farm and Passchendaele itself caused many casualties, almost wiping out the left company of the 35th Battalion, which gap was required to be filled by a company from the 36th Battalion.[383]

The Blue Line was only reached on the extreme left, by which time the battalion's numbers had been very much reduced by casualties. All available men including the reserve companies were sent forward from the Red Line to attempt to seize the line and keep up with the creeping barrage. Casualties, however, proved so heavy, that a further advance was considered impossible. The battalion's diary recorded[384]:

> Reports continued to come in from the front line troops that consolidation in face of heavy machine gun fire, snipers and 5.9 barrage was impossible and that casualties were piling up at an alarming rate.

---

[381] 36th Battalion Unit Diary October 1917 - https://www.awm.gov.au/collection/C1342694?image=5
[382] 36th Battalion Unit Diary October 1917 - https://www.awm.gov.au/collection/C1342694?image=5
[383] 36th Battalion Unit Diary October 1917 - https://www.awm.gov.au/collection/C1342694?image=5
[384] 36th Battalion Unit Diary October 1917 - https://www.awm.gov.au/collection/C1342694?image=6

During the afternoon, Boche were seen in force on PASSCHENDAELE Road advancing on our flank and from the front ENLIST FARM & ECHO COPSE. At dusk Major CARR decided that it was impossible to hold on and a new line was formed …

The battalion's casualties were reported as 14 officers and 400 other ranks.[385] Bert was one of the casualties, reported as having been killed in action on 12 October 1917, less than two weeks after having rejoined his battalion. His name appeared among those killed in action in the official casualty lists published in November 1917[386], and family notices were published on 10 and 12 November 1917 in *The Sydney Morning Herald*[387]:

SIMPSON. - Killed in action in France, 12/10/17, Bert A. Simpson, eldest son of Mr. and Mrs. Harry Simpson, Drummoyne.

SIMPSON. - Pte. Bert A. Simpson, killed in action October 12, 1917, in France. A tribute of esteem by Mr. and Mrs. W. J. Ellis. Madge, Finlay (on active service), and Irene. The Rosary.

Further family notices were published on the anniversary of Bert's death[388]:

---

[385] 36th Battalion Unit Diary October 1917 - https://www.awm.gov.au/collection/C1342694?image=7
[386] DOUBLE CASUALTY LIST. (1917, November 26). *The Sydney Morning Herald* (NSW: 1842-1954), p. 4. Retrieved April 29, 2023, from http://nla.gov.au/nla.news-article15743485 ; Latest Casualties. (1917, November 30). *The Land* (Sydney, NSW: 1911-1954), p. 11. Retrieved April 29, 2023, from http://nla.gov.au/nla.news-article102893337 ; BIG CASUALTY LIST (1917, November 25). *Sunday Times* (Sydney, NSW: 1895-1930), p. 3. Retrieved April 29, 2023, from http://nla.gov.au/nla.news-article122795987
[387] Family Notices (1917, November 10). *The Sydney Morning Herald* (NSW: 1842-1954), p. 12. Retrieved April 29, 2023, from http://nla.gov.au/nla.news-article15756155 and Family Notices (1917, November 12). *The Sydney Morning Herald* (NSW: 1842-1954), p. 6. Retrieved April 29, 2023, from http://nla.gov.au/nla.news-article15735295 . A family notice was also published by his parents on 10 November 1917 in *The Daily Telegraph* – see Family Notices (1917, November 10). *The Daily Telegraph* (Sydney, NSW: 1883-1930), p. 8. Retrieved April 29, 2023, from http://nla.gov.au/nla.news-article239244548
[388] Family Notices (1918, October 12). *The Sydney Morning Herald* (NSW: 1842-1954), p. 11. Retrieved April 29, 2023, from http://nla.gov.au/nla.news-article15806261

SIMPSON. - Our dear son, Bert, 36th Batt, killed in action at Passchendaele, October 12, 1917. The Last Post has sounded.

SIMPSON. - A tribute of lasting love to our brother, Bert, of 36th Batt, killed in action, France, October 12, 1917. Reg. (on active service), Lyle, Harrie. The supreme sacrifice.

SIMPSON. - Sacred to the memory of Private Bert A. Simpson, who paid the supreme sacrifice, October 12, 1917. Inserted by Mr. and Mrs. W. J. Ellis and family, of Redfern. The Rosary.

SIMPSON. - Everlasting memory of Bert, who gave his life Passchendaele Ridge, October 12, 1917. Always missed. Rose and Ray. A life that moved to a gracious end.

A note on Bert's service records have him as buried 100 yards northwest of Zonnebeke, west of Hill 400. After the war, Bert's grave was located, with his remains identified by his identity disc. In July 1920 Bert's body was exhumed by a GSU and reburied in Tyne Cot Cemetery.

Photograph of the grave of Bert Simpson at Tyne Cot Cemetery (author, 2018).

Joseph Marcus Harwood

Lance Corporal, No. 3055
45th Battalion, 12th Infantry Brigade, 4th Australian Division
Killed in action 13 October 1917, Passchendaele, Belgium
Buried Tyne Cot Cemetery, Passchendaele, Belgium

*Australia will have other sons but none more
honoured than these*

Photograph of Joseph Harwood. Source Ancestery.com.

Joseph Marcus Harwood was born in about 1897[389] in Rozelle, NSW, the eldest son of Joseph and Ellen Crawford Harwood. Joseph appears to be one of six children.[390] Educated at Rozelle Public School, Joseph's father had died in April 1900 when Joseph was 12 years old, as did two of his siblings.[391] His father, Joseph Harwood (Snr), had been an alderman on Balmain Council.

Joseph enlisted in the AIF on 16 July 1915 at the age of 18 years and four months.[392] Prior to his enlistment, he was employed as a farm hand and had possibly worked on a sheep station according to his application for enrolment for active service completed on 14 July 1915. On his attestation paper, Joseph specified his next of kin as his mother Ellen Harwood and her address as 41 Cary Street, Drummoyne.[393] Joseph's brother, John Michael Harwood, would also enlist in the AIF in June 1917 and join the 33rd Battalion, ultimately returning to Australia in December 1918.[394]

Initially assigned to the 10th Reinforcements to the 13th Battalion, Joseph undertook preliminary training prior to embarking from Sydney on 6 September 1915 on HMAT A70 *Ballarat* bound for the AIF training camp in Egypt. He was taken on strength with the 13th Battalion on 4 February 1916 at Moascar.

---

[389] NSW BDM Registration No. 10163/1897.
[390] Olive M (2655/1890), Cecily A (36889/1892), Nellie A (1560/1895), John Michael (10202/1898) and Arnold (28439/1899).
[391] Joseph - NSW BDM Registration No. 148/1900, Nellie - 8227/1900 and Arnold - 8191/1900.
[392] War service records accessible at https://recordsearch.naa.gov.au/SearchNRetrieve/Interface/ViewImage.aspx?B=4738535
[393] The property is also referred to by its name *Waiora* in other correspondence on Joseph's service records. In 1921, Ellen Harwood had moved to *Yenda*, Sunnyside Street, Gladesville.
[394] https://www.aif.adfa.edu.au/showPerson?pid=130376 (accessed 30 April 2023).

While the AIF was being reorganised in Egypt consequent on the withdrawal from Gallipoli and the arrival of new reinforcements from Australia, the decision was made to split the original battalions such as the 13th so that the new enlarged Australian forces would contain a mixture of experienced soldiers and newly arrived reinforcements. Joseph was one of those reinforcements originally assigned to the 13th Battalion who on 3 March 1916 were transferred to the newly formed 45th Battalion, along with B and C Companies from the 13th Battalion.[395] Reflecting the composition of the 13th, the new battalion was composed mostly of men from New South Wales. On 22 March, the newly formed battalion was inspected by HRH the Prince of Wales and Lt-General William Birdwood at Tel El Kebir.

The 45th Battalion was part of the 12th Brigade of the newly formed 4th Australian Division. At the end of March 1916, the battalion along with the rest of the 12th Brigade moved to Serapeum on the east side of the canal, and took over a section of the front-line trenches, where it remained until mid-April.[396] The battalion then travelled to Alexandria where it embarked on HMT *Kinfauns Castle* to join the BEF in France on 2 June 1916, arriving in Marseilles on 8 June 1916.

The battalion travelled by train to northern France, arriving at the town of Bailleul on 11 June 1916, and was inspected by General Plumer, the commander of the British Second Army a week later, where the unit diary notes that the general commented on the steadiness of bearing of the battalion. Further inspections were made by Lt-General Birdwood and then by the Commander-in-Chief of British Armies, General Sir Douglas Haig, with the unit diary noting that the latter 'evidently was very favourably impressed'.[397]

---

[395] Of the 361 men transferred to the 45th Battalion, 278 had experience from the Gallipoli campaign. 45th Battalion Unit Diary March 1916 - https://www.awm.gov.au/collection/C1346075?image=2

[396] 45th Battalion Unit Diary April 1916 - https://www.awm.gov.au/collection/C1346086?image=3

[397] 45th Battalion Unit Diary June 1916 - https://www.awm.gov.au/collection/C1344510?image=2

After a brief period in trenches near Sailly in July 1916,[398] by early August the battalion was preparing to take its turn in the offensive at Pozières. On 4 August, the battalion commenced its march through the town of Albert, eventually relieving the 17th, 18th and 19th Battalions on 5 August under very heavy enemy artillery fire.[399] The 45th Battalion repulsed a number of weak German counter-attacks but suffered casualties from almost continuous artillery fire both in the front and support lines. By the time the battalion came out of the line and returned to Albert on 15 August, it had suffered total killed of three officers and 84 other ranks, wounded of seven officers and 337 other ranks, and 10 missing.[400]

On 8 September 1916, the battalion entrained for Belgian Flanders, remaining in the Ypres sector until the end of October, before returning to the Somme sector at the start of November 1916.[401] By January 1917, the battalion was serving in the front-line trenches at Gueudecourt, and in February was taking up positions at Flers. It was during this time that Joseph was promoted to lance corporal on 15 February 1917.

In March 1917, Joseph was admitted to the 12th Australian Field Ambulance with 'STA Right Foot' (septic traumatic abrasions[402]), which eventually saw him transferred to the 4th Divisional Rest Station. Although discharged to his unit on 26 March, his foot infection appears to have flared up with him being readmitted to the Field Ambulance. In April 1917, the battalion moved into positions around Bapaume and Noreuil in preparation for the attack on Bullecourt. The 45th Battalion was in reserve for the 4th Division's attack on Bullecourt on 11 April 1917 and was not committed to the attack.[403]

---

[398] 45th Battalion Unit Diary July 1916 - https://www.awm.gov.au/collection/C1344511?image=2
[399] 45th Battalion Unit Diary August 1916 - https://www.awm.gov.au/collection/C1344512?image=3
[400] 45th Battalion Unit Diary August 1916 - https://www.awm.gov.au/collection/C1344512?image=3
[401] 45th Battalion Unit Diary November 1916 - https://www.awm.gov.au/collection/C1344515?image=2
[402] https://www.awm.gov.au/glossary/term-s/
[403] 45th Battalion Unit History - https://www.awm.gov.au/collection/U51485

In the first week of June 1917, the 45th Battalion had transferred to Kortepyp Camp near Ploegsteert Wood, Belgium, preparing for the forthcoming attack at Messines before moving to near Hill 63.[404] The battalion was heavily engaged during the Battle of Messines, which commenced on 7 June and suffered commensurate casualties. The battalion was relieved on 11 June and during that short period of operation had suffered casualties of eight officers and 92 other ranks killed, eight officers and 344 other ranks wounded, with 50 other ranks missing.[405]

Included among those casualties was Joseph, who suffered a gunshot wound to his left arm, and he was admitted to the 11th CCS. He was transferred to the 58th Scottish General Hospital at St Omer on 8 June 1917 and remained there for about a month. His name appeared among those listed as wounded in casualty lists published in July 1917.[406] Joseph rejoined his battalion on 4 July 1917 when it was at Kortepyp Camp.

After a period of reorganisation, training and taking on more reinforcements, the battalion returned to the front lines of the Ypres sector relieving its sister battalion, the 13th Battalion, in the reserve lines on 7 August 1917.[407] It moved into the front lines between 14 to 23 August, relieving the 48th Battalion. During that time, the battalion was occupied converting the shell holes that littered the front line into some form of coordinated defensive trench system.

After being relieved itself, the battalion moved into billets variously around Staples, Le Nieppe and Steenvoorde over the remainder of August and into September. The battalion commenced preparations for a move to Westhoek to be in the reserve lines to support the 4th

---

[404] 45th Battalion Unit Diary, June 1917 - https://www.awm.gov.au/collection/C1346082?image=2
[405] 45th Battalion Unit Diary June 1917 - https://www.awm.gov.au/collection/C1346082?image=2
[406] Australian Casualties. (1917, July 11). *Australian Town and Country Journal* (Sydney, NSW: 1870-1919), p. 16. Retrieved April 29, 2023, from http://nla.gov.au/nla.news-article263771174
[407] 45th Battalion Unit Diary August 1917 - https://www.awm.gov.au/collection/C1346084?image=2

and 13th Brigades for the next instalment of the Third Battle of Ypres, arriving there on 25 September 1917.[408] However, Joseph was to miss this next stage of the ongoing Ypres offensive as on 22 September 1917, Joseph was granted one week's leave to the UK or a 'Blighty' and did not rejoin the battalion until the start of October 1917.

Joseph's return to the battalion was just in time for the looming renewal of the Passchendaele offensive, this time with an attack to capture the village of Passchendaele itself. The battalion passed through Westhoek Ridge on the way to the front lines near Zonnebeke where it relieved the whole of the 5th Brigade in the early hours of 10 October 1917.[409] The battalion's history stated it took part in the major battle near Passchendaele on 12 October in conditions which were horrendous and in an operation that was hastily planned, resulting in failure.[410] It also described the battalion's casualties as equally horrendous.

The 12th Brigade of the 4th Division was to advance to the right of the 3rd Division, which had principal responsibility for seizing the Passchendaele Ridge, and the village beyond it. Before the attack was due to commence, the rain increased in heaviness. The leading battalions of the 12th Brigade were the 47th and 48th, with the 45th Battalion providing carrying parties. After some initial success, the attacking units from both the 3rd and 4th Divisions were forced to retire by the end of the day.

It appears from the unit diary that the 45th Battalion suffered comparatively light casualties from its time in the forward area, and certainly less than it suffered Messines.[411] Joseph Harwood was among the battalion's casualties, being killed on 13 October 1917. He was only 20 years old. News of Joseph's death was notified by family in

---

[408] 45th Battalion Unit Diary September 1917 - https://www.awm.gov.au/collection/C1346085?image=2
[409] 45th Battalion Unit Diary October 1917 - https://www.awm.gov.au/collection/C1346087?image=5
[410] 45th Australian Infantry Battalion - https://www.awm.gov.au/unit/U51485/
[411] The battalion's losses in the operation were one officer and 38 other ranks killed, seven officers and 138 other ranks wounded with ten other ranks missing - https://www.awm.gov.au/collection/C1346087?image=6

local papers[412] and family notices recording his death were published in November 1917[413]:

> HARWOOD. — Killed in action, in France, October 13, 1917, Private Joseph Marcus Harwood, the loved eldest son of the late Joseph Harwood, Weston-road, Rozelle, and Ellen Harwood, Cary-street, Drummoyne, after two years' active service, aged 20 years and 6 months.
>
> He fought the light, but ere the night
> His soul had passed away.
>
> HARWOOD. — Killed in action in France, October 13, 1917, Joseph M. Harwood, aged 20 years, eldest son of Mrs. Harwood, Drummoyne, and the late Ald. J. Harwood, Balmain.
>
> 'Thy will be done.'
>
> Inserted by his sorrowing mother, sisters and brothers.

Joseph was included among those reported killed in action in casualty lists published in December 1917[414], and his sister Cecily published a notice on the anniversary of Joseph's death in October 1918[415]:

---

[412] NEWS ITEMS. (1917, November 15). *The Gosford Times and Wyong District Advocate* (NSW: 1906-1954), p. 8. Retrieved April 29, 2023, from http://nla.gov.au/nla.news-article166852617
[413] Family Notices (1917, November 13). *The Sydney Morning Herald* (NSW: 1842-1954), p. 6. Retrieved April 29, 2023, from http://nla.gov.au/nla.news-article15745805 and Family Notices (1917, November 15). *The Gosford Times and Wyong District Advocate* (NSW: 1906-1954), p. 8. Retrieved April 29, 2023, from http://nla.gov.au/nla.news-article166852618
[414] N. S. W. CASUALTIES. (1917, December 1). *The Daily Telegraph* (Sydney, NSW: 1883-1930), p. 12. Retrieved April 29, 2023, from http://nla.gov.au/nla.news-article239234748 Latest Casualties. (1917, December 7). *The Land* (Sydney, NSW: 1911-1954), p. 11. Retrieved April 29, 2023, from http://nla.gov.au/nla.news-article102893726 ; Australian Casualties (1917, December 5). *Australian Town and Country Journal* (Sydney, NSW: 1870-1919), p. 15. Retrieved April 29, 2023, from http://nla.gov.au/nla.news-article263770807
[415] Family Notices (1918, October 10). *The Gosford Times and Wyong District Advocate* (NSW: 1906-1954), p. 8. Retrieved April 29, 2023, from http://nla.gov.au/nla.news-article166856189

HARWOOD. — In loving memory of our dear brother, Joseph Marcus Harwood, killed in France, October 12th, 1917. Thy will be done.
Inserted by Mr. and Mrs. Arch Hennessey, also Mrs. Glasson and family.

Several statements were obtained by the Red Cross in connection with its investigation of the circumstances of Joseph's death.[416] In January 1918, Private John A Hembrough (1929) said 'Joe' was in B Company, 6th Platoon and he came from Queensland. While he did not see the event, Pte Hembrough reported that near Zonnebeke, Joseph was killed outright while in the line after being hit by a shell. A similar statement was provided by Private Arthur A Rogers (1758).

Private John J Kearney (3397) also told the Red Cross that Joseph was simply called 'Joe' and provided the following statement[417]:

> Harwood was in a shell-hole near us on October 13th, on the Ypres Front, with about 30 others. A shell burst right amongst them, and we jumped up to see what we could do. There was only Harwood and a blanket left; he looked as though he had been killed by concussion. We dug and searched for the others, but found nothing. Their rations done up in a bundle were blown in the air and landed intact at our feet. We intended to bury him but were unable to. We took his effects and handed them into the Company.

Private Rockley Loftus (1952) also assisted to dig Joseph out after the shell had exploded and confirmed that he had no noticeable wounds. However, he states that he did assist to bury Joseph close to the spot straight away, in a shell hole near the trench, but the grave

---

[416] Australian Red Cross Wounded and Missing Files - https://www.awm.gov.au/collection/R1487409
[417] Australian Red Cross Wounded and Missing Files - https://www.awm.gov.au/collection/R1487409

had not been marked to his knowledge at the time.[418] Private Albert Mole (3846) did not witness Joseph's death but did advise the Red Cross that his home was in Drummoyne and that he had relations in England.

A final report was obtained by the Red Cross in February 1919 from Lance Corporal James W Graves (4170) while he was in the 4th Australian General Hospital at Randwick. The Red Cross record of the interview stated[419]:

> Informant states that they both belonged to B. Company, 6th Platoon. On 13.10.17 the Battalion was at Passchendaele holding the line. After dinner, while Harwood's section was in a trench, a shell came over and blew it in and all the section (4 men in all) were buried. Informant was about 20 yards away and saw this happen. Some of the other lads went over to the spot and dug the men out and found that they were dead. Informant could not leave his section and consequently did not see the men after they were dug out, but he saw the shell explode. He was informed that Harwood was amongst the killed and that they were reburied on the spot. ...
>
> According to Informant Harwood was very well liked by his mates.

Despite the apparent rushed and incomplete burial of Joseph's remains after he had been killed, his body was recovered after the Armistice and reinterred at nearby Tyne Cot Cemetery.

---

[418] Private Loftus also reported his belief that Joseph's home was in Katoomba, whereas Private Hembrough claimed that Joseph was from Queensland. Private Kearney said that 'his people were English' - Australian Red Cross Wounded and Missing Files - https://www.awm.gov.au/collection/R1487409

[419] Australian Red Cross Wounded and Missing Files - https://www.awm.gov.au/collection/R1487409

Photograph of the grave of Joseph Harwood at Tyne Cot Cemetery, Ypres, Belgium (author, 2018).

William Ruffley

Armourer Sergeant, No. 1539
47th Battalion, 12th Infantry Brigade, 4th Australian Division
Killed in action 13 October 1917, Passchendaele, Belgium
No known grave. Commemorated Ypres Menin Gate Memorial, Ypres, Belgium

Image of William Ruffley. Source - Reinforcements and A.L.H., Second Queensland Contingent. (1915, January 23). The Queenslander (Brisbane, Qld.: 1866-1939), p. 25. Retrieved May 1, 2023, from http://nla.gov.au/nla.news-article22293166

William Ruffley was born in St Peters, New South Wales, in about 1889.[420] There is no information available about William's parents and little information about his early life. What we can ascertain is that he had one sibling, his sister Dora, and that at some point he moved to Queensland and was working as a labourer until he enlisted at Toowoomba on 14 December 1914. On his attestation form, William disclosed that he had served for one year with D Company of the Balmain cadets, which had been disbanded, and also admitted to having been convicted of assault for which he had been fined at Gladesville Local Court.[421] William nominated his sister, Mrs Dora

---

[420] According to William's attestation paper he was born at St Peters and declared his age to be 24 years and seven months at the time of enlistment. There is no record of his birth at the NSW BDM registry.
[421] War service records accessible at https://recordsearch.naa.gov.au/SearchNRetrieve/Interface/ViewImage.aspx?B=8071409

Dundon (nee Ruffley), then living at Oatley, NSW, as his next of kin but did not tell her of his enlistment.[422]

William was assigned to the 3rd Reinforcements to the 15th Battalion as part of the 4th Infantry Brigade. The 15th Battalion was raised from late September 1914, six weeks after the outbreak of the First World War. Three-quarters of the battalion were recruited as volunteers from Queensland, and the rest from Tasmania. With the 13th, 14th and 16th Battalions it formed the 4th Brigade, commanded by then Colonel John Monash.[423] When the 4th Brigade arrived in Egypt, it became part of the New Zealand and Australian Division.

William's image appeared in the 23 January 1915 edition of *The Queenslander* as one of the contingent of reinforcements from Queensland.[424] The 3rd Reinforcements sailed from Brisbane on HMAT A49 *Seang Choon* on 13 February 1915 as part of the second Queensland contingent of reinforcements. By that time, the battalion had already landed in Egypt and was encamped at Heliopolis[425] where it remained until 11 April 1915.[426]

It is unclear from William's service records when he arrived in Egypt, it being noted that he proceeded to join MEF on 12 April 1915. This was the same day as the first contingent of the battalion left Alexandria for Lemnos in preparation for the landings on the Gallipoli peninsula.[427] From 15 April until the morning of 24 April, the troops practised disembarkation in Mudros Harbour. At 5:30 a.m. on 25

---

[422] In a letter dated 10 March 1916 to the OIC, Dora asked for any information regarding her brother as she was not aware that he had enlisted.
[423] https://www.awm.gov.au/collection/U51455
[424] Reinforcements and A.L.H., Second Queensland Contingent. (1915, January 23). *The Queenslander* (Brisbane, Qld.: 1866-1939), p. 25. Retrieved May 1, 2023, from http://nla.gov.au/nla.news-article22293166
[425] 15th Battalion Unit Diary February 1915 - https://www.awm.gov.au/collection/C1342871?image=2
[426] 15th Battalion Unit Diary April 1915 - https://www.awm.gov.au/collection/C1356103?image=2
[427] 15th Battalion Unit Diary April 1915 - https://www.awm.gov.au/collection/C1356103?image=4

April, the transports reached the entrance of the Dardanelles and witnessed the bombardment and landing of British forces.[428]

Late on the afternoon of 25 April, elements of the battalion began to disembark from their transports but were not landed until late at night,[429] with the remainder not landing until mid-morning on 26 April. The battalion took up position between the 1st and 2nd Brigades until 30 April when it moved to Monash Valley[430] and occupied Pope's Hill where it came under attack from Turkish forces.[431] After successfully repulsing the Turkish attack, on 1 and 2 May the battalion launched its own attack but were unable to hold the captured trenches without support.[432] After weathering another Turkish assault, the battalion was relieved on the evening on 3 May and bivouacked in Monash Valley.[433]

The respite from the fighting only lasted a matter of days before the battalion took up positions at Quinn's Post. Despite an initial successful assault on Turkish trenches on the night of 9–10 May, the men were forced to withdraw when they could not dislodge Turks from other parts of the trench. Throughout May 1915, the battalion exchanged punches and counter-punches with the Turks at Quinn's Post.

In early June, the battalion was withdrawn to Walker's Gully for rest. On 4 June 1915, William Ruffley was promoted to the rank of Armour Sergeant on account of Armour Sergeant RB McIntosh being promoted to regimental quarter master sergeant. In that position,

---

[428] 15th Battalion Unit Diary April 1915 - https://www.awm.gov.au/collection/C1356103?image=7
[429] 15th Battalion Unit Diary April 1915 - https://www.awm.gov.au/collection/C1356103?image=8
[430] 15th Battalion Unit Diary April 1915 - https://www.awm.gov.au/collection/C1356103?image=9
[431] 15th Battalion Unit Diary April 1915 - https://www.awm.gov.au/collection/C1356103?image=10
[432] 15th Battalion Unit Diary May 1915 - https://www.awm.gov.au/collection/C1342882?image=2
[433] 15th Battalion Unit Diary May 1915 - https://www.awm.gov.au/collection/C1342882?image=3

William was responsible for the maintenance and management of the unit's arms and ammunition.

6 August 1915 saw the battalion along with the remainder of the 4th Brigade move to the far-left flank of the ANZAC beachhead to coordinate its assault on Hill 971 adjacent the fresh landing by British forces at Suvla Bay. Units of the battalion found themselves advancing across open ground exposed to enemy fire.[434] Soon, the ground changed to rough outcrops and low scrub, which the Turks used to their advantage to provide stiff opposition to the attack. The battalion along with other elements of the brigade recommenced its attack in the early hours of 8 August, and after some initial success found its flanks exposed and under heavy Turkish counterattack. The brigade ordered a general withdraw.[435] The new offensive ultimately stalled and degenerated into static trench warfare with the Turks remaining in control of the strategic positions on the new front.

On 9 September 1915, the battalion was relieved and moved to bivouacs near Beauchop's Hill.[436] On the same day, William was admitted to the 4th Field Ambulance suffering from tonsillitis and was evacuated to 16th CCS at Mudros on Lemnos island on 13 September. The next day, he was transferred to the 25th CCS at Imbros suffering from tonsillitis and septic infection of his hands, before being admitted to the 3rd Australian General Hospital. At the same time, the brigade was withdrawn from the peninsula and evacuated to Lemnos, where it arrived on 14 September as part of a period of rest before it returned to ANZAC Cove.[437]

Within a month, William was evacuated on the hospital ship HS *Calendonia* arriving in Gibraltar on 15 October before boarding HS *Ballarat* on 25 October. William arrived in England on 31 October

---

[434] 15th battalion Unit Diary August 1915 - https://www.awm.gov.au/collection/C1342362?image=4
[435] 15th Battalion Unit Diary August 1915 - https://www.awm.gov.au/collection/C1342362?image=27
[436] 15th Battalion Unit Diary September 1915 - https://www.awm.gov.au/collection/C1342363?image=2
[437] 15th Battalion Unit Diary September 1915 - https://www.awm.gov.au/collection/C1342363?image=3

1915 where he was admitted to the Southern General Hospital, Maudlin Street, Bristol.[438] William remained in hospital until discharged on 18 November 1915 when he reported to the Australian & New Zealand Base at Abbey Wood, England, scheduled to return to join the MEF as part of the 28th draft from Weymouth. His departure, however, was delayed by reason of him being admitted to the 4th London General Hospital in February 1916 suffering from venereal sores. During this time, William's service records indicated that his pay was stopped on account of suffering from venereal disease. This would be an affliction that would follow William for some months.

Before William could rejoin his unit, he was again admitted to hospital, this time Fulham Hospital in London from 29 February to 15 March 1916, suspected to be suffering from rubella. While still in hospital, William was reassigned to the 47th Battalion on 9 March 1916. The 47th Battalion was raised in Egypt on 24 February 1916 as part of the 'doubling' of the AIF. Approximately half of its new recruits were Gallipoli veterans from the 15th Battalion, and the other half, fresh reinforcements from Australia. Reflecting the composition of the 15th the new battalion was composed mostly of men recruited in Queensland and Tasmania. The new battalion was incorporated into the 12th Brigade of the 4th Australian Division.[439]

William is recorded as having returned to duty in Egypt on 28 March 1916.[440] The newly formed battalion embarked from Alexandria on 2 June 1916 to join the BEF in France on HT *Caledonia*, arriving at Marseilles on 9 June 1916.[441] The battalion entrained and

---

[438] ROLL OF HONOUR. (1915, November 26). *Queensland Times* (Ipswich, Qld.: 1909-1954), p. 5 (DAILY.). Retrieved May 1, 2023, from http://nla.gov.au/nla.news-article113126077; The Roll Of Honour. (1915, December 4). *The Queenslander* (Brisbane, Qld.: 1866-1939), p. 10. Retrieved May 1, 2023, from http://nla.gov.au/nla.news-article22303567
[439] 47th Battalion Unit History - https://www.awm.gov.au/collection/U51487
[440] See also ROLL OF HONOUR. (1916, April 14). *The Telegraph* (Brisbane, Qld.: 1872-1947), p. 5 (SECOND EDITION). Retrieved May 1, 2023, from http://nla.gov.au/nla.news-article177996704
[441] 47th Battalion Unit Diary June 1916 - https://www.awm.gov.au/collection/C1345051?image=2

travelled north until it arrived at Bailleul West were it moved into billets near Outtersteene.[442]

The 47th Battalion entered the trenches of the Western Front for the first time on 3 July at Fleurbaix, relieving the 1st Battalion.[443] It remained in that position until 11 July when relieved by the 53rd Battalion. The battalion moved out of its billets at Outtersteene on 14 July, and by early August had taken up positions in the brickpits near Pozières, as reserve to the front line.[444] Shortly before going into action, William made his will, leaving all his pay to Miss Dorothy Wren of 90 Putney Bridge Road, Wandsworth, England. It would appear William had made a friend while hospitalised in London.

Initially, the battalion provided working parties during the 2nd Division's attack on 4 August, and then, with its own division, on 7 August the battalion commenced its relief of the 48th Battalion under artillery fire with the battalion suffering heavy casualties.[445] The battalion remained in the front-line trenches until 12 August when the slow and difficult process of relief commenced. It was not until 14 August that the battalion was able to extricate itself to reserve positions in Sausage Valley and then eventually the brickfields near Albert.[446] After a brief period of respite, the battalion was back in positions close to Pozières at the end of August[447] involved in repeated attempts to take Mouquet Farm.

After Pozières, the battalion spent the period up until March 1917 alternating between duty in the trenches, and training and rest behind the lines. On 1 January 1917, William was admitted to NZ Stationary

---

[442] 47th Battalion Unit Diary June 1916 - https://www.awm.gov.au/collection/C1345051?image=3

[443] 47th Battalion Unit Diary July 1916 - https://www.awm.gov.au/collection/C1345062?image=4

[444] 47th Battalion Unit Diary July 1916 - https://www.awm.gov.au/collection/C1345068?image=2

[445] 47th Battalion Unit Diary August 1916 - https://www.awm.gov.au/collection/C1345068?image=4

[446] 47th Battalion Unit Diary August 1916 - https://www.awm.gov.au/collection/C1345068?image=6

[447] 47th Battalion Unit Diary August 1916 - https://www.awm.gov.au/collection/C1345068?image=8

Hospital in Amiens suffering from Venereal Disease Gonorrhoea (VDG) before being transferred to the 51st General Hospital at Etaples where he remained for a month. Although discharged to base at Etaples on 10 February, he was readmitted shortly after to 18th General Hospital at Camiers, this time suspected to be suffering from mumps. Although discharged on 19 March to rejoin the depot at Etaples, within four days he was readmitted to hospital, this time to the 26th General Hospital suffering from an ingrown toenail. William remained in hospital until 23 March before returning to Etaples. During his time out of the line, William took the opportunity to write a letter to a Miss L Lynn thanking her for a Christmas parcel that she had sent him, which note was reported in an NSW Far North Coast newspaper[448]:

> Miss L. Lynn, of Riverview, has received a letter from Armorer-Sergt, W Ruffley, 47th Battalion, from France, thanking her for a parcel she sent at Xmas, which he had been fortunate enough to receive. He says during some 'pretty rough times' experienced at the front, gifts like this were very cheering.

It was not until 13 April that William rejoined his unit,[449] which meant that he had fortunately missed the disaster that was the first Battle of Bullecourt. The battalion was to provide support to the attack by the 46th and 48th Battalions scheduled to commence early on 11 April. The battalion witnessed the attack go in with only tank support, which were ineffectual in breaking down the wire: seven tanks were destroyed by direct hits, and three 'wandering about having apparently lost direction'.[450] Although the 46th Battalion and 48th Battalion each captured their objectives showing great dash and

---

[448] LOCAL AND GENERAL.. (1917, March 3). *Casino and Kyogle Courier and North Coast Advertiser* (NSW: 1904-1932), p. 2. Retrieved May 1, 2023, from http://nla.gov.au/nla.news-article234036737
[449] RETURNED TO DUTY. (1916, April 19). *Australian Town and Country Journal* (Sydney, NSW: 1870-1919), p. 50. Retrieved May 1, 2023, from http://nla.gov.au/nla.news-article263594360
[450] 47th Battalion Unit Diary April 1917 - https://www.awm.gov.au/collection/C1345053?image=7

gallantry without artillery support, there was no advance visible on the other side of Bullecourt village. Isolated, a call for reinforcements was made and the 47th Battalion became committed to the fighting.

A strong German counter-attack was successful in ousting the Australians from the captured trenches, with the 47th Battalion forced to retire to its starting positions.[451] Many men lay wounded on the German wire or in no man's land. With the stretcher bearers exhausted from their work during the fighting, 40 men from the battalion volunteered to remain behind and assist as the snow began to fall, thus saving many wounded from exposure.[452] By 13 April when William rejoined the battalion, it had reached Albert and accounted for its losses: 23 killed, 72 wounded and 68 missing.[453]

Based in Henencourt, the battalion attended to the many cases of trench foot and the other illnesses that affected the men. On 25 April, the battalion along with other units in the division commemorated ANZAC Day with sporting activities, the battalion coming in second place on aggregate points.[454] 30 April saw the men offered the opportunity to vote in the Commonwealth election, but the unit diary notes that there was little enthusiasm to vote with only about a third participating.[455]

With the arrival of new reinforcements, the opportunity was taken to get as many men as possible away on leave to England.[456] It would appear that William was the beneficiary of this indulgence as sometime in May–June 1917, William married Dorothy Alice Wren in Wandsworth, London.

---

[451] 47th Battalion Unit Diary April 1917 - https://www.awm.gov.au/collection/C1345053?image=9
[452] 47th Battalion Unit Diary April 1917 - https://www.awm.gov.au/collection/C1345053?image =9
[453] 47th Battalion Unit Diary April 1917 - https://www.awm.gov.au/collection/C1345053?image=10
[454] 47th Battalion Unit Diary April 1917 - https://www.awm.gov.au/collection/C1345053?image=12
[455] 47th Battalion Unit Diary April 1917 - https://www.awm.gov.au/collection/C1345053?image=14
[456] 47th Battalion Unit Diary May 1917 - https://www.awm.gov.au/collection/C1345054?image=5

Ruffett, Elsie	Whittaker	Leighton B.	3 b	635
Ruffle, Elvina E.	Devall	Colchester	4 a	677
Ruffles, Frederick A.	Kingsland	W.Ham	4 a	1272
Ruffley, William	Wren	Wandsworth	1 d	283
Rufford, John	Hudson	Birmingham	6 d	945

Wren, Agnes	Martland	Salford	8 d	102
— Alice R.	Massetti	Guisbro	9 d	820
— Anna C.	Vaghorn	E.Grinstead	2 b	308
— Arthur	Gibbin	Tynemouth	10 b	367
— Bertha M.	Snow	Brighton	2 b	443
— Charles	Holman	Godstone	2 a	465
— Dorothy A.	Johnson	Bristol	6 a	30
— Elisabeth M.	Ruffley	Wandsworth	1 d	945
— Emma E.	Climpson	Romford	4 a	858
— Esther M.	Kearn	E.Preston	2 b	725
	Pitts	St.Olave	1 d	

Extracts from the official register recording William Ruffley and Dorothy Wren's marriage. Source - Registration Vol 1d page 945, https://www.freebmd.org.uk accessed 13 June 2018.

On 19 May and again on 6 June 1917, William made new wills where he bequeathed his estate to Dorothy Alice Ruffley of 166A Mitcham Road, Tooting, London. At the time, the battalion had moved to Flanders and eventually made its way to Messines in Belgium, where it managed for the first time in a year a complete bath and change of clothes for the entire battalion.[457]

At the end of May 1917, the battalion's officers received instruction on the forthcoming attack, with a detailed training program for the following week. Unlike previous attacks, detailed instructions were given to not just officers, but NCOs and the ranks as to specific objectives and their roles. A model of the ground to be attacked was created for all men to observe and familiarise themselves with, by which all ranks 'were made thoroughly conversant with all details, approach routes, plans in connection with the attack and when zero hour was at last given, the Battalion was quite [a] ready player for it

---

[457] 47th Battalion Unit Diary May 1917 - https://www.awm.gov.au/collection/C1345054?image=12

which was shown by the results achieved'.[458] In describing the preparations for the forthcoming Battle of Messines, the battalion diary continued[459]:

> Never before in the history of the Bn. was so much preliminary work bestowed on a Bn. and never was it more fitted for aventure [sic] such as this.

The attack was, in comparison to other battles fought on the Western Front, a complete success, capturing Messines Ridge and beating back the expected German counter-attacks. The battalion was relieved by the 46th Battalion on 12 June, which enabled it to take stock of its losses. While regarded as a complete success, the losses suffered were still significant: the battalion's casualties alone were 15 officers and 426 other ranks killed, wounded or missing – almost half the battalion's strength.[460]

The battalion was withdrawn to Berquin, and on 28 June 1917, William was again evacuated, this time to the 53rd CCS, suffering from venereal sores. He was transferred to an ambulance train arriving at the 7th Convalescent Depot at Boulogne before being transferred to the 39th General Hospital at Le Harve on 2 July 1917. William was not discharged until 22 August 1917, when he finally rejoined his unit on 1 September 1917.

The battalion by this stage had become fully committed to the Third Battle of Ypres, or Passchendaele. In September, the battalion was based in the rear area of Fruges, undertaking training for the next stage of the battle. In a forewarning of what they would experience, the troops were issued with canvas breach covers for their rifles to ensure they would be workable in muddy conditions.[461]

---

[458] 47th Battalion Unit Diary May 1917 - https://www.awm.gov.au/collection/C1345055?image=2
[459] 47th Battalion Unit Diary May 1917 - https://www.awm.gov.au/collection/C1345055?image=3
[460] 47th Battalion Unit Diary May 1917 - https://www.awm.gov.au/collection/C1345055?image=6
[461] 47th Battalion Unit Diary September 1917 - https://www.awm.gov.au/collection/C1345058?image=3

On 25 September 1917, those men of the battalion committed to support the next attack, referred to as 'A roll', moved into the ramparts of what was left of the town of Ypres. They provided working parties to move food and ammunition forward to the 4th and 13th Brigades in their successful attack on Menin Road.[462]

After a brief period of rest and training, including on the new lethal gas being deployed by the Germans, at 5 p.m. on 10 October, the battalion moved out of Ypres and took up position on 'ANZAC Ridge'. The 4th and 5th Divisions were brought up to replace the worn-out 1st and 2nd Divisions, following the failure of the first attempt to seize the Passchendaele heights on 9 October 1917. The weather conditions were terrible, and the going was very slow with men and wagons constantly bogged down, and the country in a very bad state owing to the rain soaked land being churned up by shell-fire.[463] The conditions also prevented the Allied artillery from being brought forward to support the next stages of the attack.

On 11 October the battalion received orders for the attack on Passchendaele Ridge with the weather still very bad and the going heavy.[464] Along with the 48th Battalion from the 12th Brigade of the 4th Division, the 47th Battalion would form the right wing of the attack, with the 3rd Division's attacking brigades, the 9th and 10th on the left. The line between the 3rd and 4th Divisions was the Ypres–Roulers railway line.

At midnight on 12 October, the battalion began to move forward via Zonnebeke to the 'jumping-off' tape. Despite the land being waterlogged and shell holes full of water, the troops managed to reach their positions. At 5:45 a.m., the Germans heavily shelled the battalion's positions killing most of the signallers, runners and scouts.[465]

---

[462] 47th Battalion Unit Diary September 1917 - https://www.awm.gov.au/collection/C1345058?image=8
[463] 47th Battalion Unit Diary October 1917 - https://www.awm.gov.au/collection/C1345059?image=4
[464] 47th Battalion Unit Diary October 1917 - https://www.awm.gov.au/collection/C1345059?image=4
[465] 47th Battalion Unit Diary October 1917 - https://www.awm.gov.au/collection/C1345059?image=5

Despite the setback, the men of the battalion moved forward and captured their objective, beating back German counter-attacks.[466] Despite the failure of the 9th Brigade to seize its objective on the left flank, the battalion managed to consolidate its position but suffered the loss of its commander, Lt Col Alexander P Imlay. The battalion unit diary recorded[467]:

> The operation was a splendid achievement under most adverse conditions and men held on gamely until garrison depleted in numbers and flank in danger of being enveloped. Had 9th Bde been able to move up and give required support all would have been well.

Forced to retire along the Ypres–Roulers railway line, the battalion fought a rear-guard action until it formed a defensive line of shell holes in front of the jumping-off line.[468] In the immediate aftermath of the failed attack, stretcher bearers struggled through the bog to retrieve wounded, even finding unwounded men stuck fast in mud. The battalion suffered 305 casualties in the attack.[469]

On 13 October, the battalion was still holding a defensive line comprised of shell holes in cold, rainy conditions when it was reported that William Ruffley was killed in action. There is no information of the circumstances of William's death or of any subsequent investigation by the Red Cross. The only record is that he is reported to have been buried 1000 yards southwest of Passchendaele and 1000 yards northeast Zonnebeke.

---

[466] 47th Battalion Unit Diary October 1917 - https://www.awm.gov.au/collection/C1345059?image=6
[467] 47th Battalion Unit Diary October 1917 - https://www.awm.gov.au/collection/C1345059?image=7
[468] 47th Battalion Unit Diary October 1917 - https://www.awm.gov.au/collection/C1345059?image=6 ; Bean, page 926
[469] Bean, *Official History*, Vol. 4, p. 928.

A report of William's death appeared in the Rockhampton *Morning Bulletin* on 3 December 1917.[470] No report, however, was given to his sister, Dora, who he had nominated as his next of kin. By letter dated 15 February 1918 to the OIC, Mrs Dora Dundon then living at Buffalo Road, Ryde, advised that she kept hearing rumours of her brother's death, but she had not received any official information, despite having twice received earlier notifications of his admission to hospital. She wrote[471]:

> I am very anxious about him and shall consider it a great favour if you will let me know if he is among the casualties also if he was married, as it is strange we got no information and he has not written for sometime ..

The OIC's response followed within a week, bearing the feared news that William had been killed in action on 13 October 1917. It also advised that he had married while in England and the official notification of his death had been forwarded to his wife.[472] The OIC was unaware of Dora's relationship with William as it had merely noted that she was a 'friend' and not a relation. A statutory notice to creditors was published in July 1918 giving notice of the intention to disburse the assets of William's estate.[473]

Despite the location of William's grave being recorded, it was not identified after the war and William has no known grave. William is commemorated on the Menin Gate Memorial at Ypres.

---

[470] AUSTRALIAN CASUALTIES. (1917, December 3). *Morning Bulletin* (Rockhampton, Qld.: 1878-1954), p. 7. Retrieved May 1, 2023, from http://nla.gov.au/nla.news-article53826262

[471] War service records accessible at https://recordsearch.naa.gov.au/SearchNRetrieve/Interface/ViewImage.aspx?B=8071409

[472] In October 1922, a letter from OIC to 1st Military District requested details of the present address of William's widow, Dorothy Ruffley, in order that the Memorial Plaque could be issued to her. The response noted on the same letter records that the war gratuity was being paid to Dorothy Alice Doll of 34 Alexander Street, South Yarra, Victoria.

[473] Advertising (1918, July 13). *Daily Standard* (Brisbane, Qld.: 1912-1936), p. 8 (Second Edition.). Retrieved May 1, 2023, from http://nla.gov.au/nla.news-article179412185

Photograph of the panel inscribed with the name of William Ruffley at the Ypres (Menin Gate) Memorial, Ypres, Belgium (author, 2018).

Joseph Ignatius Connell

Private, No. 6619

8th Field Ambulance, 8th Brigade, 5th Australian Division

Killed in action 26 October 1917, Passchendaele, Belgium

Buried Lijssenthoek Military Cemetery, Ieper (Ypres), Belgium

Sweet Jesus have mercy on his soul

Joseph Ignatius Connell was one of possibly 10 sons of Thomas Christopher Connell and Johanna Connell (nee Ryan).[474] Born in about 1895 in North Sydney,[475] Joseph attended school at St Benedict's Christian Brothers, Sydney. His mother, Johanna Connell, had been abandoned by her husband in about 1913 and after 28 years of marriage petitioned the court for a divorce on the basis of cruelty in November 1914.[476] During the hearing, there was a scuffle outside the court resulting in a number of persons being charged at the Central Police Court and pleading guilty to the offence of riotous behaviour. Among those found guilty was Joseph Connell.[477]

Joseph enlisted in the AIF in April 1915 at the age of 21 years and seven months when he was working as a carpenter and joiner at York Street Workhouse in Sydney.[478] At the time, he was living at 29 Dening Street, Drummoyne, with his mother and his brother Paul.[479] Between April and August 1915, Joseph was at the AIF Infantry Depot at Liverpool undertaking his initial training. On completion, he was assigned to the 8th Field Ambulance. It is not apparent why Joseph was assigned to the Field Ambulance, as his enlistment papers do not disclose any medical condition that might preclude him from serving

---

[474] The siblings may have been Thomas W (9101/1886), John G (9505/1887), Charles (7485/1889), William L (28999/1891), Francis P (33511/1893), Stancilous P (25412/1898), Vincent A (31065/1900), Paul (2710/1903) and Peter (32921/1905).
[475] NSW BDM Registration No. 28450/1895.
[476] DIVORCE COURT. (1914, November 28). *The Sydney Morning Herald* (NSW: 1842-1954), p. 12. Retrieved May 2, 2023, from http://nla.gov.au/nla.news-article15572300. The judge ultimately dismissed the petition – see DIVORCE COURT. (1914, December 2). *The Sydney Morning Herald* (NSW: 1842-1954), p. 8. Retrieved May 2, 2023, from http://nla.gov.au/nla.news-article15550810
[477] After 28 Years (1914, November 28). *National Advocate* (Bathurst, NSW: 1889-1954), p. 3. Retrieved May 2, 2023, from http://nla.gov.au/nla.news-article157934806 .
[478] Statement of Private N V Coxon 14 January 1918, Australian Red Cross Society Wounded and Missing Bureau files 6619 Private Joseph Ignatius Connell https://www.awm.gov.au/people/rolls/R1482396/ (accessed 4 March 2015).
[479] War service records accessible at http://recordsearch.naa.gov.au/SearchNRetrieve/Interface/ViewImage.aspx?B=3277227. Sometime after Joseph's enlistment, Johanna and Paul would move to 46 College Street, Drummoyne, and the change of address is noted on the Attestation Paper.

in the infantry.[480] It is possible that owing to his trade, he was considered suitable to assist in building aid posts and hospitals.

On 10 November 1915, Joseph embarked in Melbourne on HMAT A11 *Ascanius* bound for Egypt. On arrival in Egypt, the 8th Field Ambulance was part of the 'doubling' of the AIF where new units were formed based on the experienced units that had fought at Gallipoli, and the new reinforcements arriving from Australia. The 8th Field Ambulance was attached to the 8th Brigade in the new formed 5th Australian Division.

Tents of the 8th Australian Field Ambulance on Duntroon Plateau, near Suez Canal. AWM ID No. C04414.

While stationed in Egypt, the Field Ambulance participated in many of the training routines of the other units, including forced

---

[480] For example, it was common for soldiers with less than perfect eyesight to serve in the Army Medical Corps.

marches. The training regime, the heat and the harsh environment made life extremely difficult for the troops. The 8th Field Ambulance was also responsible for assessing the hygiene of the various billets and encampments, which were generally described in the unit diary as extremely unsanitary. On 25 April 1916, the unit diary had an entry as follows: 'Anzac Day Holiday. Sport & events held'.[481] The anniversary of Australia's landing at Gallipoli just the previous year already resonated with the AIF. For the unit, a dinner and sports meeting were held, which was described by a member and author of a brief history of the unit, Langford W Colley-Priest, as the best day they had had since leaving Australia.[482] Colley-Priest would eventually also provide a statement to the Red Cross in September 1919 as part of the Red Cross' investigations into the circumstances of Joseph Connell's death.[483]

Field Ambulance companies, like the 8th Field Ambulance, were responsible for 'second line' casualty evacuation from 'first line' Regimental Aid Posts (RAP) in each battalion. The Field Ambulance would have personnel deployed forward to retrieve casualties from the field and RAP, and take them to the Field Ambulance, generally described as a Casualty Clearing Station (CCS). Stretcher bearers like Joseph would therefore be exposed to the same risks as the front-line troops. These men would be trained in basic first aid so that casualties could be evacuated. Once at the CCS, additional medical officers and supporting personnel were available to carry out surgery. Many of the cemeteries scattered through northern France and Belgium originally began alongside a CCS, and it was into one of these cemeteries that Joseph would be buried after he died of his wounds.

On 16 June 1916, along with eight officers and 205 other ranks, Joseph embarked at Alexandria bound for Marseilles aboard the

---

[481] 8th Field Ambulance Unit Diary April 1916 - https://www.awm.gov.au/collection/C1354635?image=9

[482] Colley-Priest, LW (Langford Wellman) 1919, *The 8th Australian Field Ambulance on active service: a brief account of its history and services from 4th August 1915 to the 5thMarch 1919*, Sydney, page 12.

[483] Australian Red Cross Wounded and Missing Files - https://www.awm.gov.au/collection/R1482396

Transylvania. He disembarked on 23 June 1916 and made his way with the rest of the 8th Brigade north to training camps behind the trenches of the Western Front in the Somme region.

The 5th Australian Division arrived in the Somme region of northern France. In late June and early July, the 8th Field Ambulance, along with the rest of the 5th Australian Division, made preparations for the attack at Fromelles. The 8th Field Ambulance would be one of three Field Ambulance companies in the 5th Division that would deal with the tragedy that was to be the Battle of Fromelles. This battle would account for five of the men commemorated on the Drummoyne War Memorial.

The Battle of Fromelles commenced with a bombardment at 11:00 a.m. on 19 July 1916. The unit diary reported that initial casualties were small in number[484] but this was to change markedly once the infantry assault commenced at about 6:00 p.m. The battle itself overwhelmed all of the medical assets of the 5th Division, and many soldiers would be killed in the process of trying to retrieve casualties from the battlefield. The unit diary recorded the ever-increasing stream of casualties coming in from the front. From noon 19 July until noon 20 July 1916, the 8th Field Ambulance alone admitted 224 casualties with 214 evacuated.[485] During the night of 20–21 July, the diary recorded that all the time, more cases were being brought in from no man's land, with demands for all available cars, blankets and stretchers to be brought up to assist with the evacuation of wounded.[486] From noon 20 July to noon 21 July, the unit would handle a further 317 cases, of which 307 would be eventually evacuated. Another 45 cases would be admitted in the next 24 hours, making a total of 587 cases admitted. The diary described how men from every available unit, including drivers, batmen and officers' staff, were in the field assisting

---

[484] 8th Field Ambulance Unit Diary July 1916 - https://www.awm.gov.au/collection/C1352922?image=8
[485] 8th Field Ambulance Unit Diary July 1916 - https://www.awm.gov.au/collection/C1352922?image=10
[486] 8th Field Ambulance Unit Diary July 1916 - https://www.awm.gov.au/collection/C1352922?image=11

to evacuate wounded and 'struggled on although completely exhausted'.[487]

Colley-Priest described the scene when he first made his way to the front-line trenches from the RAP to retrieve the wounded[488]:

> On reaching the old front line trenches I looked upon a terrible sight. Good God it was terrible! Dead Australians lying about; in fact they were piled up four and five deep. Had to pick our way over them to reach the wounded.

After the battle, Colley-Priest recalled watching the 59th Battalion hold a roll call in the paddock next to the aid post, and described as heart-rending the few men answering to their names.

Joseph Connell was detached to 15th Field Ambulance from 9 September 1916 until 2 November 1916, which was also part of the 5th Division. The period in which he was transferred to the 15th Field Ambulance appeared to coincide in part with when all carpenters in the unit were ordered to go to Bac St. Maur to help the 15th build a hospital.[489]

In October 1916, the 5th Division joined the 1st, 2nd and 4th Divisions on the Somme around Flers. This included taking up positions around Dernancourt. The weather at the time was universally described as terrible – cold and with continuous rain turning the churned-up ground into mud. Even marching up to the front line was a challenge; there was practically no track and men were sinking knee-deep into the mud.[490] The unit diary noted how the stretcher bearers were required to carry wounded over long distances, and with trenches in poor condition, sometimes thigh-deep in mud.[491] To escape the mud-filled trenches, the bearers carried wounded in the open,

---

[487] 8th Field Ambulance Unit Diary July 1916 - https://www.awm.gov.au/collection/C1352922?image=13
[488] Colley-Priest, *The 8th Australian Field Ambulance*, p. 20.
[489] Colley-Priest, *The 8th Australian Field Ambulance*, p. 23.
[490] Colley-Priest, *The 8th Australian Field Ambulance*, p. 25.
[491] 8th Field Ambulance Unit Diary October 1916 - https://www.awm.gov.au/collection/C1352925?image=6

thus exposing themselves to enemy fire, and all the time finding it almost impossible to keep their feet in the mud.[492]

Group photograph of the Transport Section of the 8th Field Ambulance, AIF. In the back row, first from the left is Pte L. Colley-Priest. He would give a statement to the Red Cross regarding the death and burial of Joseph Connell in September 1919, and also write a short account of the history of the 8th Field Ambulance. AWM ID No. 1115657.

The diary noted that '[a]ll bearers becoming exhausted with the exceedingly difficult conditions under which wounded are evacuated'. It also described the construction of mud sledges to assist in evacuating the wounded, reducing the time to evacuate wounded from the front line from 7 hours to 1 ½ hours.[493] The 8th Field Ambulance continued to experience difficult conditions and extreme cold until relieved shortly before Christmas and pulled back to Vignacourt. It was 'glorious to be among the green fields again, and away from the ghastly sights of the battlefield'.[494]

---

[492] 8th Field Ambulance Unit Diary October 1916 - https://www.awm.gov.au/collection/C1352925?image=6
[493] 8th Field Ambulance Unit Diary October 1916 - https://www.awm.gov.au/collection/C1352925?image=7
[494] Colley-Priest, *The 8th Australian Field Ambulance*, p. 31.

In March 1917, the Germans retreated to preprepared defences called the Hindenburg Line. Units of the 5th Division pursued the Germans, capturing Bapaume. The 8th Field Ambulance followed up the advance, entering the ruins that was the Bapaume. After providing support to the infantry units in this sector, the 8th Field Ambulance was relieved, and rested at a place called Bellevue Farm for the next four weeks. During that time, they indulged in plenty of sport including rugby league, rugby union and Australian Rules matches with other units. On 25 April, a celebration was held to mark the second anniversary of ANZAC Day.[495]

In May the 5th Division relieved the 1st Division in the Second Battle of Bullecourt. The 8th Field Ambulance went into the line[496]:

> In front of us, at Bullecourt, was raging one of the fiercest battles of the war, and all Ambulances concerned were working hard, getting the wounded away. We know now from what we saw and what we read of the terrible attacks at Bullecourt, that the Australian casualties were very heavy.
>
> ...
>
> Every evening, just as the sun was setting, and also every morning at dawn, the Germans sent a heavy barrage over our front line and supports, for fear of our infantry attacking. Only those who have experienced being in one of these barrages, can realise what it was like. It was nerve racking to sit through one of these bombardments, and on several occasions the bearers carried through this hell fire.

The unit was relieved at the end of May, by which time it had suffered some of its worst casualties of the war, but many of its individuals received awards for their conspicuous bravery in rescuing and evacuating wounded Australians from the front line.

---

[495] Colley-Priest, *The 8th Australian Field Ambulance*, p. 36.
[496] Colley-Priest, *The 8th Australian Field Ambulance*, p. 37.

After a period of further training, the 8th Field Ambulance moved into the St Omer area in July 1917, from where a number of personnel were given leave in England. Included among them was Joseph Connell, who left for England 18 September, rejoining the unit on 30 September 1917.

Unidentified members of the 8th Australian Field Ambulance parading for tea at the cookhouse, circa September 1917. AWM ID No. C00502.

In September, along with the remainder of the 5th Division, the 8th Field Ambulance was moved to the Ypres sector, in Belgium. The unit arrived at Remy Siding near Poperinghe and took over a large Divisional Rest Station. It was to this station that Joseph Connell would be evacuated after being severely wounded, and where he would die of those wounds.

Conveyed to the front lines in motor lorries, the 8th Field Ambulance stretcher bearers passed through the ruins of Ypres along the way. For the next five weeks, the bearers were in the line, going to and from the front to collect the wounded and bring them back to the clearing station. Sometimes, the bearers were too exhausted to return to the rest station, but instead found shelter in the ramparts of Ypres, exposed to hellish shell-fire. At one time, it appeared to Colley-Priest that the whole of the Menin Road was in flames, through which the ambulance drivers continuously drove their cars.[497] It was during these battles that the 8th Field Ambulance would suffer its most severe casualties.

Moving forward as the attacking Australian infantry made ground, the unit covered areas around Westhoek, Bellevarde Crater, Ideal House, Clapham Junction, Zonnebeke, Helles, Glencorse Wood, Molenhoek, Polygon Wood and The Mound. However, of all these places, there was one place that for Colley-Priest stands out: Polygon Wood. Four squads of bearers were hemmed into a pillbox for 14 hours under a severe bombardment, including many direct hits on the concrete dug-out. It was impossible to reach the wounded, and the relieving ambulance unit could not reach the dug-out. While trapped there, the Germans counter- attacked, including the use of gas. When finally relieved, the trapped bearers were suffering from the terrible strain and sick from the gas.[498]

It was in the hell that was the Third Ypres that Joseph Connell was to meet his end. On 26 October 1917, Joseph was serving in the front line. According to statements obtained by Red Cross officials in 1918–1919[499] from men who served in the 8th Field Ambulance and were present around this time, Joseph Connell was with L/Cpl William McCallum near a pillbox, and just as Joseph was stooping down to pick up a stretcher, a shell burst close to them. Shell fragments were said to have hit Joseph in the side, and he fell over mortally wounded. He was evacuated by other stretcher bearers in the unit, Privates Corrigan, Crome, Foote and one other, initially to a dressing station in Hooge Trench, and then taken to the 17th CCS at Poperinghe.

---

[497] Colley-Priest, *The 8th Australian Field Ambulance*, p. 46.
[498] Colley-Priest, *The 8th Australian Field Ambulance*, p. 47.
[499] Australian Red Cross Wounded and Missing Files - https://www.awm.gov.au/people/rolls/R1482396/

Lance Corporal Wilfred McCallum (6648) provided a statement on 8 March 1918 to the Red Cross to the following effect[500]:

> I spoke to him before they started carrying him out and he said 'I know I'm done'. I heard he was unconscious when he reached the C.C.S. He was buried in the Lijssentheok Cemetery.

Private Ernest G Musman (6645)[501] in the same report added:

> I was present when Connell died unconscious at the 17th C.C.S. I have written twice to his people at 46 College St. Drummoyne.

Joseph's name was published in casualty lists in December 1917 as having died of wounds.[502] Private Nicholas V Coxon (6620) stated in January 1918 that Joseph was buried at the cemetery just outside the CCS and 'he had a very big funeral. I know that our Fld Amb subscribed and put a cross up to hi[m].' Pte Knowles states that Connell was buried by a 'Canadian R.C. Padre'.[503]

Pursuant to a will made on 3 October 1916, Joseph Connell had left the whole of his estate to his mother, Johanna Connell. By letter dated 19 November 1917, J A Murphy of the St Mark's Branch of the Hibernian Australian Catholic Benefit Society requested the OIC for a copy of the death certificate for Joseph Connell 'so that the usual lodge payments may be paid to his mother'.[504] From 5 January 1918, Johanna Connell also began to receive a war pension.

In March 1918, Paul Connell wrote to the OIC inquiring if Joseph's kit or belongings had been returned to Australia, and if in Sydney or Melbourne, where he could go to collect them. The OIC

---

[500] Australian Red Cross Wounded and Missing Files - https://www.awm.gov.au/people/rolls/R1482396/
[501] The Red Cross report incorrectly records his regimental number as 6654.
[502] Australian Casualties. (1917, December 12). *Australian Town and Country Journal* (Sydney, NSW: 1870-1919), p. 10. Retrieved May 2, 2023, from http://nla.gov.au/nla.news-article263767497
[503] Australian Red Cross Wounded and Missing Files accessible at https://www.awm.gov.au/people/rolls/R1482396/
[504] War service records accessible at http://recordsearch.naa.gov.au/SearchNRetrieve/Interface/ViewImage.aspx?B=3277227

replied that no parcels had been returned to date but would be promptly forwarded if any come to hand. The letter also stated[505]:

> His kit being a portion of his military equipment would not be returned to you. The Authorities at the front, however, select from a deceased soldier's kit everything of sentimental value forwarding it to this Office for transmission to the next-of-kin unless testamentary instruction be received directing otherwise.

Family notices were published on the anniversary of Joseph's death in 1918 and 1919[506]:

> CONNELL. - In loving memory of Stretcher-bearer Joseph Ignatius Connell, 8th Field Ambulance, who died of wounds received at Polygon Wood, after two years' active service. Buried at Lijssenthoek Military Cemetery, Belgium. Sweet Jesus, have mercy on his soul. R.I.P.

> CONNELL. — In loving memory of Joseph Ignatius Connell, 8th Field Ambulance, aged 22, died of wounds. Polygon Wood, October 26, 1917. Rest in peace. Inserted by his mother, brothers, and sister, College-street, Drummoyne.

Notwithstanding that Joseph Connell had nominated his mother Johanna Connell as his next of kin, and left her all his estate under his will, this did not prevent Johanna from experiencing difficulty in receiving Joseph's war medals. In a letter dated 10 December 1920, the OIC wrote to Johanna Connell as follows[507]:

---

[505] War service records accessible at http://recordsearch.naa.gov.au/SearchNRetrieve/Interface/ViewImage.aspx?B=3277227

[506] Family Notices (1918, October 26). *The Sydney Morning Herald* (NSW: 1842-1954), p. 11. Retrieved May 2, 2023, from http://nla.gov.au/nla.news-article15808343 and Family Notices (1919, October 25). *The Sydney Morning Herald* (NSW: 1842-1954), p. 12. Retrieved May 2, 2023, from http://nla.gov.au/nla.news-article15849586

[507] War service records accessible at http://recordsearch.naa.gov.au/SearchNRetrieve/Interface/ViewImage.aspx?B=3277227

It is noted that you are registered on the records of the late No. 6619 Private J.I. Connell, 8th Field Ambulance as next of kin, but in order that the instructions under the 'Deceased Soldiers Estates Act 1918' may be properly complied with when disposing of War Medals, &c., I shall be glad to learn whether there are any nearer blood relations than yourself to the above named, for instance his father, still alive, if so I would be much obliged for his name and address at your earliest convenience.

The provisions of a Will have no bearing upon the distribution of medals unless they are specifically mentioned therein, such mementos being handed over in the following order of relationship, unless good and sufficient reasons for varying the procedure are stated:-

> Widow, eldest surviving son, eldest surviving daughter, father, mother, eldest surviving brother …

Other documents on Joseph Connell's war service file indicated that no reply was received to this letter so that in 1921, the OIC requested the 2nd Military District to make inquiries to try to locate Joseph's father. In November 1922, the Army advised the OIC that it had no details on file other than those of Johanna Connell at 46 College Street.

On 20 September 1923, the OIC again wrote to Johanna Connell appealing to her to respond to previous correspondence requesting advice as to the whereabouts of her husband in order that the war medals issuable to Joseph Connell could be dealt with. The letter reiterated that the Deceased Soldiers Estates Act requires that the claims of the father must be regarded before those of the mother 'unless there is good and sufficient reasons for varying the procedure'. The letter concludes with an assurance that any case which she makes to receive the medals 'will receive full and sympathetic consideration,' but[508]:

> If, however, the required information is not [forthcoming] the only course open to me is to place the mementos amongst the "Untraceables", to be in all probability, eventually destroyed.

Johanna Connell responded four days later. In her letter she wrote[509]:

> I have to state that the father of No. 6619 Pte J I Connell 8th Field Amb, my son, has been separated from his family since 1913 and is in a sense dead to us, and as I am next of kin, I fail to see why the claims of the father in the above circumstances are recognised at all.
>
> Trusting you will fully understand my position and help me to get the mementos, which I so much treasure without further delay.

The OIC made one last attempt to obtain contact details of Joseph's father from the 2nd Military District but to no avail. Finally on 17 October 1923, the OIC responded to Johanna's letter as follows[510]:

> I have to advise that I have endeavoured to get into touch with the father of the late No. 6619 Private J.I. CONNELL, 8th Field Ambulance, but without success, and, in the circumstances, am prepared to recommend that the War Medals, etc., issuable on account of the late soldier's service be handed over to you.

---

[508] War service records accessible at http://recordsearch.naa.gov.au/SearchNRetrieve/Interface/ViewImage.aspx?B=3277227
[509] War service records accessible at http://recordsearch.naa.gov.au/SearchNRetrieve/Interface/ViewImage.aspx?B=3277227
[510] War service records accessible at http://recordsearch.naa.gov.au/SearchNRetrieve/Interface/ViewImage.aspx?B=3277227

This, however, can only be done on the distinct understanding that they will be preserved with due care as memorials of deceased and returned to this Department at any time upon receipt of its demand in writing.

If you are agreeable to accept them under these conditions, I shall be glad if you will complete the attached Declaration before a Justice of the Peace and return same to me at your earliest convenience.

On 29 October 1923, Johanna Connell made a statutory declaration in the terms required by the OIC. The declaration was made before J A Murphy JP, who had also signed the letter on behalf of the St Mark's Branch of the Hibernian Australian Catholic Benefit Society in 1918. Stamped on the declaration is a note that the medals were to be given to the mother '(on bond)', with a receipt signed by Johanna on 3 December 1923. Shortly thereafter, Johanna also received the memorial plaque and memorial scroll in connection with her son's service.

Joseph is buried in Lijssenthoek Military Cemetery, 12 kms west of Ieper (Ypres), Belgium. The cemetery contains 9,901 Commonwealth burials of the First World War and is the second largest Commonwealth cemetery in Belgium. His brother Paul Connell inscribed the following on Joseph's headstone:

SWEET JESUS HAVE MERCY ON HIS SOUL

According to the Honour Roll Circular completed by Johanna Connell,[511] Joseph also had three first cousins who were killed in

---

[511] Accessible at https://www.awm.gov.au/collection/R1482396

action: Bandsman Thomas Connell, Driver Raymond Dempsey and Private F Donald Dempsey.

Photograph of the headstone of the grave of Joseph Connell, Lijssenthoek Military Cemetery (author, 2018).

Close up of the inscription on the grave of Joseph Connell, Lijssenthoek Military Cemetery (author, 2018).

Hugh McQuat

Private, No. 4962

1st Battalion, 1st Infantry Brigade, 1st Australian Division

Died of wounds 16 March 1918, Hill 60, Ypres, Belgium

Buried Outtersteene Communal Cemetery Extension,

Bailleul, France

So he giveth his beloved sleep

Hugh McQuat was born at Manor Park, Essex, England,[512] in about 1892 or 1983 to John and Sarah McQuat. Little is known of Hugh's early life and what can be gleaned from the few records is that at some time in his life he trained as a grocer before joining the Orient Line as a steward. Hugh's connection with Australia let alone Drummoyne is unclear, other than that on the Honour Roll Circular completed by his father after the war, John McQuat indicated that the Australian town Hugh was closely associated with was Sydney.[513]

Unlike most of the men commemorated on the Drummoyne War Memorial, Hugh did not enlist at an Australian recruitment office but completed his enlistment at Rollestone, Salisbury, in England in September 1916 after attesting while on board HMAT A67 *Orsova*.[514] The *Orsova* was a ship of the Orient Line built in 1909,[515] which was commandeered as a troopship in 1915.[516] It appears that Hugh was serving as a steward on SS *Orsova* before the war and continued after it was commandeered, before deciding to enlist in the AIF while on board in April 1916.[517] Hugh's date of enlistment is recorded as 14 April 1916, two days before the *Orsova* arrived at Suez with the 10th Reinforcements to the AIF.

At the time of his enlistment, Hugh gave his age as 23 years and four months and specified his father as his next of kin who was then living at 1 Sonning Villas, Exeter Road, Addiscombe, near Croydon in Surrey, England. Hugh was initially assigned to the 10th Reinforcements to the 20th Battalion and embarked to join the BEF from Alexandria on 28 May 1916, arriving in Devonport in early June.

---

[512] Hugh indicated on his attestation form that he was born in London, but the Honour Roll Circular completed by his father after the war gave his place of birth as Manor Park, Essex.
[513] Honour roll circular accessible at https://www.awm.gov.au/collection/R1648887
[514] War service records accessible at https://recordsearch.naa.gov.au/SearchNRetrieve/Interface/ViewImage.aspx?B=1959107
[515] http://www.theshipslist.com/ships/lines/orient.shtml . Other sources indicate that it was built in 1908 but registered in 1909 - https://collection.maas.museum/object/237876
[516] https://collection.maas.museum/object/237876
[517] Another steward, Henry Edward Slater (4963) also attested on board the *Orsova* on the same day as Hugh, and like Hugh was initially assigned to the 20th Battalion, 10th Reinforcements before being transferred to the 1st Battalion. Henry Slater returned to Australia in 1919 but has no known connection to Drummoyne.

Hugh, along with the other reinforcements, travelled to the Australian training base at Salisbury joining the 5th Training Battalion. By October 1916, he departed England and arrived at the Australian base at Etaples in France on 23 October 1916. Hugh, however, did not proceed to join the 20th Battalion but was transferred to join the 1st Battalion, which he did on 10 November 1916 along with another 43 reinforcements to the battalion.[518]

Immediately before Hugh's arrival with his new unit, the 1st Battalion had been involved in an action that had commenced on 5 November 1916 near Flers, which had been generally ineffectual before being relieved. The battalion then moved through various billets undertaking fatigues before arriving at Mametz in mid-December. During this period, Hugh attempted to shirk his fatigue duty responsibilities by remaining in the YMCA tent, which resulted in his being charged and found guilty of the offence of 'conduct prejudicial to good military discipline' for which he was awarded seven days' Field Punishment No.2, being heavy labouring duties.[519]

On New Year's Eve, the battalion relieved the 2nd Battalion in the front lines, leaving Bernafay Camp east of Albert on the Somme. This would signal the battalion taking turns in and out of the lines over the next few months. However, in late February 1917 it was discovered that the Germans had withdrawn to preprepared defences at what became known as the Hindenburg Line, and the Australian units were pushed forward to maintain contact with the enemy, encountering defended village outposts throughout March. In early April, the 1st Australian Division was brought up to capture the last of the German rear-guard positions. The 1st Battalion's role was limited to pushing forward some of its outposts in front of one village, Doignies, on 9 April to allow the 2nd Battalion to form up to carry out the main

---

[518] 1st Battalion Unit Diary November 1916 - https://www.awm.gov.au/collection/C1347223?image=7
[519] But not involving being restrained by handcuffs or other fetters - https://www.awm.gov.au/sites/default/files/encyclopedia/field_punishment/355_1330941_G253M_1914.pdf

assault. However, the battalion did play a key role in rushing the final village, Demicourt, later that day with the loss of 55 casualties.[520]

By early May 1917, the 1st Battalion along with the rest of the 1st Division was being thrown into the second attempt to seize the fortified village of Bullecourt, which formed part of the Hindenburg Line. Initially employed as carriers to support the attacking units of the 2nd Division, by 4 May the brigades of this division had been so badly mauled that the brigades of the 1st Division were called up. The 1st and 3rd Battalions were ordered to bomb their way to the left in the hope of joining up with the British 7th Division to close in on the village itself. In terrible fighting, which included the use of a *flammenwerfer* by the Germans against the 1st Battalion, the battalions succeeded in extending the length of captured German trenches. D Company, to which Hugh had been assigned, was moved on 5 May to replace the badly worn-out A Company that was holding the far left.[521] However, the British attack failed which left the Australian left flank badly exposed. The battalions of the 1st Brigade bravely held on under ferocious counter-attacks and shelling. Exhausted, the 1st Battalion along with the rest of the 1st Division was relieved on 7 May. The battalion's losses were five officers and 44 other ranks killed, 240 wounded and 29 missing.[522] The battalion diary recorded that[523]:

> The fighting was at close quarters and consequently grenades played a most important part, rifle grenades proving an absolute necessity, undoubtedly it was greatly owing to the range of these that the enemy were prevented from approaching our flank posts in sufficiently large numbers to rush them.

---

[520] Bean, *Official History*, Vol. 4, p. 249.
[521] 1st Battalion Unit Diary May 1917 - https://www.awm.gov.au/collection/C1347455?image=6
[522] 1st Battalion Unit Diary May 1917 - https://www.awm.gov.au/collection/C1347455?image=7
[523] 1st Battalion Unit Diary May 1917 - https://www.awm.gov.au/collection/C1347455?image=7

.... The enemy shelling during the period was exceptionally heavy destructive and constant and I cannot speak too highly of the spirit in which all ranks bore it nor of the cool and able manner in which they coped with the enemy attacks, using all weapons with judgment [sic]and skill.

The 1st Australian Division, after it emerged from Bullecourt, was sent for a rest that would ultimately extend for period of four months. Daily activities included, after training, sports and inter-unit competitions. Periods of leave were also granted. The 1st Battalion recuperated and trained for the rest of May and June, principally based around Lavieville. As the 1st Brigade was principally comprised of NSW battalions, the inter unit competitions primarily involved rugby union matches.

At the end of July, the 1st Battalion entrained for French Flanders. This was part of a broader transfer of I ANZAC Corps to act as reserve in Flanders for the forthcoming Ypres offensive. The battalion remained in the rear areas of Flanders during August and September 1917, enjoying the last period of its rest. For Hugh, this included a transfer to a summer rest camp for a week. Charles Bean noted that by the time that they emerged from their training, the divisions of I ANZAC were 'very efficient instruments indeed. The troops had never been so healthy or happy, or the battalion spirit so keen'.[524]

The battalion along with the rest of I ANZAC began to move to the Ypres sector in Belgium in mid-September 1917. The 1st Brigade relieved the 7th London Regiment on the night of 16 September on the edge of Glencourse Wood with the 1st Battalion unit diary recording its companies taking up positions near the Menin Tunnel.[525] The battalions of the 1st Brigade, however, would not lead the attack in what would be the Battle for Menin Road, which commenced on 20 September. Rather, they were to thinly hold the front lines and hand

---

[524] Bean, *Official History*, Vol. 4, p. 732.
[525] 1st Battalion Unit Diary September 1917 - https://www.awm.gov.au/collection/C1347460?image=3

over their positions to the attacking units of the 1st Division, the 2nd and 3rd Brigades, just prior to the attack commencing. While it had been intended that the 1st Brigade would be brought up shortly after the attack had gone through, the order was countermanded when it was realised that the Australian front appeared to be overcrowded. Accordingly, Hugh and his 1st Battalion comrades avoided any significant role in the battle.

Hugh also avoided involvement in the next stage of the Ypres offensive, which was an attack on Polygon Wood. Scheduled to commence on 26 September, the 1st and 2nd Australian Divisions were relieved by the 4th and 5th Australian Divisions who led the attack. This respite was not to last as the battalion was thrown into the third stage of the Ypres offensive, the attack on Broodseinde Ridge on 4 October 1917. Before their attack began, a German barrage fell on the troops of the 1st Division waiting in shell holes covered in capes against the rain. This was in fact cover for a German attack which was to commence at almost the same time, with the two attacking forces meeting each other in no man's land. The German attack was broken up, with fighting continuing from craters and pillboxes scattered across the front. The 1st Battalion quickly secured its objectives, as did almost all the Australian units involved. The inevitable German counterattack was successfully repulsed, and the battalions began the task of consolidating their gains.

While the 1st Battalion was in support lines on Westhoek Ridge carrying out fatigue duties, Hugh was slightly wounded on 8 October 1917, suffering a shell abrasion. Admitted to the 3rd Australian Field Ambulance, he was discharged back on same day to his unit. He would, however, get a longer rest when he was granted extended leave to England from 31 October to 20 November 1917. By the time Hugh had rejoined his battalion, it was in a rest camp near Verlingthun in the Pas de Calais area. By new year, it was back in Belgium and in the lines near Wytschaete experiencing freezing cold weather.[526]

---

[526] 1st Battalion Unit Diary January 1918 - https://www.awm.gov.au/collection/C1347464?image=3

On 8 February 1918, a census was undertaken of the original recruits of the 1st Battalion from 1914. There were only 69 survivors[527] from what would have originally been close to 1,000. On 28 February, the battalion moved into the front lines east of Ypres in Belgian Flanders, relieving the 52nd Battalion in what was known as the Shrewsbury Forest sector. A, B and C Companies took up posts along the front with Hugh's D Company in reserve at Hill 60.[528] It was while serving in reserve during a gas artillery bombardment by the Germans on 7 March 1918 that Hugh was badly gassed. Admitted to the 1st Australian Field Ambulance, Hugh was transferred and admitted to the 2nd CCS same day.

Statements given to the Red Cross[529] indicated that Hugh, along with a number of other men, were in a dug-out asleep when the Germans began shelling the position with gas shells. None of the men immediately showed any effects, but by the morning, Hugh had become sick.[530] He was evacuated by stretcher bearers also from D Company. Hugh did not recover and on 16 March 1918, died of poisoning from gas at the 2nd CCS.

Chaplain Gilbert Harding attached to the 2nd CCS reported to the Red Cross that Hugh had lingered but ultimately succumbed to the internal effects of the gas at 11:30 a.m. on 16 March 1918. The chaplain buried Hugh in the British Cemetery at Outtersteene near the town of Bailleul 'with all honour and reverence possible in the circumstances'.[531] Hugh's name was published in casualty lists published in April 1918 has having died of wounds.[532]

---

[527] 1st Battalion Unit Diary February 1918 - https://www.awm.gov.au/collection/C1347465?image=4
[528] 1st Battalion Unit Diary February 1918 - https://www.awm.gov.au/collection/C1347465?image=9
[529] Australian Red Cross Wounded and Missing Files - https://www.awm.gov.au/collection/R1491576
[530] Statement of CSM Leslie Mayes (864) made 28 May 1918 - https://www.awm.gov.au/collection/R1491576 . The Red Cross report incorrectly spelt his name as Mayer.
[531] Australian Red Cross Wounded and Missing Files - https://www.awm.gov.au/collection/R1491576
[532] 388th CASUALTY LIST. (1918, April 9). *The Sydney Morning Herald* (NSW: 1842-1954), p. 8. Retrieved May 3, 2023, from http://nla.gov.au/nla.news-article15788880

The only other clue of a possible connection to Australia is contained in correspondence on the Red Cross file. For reasons unclear, the Red Cross wrote three letters in May and June 1918 to a Mrs Schultz then residing at Hotel Stewart, Richmond, England, reporting on the results of its inquiries into Hugh's fate. In a separate letter from Vivienne M Davies to the Red Cross and dated 4 July 1918, Ms Davies expressed her thanks to the Red Cross in sending her information 'through Mrs Schultz (Aust. Visitor)' regarding Hugh McQuat.

Hugh is buried in Outtersteene Communal Cemetery Extension, Bailleul, France.

Photograph of Outtersteene Communal Cemetery Extension, Bailleul, France. The War Graves Project, CWGC. Reproduced with permission.

Photograph of the grave of Hugh McQuat, Outtersteene Communal Cemetery Extension, Bailleul, France. The War Graves Project, CWGC. Reproduced with permission.

Palestine 1916–1918

The British command had been long preoccupied by the threat of a Turkish attack on Egypt, particularly after the Allied evacuation from Gallipoli. Australian infantry and mounted units were therefore retained in Egypt to assist in the ongoing defence of the Suez Canal zone by occupying positions on the eastern side. By March 1916, the absence of any significant Turkish attempt to advance across the Sinai from Palestine during the winter months suggested that the threat may have passed. This enabled the gradual transfer of the Australian infantry divisions from Egypt to meet the demand for reinforcements for the Western Front. This transfer was more or less completed by June 1916 with the departure of the 5th Australian Division. Australian mounted units, however, remained behind and formed a substantial component the British mounted forces in the Sinai.

The commander of British forces in Egypt, General Sir Archibald Murray, determined to pursue a more aggressive approach, initially with raids to reconnoitre Turkish positions and strength in the Sinai. Murray ordered up the ANZAC Mounted Division, which comprised the brigades of the Australian Light Horse and New Zealand Mounted Brigade under the command of Major-General Harry Chauvel. These units assisted in the seizure of the coastal town of Romani from where they were used successfully to watch and harass Turkish forces. In August 1916, the ANZAC mounted units were instrumental in executing a major defeat of a Turkish attempt to recapture Romani. In five days of fighting, the Turks lost some 5,250 killed or wounded, with another 4,000 taken prisoner.[533]

The success at Romani opened up the possibility of an attack into Palestine. Again, General Chauvel was ordered to lead the advance of the mounted units, and in December 1916 captured the town of El Arish located on the eastern coastal side of the Sinai Peninsula, just short of Palestine. Having left the sandhills of the Sinai behind, the mounted troops were now able to undertake operations better suited to their training and their horses.

The town of Gaza, just across the Palestine border, was attacked in March 1917. The ANZAC Mounted Division skirted the town and appeared on its eastern flank cutting off the town and preventing Turkish reinforcements from reaching it, with the main attack to be launched by two British infantry divisions from the south and southwest. The British attack was slow, causing Chauvel to order two mounted divisions placed under his command to make a dismounted attack from the rear. The men knew they were racing against time as sunset drew near, the imperative being to secure water for the horses. Despite initial success and thoughts that Turkish resistance was collapsing, an order was given to withdraw. A renewed effort in April 1917 to take Gaza ended in failure and the recall of General Murray. Chauvel was placed in command of the whole Desert Mounted Corps, the first Australian to command a corps, and promoted to the rank of Lieutenant-General.[534]

---

[533] Bean, *ANZAC to Amiens*, p. 282.
[534] Bean, *ANZAC to Amiens*, p. 381. Murray's replacement would be General Allenby who arrived in June 1917.

Photograph of Sir Henry George (Harry) Chauvel. AWM ID No. J00503.

A change of approach was pursued, this time involving an inland attack on the Turkish garrison at Beersheba in October 1917. Again, the imperative was to capture the town by nightfall before mounted units would need to be withdrawn for watering. For the first time, the Light Horse were to act purely as cavalry and charge the Turkish defences with just bayonets. Starting some four miles out from the town, the troopers of the 4th and 12th Light Horse Brigades quickened to a gallop, outracing the Turkish shellfire and jumping the trench lines before descending on the bewildered defenders, many of whom promptly surrendered. The attack successfully turned the flank of the whole Turkish defensive line in southern Palestine, causing Gaza to fall in November 1917, and opened the way for the capture of Jerusalem in December 1917 as the Turkish armies withdrew northwards.

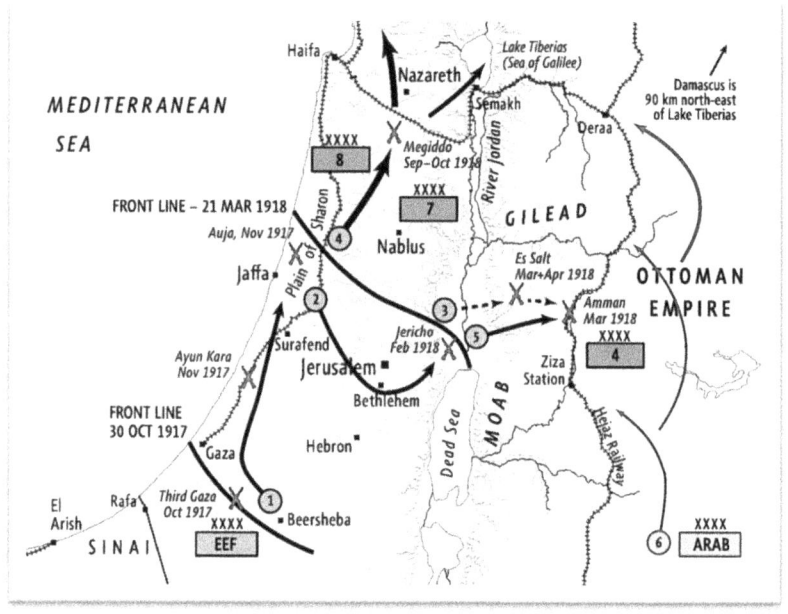

Palestine campaign 1917-18 map. Source - https://nzhistory.govt.nz/media/photo/palestine-campaign-1917-18-map (Ministry for Culture and Heritage), updated 1-Aug-2022 (accessed 7 May 2023).

The British strategy now was to push eastwards into the Jordan Valley to link up with Arab forces under the leadership of Colonel T E Lawrence (aka Lawrence of Arabia). This initially involved an attack in the direction of Amman to cut the main Turkish railway line, with British forces began the move east in February 1918 to reach the western shore of the Dead Sea, with the Light Horse entering Jericho on 21 February and then the Jordan Valley. The ANZAC Mounted Division now entered an environment that Charles Bean described as a desolate Judean wilderness and Amman as a squalid Arab town.[535]

The attack towards Amman commenced in March 1918 with the ANZAC Mounted Division working with the British 60th Division to

---

[535] Bean, *ANZAC to Amiens*, p. 497.

cross the bare, precipitous hills that led to the plateau on which the town was situated. Although the railway was cut both north and south of the town, attempts by elements of the 2nd Light Horse Brigade, the NZ Mounted Brigade and the Camel Brigade to capture the town over two days of stiff fighting were frustrated by Turkish and German resistance, with the force ordered to withdraw on 30 March 1918. The raid on Amman would result in the death of the only man commemorated on the Drummoyne War Memorial who served with the Australian Light Horse.

Amman would eventually be captured by the ANZAC Mounted Division at the end of September 1918.

George Campbell Gear

Trooper, No. 3534

6th Light Horse Regiment, 2nd Light Horse Brigade

Killed 29 March 1918, Amman, Palestine

Buried Jerusalem War Cemetery, Israel

George Campbell Gear was born in about 1883[536] to George Powell Gear and Barbara Gear. He was possibly one of seven children, his siblings including Henry Gavin, Jean Emily, Mary J, Alice C, Sidney T and Annie C.[537] In the Honour Roll Circular completed sometime after the war by his wife, Mary Jane Gear, George was said to have been closely associated with Drummoyne. On the same form, Mrs Gear noted that George's parents were deceased but gave their address as Lyons Road, Drummoyne.[538] George Powell Gear is recorded as living on the north side of Lyons Road between Hampden Road and Byrne Avenue, with the occupation of market gardener.[539]

George had married Mary Jane Capper in about 1912.[540] At the time of his enlistment on 12 May 1917,[541] the couple lived at Edgar Street, Auburn. They had three children: George Henry,[542] Jean Wingrove[543] and Hazel Mary.[544] George gave his age as 33 years and eight months, and his occupation as a wagon builder on his enlistment. Initially assigned the rank of private on enlistment, George was transferred on 23 May to the recruits training squadron at Menangle Park, and eventually assigned to serve with the Light Horse.

During his initial training George was charged on 11 August 1917 with 'soliciting alms, obscene language and using threatening language to an NCO'.[545] His punishment was initially a fine 40 shillings and 21 days' confinement to barracks, but this appears to have been reduced to a fine of 20 shillings only.

---

[536] NSW BDM Registration No. 6043/1884.
[537] NSW BDM Registration Nos. 6766/1878, 7748/1880, 4978/1882, 5315/1887, 6145/1889 and 12218/1892 respectively. Henry died in about 1884 (3174/1884), Alice in about 1890 (5013/1890) Jean in about 1909 (5208/1909),
[538] George Powell Gear died in about 1918 (5539/1918) and Barbara died in about 1924 (16348/1924).
[539] Sands General Index.
[540] NSW BDM Registration No. 4189/1912.
[541] War service records accessible at https://recordsearch.naa.gov.au/SearchNRetrieve/Interface/ViewImage.aspx?B=4104221
[542] NSW BDM Registration No. 17261/1913.
[543] NSW BDM Registration No. 16211/1914.
[544] NSW BDM Registration No. 38450/1916.
[545] War service records for George Gear accessible at https://recordsearch.naa.gov.au/SearchNRetrieve/Interface/ViewImage.aspx?B=4104221

George was allocated to the 31st Reinforcements to the 6th Light Horse and embarked from Melbourne on HMAT A73 *Commonwealth* on 28 October 1917 bound for Egypt. The transport arrived in Suez on 10 December 1917 whereupon the reinforcements marched into the Australian training camp at Moascar. George, however, was only there for a week when he was admitted to hospital. The service records indicate that he was suffering from bronchitis although another medical report on his service records suggests he was suffering from pleurisy. George was discharged from hospital on 1 January 1918 and joined the 6th Light Horse on 28 January at Wadi Hanein in Palestine where he was assigned to C Squadron.

During February 1918, the regiment interspersed its time with training and sporting matches, in between town patrols. C Squadron trialled steel helmets for the regiment on 11 February, with the unit diary noting that they were found to be unsuitable for mounted troops[546] and were eventually returned the following month.

The regiment marched out of its camp on 13 March with a complement of 20 officers and 452 other ranks, and for the next three days experienced increasingly heavier rain, which impacted on the condition of the horses. On 17 March, the regiment arrived at Jerusalem and camped outside the northwest corner of the walls, with a number of officers and men allowed to visit the old town. On 20 March, the regiment moved out with the rest of the 2nd Brigade heading for Jericho. The 6th Light Horse Regiment was the first unit to cross the Jordan River, which it did on 24 March, followed by the rest of the 2nd Brigade[547], and pushed forward to the town of Naaur before progressing along the Amman track.

The 6th Regiment formed the advance guard and made the treacherous trek up from the valley to the plateau, through the rocky defiles at night as heavy rain began to fall. At times, the ascent could only be made in single file, which stretched out the whole brigade. After three

---
[546] 6th Light Horse Regiment unit diary February 1918 - https://www.awm.gov.au/collection/C1350508?image=3
[547] *Official History of Australia in the War 1914-18*, H S Gullett, Vol. VII, 3rd Edition, Angus & Robertson, 1936, p. 557.

days and nights without rest, the units of the Mounted Division arrived on the plateau but were too exhausted to move onto Amman immediately.

Camp was set up on the evening of 26 March with C Squadron and 1 subsection of machine guns taking up defensive dispositions. After a day's rest, the attack commenced on 27 March 1918, but the Turks were aware of British intentions. The ANZACs were outnumbered and would be attacking across boggy ground without artillery support. Leaving their horses behind, elements of the 2nd Brigade including the 6th Regiment approached the town, with the terrain obscuring the visibility of the Turkish defences. Lured on, the Turks let loose a hail of shells and bullets described as being of annihilating intensity.[548] Further advance was impossible, and the units were withdrawn to positions of relative safety, with the 6th Regiment suffering casualties of one officer and 22 other ranks.[549] Attacks by the NZ Mounted Brigade and the Camel Brigade met a similar fate.

It was during the first attempt to capture Amman on 27 March 1918 that George is recorded to have been wounded and taken to the Australian Camel Field Ambulance suffering from 'H.E. Buttocks'. The next day he was transferred to the 2nd/4th London Mounted Field Ambulance with gunshot wounds to the buttocks, ankle and abdominal cavity. George died from his wounds on 29 March 1918.

The Red Cross obtained numerous statements in connection with George's wounding and subsequent death.[550] The primary differences between the various accounts are whether he was killed by an artillery shell or machine gun fire, and whether his death was instantaneous or during his evacuation.

In August 1918, Trooper Ralph L Lapworth (3598) stated that the 6th Light Horse were scattered about to the north of Amman. At about dinner time, while Gear was out reconnoitring, Lapworth saw an

---

[548] Gullett, *Official History*, Vol. 7, p. 566.
[549] 6th Light Horse Regiment unit diary March 1918 - https://www.awm.gov.au/collection/C1350510?image=5
[550] Australian Red Cross Wounded and Missing Files - https://www.awm.gov.au/collection/R1489079

explosion about 100 yards away, which he claimed killed Gear instantly and he was buried in the Jordan Valley about a ¼ mile from where he was killed. Lapwoth had come over with Gear on the *Commonwealth* and said Gear spoke constantly about 'his wife and kiddies.'[551] That George was killed by an artillery shell appears to be corroborated by the statement obtained from Sergeant Roy F Strachan (307) of the AAMC who said that George had been wounded by shrapnel and he had carried George to the dressing station. Sergeant Marseilles H J Winter (1575) and Signaller C C James (2882) also stated that George had been wounded by shrapnel from a shell.

A different story, however, is provided in the statements of Sergeant Harry B Chisholm (102) and Trooper Claud Tuckwell (3373), which attest that George had been hit by machine gun fire.[552] Tuckwell, who served with George in C Squadron, appears to provide the most reliable account. In April 1919, Major Lamb interviewed Tuckwell and recorded[553]:

> While "C" Squadron were attacking a redoubt at Amman, Gear was hit by machine gun fire. Shortly afterwards witness [Tuckwell] spoke to him [Gear] as he was being carried to the 2nd Brigade Australian Light Horse Field Ambulance. He was quite conscious, but was weak from loss of blood, and appeared far gone, and said "I'm done for".

---

[551] Australian Red Cross Wounded and Missing Files - https://www.awm.gov.au/collection/R1489079
[552] Australian Red Cross Wounded and Missing Files - https://www.awm.gov.au/collection/R1489079
[553] Australian Red Cross Wounded and Missing Files - https://www.awm.gov.au/collection/R1489079

He had had field dressings on. This was about 50 yards from where he was hit, and the advance dressing station was about 300 yards back, while the main ambulance was about 1 mile further back. Witness heard one or two days later that he had died.

The hospital records state that George's wounds were from gun shots, and the fact that he was hit numerous times is not consistent with machine gun fire.

One of George's colleagues, Jack Gray, wrote home in April 1918 providing a brief account of the travails of the Light Horse in their time in the Jordan Valley, which was published in a local newspaper[554]:

"TALK ABOUT AGONY."

Trumpeter Jack Gray (of Auburn) writes from Palestine, 3/4/'18: — "We have left the old city of Jerusalem behind, and we camped a few days above Jericho: We could see the shells bursting down on the Jordan, and at last we started down that way. On the night of the 23rd March we crossed the Jordan on a pontoon bridge. It was raining like the dickens. Blankets wet through, feet likewise; and rode all night. Talk about agony with the wet and cold! Men were groaning, and we had to get off and walk at times to keep our feet from freezing. Well, we rode until 11 a.m. on the 26th, so we were in the saddle continuously from 7 p.m. on 23rd of March until 11 a.m. on the 26th March without any sleep. Then people say the Light Horse is a catch and that they do nothing.

---

[554] "TALK ABOUT AGONY." (1918, July 3). *The Cumberland Argus and Fruitgrowers Advocate* (Parramatta, NSW: 1888-1950), p. 2. Retrieved May 7, 2023, from http://nla.gov.au/nla.news-article86212754

The Jordan was not wide where we crossed, only as wide as Duck river, but it had been raining heavily and it was running very fast. As you know, it empties into the Dead Sea, and we crossed a few miles from there; so now I can say I have seen the Dead Sea and crossed the Jordan. I might tell you that George Gear, the late drummer in Auburn Town Band, died of wounds in the fight. I am very sorry, as he was such a nice chap."

On 30 March 1918, George is recorded to have been buried in the presence of Rev. J. C. Fitzgerald at Jericho West Side, subsequently known as the Jerusalem War Cemetery. Mary Gear was initially advised of George's death on 3 April 1918, and passed on the news to a local newspaper, but which published incorrect information in relation to where George was killed[555]:

Mrs. Gear, late of Auburn and now at Annandale, has received word from the military authorities that her husband, Private George Gear, died from wounds in France on Good Friday. Deceased was well known in Auburn as a member of the town band.

A number of family notices appeared in *The Sydney Morning Herald* on 6 April 1918[556] and again a week later[557]:

---

[555] PERSONAL PARS. (1918, April 13). *The Cumberland Argus and Fruitgrowers Advocate* (Parramatta, NSW: 1888-1950), p. 6. Retrieved May 7, 2023, from http://nla.gov.au/nla.news-article86206367
[556] Family Notices (1918, April 6). *The Sydney Morning Herald* (NSW: 1842-1954), p. 12. Retrieved May 7, 2023, from http://nla.gov.au/nla.news-article15770595
[557] Family Notices (1918, April 13). *The Sydney Morning Herald* (NSW: 1842-1954), p. 12. Retrieved May 7, 2023, from http://nla.gov.au/nla.news-article15787182 . George's sister Annie Williams would die in 1923 – see Family Notices (1920, November 1). *The Sydney Morning Herald* (NSW: 1842-1954), p. 8. Retrieved May 7, 2023, from http://nla.gov.au/nla.news-article16872996

GEAR - Trooper George C Gear, died of wounds March 29, 1918, son in law and brother in law of Mr and Mrs Capper and family, of Annandale. He answered his country's call.

GEAR - Trooper George C Gear, 6th A L H., died of wounds March 29, 1918, dearly beloved husband of Mary Jane Gear, and daddy of George, Jean, and Hazel, 259 Young street, Annandale. The supreme sacrifice.

GEAR - Died of wounds March 29, 1918. Trooper George Gear, beloved nephew of Mr. and Mrs. D Hilder, and cousin of M E Hilder, Ashfield. Another Australian hero.

GEAR — Trooper George C. Gear, 6th A.L.H., died of wounds March 29, 1918. Your death has saddened us dear brother. Inserted by his loving brother and sister-in-law, Sid and Sarah Gear.

GEAR — Trooper George C. Gear, died of wounds, in Palestine, March 29, 1918, dearly loved second son of George and Barbara Gear, brother of Mary and Annie, aged 33 years. Our hero.

Mary wrote to the OIC on 21 April seeking a copy of George's death certificate in order that insurance matters could be settled. MLC wrote to the OIC on 24 April 1918 seeking the same documentation. A month later, the OIC provided a death certificate to George's wife and his insurer. Specific details of the circumstances of George's death and burial, however, were not provided to Mary until 29 July 1918.

George is the only man commemorated on the Drummoyne War Memorial who served in the Palestine theatre of First World War.

Drummoyne's Great War Volume 3

Photograph of the grave of George Gear, Jerusalem War Cemetery. The War Graves Project, CWGC. Reproduced with permission.

Photograph of Jerusalem War Cemetery. The War Graves Project, CWGC. Reproduced with permission.

Spring Offensive 1918

At about the same time as the Third Battle of Ypres came to a close, the provisional government in Russia was overthrown following the Bolshevik revolution. The Bolsheviks immediately sought an armistice with Germany, taking Russia out of the war. The Italians had also suffered a major defeat at Caporetto in October–November 1917, requiring British and French reinforcements to be transferred to secure the Italian front.

Despite these setbacks, the remaining Allies intended to renew the offensive in spring 1918 as the French Army recovered and American forces began to arrive at the Western Front in large numbers. Although the USA had declared war on Germany in April 1917, it was taking a considerable period of time for it to build up its army. The Allies, however, also fully expected Germany to take advantage of Russia's surrender by shifting many of its divisions to the Western Front. Efforts were made throughout the winter to improve defensive lines onto which the Allies would allow the Germans to batter themselves before going onto the offensive again to finish off the Germans. As it would transpire, the British sectors of the front lines would be thinly held owing to the BEF being forced to take over parts of the French lines, while being denied reinforcements from the UK.

Notwithstanding political objections to another 'Passchendaele', BEF commander Haig's plan to renew the offensive in Flanders meant that the Australian divisions wintered in this sector in anticipation of having a major role in the renewed attack. The Australian divisions, like most of the combatants, were facing a manpower crisis with the fighting of 1917 having consumed the pool of trained men such that many units were greatly under strength. The fledging 6th Australian Division in England had already been disbanded to provide reinforcements. There followed a proposal to break up the 4th Australian Division, then the weakest, to provide reinforcements to the other divisions. This potential disaster for morale was avoided when Haig agreed on 1 November 1917 to a proposal by Generals Birdwood and White to bring four Australian divisions into a single Australian Army Corps, with the 4th to become a depot division, which could then rotate with the other four divisions depending on losses from future fighting.

German General Ludendorff regarded Britain as the driving force behind the Allies, and the objective of the planned major offensive was to split the BEF from the French Army and destroy the BEF on the channel coast. The first attack, code named 'Michael', was concentrated on the Arras–Saint Quentin sector then thinly held by the British Third and Fifth Armies and commenced on 21 March 1918 with a sudden bombardment. The Germans initially overwhelmed the British Fifth Army's defences, splitting it from the British Third Army and forcing a headlong retreat. In the process, the British surrendered in just five days almost all the territory on the Somme that had been so costly won since 1916. The main road and rail junction at the city of Amiens was now threatened with capture, there being no British division between it and the advancing Germans. Covering Amiens was identified by Haig as of critical importance to Allied success in repulsing the Germans.[558]

---

[558] Haig, *War Diaries*, p. 393 (26 March 1918).

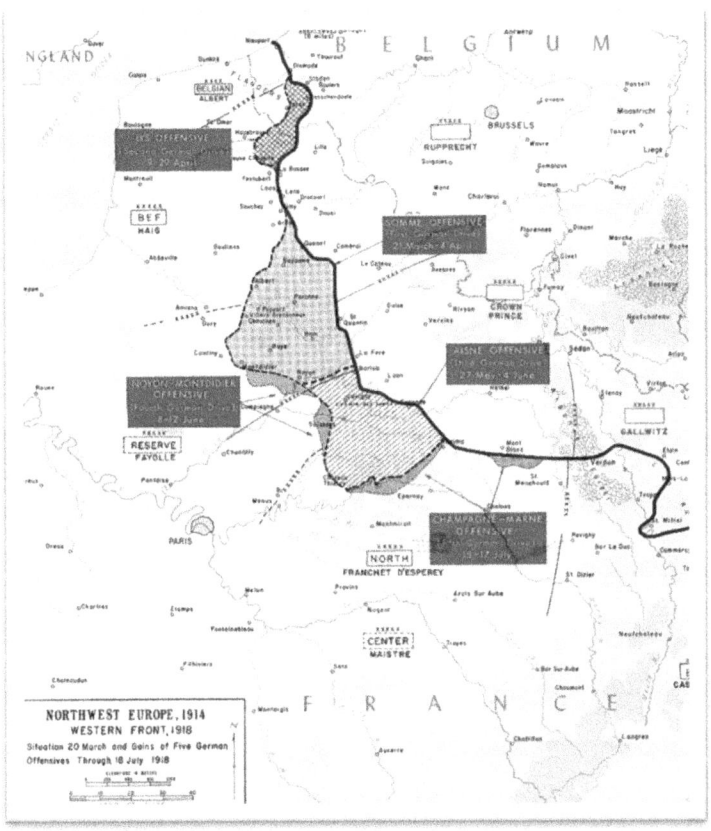

Western Front 1918 and German Spring Offensive – source https://en.wikipedia.org/wiki/German_spring_offensive (accessed 13 May 2023).

With Allied forces in retreat, reinforcements were sent from other sectors including Flanders. On 25 March 1918, the 3rd and 4th Australian Divisions began making their way south to meet the attack and relieve the pressure on the British Third Army. Within 24 hours, the 4th Division would be thrown in to close a gap in the line north of Amiens with the 4th Brigade taking up positions to defend the village of Hebuterne, where it remained for almost a month repulsing several German attempts to break through. The 12th and 13th Brigades of the 4th Division were rushed further south as the Germans had seized the town of Albert, and the 3rd Australian Division took up positions around the village of Heilly. In both instances, the Australians witnessed the panic of the retreat as French civilians, disorganised military units and stragglers fled for safety. In addition to bringing in reinforcements, the Allies finally agreed on 26 March to appoint French Marshall Ferdinand Foch as supreme commander of Allied armies in the west.[559] The town of Villers-Bretonneux was identified as critically important both in protecting Amiens but also the British right flank.[560]

On 4 April, the Germans renewed their attack in the Somme valley with one of its objectives being the capture of Villers-Bretonneux. The 9th Brigade of the 3rd Australian Division attempted to stabilise the line in front of the village, while the 12th and 13th Brigades of the 4th Australian Division were heavily attacked near Dernacourt. Each succeeded in repulsing the German efforts with the 2nd Australian Division arriving from Messines on 5 April to relieve the 4th Division.

The Germans now launched their second major blow on 9 April, named Operation Georgette,[561] focused in Flanders and with the objective of capturing the crucial railroad junction at Hazebrouck to force a British withdrawal from the Ypres salient. The Germans fell upon many tired British units that had been involved in the recent fighting on the Somme but had been sent north for rest. The Germans captured Messines, forcing a withdraw from the Passchendaele salient that had cost so many lives in 1917 and threatened to capture Hazebrouck. Given the seriousness of the situation, Field Marshal Haig was compelled on 11 April to issue an order of the day that included the following entreaty[562]:

---

[559] Haig, *War Diaries*, p. 394 (26 March 1918).
[560] Haig, *War Diaries*, p. 396 (1 April 1918).
[561] Sometimes referred to as the Battle of the Lys, or the Fourth Battle of Ypres.
[562] Bean, *Official History*, Vol 5, p. 437.

Every position must be held to the last man: there must be no retirement. With our backs to the wall and believing in the justice of our cause each one of us must fight to the end.

The 1st Australian Division, which had only just reached Amiens, was ordered to return north where it arrived on 12 April[563] to defend Hazebrouck and save the situation.[564] The German northern attack ultimately stalled and with that front now stabilised, the Germans turned their attention back to Amiens.

The Australian divisions, which in April had been deployed stretching from Dernacourt to south of Villers-Bretonneux defending the Somme sector, were relieved by two tired British divisions. This was completed just before the Germans renewed their attack on Villers-Bretonneux on 24 April. The Germans succeeded in capturing the village. Immediately, British commanders ordered the 15th Brigade from the 5th Australian Division and the 13th Brigade from the 4th Australian Division to launch a counter-attack, which went in at 10 p.m. on the night of 24 April without any preliminary bombardment. The 15th Brigade attacked north of the village and the 13th Brigade to the south in a pincer movement, and succeeded in driving the Germans out, entering the village in the early hours of the morning on 25 April 1918, the third anniversary of the landings at ANZAC Cove.

As German attention now shifted to attacking the French on the Aisne (called Operation Roland), the Australian divisions adopted an aggressive patrolling tactic described as 'peaceful penetration' but which Charles Bean described as 'Australia's private war against the Germans'.[565] Throughout May and June 1918, the Australian sectors of the front from Amiens to Hebuterne and Hazebrouck remained active, with the tactic often succeeding in capturing large sections of German outpost defences and with it many prisoners.

---

[563] Bean, *ANZAC to Amiens*, p. 428.
[564] Haig, *War Diaries*, p. 405 (18 April).
[565] Bean, *ANZAC to Amiens*, p. 445.

His Majesty King George V, knighting Lieutenant-General Sir John Monash, 12 August 1918 at Chateau de Bertangles. This was the first time in 200 years that a British monarch had knighted a commander on the battlefield. AWM ID No. E02964.

In June 1918, a change of command occurred in the Australian Corps with General Monash being appointed to take over from General Birdwood, who was appointed to command British Fifth Army. Monash was highly regarded by Haig, who considered him to be a most thorough and capable commander.[566] Monash's first operational task as Corps commander was the attack on the German strongpoint at Hamel on 4 July 1918, which proved to be a brilliant success. Although essentially a small-scale action, it is nevertheless regarded as one of the most significant of the entire war.[567] Combining some 60 new British Model V tanks advancing behind a creeping barrage, with infantry closely following, and being resupplied from the air and by carrier tanks, units of the 4th Australian Division seized the heights at

---

[566] Haig, *War Diaries*, p. 425 (1 July 1918).
[567] *Forgotten Victory*, Gary Sheffield, Headline Book Publishing, London, 2002, p. 235.

Hamel in a battle that took only 93 minutes, capturing some 1,470 prisoners. Entirely devised by General Monash, it is considered one of the first 'all-arms' battles in which infantry, artillery, tanks and aircraft were effectively combined to achieve victory.[568] The plan of the attack was to become a model on which instructions were quickly issued throughout the British Army for future attacks involving tanks[569] and which Haig impressed on his commanders in their training.[570]

The rate of 'peaceful penetrations' by Australian units on the Somme front now increased, putting significant strain on the Germans and preventing them from properly fortifying their positions. This influenced Haig to switch the point of his planned major offensive from Flanders to the Somme believing the German positions to be weaker and the land more favourable for the use of tanks. Preparations were made for a new offensive to commence in early August in which the Australian Army Corps would feature prominently.

---

[568] Sheffield, *Forgotten Victory*, p. 237.
[569] Bean, *ANZAC to Amiens*, p. 462; Sheffield, *Forgotten Victory*, pp. 235-6.
[570] Haig, *War Diaries*, p. 436 (31 July 1918).

Gainsford Wilton Evans

Private, No. 7114

13th Battalion, 4th Infantry Brigade, 4th Australian Division

Killed in action 11 April 1918, Villers-Bretonneux, France

No known grave. Commemorated Australian National Memorial, Villers-Bretonneux, France

Photograph of Gainsford Evans. Source - https://vwma.org.au/explore/people/182223

Gainsford Wilton Evans was the son of Walter Glendower Evans and Sarah Evans. Born in Bega, NSW, in 1894,[571] he attended Balmain Public School and was employed as a coal lumper.[572] Gainsford first applied to enlist in the AIF on 31 January 1916 and gave his postal address as 10 Day Street, Drummoyne.[573] Aged 22 years old, Gainsford was only 5 feet 2 ½ inches when he enlisted. When war broke out, enlistment standards for the AIF required a minimum of 5 feet 6 inches for its recruits, but by June 1915, this had been reduced to 5

---

[571] NSW BDM Registration No. 6084/1894. According to those records, his name was Wilton G H Evans. He was possibly the youngest of ten children, the others being Walter Spencer S (4574/1882), Jessie L S (4442/1883), Herbert A W (20308/1885), Owen C J (21368/1886), Alice E M (22024/1887), Allan S G (21399/1889), twins Muriel F B (6612/1891) and Vera D B (6613/1891), and Alice E P (6601/1893) who were variously born in the districts of Balmain/Leichhardt, Grafton and finally Bega.

[572] For more information on the occupation, see http://www.dictionaryofsydney.org/entry/coal_lumpers

[573] War service records accessible at https://recordsearch.naa.gov.au/SearchNRetrieve/Interface/ViewImage.aspx?B=1909155

feet 2 inches.[574] Initially assigned to the 20th Battalion, Gainsford's enlistment lasted only 21 days. It is unclear why but he was discharged from the AIF on 21 February 1916 with the reason given simply as 'services no longer required'.[575] However, on the second lot of attestation papers that Gainsford completed when he applied to enlist in the AIF on 10 November 1916, he disclosed that he had been discharged for 'missing early morning parade'.[576] At the time of his second enlistment, Gainsford's parents were living at *Woodlyn House*, Renwick Street, Drummoyne.[577]

Gainsford was assigned to the 23rd Reinforcements to the 13th Battalion and embarked for overseas only a fortnight later on HMAT A72 *Beltana* on 25 November 1916 from Sydney. He arrived in Devonport England on 29 January 1917 and marched into the 4th Training Battalion at Codford the next day. For the next 6 months, Gainsford undertook training in advance of being posted to France. He departed Folkestone bound for the BEF on 2 July 1917 and was one of 12 other ranks taken on strength by the 13th Battalion on 21 July when the battalion was based in Belgium and had just come out of the Battle of Messines. Billeted in Vieux-Berquin, the battalion was resting and recuperating. Gainsford arrived just in time for an inspection by the commander of the Second Army, General Plumer, and by General Birdwood.[578]

Late July saw the battalion return to the front lines where it relieved the 15th Battalion. For the next month, the battalion was involved in patrolling no man's land around Houthem, while experiencing

---

[574] AIF Enlistment Standards - https://www.awm.gov.au/encyclopedia/enlistment/. The standard was reduced again to 5 feet in April 1917.
[575] War service records for Gainsford Evans accessible at https://recordsearch.naa.gov.au/SearchNRetrieve/Interface/ViewImage.aspx?B=1909155
[576] War service records - https://recordsearch.naa.gov.au/SearchNRetrieve/Interface/ViewImage.aspx?B=1909155
[577] His parents had a number of addresses including 118 Hereford Street, Forest Lodge, '*Gordonville*', Ewell Street, Rozelle, 96 Beattie Street, Balmain and 463 Balmain Road, Leichardt.
[578] 13th Battalion Unit Diary July 1917 - https://www.awm.gov.au/images/collection/bundled/RCDIG1017511.pdf

periodic heavy enemy shelling. Relieved on 29 August by the 16th Manchester, the battalion took up billets at Verte Rue.[579]

By 1 September 1917, the unit diary notes that the battalion was 'brightening up generally' and benefiting from clean clothes in advance of a move to the Hazebrouck area of Belgium.[580] The battalion undertook further training as it moved billets until arriving back at Ypres on 22 September 1917 when it relieved the 23rd Battalion in the front lines. Gainsford missed out on this initial experience in the trenches since on 17 September 1917, he was admitted to the 4th Australian Field Ambulance with pyrexis (or fever) of unknown origin. The next day he was admitted to the 58th CCS before being admitted to the 11th General Hospital on 22 September 1917 at Camiers.

Gainsford did not rejoin his battalion for a month, arriving back on 24 October 1917. During his absence, the battalion, along with the other units of the 4th Australian Division, had been involved in operations as part of the Third Battle of Ypres, which commenced on 26 September in the Zonnebeke sector. After a period of rest and training, the battalion returned to the front lines near Zonnebeke on 18 October. Gainsford rejoined the battalion after it had been withdrawn and was resting near Reninghelst. He was among nine officers and 193 other ranks who rejoined the battalion on that day.[581]

After a brief spell in the Somme sector undertaking general training,[582] the battalion returned to the Ypres sector in Belgium in late January 1918[583], which was relatively quiet throughout all February.

The battalion moved to La Herliere, north of Amiens in France, in March 1918 with Gainsford going on leave in France on 18 March, and not to rejoin his battalion until 8 April 1918. The Germans had

---

[579] 13th Battalion Unit Diary August 1917 - https://www.awm.gov.au/images/collection/bundled/RCDIG1004157.pdf
[580] 13th Battalion Unit Diary August 1917 - https://www.awm.gov.au/images/collection/bundled/RCDIG1004157.pdf
[581] 13th Battalion Unit Diary October 1917 - https://www.awm.gov.au/images/collection/bundled/RCDIG1004552.pdf
[582] 13th Battalion Unit Diary November 1917 - https://www.awm.gov.au/images/collection/bundled/RCDIG1017737.pdf
[583] 13th Battalion Unit Diary January 1918 - https://www.awm.gov.au/images/collection/bundled/RCDIG1004650.pdf

broken through the Allied lines with the unit diary noting that they had reached Hubeterne. The battalion received orders on 26 March to move on the village and for the next two weeks were engaged in resisting German attacks to retake it. On 9 April 1918, the battalion received the following message from General Brand, the general officer commanding the 4th Brigade[584]:

> I regret that the relief of your Battalion has been postponed from 10/11 April till 13/14 April. After 15 days strenuous work all higher commanders would have liked to see your men get a few days rest, but the holding of HUBETERNE is all important to the IV Corps, it has therefore been arranged that the 4th Brigade carry on the good work rather than be relieved.
>
> …
>
> The importance of the British holding the Germans and allowing him to expend his fresh Divisions whilst the French and American counter offensive is maturing, will be appreciated by all thinking officers, NCO's and Men. From what one can gather the British have very few fresh Divisions so that all our efforts have to be redoubled.
>
> …
>
> Please let all ranks know that the best service they can do is to stick to it.

The extension of the battalion's time in the front lines would prove fatal for Gainsford. While there is no information regarding the circumstances of Gainsford's death, and the unit diary does not detail any significant enemy action on 11 April, his service records include an entry on 13 April that Gainsford was killed in action on 11 April 1918. He was one of two other ranks killed on that day in what

---

[584] 13th Battalion Unit Diary April 1918 - Appendix 1, pages 13-14 - https://www.awm.gov.au/images/collection/bundled/RCDIG1004654.pdf

appears to have been light combat, with the intelligence summary report noting that enemy activity was limited to artillery landing around posts and the front line, with twelve direct hits being registered in the morning, and five in the afternoon.[585]

No information exists in relation to the fate of Gainsford's remains. There is no Red Cross file that might contain statements from any of his comrades in the battalion regarding the circumstances of his death or if he was buried.

A Roll of Honour notice was published in *The Blue Mountain Echo* on 31 May 1918[586]:

> EVANS — Killed in action in France, April 11, 1918, Pte. Gainsford Evans, aged 20, 13th Battalion, beloved youngest son of Mr. and Mrs. W. G. Evans, of Paddington, and grandson of the late Dr. O. S. Evans, of Balmain; brother of Surrey, Bert and Spencer (on active service), Jessie, Evelyn, Muriel, Vera and Alice; brother-in-law of R. Bell, A. Hannah, S. F. Driscoll and L. Peterie (both on active service) and J. W. Webb, of Mort Street (returned).
>
> The supreme sacrifice.

Gainsford's photograph subsequently appeared in the *Australian Town and Country Journal* on 3 July 1918 among those either killed or wounded in action.

---

[585] 13th Battalion Unit Diary April 1918 – Appendix 1, pages 20, 32-33 - https://www.awm.gov.au/images/collection/bundled/RCDIG1004654.pdf
[586] Family Notices (1918, May 31). *The Blue Mountain Echo* (NSW: 1909-1928), p. 2. Retrieved May 21, 2023, from http://nla.gov.au/nla.news-article108244293 . Although the notice states that Gainsford was 20 years old, this does not reconcile with his date of birth which would have made him 23 or 24 at the time he was killed.

Pte. G. W. Evans (OF PADDINGTON), killed in action.

Photograph of Gainsford Evans. Source - N.S.W. Soldiers Reported Wounded. (1918, July 3). *Australian Town and Country Journal* (Sydney, NSW: 1870-1919), p. 17. Retrieved May 21, 2023, from http://nla.gov.au/nla.news-article263628162

Gainsford's personal effects were consigned from England on the HMAT A43 *Barunga* on 21 June 1918. The *Barunga* was on its way to Australia with more than 800 sick and wounded on board when it was torpedoed at 4:30 p.m. on 15 July 1918 by U108. Destroyers that had been some miles away were quickly on the scene to pick up survivors and returned them to Plymouth. All hands were saved before the *Barunga* subsequently sank with the loss of all its cargo.

Gainsford has no known grave and is commemorated at the Australian National Memorial, Villers-Bretonneux, France.

Robert Alexander Smith

Private, No 7325

2nd Battalion, 1st Infantry Brigade, 1st Australian Division

Died of wounds, 13 April 1918, Namps-au-Val, France

Buried Namps-au-Val British Cemetery, Amiens, France

Robert Alexander Smith was born in Crudine, NSW, in 1885 in the district of Sofala.[587] He was the son of William Henry and Matilda F Smith and is perhaps one of seven children, the others being Charles Henry, William George Moses, Albert Leslie, Esther Matilda, Catherine M and Teresa May.[588] The second youngest of the family, Robert attended the local Crudine Public School.

Robert was living in the town of Capertee, east of Crudine, in November 1916 at the time of his enlistment in the AIF.[589] Employed as a labourer, he nominated his mother Matilda then living at Torbane north of Lithgow as his next of kin. A handwritten note on Robert's attestation paper states that by nominating his mother as his next of kin 'the answer to this question shall not be construed as in the nature of a will'.[590] Uncertainty over whether Robert had made a will would ultimately end in a dispute between his brothers and sister over who was entitled to receive his war medals and personal effects after the end of the war.

Declaring his age to be almost 33 years old at the time of his enlistment at Bathurst,[591] Robert disclosed on his attestation form that he had previously attempted to enlist but had been rejected on medical grounds. It is not apparent from the records the reason he was determined to have been medically unfit but on this occasion his application as successful.

Initially assigned to the 8th Reinforcements to the 56th Battalion, on 30 January 1917 he was transferred to the 24th Reinforcements to the 2nd Battalion. Robert embarked from Sydney on 10 February 1917 on board RMS *Osterley*, disembarking at Plymouth, England, on 11 April 1917.

---

[587] NSW BDM Registration No. 14602/1885. The entry on the register has his name as Alexander Robert Smith.
[588] NSW BDM Registration Nos. 17724/1871, 18720/1873, 20288/1876, 23325/1879, 11853/1882 and 16229/1888 respectively.
[589] War service records for Robert Alexander Smith accessible at https://recordsearch.naa.gov.au/SearchNRetrieve/Interface/ViewImage.aspx?B=1787989
[590] By this time, his father had died.
[591] He declared his age to be 32 years and 11 months but based on his date of birth he is likely to have been 31 years old.

Robert marched into the 1st Training Battalion in Durrington Camp, England, where he remained for the better part of five months undertaking training. It was not until 25 September 1917 that Robert finally proceeded overseas to France, embarking from Southampton. Taken on strength with the 2nd Battalion on 8 October 1917, the battalion had just been relieved fighting around Westhoek Ridge in Belgian Flanders as part of the Third Battle of Ypres. In the cold and increasingly wet weather that characterised the closing stages of the battle, the battalion settled in to providing working parties and training until, at the end of the month, it was back in Ypres.[592] With a complement of 25 officers and 637 other ranks,[593] the battalion relieved the 9th Battalion near Zonnebeke on 5 November and took up positions along the front, including near a regimental aid post at Tyne Cottage.[594] During its time in the front lines, the fighting to capture the village of Passchendaele continued with the battalion exposed to heavy German shelling and enduring the cold and muddy conditions. The mud and shelling caused difficulties in supplying the front-line troops resulting in shortages, with the carrying parties resorting to bringing up water in petrol tins on pack horses.[595]

The battalion was relieved on 8 November and returned to the support lines from where it provided a large number of working and carrying parties. The battalion was eventually moved back to the hutted 'Halifax Camp' where the men could escape the wet and mud, and an account taken on the losses and the men's deteriorated condition, including trench foot cases. The battalion was moved further back to

---

[592] 2nd Battalion Unit Diary October 1917 - https://www.awm.gov.au/collection/C1347983?image=11
[593] 2nd Battalion Unit Diary November 1917 - https://www.awm.gov.au/collection/C1347984?image=2
[594] 2nd Battalion Unit Diary November 1917 - https://www.awm.gov.au/collection/C1347984?image=3 . Tyne Cottage was the name given to a barn by British soldiers around which the Germans had constructed strong defensive positions including a number of concrete pillboxes, which had been captured by the 3rd Australian Division on 4 October 1917. It would become the site of the future Tyne Cot Cemetery, the largest Commonwealth war cemetery in the world.
[595] 2nd Battalion Unit Diary November 1917 - https://www.awm.gov.au/collection/C1347984?image=6

the village of Frencq, near the Australian depot base at Etaples, where it undertook training and re-equipment, with the men able to take advantage of hot baths. It was while in billets on 29 November 1917 that Robert was charged with drunkenness and creating a disturbance. He was found guilty, awarded ten days' close confinement and forfeited four days' pay.

Australian troops of the 1st Division enjoying a well-earned spell in the vaults beneath the ramparts of Ypres, in Belgium, after supporting the flank of the Canadian Divisions in the fight for Passchendaele. 7325 Pte Robert Alexander Smith (right foreground, sitting). 1 November 1917. AWM ID No. E01399.

By the end of December 1917, the battalion was back in the frontlines near Kemmel,[596] southwest of Ypres, where it remained through January 1918, enduring bitter and freezing conditions. On 13 January while the battalion was still in the line, Robert was evacuated to the

---

[596] 2nd Battalion Unit Diary December 1917 - https://www.awm.gov.au/collection/C1347985?image=8

2nd Australian Field Ambulance suffering from furunculosis.[597] He was later transferred to hospital at Wimereux. Robert remained in various hospitals and convalescent camps in France during which time he again committed a crime, although less serious than previously, charged with being unshaven at the 9 a.m. inspection parade. On this occasion, Robert was awarded seven days' confinement to barracks.

Robert remained incapacitated until he rejoined the 2nd Battalion on 3 April 1918 when it was based at Devonshire Camp near Reninghelst southwest of Ypres. In just over a week after rejoining his unit, however, Robert would be mortally wounded.

The battalion entrained from Godewaersvelde on 6 April heading for Amiens[598] and the Somme sector where the Germans had succeeded in breaking through the Allied line. Arriving at St Roche railway station the same day, the battalion moved out to Cardonette, but by 10 April, had received orders to return to Amiens to entrain and return north with the rest of the 1st Australian Division in response to the opening on the German 'Georgette' offensive in the Ypres sector of the front. The battalion returned to St Roche railway station at Amiens where it acted as the loading party for the entrainment of the 1st Brigade. During the night of 11 April, the Germans shelled the railway station where D Company was working, as well as some of the battalion's billets. The shelling is reported to have killed one officer and two other ranks and wounded 13 others.[599]

It is probable that Robert was one of the casualties from the shelling at St Roche railway station that evening. He is reported to have suffered shell wounds to his arm and face and was admitted to the 2/3 Home Counties Field Ambulance on 11 April and then transferred to the 41st CCS where he died of his wounds on 13 April 1918. The 41st CCS was a casualty clearing station, which had relocated to

---

[597] A deep infection of the hair follicle leading to abscess formation with accumulation of pus and necrotic tissue sometimes called boils - https://www.ncbi.nlm.nih.gov/pmc/articles/PMC3934592/
[598] 2nd Battalion Unit Diary April 1918 - https://www.awm.gov.au/collection/C1355279?image=4
[599] 2nd Battalion Unit Diary April 1918 - https://www.awm.gov.au/collection/C1355279?image=6

Namps-au-Val on account of the German offensive.[600] Robert's name appeared in the casualty list published on 10 May 1918 as having been wounded[601] before reported to have died of wounds three days later.[602]

According to an extract from Robert's pay book on his service file, he made a will dated 9 February 1917, which had been lodged with Mrs Alvina Ann Smith of Torbane, NSW. On 11 April 1919, the OIC wrote to Mrs Alvina Smith requesting a copy of Robert's will in order to deal with his 'military affairs'.

In a letter dated 24 May 1920 from Mr George Smith[603] living at Dunedoo to Captain W F Dunn MLA, George claimed that Robert had made a will before he embarked 'to my wife Mrs E A Smith'.[604] He noted that his wife had received a letter from the matron in France stating that she was sending all Robert's belongings to her, but nothing had been received. The letter was passed to the OIC, which responded in a letter dated 15 June 1920 to Mrs E A Smith at Torbane Mine, Torbane, in which she was advised that one package of Robert's personal effects had been lost to enemy action with the sinking of SS *Barunga*, but that an additional package was held, pending receipt of Robert's will.[605]

Alvina Smith's letter dated 16 June 1921 to the OIC noted that Robert had never married and that as his father and mother were both dead, her husband George M Smith was the oldest surviving brother 'and therefore next of kin'.[606] A handwritten note on the letter was made by the OIC that Robert's war medals were to be issued to the

---

[600] https://www.cwgc.org/find-a-cemetery/cemetery/4002/namps-au-val-british-cemetery/
[601] CASUALTY LISTS. (1918, May 10). *The Sydney Morning Herald* (NSW: 1842-1954), p. 5. Retrieved May 21, 2023, from http://nla.gov.au/nla.news-article15763381
[602] 399th CASUALTY LIST. (1918, May 13). *The Sydney Morning Herald* (NSW: 1842-1954), p. 4. Retrieved May 21, 2023, from http://nla.gov.au/nla.news-article15768191
[603] George Smith was born William George Moses Smith in 1873 (NSW BDM Registration No. 18720/1873).
[604] War service records - https://recordsearch.naa.gov.au/SearchNRetrieve/Interface/ViewImage.aspx?B=1787989
[605] War service records - https://recordsearch.naa.gov.au/SearchNRetrieve/Interface/ViewImage.aspx?B=1787989
[606] War service records - https://recordsearch.naa.gov.au/SearchNRetrieve/Interface/ViewImage.aspx?B=1787989

eldest brother.⁶⁰⁷ Receipts on Robert's service file signed by G M Smith acknowledge receipt of Robert's medals, memorial scroll and war memorial plaque over the course of 1921–1923.

The propriety of the disposal of Robert's war medals and mementos was first raised in January 1924 when Robert's sister, Teresa May Hanslow⁶⁰⁸, then living at 47 Parramatta Road, Annandale, wrote to the OIC inquiring whether she could make a claim for the gratuity bond payable on account of Robert's service.⁶⁰⁹ The following month, Teresa again wrote to the OIC inquiring if anyone had claimed Robert's war medals as 'if not have I any claim to them as I am his only sister alive as far as I know. I would like to have something in [remembrance] of him as he [has helped] to fight to save us and our country and lost his life.'⁶¹⁰

On 22 February 1924, the OIC responded to Teresa's letter advising that Robert's medals had been issued to his eldest brother, Mr G M Smith. Teresa responded promptly to this advice⁶¹¹:

> Referring to your letter which I received today saying that G M Smith was the eldest brother of the late Private R A Smith if he [has] put himself the eldest brother he [has] made a false statement. C H Smith is the eldest brother of our family and I know he knows nothing about it because I am saying to get his [brother's] war bond as he is a cripple and also lost of one eye. Could the eldest brother claim those medals as the other brother has made a false statement?

---

⁶⁰⁷ War service records - https://recordsearch.naa.gov.au/SearchNRetrieve/Interface/ViewImage.aspx?B=1787989
⁶⁰⁸ Theresa May Smith was born in 1888 (NSW BDM Registration No. 16229/1888) and married Joseph J Hanslow in Bathurst in 1908 (NSW BDM registration no. 10259/1908).
⁶⁰⁹ War service records - https://recordsearch.naa.gov.au/SearchNRetrieve/Interface/ViewImage.aspx?B=1787989
⁶¹⁰ War service records - https://recordsearch.naa.gov.au/SearchNRetrieve/Interface/ViewImage.aspx?B=1787989
⁶¹¹ War service records - https://recordsearch.naa.gov.au/SearchNRetrieve/Interface/ViewImage.aspx?B=1787989

On 3 March 1924 the OIC advised Teresa that in reply to an enquiry addressed to Robert's late mother, it was advised on 23 May 1921 by Mrs A A Smith of Torbane that her husband, G M Smith, was the eldest surviving brother. As both Robert's parents were deceased, the OIC concluded that G M Smith was Robert's legal next of kin.[612]

The eldest brother, Charles Henry Smith,[613] engaged Norman J Palmer solicitors of Moree to write to the OIC on 21 March 1924 in response to OIC's letter dated 3 March to Teresa Hanslow. In the letter, the solicitors asked whether a receipt for deferred pay had been signed by Matilda Smith as there was a suspicion that her daughter-in-law may have forged Matilda's signature since Matilda had died some few weeks before the deferred pay was available.[614]

The OIC's letter to the AIF finance officer a week later, referring to the letter from the lawyers, stated that the daughter-in-law referred to is understood to be identical to Mrs Alvina Smith of Torbane, who had advised the OIC that her husband G M Smith was the eldest surviving brother. The OIC confirmed that war medals and other mementos were disposed of in favour of G M Smith. The OIC's letter of the same date in reply to Norman J Palmer stated[615]:

> In the present instance it would appear therefore that your client, Mr C H Smith, as the eldest surviving male relative is fully entitled to possession, and the legality of the claim cannot be reasonably disputed by his younger brother.

In a letter dated 7 January 1925 to the OIC, Teresa Hanslow stated that 'G M Smith as [sic] got Pte R A Smith Medals by saying he was

---

[612] War service records - https://recordsearch.naa.gov.au/SearchNRetrieve/Interface/ViewImage.aspx?B=1787989
[613] Charles Henry Smith was born in 1871 (NSW BDM Registration No. 17724/1871).
[614] War service records - https://recordsearch.naa.gov.au/SearchNRetrieve/Interface/ViewImage.aspx?B=1787989
[615] War service records - https://recordsearch.naa.gov.au/SearchNRetrieve/Interface/ViewImage.aspx?B=1787989

the eldest brother which he is not as you will see in the form.'[616] The letter enclosed a statutory declaration made by Teresa Hanslow declaring that Charlie H Smith of Balo Street, Moree was Robert's eldest brother. The reply from the OIC dated 13 January 1925 noted that any enquiries regarding payment of the war gratuity needed to be directed to the District Finance Officer but continued[617]:

> I may say that the late soldier on enlistment nominated Mrs Matilda Smith of Torbane, Mudgee Line, NSW as next-of-kin in the relationship of mother. Notwithstanding that the deceased's war medals and other memorial items have been disposed of in favour of Mr G M Smith, it would appear that Mr C H Smith as the eldest surviving brother is the person most entitled to receive, and it is suggested that suitable representations be made to the present recipient with a view to their recovery.

Charlie Smith finally wrote to the OIC in March 1925 in plaintive terms[618]:

> I am [writing] to you in regard to my deceased brother R A Smith [medals] as I am the eldest brother I think I am [entitled] to war [medals] and property belong[ing] to him as my father and mother are dead. Would you let me know if I could get anything belonging to him and oblige the same.

The OIC acknowledged receipt of Charlie's letter, excusing the fact that it had disposed of Robert's war medals and other memorials on account of the incorrect advice that had been provided by Alvina Smith, but otherwise asserted that it had acted in good faith and in accordance with the provisions of the *Deceased Soldiers' Estate Act* 1918.

---

[616] War service records - https://recordsearch.naa.gov.au/SearchNRetrieve/Interface/ViewImage.aspx?B=1787989
[617] War service records - https://recordsearch.naa.gov.au/SearchNRetrieve/Interface/ViewImage.aspx?B=1787989
[618] War service records https://recordsearch.naa.gov.au/SearchNRetrieve/Interface/ViewImage.aspx?B=1787989

The OIC's letter enclosed a copy of the letter received from Alvina Smith 'for civil action you may wish to take toward recovery of the mementoes.'[619]

In June 1925, Charles Henry Smith brought proceedings against his brother, William George Moses Smith, in Moree Magistrates Court to recover Robert's war medals and mementos. In what was widely reported at the time as a remarkable case, Charles was unsuccessful in obtaining what had been issued to George Smith despite the sympathy of the presiding magistrate. *The Richmond River Herald and Northern Districts Advertiser* reported the case in the following terms, which was picked by many other newspapers[620]:

An Extraordinary Case.

BROTHER v. BROTHER.

The Police Magistrate at Moree, Mr. A. E. Chapman, had rather an unusual case before him on Thursday, when Charles Henry Smith, a drover, of Moree, proceeded against William George Moses Smith, his brother, for detention of property — a memorial scroll and plaque; and a British War Medal and victory medal.

---

[619] War service records https://recordsearch.naa.gov.au/SearchNRetrieve/Interface/ViewImage.aspx?B=1787989

[620] An Extraordinary Case. (1925, June 12). *The Richmond River Herald and Northern Districts Advertiser* (NSW: 1886-1942), p. 6. Retrieved February 25, 2024, from http://nla.gov.au/nla.news-article125959447 . See also BROTHERS AT LAW (1925, June 11). *The North Western Courier* (Narrabri, NSW: 1913-1955), p. 4. Retrieved February 25, 2024, from http://nla.gov.au/nla.news-article133460584 ; Remarkable Case. (1925, June 9). *The Armidale Express and New England General Advertiser* (NSW: 1856-1861; 1863-1889; 1891-1954), p. 8. Retrieved February 25, 2024, from http://nla.gov.au/nla.news-article192067028 ; A PECULIAR CASE. (1925, June 10). *Lithgow Mercury* (NSW: 1898-1954), p. 1. Retrieved February 25, 2024, from http://nla.gov.au/nla.news-article219247047 ; Brother Sues Brother. (1925, June 4). *North West Champion* (Moree, NSW: 1915-1954), p. 5. Retrieved February 25, 2024, from http://nla.gov.au/nla.news-article181563322 ; BROTHER SUES BROTHER (1925, June 18). *Mullumbimby Star* (NSW: 1906-1936), p. 4. Retrieved February 25, 2024, from http://nla.gov.au/nla.news-article125184329 ; BROTHERS AT LAW. (1925, June 8). *The Sydney Morning Herald* (NSW: 1842-1954), p. 8. Retrieved February 25, 2024, from http://nla.gov.au/nla.news-article16232292 ; News from Everywhere (1925, June 15). *Wellington Times* (NSW: 1899-1954), p. 1. Retrieved February 25, 2024, from http://nla.gov.au/nla.news-article141219246

Charles Smith said he had a brother who was killed in the war, and produced his own and his brother's birth certificates. The property in dispute had belonged to the brother now dead. Witness wrote to Victoria Barracks, and received a reply from the Officer in Charge of Base Records, which he produced. He claimed the property as the eldest brother and next-of-kin. His solicitor had written to his brother, the defendant, claiming the property, but had received no reply.

His Worship said he would rather they settled the matter between them, and shake hands. 'Life was too short to quarrel on matters like that.' He was of opinion that the elder brother was entitled to the medals.

Defendant said plaintiff claimed to be his brother, but he did not know who he was.

The Magistrate pointed out that the birth certificates were evidence.

Giving evidence the defendant, William George Moses Smith, said he was a laborer, living at Torbane, on the Mudgee line. The brother who was killed had claimed witness as his eldest brother. Witness' wife had written to the Base Records office for the property stating 'her husband was the next of kin'. Witness declared he would not give up the property of his poor dead brother, with whom he had lived for 25 years. He was going to keep those medals until they made him give them up.

The Magistrate: We can soon make you give them up, but want you to settle the. matter voluntarily. His Worship quoted a case and said the application for the return of the property must be made by the complainant going personally to the place and demanding delivery from the defendant.

It was pointed out that had had been done.

His Worship also mentioned a Queensland case, which laid it down that the complainant must sue in the district where the property was detained. He could not find a similar case in New South Wales. In the circumstances he must dismiss the application.

Defendant then said he had been brought over 500 miles just for those medals, and asked for his expenses. He had no money left.

The case was dismissed, complainant being ordered to pay £3, defendant's train fare, in default 21 days' hard labor.

It is unknown if Charles made any further attempts to recover Robert's war medals and mementos. Robert is buried at Namps-au-Val British Cemetery, 11 miles southwest of Amiens.

Photograph of Namps-au-Val British Cemetery. The War Graves Project, CWGC. Reproduced with permission.

Photograph of the grave of Robert Smith, Namps-au-Val British Cemetery. The War Graves Project, CWGC. Reproduced with permission.

Claude Edward Pierpoint

Private, No. 6840

8th Battalion, 2nd Infantry Brigade, 1st Australian Division

Killed in action 16 April 1918, Hazebrouck, France

Buried Nieppe-Bois (Rue-Du-Bois) British Cemetery, Viserquin, France

Claude Edward Pierpoint was one of six children of William and Emily Jane (nee Alton) Pierpoint, but his parents died during his infancy and he was raised by his sister Emily. Claude was born in Richmond, Victoria, in 1881[621] and his early education is unknown. He first applied to enlist in the AIF in November 1915 at the declared age of 35 years and 11 months, which would mean that he was born in about 1879.[622] A labourer and cook by occupation, Claude named his sister Emily Theresa Spencer then living at *Warning Camp*, 27 Dening Street, Drummoyne, as his next of kin.[623]

Originally given a regimental number of 287 at the AIF Base in Armidale, New South Wales, in November 1915, Claude's enlistment was short-lived as on 21 January 1916 he was discharged for being absent without leave for a period of eight hours on 6 January 1916, and for drunkenness.

Claude re-enlisted on 28 October 1916, and despite the passage of time declared his age to be 35 years and 10 months. Although he initially specified a friend, Alfred Dixon of Gravesend, as his next of kin, at some later date this was crossed out and his sister's details inserted in their place. Pertinently, Claude declared on his attestation paper that he had not previously been discharged from, nor had he previously served in, any part of His Majesty's Forces. Given a new regimental number of 6840, he was assigned to the 22nd Reinforcements to the 8th Battalion.

The 22nd Reinforcements embarked from Sydney on SS *Port Napier* on 17 November 1916, arriving in Devonport, England, at the end of January 1917. Claude joined the 2nd Training Battalion and after a three-month period of training, embarked from Folkestone in April 1917 to join his battalion in Etaples, France. He was taken on strength with the 8th Battalion on 13 May 1917 after the battalion had

---

[621] Victorian BDM Registration No. 5050/1881.
[622] War service records for Claude Edward Pierpoint accessible at https://recordsearch.naa.gov.au/SearchNRetrieve/Interface/ViewImage.aspx?B=8011989
[623] Emily was born in 1863 in Balranald, NSW (NSW BDM Registration No. 4761/1863).

participated in operations to follow-up the German withdrawal to the Hindenburg Line.[624]

In May 1917, the battalion had taken up front lines positions adjacent the Hindenburg Line to the right of Bullecourt and successfully repulsed a strong enemy raid. Relieved, the battalion was assigned billets in Brevilliers, where it rested and undertook specialised training.[625] The battalion's routine continued into June with manoeuvres undertaken, which involved the battalion periodically changing billets. On 12 July 1917, the battalion as part of the 2nd Brigade assembled on the main Amiens–Albert Road near Bresle, where it was inspected by the king as he was passing through.[626]

By September 1917, the 8th Battalion had moved to the Ypres sector to join the Third Battle of Ypres. In preparation for what was to come, the battalion received training to assist them to determine their location on a field of battle when permanent objects had been obliterated.[627] They also received training in the new method of attack to be adopted in the offensive, being the 'bite and hold' tactic, as well as inspect models of the area over which it would attack.

On 15 September, the battalion moved forward to the Chateau Segard Bund Dugouts and from 7 p.m. on 19 September began to move forward to the assembly areas just as rain began to fall. The objective of this attack was the Menin Road Ridge. The rain caused delays and confusion in the assembly areas as other units were slow to move out. Notwithstanding these difficulties, the battalion had secured its three objectives by mid-morning on 20 September and began consolidating its new positions.[628] The expected enemy counter-attack was successfully broken up by coordinated artillery barrages.

---

[624] https://www.awm.gov.au/collection/U51448
[625] 8th Battalion Unit Diary May 1917 - https://www.awm.gov.au/collection/C1340716?image=5
[626] 8th Battalion Unit Diary July 1917 - https://www.awm.gov.au/collection/C1340718?image=4
[627] 8th Battalion Unit Diary September 1917 - https://www.awm.gov.au/collection/C1355739?image=2
[628] 8th Battalion Unit Diary September 1917 - https://www.awm.gov.au/collection/C1355739?image=5

In was during the attack on 20 September 1917 that Claude was wounded in action, said to have suffered a gunshot wound to the thumb and back. Admitted to the 6th Australiann Field Ambulance, he was transferred to the 17th CCS and then onto an ambulance train before being admitted to 14th General Hospital at Wimereux. The wound to his back was sufficiently serious that on 2 October 1917, Claude was evacuated to England on the hospital ship *St Andrew* and admitted to the Royal Victoria Hospital, but he was only there for a short time. He was reported as wounded in action in casualty lists published in October 1917.[629]

Emily was notified by the OIC on 1 November 1917 that Claude had been admitted to the Royal Victoria Hospital suffering from a gunshot wound to the head and contusions. According to the medical reports, Claude was reported to have been buried by a shell explosion and suffered from sprained muscles in his back and neck, with bruising over the lower lumbar. He was transferred later in October 1917 to the 3rd Auxiliary Hospital where it was noted that he had much improved and walking about quite well. By 29 October he was discharged for leave with orders to report to No.3 Depot at Hurdcott two weeks later on 14 November 1917. At the depot, Claude was given a fitness classification of B1A3[630] and underwent further treatment with the conclusion that by 3 January 1918, he was suffering from no obvious disability. He remained at Hurdcott until 9 January 1918 when he was transferred to the Overseas Training Brigade at Longbridge, Deverell.

On 1 February 1918, Claude proceeded overseas via Southampton, eventually rejoining his unit a week later when the battalion was billeted in the Belgian village of Locre (Loker), southwest of Ypres. The 8th Battalion was resting, training and undefeated in the inter-unit

---

[629] AUSTRALIAN CASUALTIES. (1917, October 25). *The Sydney Morning Herald* (NSW: 1842-1954), p. 8. Retrieved May 21, 2023, from http://nla.gov.au/nla.news-article15754165
[630] Fit for overseas training camp in two to three weeks - Australian Department of Veteran Affairs handbook https://www.dva.gov.au/sites/default/files/files/consultation%20and%20grants/repatriation/PO_HBook_ch5.pdf

divisional competitions under Australian rules.[631] At the end of February, the battalion was warned of an impending enemy attack, and prepared to move at a moment's notice.[632] Preparations in anticipation of the threatened German attack would continue through the first three weeks of March with leave cancelled, and more training undertaken and working parties deployed. At 9 p.m. on 22 March 1918, the battalion received notice to stand by ready to move, and 90 minutes later, received orders to relieve the 54th Battalion in the Wytschaete sector near Ypres.

What would unfold for the battalion and the entire Allied front was the opening of the German spring offensive that would in a matter of weeks recapture all the territory that had been so costly won by the Allies since 1916. The initial German attack occurred in the Somme sector with reinforcements sent from other sectors including Belgian Flanders.

So it was that on 5 April, the battalion was relieved and proceeded south to St Ouen where it arrived a day later. When there, the battalion commanders were briefed on the 'general situation'. Their stay was short-lived as on 8 April orders were received to move to Vignacourt.[633] Over the course of the next few days, the battalion progressively moved south reaching the railway junction at Amiens–St Roch on 12 April 1918. However, with the Germans switching the point of attack to Flanders, the battalion along with the whole 1st Australian Division was sent back to take up positions and construct defensive lines for what was emerging as the Battle of Hazebrouck.

According to accounts recorded by Charles Bean, all was chaos and men in the forward lines did not know what units were in their neighbourhood beyond their own.[634] On the morning of 13 April, the 8th Battalion witnessed fierce fighting in front of them in the village of

---

[631] 8th Battalion Unit Diary February 1918 - https://www.awm.gov.au/collection/C1343739?image=5
[632] 8th Battalion Unit Diary February 1918 - https://www.awm.gov.au/collection/C1343739?image=5
[633] 8th Battalion Unit Diary April 1918 - https://www.awm.gov.au/collection/C1343741?image=5
[634] Bean, *Official History*, Vol 5, pp. 449 and 455.

Vieux-Berquin held by the 4th Guards Brigade.[635] By the afternoon, the guards were being forced back and began to retire through the battalion's lines.

At 1 a.m. on 14 April, a group of 100 Germans was observed approaching the battalion's positions. The Germans were allowed to come within 25 yards of the battalion's positions whereupon Lewis guns and rifles opened up[636] causing the enemy to withdraw in confusion, suffering losses of one officer and two other ranks killed, and six machine guns being captured.[637] On 15 April, the Germans renewed their attack, this time in considerable force. Although this attack was also beaten off, a German minenwerfer destroyed one post killing the whole garrison except for one officer and one other rank who managed to fight their way back to the Australian lines.

The fighting continued during 16 April, with each side exchanging artillery and mortar fire, and patrols being pushed out to identify the enemy's location.[638] It was during this fighting that Claude was killed, one of 18 other ranks of the battalion killed during the fighting on 16 April.[639]

Although we have no information as to the circumstances of his death, it is possible that Claude was initially wounded given that his name was included in casualty list as such.[640] Any uncertainty was resolved by May with a Roll of Honour notice published in *The Sydney Morning Herald* on 15 May 1918[641]:

---

[635] 8th Battalion Unit Diary April 1918 - https://www.awm.gov.au/collection/C1343741?image=6
[636] 8th Battalion Unit Diary April 1918 - https://www.awm.gov.au/collection/C1343741?image=6
[637] 8th Battalion Unit Diary April 1918 - https://www.awm.gov.au/collection/C1343741?image=7 . Bean records the German losses as one officer and twenty men dead (Bean, *Official History*, Vol 5, p. 465).
[638] 8th Battalion Unit Diary April 1918 - https://www.awm.gov.au/collection/C1343741?image=8
[639] 8th Battalion Unit Diary April 1918 - https://www.awm.gov.au/collection/C1343741?image=9
[640] Australian Casualties. (1917, October 31). *Australian Town and Country Journal* (Sydney, NSW: 1870-1919), p. 43. Retrieved May 21, 2023, from http://nla.gov.au/nla.news-article263767881
[641] Family Notices (1918, May 15). *The Sydney Morning Herald* (NSW: 1842-1954), p. 10. Retrieved May 21, 2023, from http://nla.gov.au/nla.news-article15788627 . An identical

PIERPOINT. — Killed in action, France, April 16, 1918, Private Claude Edward Pierpoint, beloved youngest brother of Mrs. C. Spencer, Denning-street, Drummoyne, Mrs. A. Harlor, Balmain, and brother, of Hawkesbury River. Deeply mourned by his sorrowing relatives.

On 4 April 1919, almost a year after Claude's death, Emily wrote to OIC inquiring as to the whereabouts of Claude's personal effects, which she was most anxious to have returned to her 'as the one sister most nearly associated with him all his life having raised him from infancy. Both father and mother dying at that time.' The personal effects she stated would be highly prized by her 'as the last link between us.'[642]

Unfortunately, there was to be further bad news for Emily as on 9 April 1919, the OIC replied to Emily's letter advising that HMAT *Barunga*, on which the personal effects of Claude and some 5,000 other soldiers had been placed, was lost at sea by enemy action.[643] All that was eventually provided to Emily was a copy of the inventory for the package that had contained Claude's personal effects.

In May 1921, the OIC wrote to Emily asking for details of Claude's brothers and sisters in order that Claude's war medals could be issued in accordance with the requirements of the *Deceased Soldiers Estates Act 1918*. Quickly replying, Emily advised[644]:

> I beg to state that I am the eldest sister. His eldest brother's name is Percy Alton but his address is unknown to me not hearing of him for some time. He is younger than myself.

---

notice was published in *The Daily Telegraph* on the same date - Family Notices (1918, May 15). *The Daily Telegraph* (Sydney, NSW: 1883-1930), p. 8. Retrieved May 21, 2023, from http://nla.gov.au/nla.news-article239259242

[642] War service records - https://recordsearch.naa.gov.au/SearchNRetrieve/Interface/ViewImage.aspx?B=8011989

[643] War service records - https://recordsearch.naa.gov.au/SearchNRetrieve/Interface/ViewImage.aspx?B=8011989

[644] War service records - https://recordsearch.naa.gov.au/SearchNRetrieve/Interface/ViewImage.aspx?B=8011989

The OIC's response in June 1921 requested details of the second eldest surviving brother, noting that brothers have prior claims to sisters 'unless there are good and sufficient reasons for varying the procedure.'[645] Emily promptly responded noting the names of Claude's other brothers; William Arthur (1870), Ernest Edwin (1874) and James Herbert (1879), but that their addresses were unknown to her and had been for some time.[646]

On 11 July 1921, the OIC advised Emily of its decision to hand over Claude's war medals to her 'but only on the distinct understanding that they will be preserved with due care as memorials of his services and produced to this Department upon receipt of its demand in writing should any of your brothers at any time prefer a claim which is upheld by the Minister.'[647] Emily was requested to complete and return a statutory declaration to that effect, which she did, and the next month she received the British War Medal, and two years later, the Victory Medal.

The OIC also corresponded with Emily in relation to the inscription that she would like to include on Claude's headstone. In March 1922, Emily advised[648]:

> I have decided to have his name on the family grave here. Having buried Mr Spencer last Wednesday after an illness of six months and it was his wish to do so when he died. There are no others in the family that would wish otherwise, as far as I know.

---

[645] War service records - https://recordsearch.naa.gov.au/SearchNRetrieve/Interface/ViewImage.aspx?B=8011989
[646] There would appear to be three other sisters, Edith Pierpoint born in 1876 (Vic BDM 25290/1876) and Florence Annie Pierpoint born in 1872 (Vic BDM 2764/1872) and Mary Pierpoint born in 1862 in Hay, NSW (NSW BDM 4502/1862). The NSW BDM also records another son, Percy born in 1868 (5551/1868), and an unnamed female born in 1865 (5163/1865), both in Hay, NSW.
[647] War service records - https://recordsearch.naa.gov.au/SearchNRetrieve/Interface/ViewImage.aspx?B=8011989
[648] War service records - https://recordsearch.naa.gov.au/SearchNRetrieve/Interface/ViewImage.aspx?B=8011989

Emily's husband, Thomas Charles Spencer, had died on 6 March 1922 at their home, aged 66.⁶⁴⁹ Thomas is buried in the Field of Mars Cemetery, Ryde. As a consequence, there is no inscription of Claude's headstone other than his name, unit, rank, regimental number and date of death.

Photograph of the grave of Claude Pierpoint at Nieppe-Bois (Rue-Du-Bois) British Cemetery, Vieux-Berquin (author, 2018).

Claude Pierpoint is buried in Nieppe-Bois (Rue-Du-Bois) British Cemetery, Vieux-Berquin.⁶⁵⁰ In addition to the Drummoyne War Memorial, Claude is commemorated on the Moree ANZAC Centenary War Memorial.⁶⁵¹

---

⁶⁴⁹ Family Notices (1922, March 8). *The Sydney Morning Herald* (NSW: 1842-1954), p. 12. Retrieved September 12, 2023, from http://nla.gov.au/nla.news-article15991784
⁶⁵⁰ On 17 December 1918, the OIC advised Emily that Claude had been buried at Bois D'Aval Military Cemetery, three miles south of Hazebrouck, France. This cemetery is located close by, but this advice was given in error.
⁶⁵¹ https://www.warmemorialsregister.nsw.gov.au/content/private-claude-edward-pierpont

John Stephen Coolahan MC

Lieutenant

5th Machine Gun Company, 2nd Australian Division

Died of wounds 3 May 1918 in captivity

Buried Valenciennes Communal Cemetery, France

THE LATE LIEUT. J. S. COOLAHAN, M.C.

Photograph of John Coolahan. Source - "AUSTRALIAN NOTES" *Sunday Times* (Sydney, NSW: 1895-1930) 30 December 1917: 3. Web. 22 May 2023 http://nla.gov.au/nla.news-article122782567

John Stephen Coolahan was born in Tamworth, NSW, on 30 October 1882,[652] one of four children of Patrick and Maria Coolahan.[653] Described by Charles Bean as a 'big, brave, raw-boned Irish-Australian,' John was a single 33-year-old when he enlisted in the AIF on 13 December 1915, and may well have enlisted on the same date as his brother, Arthur Francis Coolahan.[654] At the time of enlistment, John's occupation was that of a salesman and he gave his address as *Latonaville*, St Georges Crescent, Drummoyne (now 1A Queen Victoria Place). He named his mother of the same address as his next of kin,[655] his father Patrick having died in or about the same time.[656]

Initially appointed as an acting sergeant in B Company of the 1st Training Battalion between 8 March and 1 August 1916, John undertook Officer Training School at Duntroon and was promoted to second lieutenant at the Cootamundra Camp on 4 October 1916, before moving to Liverpool to await embarkation on 8 November 1916 aboard the *SS Port Nicholson*.

He arrived in England on 10 January 1917 before making his way to a camp in Durrington. John undertook a training course with the Australian Machine Gun training depot at Grantham, before he was posted to the Australian Machine Gun Corps. He embarked for

---

[652] NSW BDM Registration No. 27166/1881. His surname is misspelt Coolalan.
[653] The other children were Thomas (24757/1880), Arthur Francis (30688/1883) and Mary (34078/1886).
[654] https://www.aif.adfa.edu.au/showPerson?pid=61423
[655] War service records of John Stephen Coolahan accessible at http://recordsearch.naa.gov.au/scripts/Imagine.asp?B=3403437 ; Roll of Honour Circular accessible at https://www.awm.gov.au/people/rolls/R1729053/
[656] NSW BDM Registration No. 8786/1916.

France in April 1917, whereupon he joined the 5th Machine Gun Company on 5 May 1917 as part of the 2nd Australian Division. On 6 July, John was promoted to lieutenant.

Lt Coolahan appears to have seen his first major action in September 1917 in the Ypres Salient at Westhoek, Belgium. As part of the Third Battle of Ypres, the 2nd Division was engaged in action at Menin Road, Broodseinde and, ultimately, Passchendaele Ridges.

On 19 September 1917, sections of the company were assigned to support individual battalions in the 2nd Division, with Lt Coolahan's machine gun section assigned to support the 17th Battalion.[657] Even before any attack commenced, one gun in Lt Coolahan's section was knocked out by shellfire, with two killed and two wounded. Part way into the advance, another gun was knocked out. With replacement guns and teams called up from reserve, the fight continued throughout 19 to 23 September. At one point, a German plane was shot down by one of the guns in the section.

It was during the attack around Westhoek that Lt Coolahan's actions resulted in him being awarded the Military Cross. The recommendation for the award from the commander of the 5th Infantry Brigade, Brigadier General Robert Smith, and approved by Major-General N. M. Smythe of the 2nd Australian Division, dated 25 September 1917, reads[658]:

> This officer on 20th September, 1917, at WESTHOEK, by great exertion got his Vickers Machine Guns and ammunition in position just in the rear of the 3rd objective as soon as it was taken by the 17th Battalion. He showed splendid pluck and cheerfulness under very heavy shell fire, setting a very good example to all his men.

---

[657] 5th Machine Gun Company Unit Diary, September 1917 - https://www.awm.gov.au/collection/C1344745?image=10
[658] Recommendation reference accessible at https://www.awm.gov.au/people/rolls/R1580745/

He also visited all M.G. positions on the front of his Brigade [5th Brigade] and through his good grip of the situation was of great assistance to the Battalion commander, relieving him of much of his anxiety by the splendid manner in which he handled his guns.

This was particularly apparent when the enemy was seen to be massing for a counter attack. This officer with great promptitude opened fire and helped materially in preventing the counter attack from developing. This is the first time Lieut. COOLAHAN had been under fire.

The Unit Diary of the 5th Machine Gun Company for October 1917 refers to the recommendation[659] and includes the following statement from the Officer Commanding – Captain R A P Hamilton[660]:

...I wish to state that I was personally much impressed with the excellence of his work which was on a level with the usual high standard of efficiency which he has shown since joining the Company. His men speak of him in the highest terms – it is his personal courage & energy that were great factors in achieving the results shown by his Section of [guns] in the attack of the 21st inst.

Although the Military Cross is recorded in his personal records as having been awarded to Lt Coolahan on 26 March 1918, the fact of

---

[659] The recommendation appears to have come from a Lt Colonel Martin, 5th Machine Gun Company, October 1917 (AWM ID No. AWM4 24/10/14) accessible at https://www.awm.gov.au/collection/AWM4/24/10/14/
[660] 5th Machine Gun Company Unit Diary, October 1917 - https://www.awm.gov.au/collection/C1344746?image=11

the award was published is both the Australian and London Gazettes at various dates.[661] The citation in the *Commonwealth Gazette* states[662]:

> For conspicuous gallantry and devotion to duty. This officer by great exertions got his machine guns and ammunition into position in rear of the objective as soon as it had been gained. He showed splendid pluck and cheerfulness under heavy shell fire. Through his grip of the situation he rendered great assistance to the battalion commander by the splendid manner in which he handled his guns, and by his promptitude in opening fire, preventing the counter attack from developing.

As the Ypres offensive continued into October 1917, Lt Coolahan saw further action around Zonnebeke, Belgium. On 4 October, Lt Coolahan was sent to take charge of E Battery to replace Lt Dickinson, who was wounded. During its attack, the company experienced considerable difficulty in getting its guns forward due to a swamp near Zonnebeke and heavy enemy artillery fire.

On about 8 October, Lt Coolahan was in charge of the 4th section of the company and prepared his section for an attack to occur on 9 October. It was during this attack that Lt Coolahan was one of four officers in the company who was wounded. He suffered gunshot wounds to the left arm and shoulder. He also suffered a severe compound fracture of the radius and injury to the radial artery that needed to be tied. His wounds required him to be evacuated to England on 12 October 1917 where he was admitted to the Prince of Wales Hospital. John's name appeared in casualty lists in November 1917[663] and

---

[661] It was published in the *Commonwealth Gazette* on 14 February 1918 (page 285, position 32) and the citation on 25 July 1918 (page 1596, position 1). See Government Gazette Proclamations and Legislation (1918, February 14). *Commonwealth of Australia Gazette* (National: 1901 - 1973), p. 284. Retrieved May 22, 2023, from http://nla.gov.au/nla.news-article232463511 It was published in the *London Gazette* on 27 October 1917 (page 11110, position 16) and the citation on 18 March 1918 (page 3436, position 13).
[662] Government Gazette Proclamations and Legislation (1918, July 25). *Commonwealth of Australia Gazette* (National: 1901 - 1973), p. 1587. Retrieved May 22, 2023, from http://nla.gov.au/nla.news-article232461968
[663] BIG CASUALTY LIST (1917, November 25). *Sunday Times* (Sydney, NSW: 1895-1930), p. 3. Retrieved May 22, 2023, from http://nla.gov.au/nla.news-article122795987

his hospitalisation was reported along with a portrait in the *Sunday Times* on 30 December 1917.[664]

During Lt Coolahan's hospitalisation, he appears to have been diagnosed with fibrosis of the right lung and assessed for tuberculosis (which proved negative) because of a persistent cough that had worsened over the last two months. After a period convalescing, Lt Coolahan was discharged and returned to France in early March 1918, eventually rejoining his company on 8 March 1918.[665] By this time, the Australian Machine Gun Battalions were formed by joining four machine gun companies in each division. The 5th Machine Gun Company became part of the 2nd Machine Gun Battalion allocated to the 2nd Australian Division. In March 1918, Lt Coolahan is reported to have been awarded a bar to his Military Cross[666] but this appears to be an error as his service records contain no mention of a second award and in fact the award of his Military Cross was not formalised until March 1918.[667]

In March 1918, the Germans launched their major offensive to try to break through the Allied lines before large numbers of American troops began to arrive in France. The unit diary recorded increasing enemy activity around this time.[668] The offensive included an attack in the Somme region heading towards Amiens. Australian divisions were rushed to the front to try to re-establish a defensive line in proximity to Villers-Bretonneux.

On 6 April 1918, the unit diary noted that at 6:00 a.m., Lt Coolahan, who was at the time the officer commanding no. 3 section in

---

[664] "AUSTRALIAN NOTES" *Sunday Times* (Sydney, NSW: 1895-1930) 30 December 1917: 3. Web. 22 May 2023 http://nla.gov.au/nla.news-article122782567
[665] 5th Machine Gun Company Unit Diary, March 1918 - https://www.awm.gov.au/collection/C1344751?image=5
[666] ANZAC HONORS. (1918, March 20). *Geelong Advertiser* (Vic.: 1859-1929), p. 4. Retrieved May 22, 2023, from http://nla.gov.au/nla.news-article119713642
[667] GALLANT AUSTRALIANS. (1918, March 20). *The Sydney Morning Herald* (NSW: 1842-1954), p. 11. Retrieved May 22, 2023, from http://nla.gov.au/nla.news-article15766676
[668] 5th Machine Gun Company Unit Diary, March 1918 - https://www.awm.gov.au/collection/C1344751?image=6

the company, took a German soldier prisoner.[669] Charles Bean briefly noted the encounter in the *Official History* as follows[670]:

> The Germans also were evidently doubtful as to the line held. In the small hours of the 6th Lieut. J. S. Coolahan – big, brave, raw-boned Irish-Australian of the 5th Machine Gun Company – is said to have collided in the dark with a German outside the support company headquarters. Coolahan 'grabbed the Jerry', wrote Captain V. R. Portman, 'and threw him into the 'bivvy' like a bundle of skins.'

On 7 April, the diary recorded that during operations, the machine guns of the company were constantly engaged firing on small parties of Germans entering to the south of Bois de Hangard[671] causing many casualties, and that enemy snipers and machine guns were busy. It was on this date that the unit diary noted that Lt Coolahan was wounded along with two other ranks.[672] The diary contains no further reference to Lt Coolahan but his personal service records noted that he was reported as wounded in action on the second occasion on 13 April 1918. This was changed on 26 April 1918 to record that Lt Coolahan 'is now reported wounded and missing'.[673]

Lt Coolahan's machine gun company supported the 5th Australian Infantry Brigade's attack on Hangard Wood, carried out by the 19th and 20th Battalions. The attack commenced on 7 April 1918 but foundered quickly in the absence of accurate maps of the area.[674] The attack came under heavy German machine gun fire, and although part of it eventually attained its objective, the ground was determined to be untenable, and by nightfall, the battalions had fallen back to their start line. It is during this attack that Lt Coolahan, accompanied by a

---

[669] 5th Machine Gun Company Unit Diary, April 1918 - https://www.awm.gov.au/collection/C1344753?image=4
[670] Bean, *Official History*, Vol. 5, p. 504n.
[671] Almost immediately south of Villers-Bretonneux.
[672] 5th Machine Gun Company Unit Diary, April 1918 - https://www.awm.gov.au/collection/C1344753?image=5
[673] War service records - http://recordsearch.naa.gov.au/scripts/Imagine.asp?B=3403437
[674] McLachlan, *Walking with the ANZACS*, p. 175.

runner, Private Callaghan, and looking to find a position to set up a machine gun, was wounded.[675] He had just sent the runner back to the gun crew under the command of Corporal Noble when he was hit, and by the time Corporal Noble had reached the position, he was reported to have found Lt Coolahan apparently dead.[676] Lt Coolahan fell into German hands during the withdrawal.

On 2 May 1918, the Red Cross reported to Captain Webb of the 5th Machine Gun Company that 'we are glad to inform you that [Lt Coolahan] is reported from Copenhagen to be a prisoner of war and his address at present is unknown.'[677] On 13 May 1918, it was recorded that Lt Coolahan was a prisoner of war in Germany, and on 22 May 1918, a letter from the Central Prisoner of War Commission stated that as at 29 April, he was 'in German hands'.[678] John's name appeared in casualty lists published in May initially as having been wounded[679] before reported as being a prisoner of war.[680]

It was not until 28 August 1918 that it was reported that Lt Coolahan had died while a prisoner of war on 3 May 1918, as a result of wounds to the 'right lung and side of breast' at the Kriegslasarett Valenciennes, France. The Red Cross reported that Lt Coolahan was shot in the left breast and hip and 'it seems that from the beginning there was no hope for his recovery'.[681] Captain R C Webb of the 5th Machine Gun Company in a letter to the Red Cross in reply, stated that '[i]t was a terrible shock to me and his friends to receive such news.'[682]

---

[675] Bean, *Official History*, Vol 5, p. 509.
[676] Bean, *Official History*, Vol. 5, p. 510.
[677] Australian Red Cross Wounded and Missing Files for John Stephen Coolahan - https://www.awm.gov.au/people/rolls/R1478910/
[678] Australian Red Cross Wounded and Missing Files - https://www.awm.gov.au/people/rolls/R1478910/
[679] Australian Casualties. (1918, May 8). *Australian Town and Country Journal* (Sydney, NSW: 1870-1919), p. 16. Retrieved May 22, 2023, from http://nla.gov.au/nla.news-article263624147
[680] APRIL FIGHTING (1918, May 20). *The Sun* (Sydney, NSW: 191 1954), p. 2. Retrieved May 22, 2023, from http://nla.gov.au/nla.news-article221954846
[681] Australian Red Cross Wounded and Missing Files -https://www.awm.gov.au/people/rolls/R1478910/.
[682] Australian Red Cross Wounded and Missing Files - https://www.awm.gov.au/people/rolls/R1478910/

Lt Coolahan was reported buried at Ebrenfried Valenciennes, France, 'by German hands' on 14 October 1918. A brief handwritten note purporting to be an extract from a statement from Lt Boase of the 52nd Battalion states that 'I saw Lieut. Coolahan 5MG Co. die at Valenciennes Hospital in April – I do not remember the date.' Another statement in Red Cross files from Lt William Hardy of the 8th Machine Gun Company says 'Lieut. Coolahan died of wounds in hospital at VALENCIENNES. I was lying wounded in the same hospital and saw him dead. He was buried at Valenciennes.'[683]

A family notice was published in the *Sunday Times* on 13 October 1918 along with John's portrait[684]:

> The Late Lieut. J. S. Coolahan MC of the 5th Machine Gun Company, died of wounds whilst a prisoner of war. Lt. Coolahan enlisted in November, 1915, passed through Duntroon Military College, gained his commission, and sailed on November 18, 1916. He was awarded the Military Cross for gallantry on the field in the Westhoek attack on Sept 20, 1917. Later he was severely wounded, invalided to England, and further awarded a bar to his M.C. On returning to France he was again wounded and captured. The deceased officer was very popular, and his death is deeply regretted by many friends. His mother resides at St. George's Crescent, Drummoyne.

Over several months, the personal effects of Lt Coolahan began to make their way back to Australia and were forwarded to Maria Coolahan at *Latonaville*. First was an envelope from Germany containing a wallet, some coins, letters, photos and '5 religious charms.' These were then followed from 'the field' a sealed brown valise and a sealed

---

[683] Australian Red Cross Wounded and Missing Files - https://www.awm.gov.au/people/rolls/R1478910/

[684] FASCINATING SPORT OF STRAFING SUBMARINES (1918, October 13). *Sunday Times* (Sydney, NSW: 1895-1930), p. 16. Retrieved May 22, 2023, from http://nla.gov.au/nla.news-article123133527 . An earlier family notice was published in Family Notices (1918, September 25). *The Sydney Morning Herald* (NSW: 1842-1954), p. 10. Retrieved May 22, 2023, from http://nla.gov.au/nla.news-article15804096

suitcase containing clothes and '1 rosary'. It would have been little consolation to Maria Coolahan when she received a letter from the OIC on 7 August 1918 advising of the fact that her son's award of the Military Cross had been published in the *London Gazette*.

John Coolahan also had a brother, Arthur Francis Coolahan, of the same address. While his Attestation Paper and the Nominal Roll indicate that Arthur joined on 13 December 1915, the same date as John Stephen Coolahan, the service records show him as having enlisted on 10 January 1916.[685] Arthur was 31 at the time of enlistment, and like John was a salesman. Arthur served with the Field Artillery, initially as a gunner with the 7th Field Artillery Brigade, Battery 26. After arriving in England in May 1916, he was transferred to the 3rd Division's Light Trench Mortar Brigade, before finally being assigned to the 34th Battalion in August 1917.

Arthur was quickly promoted during the course of 1917, until commissioned as a second lieutenant on 19 November 1917, and eventually as a lieutenant on 16 March 1918. Arthur Coolahan survived the war, returning to Australia in July 1919. Based on correspondence in his service records, it appears that Arthur lived on Bowman Street, Drummoyne in about 1922–23. It is possible that Mrs Maria Coolahan also moved to the same address, as the service records for John Stephen Coolahan show that at some point in time, Maria's address changed to Bowman Street.

Although it is not clear, there is a possibility that John and Arthur also had a cousin, James Dudley Coolahan, who died on 3 October 1916, aged 33 years, from illness while serving in France.[686]

---

[685] War service records for Arthur Francis Coolahan accessible at http://recordsearch.naa.gov.au/scripts/Imagine.asp?B=3403426; Nominal Roll for Arthur Francis Coolahan accessible at https://www.awm.gov.au/collection/R2179721
[686] War service records for James Dudley Coolahan accessible at http://recordsearch.naa.gov.au/scripts/Imagine.asp?B=3403426.

Valenciennes (St. Roch) Communal Cemetery, France. The War Graves Project, CWGC. Reproduced with permission.

The Honour Roll Circular for James that was completed by his father, Edward Francis Coolahan, contains a handwritten note that, in addition to having a 'brother service corps,'[687] he had a 'cousin Leiut Stephen Coolahan wounded and died.'[688]

---

[687] This is likely to be Maurice Stanley Coolahan as they shared the same address in Randwick and Edward Francis Coolahan as their next of kin – see NAA WWI Service records for Maurice Stanley Coolahan accessible at http://recordsearch.naa.gov.au/scripts/Imagine.asp?B=3403441. Maurice was present at Dudley's funeral according to Red Cross Records https://www.awm.gov.au/people/rolls/R1478909/.
[688] The Honour Roll Circular accessible at https://www.awm.gov.au/people/rolls/R1728310/

John Coolahan is buried at the Valenciennes Communal Cemetery, France.[689]

Grave of John Stephen Coolahan, Valenciennes (St. Roch) Communal Cemetery, France. The War Graves Project, CWGC. Reproduced with permission.

---

[689] Commonwealth War Graves Commission http://www.cwgc.org/find-a-cemetery/cemetery/63800/VALENCIENNES%20(ST.%20ROCH)%20COMMUNAL%20CEMETERY

Robert James Henderson MC and Bar

Captain

13th Battalion, 4th Infantry Brigade, 4th Australian Division

Died of wounds 13 May 1918

Buried Etaples Military Cemetery, Etaples, France

Capt. R. J. Henderson, M.C., Drummoyne, Sydney, who was awarded the Military Cross for bravery on the battlefield.

Photograph of Robert Henderson. Source – 19 June 1918, Sydney Mail (NSW: 1912-1938), p. 20. Retrieved May 23, 2023, from http://nla.gov.au/nla.news-article159026484

Robert (Bob) James Henderson was born in Sydney on 13 December 1885.[690] He was one of five children to James and Amy Violet Henderson. His father James emigrated to Australia from Scotland in 1878 on RMS *Chimborazo*, which was wrecked near Jervis Bay on its journey to Sydney. Along with all the passengers, James was rescued. James gained employment with the Bank of New South Wales in Sydney where he worked until his retirement in 1916. In 1882, he married Amy Violet Richardson (the daughter of R P Richardson of

---

[690] NSW BDM Registration No. 5277/1886.

Richardson & Wrench), and they had three sons, Robert, Leonard[691] and Stewart,[692] and two daughters, Lorna Violet[693] and Isabel Jane.[694]

Robert was the eldest son and attended Fort Street High School and Sydney Grammar School before training and working as an electrical engineer employed with the Electric Light Co.[695] Robert is also reported to have been a member of Balmain District Cricket Club.[696] He enlisted in the AIF on 23 May 1915 with service number 2392 at the declared age of 29 years and five months.[697] Robert specified his father as his next of kin who at the time was living at *Wahnfried*, 133 St Georges Crescent, Drummoyne. On leaving his employer, Robert received a wristlet watch from his colleagues as 'a token of esteem on the eve of his departure for war.'[698]

Robert was a prolific correspondent during his period of service, writing letters to his family and in particular to his mother, on a regular basis and in some instances within days of previous letters. The correspondence from Robert to his family was donated to the Australian

---

[691] NSW BDM Registration No. 6140/1889. Leonard was born in about 1889 and was employed as a bank clerk at the time of his enlistment as the age of 26 years. Leonard saw service at Gallipoli with the 13th Battalion, and in France as part of the 45th Battalion where he was commissioned as a Lieutenant. Leonard survived the war and returned to Australia on 14 January 1919 - https://www.aif.adfa.edu.au/showPerson?pid=134309

[692] His correct name was Hamilton Stewart (NSW BDM Registration No. 12206/1892). Stewart, who Robert referred to in his letters as 'Mick', was articled as a solicitor with Messrs Leibius, Black & Wray. Stewart would ultimately apply for probate of Robert's Will, which was provided to the OIC in January 1919.

[693] NSW BDM Registration No. 8883/1884. Lorna married Jack Tivey and subsequently moved to the United States.

[694] NSW BDM Registration No. 5585/1887. An obituary for James Henderson published in *The Sydney Morning Herald* on 19 July 1923 states that he was survived by his wife, two sons and two daughters with another son killed on active service. A notice published in February 1917 marking James' retirement states that he has three sons and one daughter – see A RETIRED BANKER. (1917, February 1). *The Sydney Morning Herald* (NSW: 1842-1954), p. 3. Retrieved May 23, 2023, from http://nla.gov.au/nla.news-article15730094

[695] AWM biography https://www.awm.gov.au/people/P10677467/

[696] 1916 'CRICKET.', *The Daily Telegraph* (Sydney, NSW: 1883-1930), 26 July, p. 14. , viewed 16 Sep 2023, http://nla.gov.au/nla.news-article239220101 ; WAR CASUALTIES. (1918, June 15). *The Sydney Morning Herald* (NSW: 1842-1954), p. 14. Retrieved May 23, 2023, from http://nla.gov.au/nla.news-article15766069

[697] War service records for Robert James Henderson accessible at https://recordsearch.naa.gov.au/SearchNRetrieve/Interface/ViewImage.aspx?B=5338768

[698] FAREWELLS TO SOLDIERS. (1915, June 30). *The Daily Telegraph* (Sydney, NSW: 1883-1930), p. 11. Retrieved May 23, 2023, from http://nla.gov.au/nla.news-article239044813

War Memorial, along with some photographs and postcards that he also sent home.[699]

Robert was assigned as a private to the 7th Reinforcements to the 13th Battalion and undertook initial training at Liverpool. His brother, Leonard, enlisted in July 1915 and was also assigned to the 13th Battalion's reinforcements and both embarked from Sydney on 20 August 1915 on board HMAT A9 *Shropshire*. Robert was promoted to the rank of acting corporal as part of the reinforcement detail. The battalion's reinforcements were commanded by Robert's friend, Lieutenant Harold Leslie Henley.[700] Lt Henley wrote to Robert and Leonard's father on 14 September 1915 while at sea to reassure him that his sons were in the best of health and spirit.[701]

The brothers arrived in Egypt where they undertook further training at Zeitoun, all the time on 24 hours' notice of possible assignment to either Gallipoli or Salonika. During this time, Robert met plenty of men that he knew, including the Kirkwoods,[702] and came into contact with men who had served at Gallipoli and been evacuated. Robert wrote in one of his letters to his mother[703]:

> Everybody here has a terrible set on Kitchener's Army at the front say they are no good at all in fact the Indians will not fight with them and all say that had there been enough Australians in the first landing things would have been very different.

While in Egypt, Robert applied to join the machine gun training school. He was one of three of the thirty applicants who was chosen to attend the school, which Robert noted in his letters made him feel

---

[699] Robert's correspondence accessible at https://www.awm.gov.au/collection/C92650
[700] Lt Harold Leslie Henley is also commemorated on the Drummoyne War Memorial. See his separate account.
[701] Letters from Robert James Henderson, 1915 - https://www.awm.gov.au/collection/C2134042?image=11
[702] Noel, John, William and Phillip Kirkwood all enlisted. William and Phillip were killed in action and are commemorated on the Drummoyne War Memorial. See their separate accounts.
[703] Letters from Robert James Henderson, 1915 - https://www.awm.gov.au/collection/C2134042?image=13

'quite hot stuff.' As a consequence, however, Robert missed out on sailing with his brother and the other reinforcements to the 13th Battalion who embarked from Alexandria on 18 October 1915 for service on the Gallipoli peninsula. Robert completed his training on machine guns and enjoyed the additional time to socialise with Australian nurses and explore Cairo and the surrounding environs.

After completing his course, Robert qualified to be a machine gun sergeant but was uncertain if any position was available or when he would join his battalion. In one letter to his mother, he commented that machine gunners considered themselves 'too high and mighty to mix with the infantry.'[704] While he awaited orders, Robert kept himself entertained in Egypt noting that Cairo was the most immoral place but at the same time he found himself becoming more extravagant, needing his father to transfer money to help him to keep up his social and entertainment activities. All the time, Robert heard no news of his brother Leonard.

Robert's time in Egypt abruptly ended on 12 November 1915 when after returning from a night on the town at about 10:30 p.m., and with theatre plans and a trip organised with one of the nurses for the weekend, he received orders to leave Zeitoun for Alexandria at 6 a.m. the next morning. After a five-hour train journey, Robert embarked on HT *Argylshire* from Alexandria on 14 November 1915. While at sea he wrote that he still did not know where he was headed but guessed Lemnos Island. He was correct and would spend the next three weeks on board the *Argylshire* moored in Mudros Harbour enduring the monotony of life on the ship, eager to get to the peninsula.

---

[704] Letters from Robert James Henderson, 1915 - https://www.awm.gov.au/collection/C2134042?image=28

Brendan Bateman

A postcard from Robert to his sister Jane being a photo of Robert and some comrades enjoying the pyramids by camel and donkey. Photographs relating to Robert James Henderson, 1916-1918 - https://www.awm.gov.au/collection/C2134051?image=1

Robert finally joined his battalion on Gallipoli on 8 December 1915, as one of 36 reinforcements who arrived on that day.[705] After a three and half mile march through the cliffs from the beach, he arrived at Durrant's Post where the 4th Brigade was situated. Robert quickly met up with his brother Leonard and Leslie Henley, as well as many other men he recognised. Robert lost his temporary rank and was assigned to the machine gun section of the 13th Battalion.

Robert arrived just before the decision was made to evacuate Australian forces from ANZAC Cove. His stay on the peninsula was to last only two weeks before he was evacuated. While at sea after his evacuation, Robert wrote to his mother on 30 December 1915[706]:

> We are on our way to Egypt 'again' travelling on a boat about 11,000 tons belonging to the Allen Line. Suppose you have had all sorts of reports about the evacuation from the peninsula. Everything went off very well about 140,000 troops being taken away in 2 days and nights without any casualties. The machine gun sections were about the last to get off. It was a beautiful moonlight night and the last night there every section moved away at specified time and embarked. Mr Turk all unconscious of the move was blazing away. Would like [to] know what he thought when he discovered no-one was there.
>
> We had great fun setting bayonets, tins etc in the ground so that when anyone pulled them out, off would go a bomb. Then all sorts of messages were left in the dugouts wishing the Turks the compliments of the season etc in all sorts of language.

---

[705] 13th Battalion Unit Diary December 1915 - https://www.awm.gov.au/collection/C1342716?image=3
[706] Letters from Robert James Henderson, 1915 - https://www.awm.gov.au/collection/C2134042?image=42

I had about a fortnight there it was a dreary place and am glad to get away although it hurt some sneaking away all the graves of the fellows who fell before, still suppose it was for the best. Do not know where we will go next. All sorts of rumours about going to London then to France also fighting on the Suez Canal.

Robert arrived in Alexandria on 3 January 1916 via Lemnos on HT *Tunisian* and moved to a new camp at Ismailia before heading to the Suez Canal at Moascar. While the battalions were being refitted and reinforced, he received news from Leslie Henley, then second in command of B Company, that Leslie's mother and sister, Millicent (Millie) would be arriving in Alexandria on 13 February 1916.

Mrs Henley, Leslie Henley, Robert Henderson and Captain Fox in Egypt 1916. Photographs relating to Robert James Henderson, 1916-1918 - https://www.awm.gov.au/collection/C2134052?image=49

On about 20 February 1916, the battalion moved to Tel El Kebir, and Robert wrote to his sister Jane recording that the division was to be split from the New Zealanders to form a purely Australian division. He wrote 'everybody is dreadfully upset both our chaps and the New Zealanders'[707] and in a letter a week later, Robert informed his mother of their arrival in Tel El Kebir noting 'we are all going to be reformed and adjusted and expect to put in about 4 weeks hard work then to imshi to France and have a go at the square heads.'[708] In addition to expressing the opinion that the war would end in that year, Robert also conveyed news that he had been recommended for a commission, which came as 'a hell of a shock'.[709]

Robert was transferred to Zeitoun to undertake the infantry training course for officers, and while on the way, went shopping in Cairo to 'make myself presentable',[710] which resulted in another cable to his father requesting further money. He wrote his mother on 5 March 'this is all quite a treat to have but damned expensive but if one takes on these swank jobs one must be prepared to live up to them I suppose.'[711] Robert particularly enjoyed the benefits of having a batman to clean his boots and make his bed.

In the same letter, Robert reported on Leonard's transfer to the 45th Battalion during 'this splitting up business.' He noted 'I could easily claim him and get him back with me but think it rather a good idea to be separated.'[712]

---

[707] Letters from Robert James Henderson, January - June 1916 - https://www.awm.gov.au/collection/C2134043?image=25
[708] Letters from Robert James Henderson, January - June 1916 - https://www.awm.gov.au/collection/C2134043?image=26 . The word 'imshi' is Australian military slang, meaning to go away or to be off. It is thought to be an adoption of an Arabic word of the same meaning - https://www.collinsdictionary.com/dictionary/english/imshi#
[709] Letters from Robert James Henderson, January - June 1916 - https://www.awm.gov.au/collection/C2134043?image=31
[710] Letters from Robert James Henderson, January - June 1916 - https://www.awm.gov.au/collection/C2134043?image=33
[711] Letters from Robert James Henderson, January - June 1916 - https://www.awm.gov.au/collection/C2134043?image=34
[712] Letters from Robert James Henderson, January - June 1916 - https://www.awm.gov.au/collection/C2134043?image=35

After completing his three-week officer training course, Robert was promoted to second lieutenant on 16 March 1916[713] and assigned to A Company in the 13th Battalion, but still managed some time in Cairo to catch up with members of the Henley family. In April, he wrote to his brother Stewart (whom he referred to as 'Mick') that although the higher pay as an officer was most welcome, 'mess accounts, batman, drinks, cards etc all of which one must indulge in, it does not go very far.'[714]

Photo of the Officers Class School of Instruction, Zeitoun, attended by Robert Henderson. Photographs relating to Robert James Henderson, 1916-1918 - https://www.awm.gov.au/collection/C2134051?image=3

By early April 1916, the battalion was based at Serapeum. With his platoon, Robert was involved in the planning for ANZAC Day, commemorating the landing 12 months prior, which he regarded as quite

---

[713] Official notice was published in the Commonwealth Gazette in June 1916 – see 1916 'AUSTRALIAN IMPERIAL FORCE.', *Commonwealth of Australia Gazette* (National: 1901-1973), 29 June, p. 1472, viewed 16 Sep 2023, http://nla.gov.au/nla.news-article232469407
[714] Letters from Robert James Henderson, January - June 1916 - https://www.awm.gov.au/collection/C2134043?image=72

a success with a swimming carnival organised at the Suez Canal. The only thing spoiling the day was the terrible heat.[715]

The monotony of routine drilling in the camp and the overbearing heat wore down the patience of the troops, and not the least that of Robert. On 14 May 1916, Robert advised his brother Stewart in a letter[716] that he had converted to Church of England[717] in order to get a day trip to Cairo and participate in a confirmation service officiated by the Bishop of Jerusalem. A trip to the pub before and after the service raised the spirits of the participating men immeasurably. On returning to the camp, Robert reported that the extreme heat continued for several days after. On one occasion, the heat was so intense that the men were dismissed from further duty at 8:30 a.m., and Robert decided to spend all day in silk pyjamas that he had brought from Australia[718]:

> Of course, I got a cheer but was generally envied by all. It was terribly hot and I was the most comfortable which is not saying much. However, my pyjamas seemed to send everybody mad for after dinner everyone got into some sort of fancy dress, swimming costumes, pyjamas of all colours etc.

There then followed a procession to the officers' messes of the neighbouring battalions, inviting them back to the 13th Battalion officers' mess until about 60 officers were in attendance where songs were sung and at least four cases of beer and several bottles of whiskey were consumed.

---

[715] Letters from Robert James Henderson, January - June 1916 - https://www.awm.gov.au/collection/C2134043?image=80 . In the same letter to his mother dated 28 April 1916, Robert noted that he had met with John (Jack) Kirkwood who was a second lieutenant in the 45th Battalion which was the sister battalion of the 13th Battalion.
[716] Letters from Robert James Henderson, January - June 1916 - https://www.awm.gov.au/collection/C2134043?image=85
[717] Robert noted his religion as Presbyterian on his attestation papers.
[718] Letters from Robert James Henderson, January - June 1916 - https://www.awm.gov.au/collection/C2134043?image=87

Kit inspection by the Brigadier at Serapeum just before leaving for France. Photographs relating to Robert James Henderson, 1916-1918 - https://www.awm.gov.au/collection/C2134052?image=55

While Robert and his colleagues expected to be posted to France at any time, the delay caused concern that they were destined to remain in the defence of Egypt, and continue to endure the heat and sandstorms, or be posted to another difficult environment. Relief finally occurred at the end of May 1916 when the battalion received orders to entrain for the Port of Alexandria. The majority of the battalion embarked from Alexandria on HMT *Transylvania* on 1 June 1916, arriving at Marseilles on 8 June.

The journey from Marseilles to the battlefields of northern France by train was a delight for Robert compared to the landscape of Egypt. In a letter to his mother dated 11 June 1916, Robert recorded the absolute pleasure in 'passing through a huge park the whole way. I have never seen anything that could come anywhere near the beauty and picturesqueness of the country. .. I never thought that anything like this could exist and I simply enjoyed every minute of the trip.'[719] So taken with the country that on one stop, Robert was among a number of others who missed the departure time of the troop train. On the journey to catch up with his unit, Robert reported to his mother that the crisis had considerably improved his French.

The proximity of the front to London, however, enticed Robert to think of a possible trip for which he would need money and decided to cable his father to send £50 to the Commonwealth Bank in London to fund his future adventures. For the time being, however, Robert decided to defer any leave until he had had a 'smack at the Germans.' Other motivations may have been in play as he also advised his mother[720]:

> Please excuse the rambling, disjointed letter but I seem to be in a perfect whirl at present everything is so novel and new, and such a pleasant change from Egypt. Tell Mick the girls are simply bosca here, they look so clean and fresh after Egypt but all without exception are as hot as mustard. This country will always do me.

Robert also received correspondence from Ms Hope Davies who lived in Liverpool, England, which had started when Robert was in Egypt. Although Robert reported to his mother in a letter dated 18

---

[719] Letters from Robert James Henderson, January - June 1916 - https://www.awm.gov.au/collection/C2134043?image=96
[720] Letters from Robert James Henderson, January - June 1916 - https://www.awm.gov.au/collection/C2134043?image=98

June 1916 that Ms Davies was 'some hard nut by her letters, it is great fun writing to people you do not know both saying all sorts of mad things.'[721] In addition to receiving a 'bosca' photo of Ms Davies from her, Robert noted that as he was now within a day's travel to London, he was greatly looking forward to 'seeing this little lass for she looks some class.' In a later letter, Robert confessed he and Ms Davies 'are having a great flirt in our correspondence.'[722]

Photograph of Hope Davies, the girl from Liverpool, England, with whom Robert had a flirtatious relationship by correspondence. Robert believed she was in love with him but the feelings were not reciprocated. Photographs relating to Robert James Henderson, 1916-1918 - https://www.awm.gov.au/collection/C2134052?image=5 (public domain).

---

[721] Letters from Robert James Henderson, January - June 1916 - https://www.awm.gov.au/collection/C2134043?image=103
[722] Letters from Robert James Henderson, January - June 1916 - https://www.awm.gov.au/collection/C2134043?image=109

Robert and his colleagues quickly discovered that the conditions at the front were very different from that at Gallipoli. In addition to having to go everywhere with a gas mask and undertake specialist training in gas attacks, the impact of the German artillery was on another level. Shortly after arriving at the front, units of the battalion rotated through the front-line trenches near Bois Grenier for three days to become acclimatised the trench warfare on the Western Front.[723] As their time in the trenches increased, Robert noted[724]:

Fighting on the Peninsular as far as my experience goes was a baby to this and all the old hands are of a similar experience.

Another new feature in trench warfare on the Western Front was the specialist role of bombardiers in raiding enemy trenches. Robert was sent to specialist training at a bombing school and eventually became the battalion's bombing officer. A very tricky job, Robert expected to be blown up sooner or later by 'the rotten things,' but recognised it was 'all in the game.' He attributed his skill for throwing bombs to his cricket such that 'given a fair duel with any Germans feel sure he would get the worst of it.'[725]

The 13th Battalion had its first major action of the Western Front at Mouquet Farm, near Pozières, in August 1916. On 7 August, the battalion less C Company moved into Sausage Valley as the reserve battalion, employed in ration fatigues and sapping towards the new firing line. Even in the reserve position, the battalion suffered casualties of one killed and 32 wounded from enemy artillery.[726] On 9 August, A Company moved forward to support the 16th Battalion to take its position in the trenches as the 16th Battalion advanced. The battalion then relieved the 15th Battalion at Pozières in the afternoon

---

[723] 13th Battalion Unit Diary June 1916 - https://www.awm.gov.au/collection/C1342723?image=5
[724] Letters from Robert James Henderson, July - December 1916 - https://www.awm.gov.au/collection/C2134047?image=4
[725] Letters from Robert James Henderson, July - December 1916 - https://www.awm.gov.au/collection/C2134047?image=7
[726] 13th Battalion Unit Diary August 1916 - https://www.awm.gov.au/collection/C1342725?image=3

of 10 August, with A and C Companies in the front line. While waiting to advance, these companies were subject to intense German artillery fire. At 1:00 a.m. on 11 August, the attacking companies of the battalion advanced under a covering barrage. Although the companies captured and had commenced consolidating their positions by 2:00 a.m., they became subjected to a fierce German artillery bombardment, which increased in intensity until 9:00 p.m. before decreasing to 'normal' at 5:00 a.m. on 12 August.

The attack was renewed on the evening of 12 August, which attracted intense and sustained artillery fire. A further attack by the battalion took place on 14 August, enjoying a modicum of success. The 13th Battalion was in the centre of the line with the 50th Battalion and 51st Battalion on either side. The 13th Battalion achieved some success, with the attacking waves led by Captain Harry Murray securing about 200 yards of the German *Fabeck Graben* trench. However, the attacking companies of the 13th Battalion were badly exposed as neither the 50th nor 51st Battalion had managed to make any headway.

The battalion's flanks almost immediately came under heavy counter-attack from three sides, forcing Captain Murray to withdraw his men. Captain Murray organised a fighting withdrawal to enable the wounded to be evacuated, stationing posts at intervals. The Germans pressed their attack with bombs being thrown by each side to drive the other back. By the time Captain Murray's men had reached the second last post, they were down to only six bombs. As wounded still needed to be evacuated, the position was critical. It was at this moment that Robert Henderson arrived with two sections, each man carrying thirty bombs, which enabled the advancing Germans to be driven off, and the 13th Battalion to withdraw over no man's land entirely unmolested.[727]

Captain Murray later recounted the events of the withdrawal[728]:

---

[727] Bean, *Official History*, Vol. 3, pp. 766-769.
[728] G Franki and C Slayter, *Mad Harry: Australia's Most Decorated Soldier*, Kangaroo Press, Sydney, 2003, p62 cited in *Diggers in France: Australian Soldiers on the Western Front*, R Travers, ABC Books, Sydney, 2008

It looked as if we were to be reduced to our last resort – the bayonet – but then I heard dear old Bob Henderson's voice calling for me. He was our bombing officer and I called out promptly. 'Here I am Bob – have you any bombs?' and back came his reply, like a returning wave, and couched in strong Australianese, 'ANY BLOODY AMOUNT! THROWERS TO THE FRONT'.

Robert wrote to his mother on 18 August 1916, having just come out of the firing line[729]:

> ... believe me those of us who are left [have] been through hell about six times. It is not a bit of use trying to tell you anything about it, the whole thing is so ghastly as to be indescribable and doing my level best to get the whole thing out of my mind which is indeed hard.

Robert noted in his letter that only about half the battalion managed to come out of the line, and of the 23 officers that went in, 17 were lost.[730] One of those officers was Robert's friend Leslie Henley who by that stage had been promoted to captain. Robert was near Leslie on their way out of the trenches and well behind the firing line when a shell burst killed him.

During the battle, Robert's bombing platoon had suffered extensive losses having 'hand to hand goes with the Huns.' In one instance, Robert recorded how he and a couple of men had approached a German trench that had a 30-feet deep dug out. After Robert threw in a smoke bomb and called on 'Fritz' to come out, three Germans came out. When asked if there was anyone else in the dugout, one German replied no. A couple of minutes later, another German came out

---

[729] Letters from Robert James Henderson, July - December 1916 - https://www.awm.gov.au/collection/C2134047?image=11

[730] According to the 13th Battalion Unit Diary, total casualties from 7-15 August 1916 were officers one killed, 12 wounded, four missing and one prisoner of war, and other ranks 37 killed, 302 wounded, 28 missing and one prisoner of war - https://www.awm.gov.au/collection/C1342725?image=11

where upon one of Robert's men singled out the German who had said that there was no one else in the dugout, called him a liar and promptly bayoneted him. Robert wrote[731]:

> It seems cold hearted but he deserved it and one cannot be too careful. If he had worked along the trench this fellow would have come out and shot us from behind.

Robert's conduct during the attack came to the attention of his commanders, with his colonel reporting Robert's bravery to General Cox, the division commander who wrote Robert a congratulatory card.

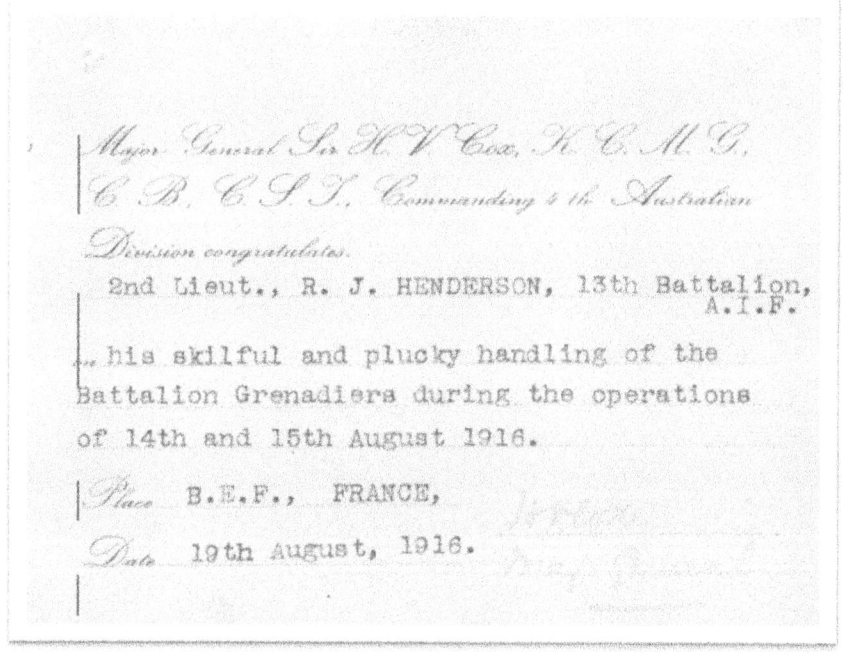

The first of three congratulatory cards that Robert would receive for his gallantry in action. Material relating to the promotion and awards of Robert James Henderson, 1916-1919 - https://www.awm.gov.au/collection/C2134053 (public domain).

---

[731] Letters from Robert James Henderson, July - December 1916 - https://www.awm.gov.au/collection/C2134047?image=13

Robert joked in his letter to his mother that people would now have to pay to speak to him, with all the shaking of hands and being congratulated by the general. He also lamented that the worst thing about this was that he now has a reputation to live up to, which will entail all sorts of risks, 'but this sort of thing must go on.'[732]

Robert was promoted to full lieutenant on 19 August 1916[733] and reported to his mother that he had received another great letter from Hope Davies and predicted that he would have a great time in England if he was ever lucky enough to get across there. However, he predicted that the only chance may be to 'get a decent sort of a wound, leave being out of the question.'[734]

Robert would get that chance in the next attempt to capture Mouquet Farm. This time the 13th Battalion was to attack along the same route but with the 16th Battalion on its left. The left company of the 13th Battalion under Captain Harry Murray succeeded in capturing its objective. Robert Henderson, leading the regimental bombers, attacked the German posts, enabling Captain Murray's men to seize the *Fabeck* trench, but with tremendous loss. On the left flank, initially meeting strong opposition, Robert was reported to have cleverly forced his way forward under cover of a Stokes mortar barrage to form a junction with Captain Murray, thus temporarily occupying 150 yards of the German trench.[735] Captain Murray arranged his men into seven posts of three men each, with a party of five bombers under Lt Henderson and a roving commission to reinforce wherever the enemy counter- attacked. Each German attack was met with a dense shower of bombs, as Lt Henderson had ensured that his bombers brought a large supply.

---

[732] Letters from Robert James Henderson, July - December 1916 - https://www.awm.gov.au/collection/C2134047?image=14
[733] Notice of Robert's promotion was not published in the Commonwealth Gazette until January 1917 – see AUSTRALIAN IMPERIAL FORCE. (1917, January 18). *Commonwealth of Australia Gazette* (National: 1901-1973), p. 70. Retrieved September 16, 2023, from http://nla.gov.au/nla.news-article232452639
[734] Letters from Robert James Henderson, July - December 1916 - https://www.awm.gov.au/collection/C2134047?image=15
[735] Bean, *Official History*, Vol. 5 p. 831-832.

Like the previous attack on Mouquet Farm, the units on the flank failed to secure their objectives, leaving Captain Murray and his men badly exposed. A fighting withdrawal was needed again.[736] Just before midnight on 29 August 1916, while advancing across no man's land, Robert was wounded by machine gun fire suffering a gunshot wound to the right thigh, just above the knee.[737] For his conduct during the fighting at Mouquet Farm, Robert received a further congratulatory card from General Cox 'for his gallantry as bombing officer' on 29-30 August 1916.[738] Robert diminished the recognition telling his mother that he did not deserve 'all this rubbish and shall be getting a swelled head if this sort of thing goes on.'[739] Robert's name appeared in casualty lists published in September 1916.[740]

In a letter to his mother dated 3 September 1916 written while on the hospital ship, Robert reported how the machine gun bullet had passed right through his leg, without touching a bone. Despite being hit, he carried on fighting for another hour, then after having the wound temporarily dressed, walked five hours until he became lost. Falling upon a 'Tommy' dressing station, he was sent onto the town of Albert, from where he was moved by motor ambulance to Warloy and eventually put on a hospital train at Rouen bound for Calais, from whence he would travel by hospital ship to England. Robert was admitted to the 4th London General Hospital at Denmark Hill, in southeast London, finally getting his wish for a trip to the capital. Although only expecting to be out of action for no more than a month, Robert's wound turned septic, which required an operation and

---

[736] Bean, *Official History*, Vol. 5 p. 835.
[737] The 13th Battalion Unit diary contains an appendix reporting on the further attack on 29-30 August and states that Robert, along with Captain Murray, were wounded on 30 August 1916 during the fighting withdrawal -
https://www.awm.gov.au/collection/C1342725?image=14
[738] Material relating to the promotion and awards of Robert James Henderson, 1916-1919 -
https://www.awm.gov.au/collection/C2134053?image=2
[739] Letters from Robert James Henderson, July - December 1916 -
https://www.awm.gov.au/collection/C2134047?image=14
[740] NEW SOUTH WALES. (1916, September 30). *The Sydney Morning Herald* (NSW: 1842-1954), p. 10. Retrieved September 16, 2023, from http://nla.gov.au/nla.news-article15677027

extensive care. In all, Robert would be in hospital or convalescing for more than six months.

Although the slow recovery of Robert's leg would drive him to despair, he wasted no time in organising his social calendar so that when the chance finally arose, he could take in the sights, sounds and girls of London. Even while still on the hospital ship on the way to England, he announced to his mother that he intended to cable his father for more money to assist in meeting his anticipated expenses. He also proposed to look 'the good Hope Davies up and see what sort of a lass she is.'[741] Among the more solemn duties that Robert intended to perform while in England was to visit Leslie Henley's family. He had not written to them since Leslie's death as, although he had tried, he had not been able to bring himself to do so. He preferred to see them personally and explain the circumstances of Leslie's death.[742]

Among the other excitements that Robert experienced in London was a Zeppelin overnight raid in the first few weeks of his stay in hospital with the bombs and gun fire waking up the patients. The disturbance, however, paled in comparison to the shelling he experienced on the Western Front, so he just rolled over in his bed and went back to sleep.[743] By early October, Robert was allowed out for short day trips into the city, with his first involving lunch at the Regent Palace Hotel. Shortly after, he obtained permission to stay out later in the night, and in the company of a Canadian officer attended a 'flash joint for tea [and] lost my heart 30 times in 30 minutes.'[744]

While Robert harboured the ambition to meet up with Hope Davies, who lived in Liverpool, he first went out with her sister Gwen, who worked in London. Like her sister, and most of the women that

---

[741] Letters from Robert James Henderson, July - December 1916 - https://www.awm.gov.au/collection/C2134047?image=23
[742] Letters from Robert James Henderson, July - December 1916 - https://www.awm.gov.au/collection/C2134047?image=28
[743] Letters from Robert James Henderson, July - December 1916 - https://www.awm.gov.au/collection/C2134047?image=39
[744] Letters from Robert James Henderson, July - December 1916 - https://www.awm.gov.au/collection/C2134047?image=46

Robert came across in London for that matter, Gwen was 'some hot stuff'[745] and they arranged for more outings. Unfortunately, Robert's social activities were severely curtailed when in mid-October 1916, his leg wound turned bad again. Although he avoided another operation, he was confined to hospital to bring the infection under control. Robert's confinement did not last long as he used his charm on the nurses to persuade them to allow him out to town. Concerts, theatre and opera filled his busy social diary interspersed with lunches, teas and dinners at various hotels, clubs and venues such as the Trocadero. On many occasions, Robert ended up in the company of ladies who gave him the 'glad eye.' Robert wrote to his mother on 24 October[746]:

> I have been in Cairo and Alexandria in Egypt, such places as Marseilles, Amiens, Rouen in France and London, and consider the last named the worst morally – this place is simply the limit.

And Robert pushed the limit during his extended time in London. He wrote to his sister Jane at the end of November[747]:

> Of course am having the time of my life here in London, the hospital is more or less a boarding house for me now, go out every day and night which of course requires tons of money for believe me this is the city to spend it in. .. There is absolutely no place like London for having a good time and believe me I am taking advantage of my opportunity.

By the end of November, Robert's leg wound was healing nicely, with only a little limp evident. He was resigned to remaining in London over Christmas and the New Year, but with the onset of the cold weather, he felt both relieved and guilty that he was not in the front lines. The feeling of guilt, however, soon passed as Robert attended

---

[745] Letters from Robert James Henderson, July - December 1916 - https://www.awm.gov.au/collection/C2134047?image=52
[746] Letters from Robert James Henderson, July - December 1916 - https://www.awm.gov.au/collection/C2134047?image=59
[747] Letters from Robert James Henderson, July - December 1916 - https://www.awm.gov.au/collection/C2134047?image=77

numerous 'swank' functions and attended on an equal number of ladies. In a sign of the social changes brought about by the war, Robert remarked to his brother that these ladies 'smoke their cigarettes and drink their whiskey & soda with consummate ease, in fact it is quite in order to take girls into a pub and have a drink with them. I mean quite respectable people you know.'[748]

The invitations flowed to attend 'at home stunts' where high society ladies invited a group of wounded officers to attend their homes for lunch or afternoon tea, in some cases involving butlers and footmen. On one occasion, in December 1916, Robert met Lady Birdwood, the wife of the commander of I ANZAC Corps, and who had commanded ANZAC forces at Gallipoli. Robert described Lady Birdwood as very charming, 'but not more so than the General, he is a great man and well-liked by all,'[749] confirming the warmth with which General Birdwood was regarded by the Australians.

Robert finally committed to travel to Liverpool at the invitation of Mrs Davies to spend Christmas with her family, including the great flirt, Hope Davies. But the long-awaited meeting was not to be as just before Christmas, Robert was advised that Mr Davies had come down seriously ill and the event cancelled. In his letters, Robert betrays that the change in circumstance was not overly disappointing, as he would happily remain in London over Christmas where he expected to have a 'ripping time.'[750]

Early January 1917 saw Robert on a jaunt to his father's birthplace, Scotland. Largely unimpressed by Edinburgh, he considered it quite a dead city compared to London. One thing that was to his liking was the fine whiskey that the Scots brewed, in which he regularly imbibed. As time passed, and his leg improved, Robert expected to be discharged before the end of January so he would be back with his unit

---

[748] Letters from Robert James Henderson, July - December 1916 - https://www.awm.gov.au/collection/C2134047?image=87
[749] Letters from Robert James Henderson, July - December 1916 - https://www.awm.gov.au/collection/C2134047?image=97
[750] Letters from Robert James Henderson, July - December 1916 - https://www.awm.gov.au/collection/C2134047?image=108

by mid-February. This, however, was not to be as the Medical Board was concerned that his leg would not withstand the rigours of front-line action, at most recommending him for light duties. This would condemn Robert to being posted to a training camp somewhere in England, the idea of which was abhorrent to him.

While at dinner on the night of 19 January 1917, Robert also experienced one of the tragic events in wartime London, with the explosion at a munitions factory in the east end. Robert remarked to his mother that it was a terrific explosion, with the concussion so bad that windows cracked. Initially, Robert thought that it might have been bombs from a Zeppelin, but subsequently ascertained that a munitions factory some three miles away had blown up. He commented that the damage and loss of life was bad but that the information coming through was very vague, with the press not able to say much about these things.[751] The explosion at the Silvertown munitions factory killed 73 people, wounded more than 400 and destroyed or badly damaged approximately 900 properties in close proximity to the factory. It is estimated 60,000 further properties suffered some damage from the explosion including shattered or broken windows.[752]

Resigned to a further extension of his stay in hospital, Robert was also resigned to not meeting with Hope Davies. In a letter dated 27 January 1917 to his brother Stewart, Robert wrote[753]:

> As for Hope the dear little thing I have never yet seen her and probably never shall you know. I think everything would be spoilt if we ever met.

Two days later, Robert's frustration was exacerbated when he was advised by his doctor that he would not discharge him from the

---

[751] Letters from Robert James Henderson, January - June 1917 - https://www.awm.gov.au/collection/C2134048?image=17
[752] https://livesofthefirstworldwar.org/community/2397
[753] Letters from Robert James Henderson, January - June 1917 - https://www.awm.gov.au/collection/C2134048?image=19

hospital owing to the continuing weak strength of his leg. Although disheartened by the news, in a letter to his mother he wrote[754]:

> Of course I could trade in this leg and say weakness etc and in all probability stay here for the duration without any difficulty, but not this chicken. .. [I will] make a point of getting back before the next offensive and do my bit.

Robert's state of mind was not so committed, as the fear of being killed if he went back to the front was clearly ever present. He confided this fear indirectly to his sister Lorna[755]:

> Say old girl what a shame if a fellow goes back to France and gets slugged after seeing, doing and learning so much in the past 18 months or so, I shall be most annoyed.

Robert took full advantage of his extra time in London, bragging about his social successes at the many afternoon teas to which he was invited at high society homes. Some of these events were also attended by girls who were invited to keep the officers company, and on one occasion taught Robert the fox trot, which he described as all the rage, and regarded himself as 'quite hot stuff at it now.'[756] He was also formally invited to the opening of Parliament House where he enjoyed an excellent view of the king and queen, referring to the king as 'Cousin George.'[757]

February brought Robert some good news – he finally heard from his brother Leonard who had been sent to undertake an officer training course at St John's College, Cambridge. Robert immediately travelled to Cambridge to be reunited with his brother. He was greatly cheered by his brother's presence in England, and the fact that for at

---

[754] Letters from Robert James Henderson, January - June 1917 - https://www.awm.gov.au/collection/C2134048?image=31
[755] Letters from Robert James Henderson, January - June 1917 - https://www.awm.gov.au/collection/C2134048?image=39
[756] Letters from Robert James Henderson, January - June 1917 - https://www.awm.gov.au/collection/C2134048?image=80
[757] Letters from Robert James Henderson, January - June 1917 - https://www.awm.gov.au/collection/C2134048?image=43

least six months he would be safe from death. The reunion, however, was a brief one as Robert needed to return to hospital for his next appointment with the Medical Board. Although kept waiting for almost four hours, he at last received the news he was awaiting – that he was once again fit for general service.[758] Granted 14 days' leave, Robert was to report to Perham Downs near Tidworth on 14 March, but this was delayed for another week to allow him to deal with some troublesome dental problems.

Robert arrived in Perham Downs and had great difficulty adjusting to the Spartan life on an army base after more or less six months of soft beds and clean sheets. He complained that he would 'go dippy' if he had to stay in 'this hole' for long.[759] Robert's first assignment was to take a draft of 90 reinforcements across to Boulogne from Folkestone, and onto the Australian base at Etaples. This was a soft introduction back to active service as he was required to return to England. After reporting back at Perham Downs, he quickly travelled to London to remind himself of the luxuries of the city again if only for a brief period.

Unfortunately, Robert's time in the 'hole' that was Perham Downs dragged on into mid-April 1917. It ended on 22 April 1917 when he reported to Lark Hill and received orders to proceed overseas with a draft of men for France, from whence he would finally rejoin his battalion. During the period that Robert's time in England had been extended, the battalion had been badly cut up in the fighting around Bullecourt.[760] Robert therefore expected that when he arrived, the battalion would be in need of reorganisation and filling out again with reinforcements, and therefore it would be a little while before it was in action again.

---

[758] Letters from Robert James Henderson, January - June 1917 - https://www.awm.gov.au/collection/C2134048?image=62
[759] Letters from Robert James Henderson, January - June 1917 - https://www.awm.gov.au/collection/C2134048?image=93
[760] The 13th Battalion's casualties during the Battle of Bullecourt totalled 21 officers and 489 other ranks, more than half the battalion's strength prior to the battle. Appendix B.42 to the 13th Battalion's unit diary, April 1917 - https://www.awm.gov.au/collection/C1342732?image=13

Robert proceeded overseas from England on 25 April 1917 and rejoined the battalion on 30 April 1917. The weather in the northern French spring was 'simply glorious .. It will be quite a pleasure to fight and die if need be under climatic conditions such as exist at present.'[761] Robert also noticed significant changes in the battalion. There were very few of the 'old fellows being left',[762] and the companies were very under strength. Assigned to second in command of A Company under Captain Harry Murray VC DSO (Bar) DCM, Robert felt the weight of expectation of serving under such a decorated and highly respected soldier.

The pressure was to grow on Robert as within a month of his arrival, Captain Murray was sent on leave to England and Robert assumed command of the company just before it moved into Belgian Flanders for its next 'stunt'. Shortly before its move, Robert wrote to his brother Mick congratulating him on him graduating with a law degree. He added[763]:

> Do not worry about coming over – the family is well represented. Besides you will be wanted at home to look after Mother and Father.

In early June, the battalion moved to Belgium and was engaged in the Battle of Messines as a prelude to the opening of the Third Battle of Ypres. Robert was wounded again in the right thigh, this time as a result of shrapnel from a high explosive shell. He was admitted to the 77th Field Ambulance on 12 June 1917, and from there evacuated to the 2nd CCS. While at the CCS, Robert wrote a letter to his mother dated 13 June 1917, in which he described his wound as 'very slight'.[764] He complained that he should not have needed to leave the line if the

---

[761] Letters from Robert James Henderson, January - June 1917 - https://www.awm.gov.au/collection/C2134048?image=114
[762] Letters from Robert James Henderson, January - June 1917 - https://www.awm.gov.au/collection/C2134048?image=116
[763] Letters from Robert James Henderson, January - June 1917 - https://www.awm.gov.au/collection/C2134048?image=129
[764] Letters from Robert James Henderson, January - June 1917 - https://www.awm.gov.au/collection/C2134048?image=136

doctor had managed to get the fragment out, but after probing about, it could not be located. As a consequence, Robert was transferred to a hospital train for Boulogne. He feared returning to England after only recently rejoining his battalion, and fully intended to get fixed up in Boulogne and remain in France. Of the battle, Robert wrote[765]:

> We have been in the push at Messines which no doubt you will have read all about by the time you get this note – it was quite a successful show but of course we suffered heavily as per usual .. was on my way to BHQ [Battalion Headquarters] to see the Colonel re the show when I was caught. Heard the shell coming and took a flying dive into a shell hole but it was too quick for me.

Robert tried to persuade the colonel to let him stay for the 'show' but the doctor would have none of that.

Although the fragment could not be located, Robert received his wish and was moved to the 2nd ANZAC Rest House at La Motte near Le Harve. A memo dated 22 June 1917 from the OIC advised Robert's father that Robert had been wounded for the second time but this does not appear to have been received by him.[766] A telegram from James Henderson dated 4 July 1917 to the OIC complains that no official information had been communicated in connection with Robert's wounding, presumably in response to Robert's name appearing on a casualty list.[767]

Robert was absent for only 10 days and was back with his company and in the front line by July 1917. Not long after, Robert was informed that he had been awarded the Military Cross for valour in action, which was presented to him by the commander of II ANZAC Corps,

---

[765] Letters from Robert James Henderson, January - June 1917 - https://www.awm.gov.au/collection/C2134048?image=137
[766] War service records accessible at https://recordsearch.naa.gov.au/SearchNRetrieve/Interface/ViewImage.aspx?B=5338868
[767] Australian Casualties. (1917, July 4). *Australian Town and Country Journal* (Sydney, NSW: 1870-1919), p. 15. Retrieved September 16, 2023, from http://nla.gov.au/nla.news-article263769981

General Godley on 10 July 1917.[768] He hoped that on his next trip to London, he would be lucky enough to be interviewed by 'Cousin George' and receive his medal.[769] The full citation published in the *Gazette* relating to the awarding of the Military Cross to Robert was as follows[770]:

> During the operations near MESSINES from 8th to 11th June 1917, this officer rendered valuable service in Command of a Company. While in process of relief his Company was twice caught in heavy barrages in the open and on each occasion his coolness and courage saved the situation.
>
> His Company was under heavy shell fire for three days near BETHLEHEM FARM, but he set his Company to work and consolidated the position in a most creditable manner.
>
> His personal reconnaissance reports from the front line were most valuable.

One of Robert's responsibilities and one in which he excelled was in organising the inter-Brigade sporting competitions while the battalions were in rest camps. Robert trained and captained the 13th Battalion's cricket team, and the competition between the units was fierce but friendly. The brigade commanders took a particular interest

---

[768] 13th Battalion Unit Diary July 1917 - https://www.awm.gov.au/collection/C1356089?image=13 . Notice was also published in BRAVE AUSTRALIANS. (1917, August 27). *The Argus* (Melbourne, Vic.: 1848-1957), p. 4. Retrieved September 16, 2023, from http://nla.gov.au/nla.news-article1645418 and THE AUSTRALIANS (1917, September 1). *Chronicle* (Adelaide, SA: 1895-1954), p. 38. Retrieved September 16, 2023, from http://nla.gov.au/nla.news-article87411259

[769] See also Letters from Robert James Henderson, July - December 1917 - https://www.awm.gov.au/collection/C2134049?image=2

[770] See Material relating to the promotion and awards of Robert James Henderson, 1916-1919 - https://www.awm.gov.au/collection/C2134053?image=10 ; The notice published in the *London Gazette* on 24 August 1917 stated that Robert displayed great 'coolness and courage on two critical occasions, when his company had been caught in heavy barrage in the open. He also worked at the consolidation of a position for three days under heavy shell fire, successfully completing the task.' The official notice was published in the *Commonwealth of Australia Gazette* on 20 December 1917. It is noted that the reference to Bethlehem Farm is an error as the location is more likely Bethleem Farm.

in the successes of their brigades in such competitions. The 4th Brigade won its fair share of trophies, with Robert ensuring that the collection was recorded for posterity.

The sporting trophies won by the 4th Infantry Brigade. Photographs relating to Robert James Henderson, 1916-1918 - https://www.awm.gov.au/collection/C2134051?image=9 (public domain).

Robert had been running A Company in place of (now) Major Murray for three months. In recognition of his responsibility, but also the casualties among the officer cadre, Robert was promoted to captain on 16 August 1917.

As the pressure of his time in the front lines grew, and the responsibilities of command weighed on him, Robert's attention turned to a possible sojourn in Paris or London. His letters betray a desire to go back to a city where he certainly knew how to have a good time or try an unfamiliar but famous city. In September 1917, Robert wrote to his mother that he expected to be back in action for another 'stunt' in about another three weeks[771]:

> Am getting full of these hop overs not for myself but for all these chaps under one's care. When you come to think of it, it is a huge responsibility to take a Company into action and of course officers and men must be killed and wounded etc. The whole thing is rotten.

In a further letter, just before the start of the coming offensive, Robert informed his mother that fortunately or unfortunately, he expected to be left out of the forthcoming stunt, as a result of orders to leave out two company commanders. Robert wrote[772]:

> I don't want it. Would sooner go in and have done with it, however, on the other hand, feel a spell from a show will do me no harm.

Robert was allowed to go on ten days leave to England, arriving in London on 23 September 1917 just as the 13th Battalion was moving back into the front lines outside of Ypres to join in support of the attack by the 5th Australian Division on Polygon Wood. Immediately on his arrival in London, he thought of going to Liverpool to see Hope Davies, but in a letter to his mother wrote that he did not know if he would be able to tear himself away from London. Robert did manage to tear himself away, finally meeting with Hope Davies on 29

---

[771] Letters from Robert James Henderson, July - December 1917 - https://www.awm.gov.au/collection/C2134049?image=17
[772] Letters from Robert James Henderson, July - December 1917 - https://www.awm.gov.au/collection/C2134049?image=24

September and gave her a good 'fly around'.[773] Perhaps in a sign that the mystery of the unknown was more exhilarating that the reality, Robert described Hope unenthusiastically as 'quite a nice kid and certainly enjoys being taken around and a good time.'[774] To his sister Jane, he advised that 'there is nothing doing, although I have lots of fun with these girls.'[775] Finally, cruelling any ambition on the part of his mother of a wartime romance, Robert wrote[776]:

> Glad you dote on Hope. She is a nice kid afraid she is madly in love with me but there is nothing doing. Am not likely to marry anyone on this side of the world. Tell Mick I shall reserve her for him.

Robert was only in Liverpool for two days before he returned to London. Late at night on 2 October 1917, he received a message from the battalion ordering his immediate return. Back with the battalion, he ascertained that there would shortly be another 'stunt' and that all officers were required on duty. At about the same time, Robert noted that the weather was raining and bitterly cold, a hallmark of the last stages of the Passchendaele offensive.

Although the 4th Brigade was not directly involved in the next period of fighting, which entailed the attack on Broodseinde Ridge, he was exposed to poison gas, resulting in the loss of his voice and blistering. Robert described the gas to his mum as 'beastly stuff'.[777] The effects of the gas lasted for some time, with Robert not fully recovering until February 1918.

---

[773] Letters from Robert James Henderson, July - December 1917 - https://www.awm.gov.au/collection/C2134049?image=35
[774] Letters from Robert James Henderson, July - December 1917 - https://www.awm.gov.au/collection/C2134049?image=35
[775] Letters from Robert James Henderson, July - December 1917 - https://www.awm.gov.au/collection/C2134049?image=46
[776] Letters from Robert James Henderson, 1918 - https://www.awm.gov.au/collection/C2134050?image=22
[777] Letters from Robert James Henderson, July - December 1917 - https://www.awm.gov.au/collection/C2134049?image=60

In December 1917, the battalion was moved to a forward area near Moislains, with Robert describing the accommodation as most uncomfortable and a 'hole'.[778] The battalion would serve Christmas and the New Year in Templeux La Fosse, northeast of the town of Péronne.

Robert Henderson winter 1917–1918 from personal photographs sent to his mother. On the reverse, it has in Robert's handwriting 'You see I [sic] just the same long skinny being.' Photographs relating to Robert James Henderson, 1916-1918 - https://www.awm.

---

[778] Letters from Robert James Henderson, July - December 1917 - https://www.awm.gov.au/collection/C2134049?image=67

By March 1918, while the battalion was based at Neuve Eglise in Belgium,[779] Robert reported that 'Fritz' was expected to launch a big attack at any time.[780] In a letter to his sister Lorna on 19 March 1918, he reported that the night before he had arrived back at his billets at 1:30 a.m. and had just gone off to sleep when the Germans started shelling the place with 'big stuff'.[781] This marked the start of the last major German offensive of the war. By 22 March 1918, the battalion's billets at Neuve Eglise came under artillery fire.[782]

Robert's next letters to his family are rushed but display an excitement of the events in April 1918 as Australian forces are thrown in to stop the German advance and fill the gaps appearing in the Allied front lines. The 4th Brigade had been given the objective of driving the Germans out of the village of Hebuterne, located northeast of Villers-Bretonneux. In a letter to his mother dated 7 April, Robert wrote of the fighting around Hebuterne as follows[783]:

> We are doing fine work here rushed up at a critical time. Drove the Hun out of the village and are keeping him at bay. Most thrilling experiences and hair breath escapes but so far am going strong. No news of any relief yet all are very weary. Have been going strong for the past eleven days. .. Of course, our casualties are heavy but the enemy's much heavier.

The commander of the 4th Brigade believed that it was necessary for the 13th and 14th Battalions to remain in the defence of Hebuterne in order to ensure that the village was held against the incessant German attacks and artillery fire, with only the 15th and 16th Battalions

---

[779] 13th Battalion Unit Diary March 1918 - https://www.awm.gov.au/collection/C1343231?image=4 . The town is also referred to as Nieuwkerke.
[780] Letters from Robert James Henderson, 1918 - https://www.awm.gov.au/collection/C2134050?image=25
[781] Letters from Robert James Henderson, 1918 - https://www.awm.gov.au/collection/C2134050?image=31
[782] 13th Battalion Unit Diary March 1918 - https://www.awm.gov.au/collection/C1343231?image=6
[783] Letters from Robert James Henderson, 1918 - https://www.awm.gov.au/collection/C2134050?image=34

provided relief.[784] The 13th and 14th Battalions were not relieved until 13 April 1918, with the 13th Battalion moved to Coigneux for rest and refitting.[785]

On 21 April 1918, Robert would write his final letters to his mother and brother. In those letters, Robert expected that they would have read about all the fighting that was now taking place around Villers-Bretonneux. In his letter to his mother, he wrote[786]:

> … and as far as the Australians are concerned far from being beaten they are doing wonderful work and have saved the situation on many occasions lately. [T]he highest praises has come and still comes to us from all the Heads. Of course, we are losing men but what else can be expected of you; do your job and after all it is good fun having a crack at the oncoming thousands of Huns even if one loses one's life eventually. Of course, those of us who are still going have had wonderful escapes to date, hard times, soft times, exciting times and very interesting times, worrying times and all the rest of it. Sometimes sad, sometimes humorous, wonderful experiences many of which could not be told.

In his letter to his brother, Robert was franker about the experience, describing how there was tons of fighting, and the Australians had saved the situation on more than one occasion. He also recorded how many 'originals' who had landed on Gallipoli had been killed in the most recent fighting, so that 'apparently, it is only a matter of time'. Robert went on[787]:

---

[784] 13th Battalion Unit Diary April 1918 – Appendix 1 - https://www.awm.gov.au/collection/C1343235?image=1
[785] 13th Battalion Unit Diary April 1918 - https://www.awm.gov.au/collection/C1343232
[786] Letters from Robert James Henderson, 1918 - https://www.awm.gov.au/collection/C2134050?image=40
[787] Letters from Robert James Henderson, 1918 - https://www.awm.gov.au/collection/C2134050?image=45

I am easy kid on the whole matter. One must look at this game from a philosophical stand point.

Robert also passed on a rhyme to his brother that had been sent to him by an English girl he had met, which he thought his brother might enjoy[788]:

There was a young lady of fashion
Who loved a man with great passion
and she smilingly said as she jumped into bed
'There's one thing that Lord Rhondda can't ration'.

On 28 April, the battalion moved back to the front lines relieving the 59th Battalion late in the evening, east of Villers-Bretonneux. Captain Henderson's A Company was in the front line on the right, with B Company on the left, and the other companies being in reserve.[789] The right part of the 13th Battalion's front occupied by A Company was regarded as the most vulnerable point. At 3:30 a.m. on 30 April, the A and B Companies pushed forward in conjunction with units from the adjoining the 46th Battalion to establish a new front line of posts.

On 1 May 1918, the commander of the battalion issued orders for A and B Companies to push posts further out to keep pressure on the enemy and prevent them from occupying key strong points. Captain Henderson was appointed to command this operation, after which he was to establish a new line and hand it over the C and D Companies the following morning. The operation was to commence at 2:00 a.m. on the night of 1–2 May.

According to the battalion's summary of operations report, the first phase of the operation had been successful notwithstanding

---

[788] Letters from Robert James Henderson, 1918 - https://www.awm.gov.au/collection/C2134050?image=46 . David Alfred Thomas, 1st Viscount of Rhondda, or commonly called Lord Rhondda, was appointed Minister for Food in June 1917 and responsible for introducing rationing in Britain during the last years of the war.

[789] 13th Battalion Unit Diary May 1918 –Appendix 1A Summary of Operations - https://www.awm.gov.au/collection/C1343236?image=8

heavy German machine gun fire. The second phase involved a raid on an enemy post. Before this could be launched, Captain Henderson was informed that the 47th Battalion had fallen back to their original position, thus leaving the 13th Battalion's flank in a precarious position. Ordering his raiding party to stand fast, Captain Henderson attended 'assiduously to the organisation of his new position', despite heavy German machine gun fire from the front and both flanks and even after daylight had broken. The commander of the battalion, Colonel D G Marks went onto to state[790]:

> I regret to say that he has been severely wounded by M.G. fire. His gallantry will form the subject of a special recommendation.

Robert's brother Leonard made inquiries of the battalion's officers regarding the circumstances of Robert's wounding and subsequent death and reported this to his family in a letter dated 24 May 1918. He further advised that Robert was hit in the left thigh by machine gun fire, causing a compound fracture of the femur, and it was this wound that would ultimately prove fatal.

According to a statement provided by Private Bruce Gough (1341) to the Red Cross,[791] he was the captain's runner, and after having secured their position, the captain decided to go over to B Company. This required traversing about 15 yards of open space. As soon as they started, a German machine gun opened up on them. When they had gone about ten yards, the captain was hit in the thigh and called out to Private Gough that they had 'got him'. Private Gough lay next to the captain for about fifteen minutes dressing his wound until stretcher bearers came and helped take him away. Private Gough saw the captain at the dressing station, and commented that he 'seemed very cheerful and told [Private Gough] that he would see him in England'.

---

[790] 13th Battalion Unit Diary May 1918 - https://www.awm.gov.au/collection/C1343236?image=9
[791] Australian Red Cross Wounded and Missing Files - https://www.awm.gov.au/collection/R1490825

Private Charles H Heathfield (168) who was at the dressing station and helped dress his wounds confirmed that Captain Henderson was very cheerful and chatted freely to those around him. Pte Gough added that Captain Henderson was one of the most popular officers in the battalion and that everyone felt his loss, sentiments echoed by Pte Heathfield, Private Robert J Freeman (1006) and Private George McGregor (1341) in their statements to the Red Cross.[792] All these reports were passed on by the Australian Red Cross to Millie Henley who was working in London with the Australian Comforts Fund.

Robert was evacuated on 2 May and admitted to the 12th Australian Field Ambulance and transferred to the 61st CCS at Vignacourt. On 3 May, he was transferred to Ambulance Train 7 and admitted to the 1st Canadian General Hospital, Etaples, France on 4 May. A letter from the officer commanding the hospital to the Australian Red Cross dated 29 May 1918 summarised the notes on Robert's field medical card. These indicated that Robert was admitted with a severe wound to the thigh which had fractured his femur longitudinally for about two-thirds of its length, resulting in about one-third of the shaft being removed in loose pieces. The report went on to state that Robert had been admitted to the hospital in a poor condition but the attending medical staff had hopes that he would recover. Robert was doing fairly well until 13 May 1918 when he suffered a secondary haemorrhage 'but in his low condition it was enough to result in his death, which took place a few hours later'.[793]

Robert was 32 years old. He was buried at the nearby Etaples Military Cemetery and his name appeared in casualty lists published on 30 May 1918.[794] Numerous family notices reporting Robert's death were also published in May and June 1918.[795] A memorial service was

---

[792] Australian Red Cross Wounded and Missing Files - https://www.awm.gov.au/collection/R1490825
[793] Australian Red Cross Wounded and Missing Files - https://www.awm.gov.au/collection/R1490825
[794] CASUALTY LIST (1918, May 30). *The Sun* (Sydney, NSW: 1910-1954), p. 6 (FINAL EXTRA). Retrieved May 23, 2023, from http://nla.gov.au/nla.news-article221936830
[795] Family Notices (1918, May 21). *The Daily Telegraph* (Sydney, NSW: 1883-1930), p. 4. Retrieved May 23, 2023, from http://nla.gov.au/nla.news-article239262262 ; Family Notices

conducted in Drummoyne by Rev. S B Reid later that month[796] and the following appeared in a tribute by the Balmain District Cricket Club published in the *Arrow* on 19 July 1918[797]:

> This gallant soldier was one of the most popular members of the club. His ever-smiling face and jovial and good-natured ways will always be missed by us. We sincerely sympathise with his parents in their great loss.

The New South Wales Cricket Association acknowledged Robert's death at its annual meeting in July 1918, among other members who had been recently killed in fighting.[798]

For his action during the fighting, Robert was posthumously awarded a bar to his Military Cross. The citation published in the *London Gazette* on 16 September 1918 states[799]:

> For conspicuous gallantry and devotion to duty. This officer, in command of a flank company in the front line, advanced his line to a point about 300 yards forward under heavy fire, but so effectively did he dispose his covering party that the remainder of the company was able to dig in with very few casualties.

(1918, May 21). *The Sydney Morning Herald* (NSW: 1842-1954), p. 6. Retrieved May 23, 2023, from http://nla.gov.au/nla.news-article15768418 ; Family Notices (1918, May 22). *The Sydney Morning Herald* (NSW: 1842-1954), p. 10. Retrieved May 23, 2023, from http://nla.gov.au/nla.news-article15768108 ; Family Notices (1918, May 28). *The Sydney Morning Herald* (NSW: 1842-1954), p. 6. Retrieved May 23, 2023, from http://nla.gov.au/nla.news-article15788783 ; 1918 'WAR CASUALTIES.', *The Sydney Morning Herald* (NSW: 1842-1954), 15 June, p. 14. , viewed 16 Sep 2023, http://nla.gov.au/nla.news-article15766069

[796] Advertising (1918, May 25). *The Sydney Morning Herald* (NSW: 1842-1954), p. 10. Retrieved May 23, 2023, from http://nla.gov.au/nla.news-article15785655

[797] CRICKET (1918, July 19). *Arrow* (Sydney, NSW: 1916-1933), p. 5. Retrieved May 23, 2023, from http://nla.gov.au/nla.news-article103524068

[798] CRICKET. (1918, July 30). *The Sydney Morning Herald* (NSW: 1842-1954), p. 9. Retrieved September 16, 2023, from http://nla.gov.au/nla.news-article15795817

[799] War service file - https://recordsearch.naa.gov.au/SearchNRetrieve/Interface/ViewImage.aspx?B=4104221

At dawn next morning he learnt that the unit on his right had withdrawn, so he had to go and adjust his posts to make a defensive flank, which he did under heavy fire, being severely wounded just as his task was completed.

The report of the award was published in newspapers in September 1918[800] with official notification of the award provided to James Henderson by letter dated 13 February 1919.[801] The original Military Cross and bar were sent to Robert's parents in March 1919.[802]

During the First World War, the area around Etaples was the scene of immense concentrations of Commonwealth reinforcement camps and hospitals. In 1917, 100,000 troops were camped among the sand dunes and the hospitals, which included eleven general, one stationary, four Red Cross hospitals and a convalescent depot. Etaples Military Cemetery, which was established next to the camp, contains 10,771 Commonwealth burials of the First World War, and is the largest cemetery in France maintained by the Commonwealth War Graves Commission.[803]

---

[800] AUSTRALIANS HONORED (1918, September 21). *The Sun* (Sydney, NSW: 1910-1954), p. 5 (FINAL SPORTING). Retrieved September 16, 2023, from http://nla.gov.au/nla.news-article221417202 . See also Material relating to the promotion and awards of Robert James Henderson, 1916-1919 - https://www.awm.gov.au/collection/C2134053?image=12

[801] The official notice was published in the *Commonwealth of Australia Gazette* on 4 February 1919.

[802] PERSONAL. (1919, March 4). *The Daily Telegraph* (Sydney, NSW: 1883-1930), p. 6. Retrieved May 23, 2023, from http://nla.gov.au/nla.news-article239592089 ; UNITED SERVICE. (1919, March 6). *Camden News* (NSW: 1895-1954), p. 1. Retrieved May 23, 2023, from http://nla.gov.au/nla.news-article136646234

[803] http://www.cwgc.org/find-a-cemetery/cemetery/56500/ETAPLES%20MILI-TARY%20CEMETERY

Drummoyne's Great War Volume 3

The Grave Registration Card and photograph provided to Robert's parents.
Photographs relating to Robert James Henderson, 1916-1918 -
https://www.awm.gov.au/collection/C2134052

Photograph of Etaples Military Cemetery. The War Graves Project, CWGC.
Reproduced with permission.

Photograph of the grave of Robert Henderson at Etaples Military Cemetery. The War Graves Project, CWGC. Reproduced with permission.

Bertie George Englert

Private, No. 7342

14th Battalion, 4th Infantry Brigade, 4th Australian Division

Killed in action 31 May 1918, Allonville, France

Buried Allonville Communal Cemetery, France

Gently sleeping till the day dawns

Studio portrait of Bertie Englert (courtesy Englert family).

Bertie George Englert was born on 1 March 1887 in Dungog, NSW.[804] Bertie was one of eight children and the eldest son of George Anton and Elizabeth Englert. His siblings were Guerle,[805] Eldred Anton,[806] Nellie Kathleen Carmen,[807] Bismark Carl,[808] Jack Rivis,[809] Dorothy

---

[804] NSW BDM Registration No. 20082/1887. Additional information provided by the Englert family – see https://georgeantonenglert.wordpress.com/bertie/ and https://vwma.org.au/explore/people/352453
[805] NSW BDM Registration No. 30058/1892. Sometimes spelt Gurle.
[806] NSW BDM Registration No. 28090/1894. Relatives believe his name was also spelt Eldrid.
[807] NSW BDM Registration No. 16832/1896.
[808] NSW BDM Registration No. 16268/1898. Relatives believe that his name was Carl Bismark.
[809] NSW BDM Registration No. 35026/1899.

Myrtle[810] and Audrey Phyllis.[811] By the time of the outbreak of the war, Bertie's parents had moved to Sydney and resided at 1 Napier Street, Drummoyne. Bertie married Ruth Zara Higgins in 1916[812] and lived with his in-laws at *Frampton*, 13 Westbourne Street, Drummoyne.[813]

A painter by occupation at the time of his enlistment on 9 October 1916 at The Royal Agricultural Showground camp, Sydney, Bertie was allocated to the 24th Reinforcements to the 14th Battalion.[814] Records created by family also report that Bertie was a pianist, trumpet player and bugler.[815] Bertie's younger brother Eldred also enlisted in the AIF, in November 1916.[816] As apparent from the marriage notice published in *The Sydney Morning Herald* on 16 December 1916, Bertie had already enlisted when he married Ruth[817]:

> ENGLERT- HIGGINS. - November 20, 1916, at St. Thomas', Balmain West, by Rev Luke Parr. Pte. Bertie George Englert, eldest son of Mr. and Mrs. Anton Englert, of Napier-street, Drummoyne, to Ruth Zara Higgins, second eldest daughter of Mr. and Mrs. Edmond Higgins, Frampton, Westbourne street, Drummoyne.

---

[810] NSW BDM Registration No. 36259/1901.
[811] NSW BDM Registration No. 26349/1908.
[812] NSW BDM Registration No. 13338/1916.
[813] Edmond J Higgins is recorded as residing at the property according to the General Index.
[814] War service records for Bertie George Englert accessible at https://recordsearch.naa.gov.au/SearchNRetrieve/Interface/ViewImage.aspx?B=3542972
[815] https://www.imdb.com/title/tt24638514/plotsummary/?ref_=tt_ov_pl
[816] https://aif.adfa.edu.au/showUnit?unitCode=CYC.ACB1R9
[817] Family Notices (1916, December 16). *The Sydney Morning Herald* (NSW: 1842-1954), p. 12. Retrieved May 25, 2023, from http://nla.gov.au/nla.news-article15702819

Brendan Bateman

Eldrid Anton Englert (left); Bertie George Englert (middle); unknown friend (right). Source – Englert family (https://georgeantonenglert.word-press.com/bertie/).

Bertie at Drummoyne. Source – Englert family (https://georgeantonenglert.wordpress.com/bertie/).

While at the general depot at Seymour, in early January 1917, Bertie was charged with being absent without leave for 8 days, for which he was fined £5 and sentenced to 40 days confinement to barracks. Shortly after his sentence expired, Bertie found himself embarking from Melbourne on 19 February 1917 bound for England on board HMAT A70 *Ballarat*.

A group of members of the 24th Reinforcements, 14th Battalion, prior to the departure of HMAT Ballarat (A70). AWM ID No. PB0205.

When in the English Channel on 25 April 1917, the *Ballarat* was attacked and sunk by a German U-boat, but without any casualties being suffered – all men on board were evacuated successfully before it sank. Bertie disembarked at Devonport on 25 April 1917, and three days later had arrived at the Australian training depot at Codford, joining the 4th Training Battalion.

Drummoyne's Great War Volume 3

The transport HMAT Ballarat after being torpedoed by a German submarine off the southern English coast. In the background a British destroyer is standing by to take the troops. 25 April 1917. AWM ID No. C01592.

Bertie undertook further training in preparation for joining the 14th Battalion. In August 1917, while still at Codford, Bertie was admitted to the group hospital suffering from renal calculus (kidney stones). Given his apparent musical capabilities, Bertie was a bugle player in the 14th Battalion band, and can be seen on parade here at Codford, England in 1917.[818]

---

[818] https://georgeantonenglert.wordpress.com/bertie/

Photograph of the 14th Battalion band at Codford, England c. 1917. Bertie Englert was a bugle player in the band. Source – Englert family (https://georgeantonenglert.wordpress.com/bertie/).

In November 1917, Bertie transferred to the 13th Training Battalion also at Codford, and by April 1918 had transferred to the 12th Training Battalion at Folkestone in preparation for embarkation for France. He arrived at the Australian main camp at Etaples, France, on 17 April 1918. Bertie was taken on strength by the 14th Battalion on 27 April 1918.

Established in September 1914 primarily with recruits from Melbourne and its surrounding suburbs, the 14th Battalion along with the 13th, 15th and 16th Battalions, formed the 4th Infantry Brigade commanded by then Colonel John Monash. The 4th Brigade landed at Gallipoli on the afternoon of 25 April 1915 and served at ANZAC Cove until evacuation in December 1915. The 14th Battalion became known as 'Jacka's Mob' owing to the heroics of Albert Jacka who was awarded the AIF's first Victoria Cross. In Egypt in 1916, the battalion was split, providing experienced men for the newly established 46th

Battalion. The 14th Battalion became part of the newly established 4th Division and served on the Western Front, seeing action at Pozières, Bullecourt and Ypres, before returning to the Somme in March 1918 to help stop the German spring offensive.[819]

Bertie was one of 221 other ranks who joined the battalion as reinforcements in April 1918. At the time he joined his battalion, it was at Foret de Mail just outside Amiens. The battalion paraded at 9:30 a.m. on 26 April with the commanding officer addressing the battalion and saying a few words of welcome to the newly arrived reinforcements.[820] On the same day, the battalion received orders that the 4th Australian Division was to replace the British 8th Division. They moved out on 27 April 1918, arriving at Villers-Bretonneux on 28 April. On 30 April, the battalion's strength included 27 officers and 561 other ranks in the front line, with 14 officers and 168 other ranks forming part of a rear detail at Allonville.[821]

During May 1918, the battalion was in and out of the front lines around Villers-Bretonneux, and on several occasions, came under gas attacks. On 22 May, the 4th Brigade moved to the Allonville area where it undertook training, interspersed with cricket games. In the same month, the Germans are said to have captured a handful of Australians who under interrogation divulged the location of the 4th Division's headquarters at Allonville.[822]

On 30 May, the battalion commenced preparations to move back to the front lines but during the night of 30–31 May 1918, the battalion diary recorded[823]:

---

[819] 14th Australian Infantry Battalion, Australian War Memorial - https://www.awm.gov.au/unit/U51454/
[820] 14th Battalion Unit Diary April 1918 - https://www.awm.gov.au/collection/C1343776?image=7
[821] 14th Battalion Unit Diary April 1918 - https://www.awm.gov.au/collection/C1343776?image=8
[822] Bean, *Official History*, Vol. 6, p. 109 fn2. McLachlan, *Walking with the ANZACS*, p. 194.
[823] 14th Battalion Unit Diary May 1918 - https://www.awm.gov.au/collection/C1343777?image=8

At about 1.15 a.m. the enemy shelled ALLONVILLE and one shell landed right in the large barn occupied by "A" Company, cutting it in halves. 13 O/Ranks killed; 56 wounded. Another shell landed in the barn occupied by "C" Company and Headquarters, causing 17 casualties. The behaviour of the men was excellent, as men were buried in the debris and had to be dug out and some of the wounds (the majority) were awful.

Total casualties at Allonville were 18 other ranks killed, and 68 wounded.[824] Among the dead was Bertie Englert. Charles Bean described the shell that hit the first barn at Allonville as the largest loss of life in the AIF from a single shell burst and further noted that[825]:

The occurrence inflicted a terrible shock, but some very brave rescue work was done. Of the wounded, one, with both legs cut off above the knee said to the rescuers: 'I'm all right-get the badly wounded boys out'. Another whose arm was shattered would not let his friends light his cigarette – 'I'll have to learn to do it with one hand.' he said, 'may as well begin now!'

In a statement given to the Red Cross in April 1919, Private Clarence P Carroll (7349) said he saw Bertie on the night of 30 May 1918, and the next morning, he was one of the 18 men that were killed outright by one shell[826]:

He and his pal were dead alongside one another in their billet. He was much torn about on the whole of one side of his body. I saw him dead at Alonville [sic] and saw him buried in the cemetery at Allonville Village – A week later I saw a cross on the grave – the grave was in good condition.

---

[824] 14th Battalion Unit Diary May 1918 - https://www.awm.gov.au/collection/C1343777?image=8
[825] Bean, *Official History*, Vol. 6, p. 110fn. Bean stated that the first shell killed 13 and wounded 56, the second shell killing five and wounding a further 12 men.
[826] Australian Red Cross Wounded and Missing Files - https://www.awm.gov.au/collection/R1485656

13 others including his mate were buried alongside him. His mate Wootten only got shifted from another cc., about a week previously so as to be with Englert and they both died at the same time alongside one another - buried alongside each other.

Barns at the old racing stable at Allonville, shelled just before the Villers-Bretonneux stunt, when they were used as billets for the 14th Battalion. AWM ID No. A02632.

A graveyard at the Allonville Communal Cemetery near Amiens, France. The graves are of the men of the 14th Battalion who were killed on 31 May 1918 when a German shell exploded in the barn in which they were sleeping, c 1918. AWM ID No. P05740.002.

A number of family notices were published on the anniversary of Bertie's death in 1919 in *The Sydney Morning Herald*[827]:

> ENGLERT. — In loving memory of our dear son. Pte. Bertie George Englert. Killed in action in France May 31, 1918, aged 31 years. R.I.P.
> This is the day that is sad to recall,
> This is the day of remembrance to all.
> Inserted by his loving parents.

---

[827] Family Notices (1919, May 31). *The Sydney Morning Herald* (NSW: 1842-1954), p. 16. Retrieved May 25, 2023, from http://nla.gov.au/nla.news-article15841282

ENGLERT. - In loving memory of my dear husband, Bert, killed in action, France, 31 May 1918.
In a soldier's grave he sleeps,
Far from those he loved.
Inserted by his loving wife, Zara.

ENGLERT. — In loving memory of our dear brother, Pte. Bertie George Englert, killed in France. May 31, 1918.
One thing death cannot sever—
Loving remembrance lasts for ever.
Inserted by his loving brothers and sisters and brothers-in-law.

ENGLERT. — In loving memory of or dear son-in-law and brother-in-law. Bert, killed in action France, May 31, 1918, Inserted by Mr. and Mrs. Edmond Higgins, Mr. and Mrs. V. Higgins, Mr. and Mrs. S. Wright, Mr. and Mrs. E. Higgins, Mr. and Mrs. A. Stokes and Archie and Nerida Higgins.

Bertie Englert is buried in the Allonville Communal Cemetery. The communal cemetery was used from August 1916 to February 1917 by the 39th CCS then posted at Allonville, and from April to July 1918, by Australian fighting units.[828]

---

[828] http://www.cwgc.org/find-a-cemetery/cemetery/64903/ALLONVILLE%20COMMUNAL%20CEMETERY

Photograph of the grave of Bertie Englert, Allonville Communal Cemetery (author, 2018).

Arvan James Prichard

Lieutenant
22nd Machine Gun Company, 2nd Australian Division
Killed in action 18 July 1918, Villers-Bretonneux, France
No known grave. Commemorated Australian National Memorial, Villers-Bretonneux, France

Studio portrait of 1383 Private (Pte) Arvan James Prichard, 20th Battalion, made Sydney c. 1916 [sic], *Sydney Mail*. AWM ID number P05301.081. Public domain.

Arvan James (Jimmy) Prichard was born in Townsville, Queensland, on 26 June 1898,[829] the son of William Gordon Prichard and Kathleen May Prichard (nee Kelly). Due to differences in spelling of the surname on official records,[830] it appears that Arvan was the second of two sons, the other being William Roy Prichard[831] although subsequent newspaper notices indicate that he also had a sister.[832] At some point prior to enlistment, he moved to New South Wales with

---

[829] Queensland BDM Registration No. 1898/C/11012 however the surname is spelt Pritchard.
[830] The surname is misspelled Pritchard on the St Mark's Memorial Board and the Drummoyne War Memorial. They are not alone as correspondence on the birth records, service records and Red Cross records also have the surname misspelled, although some have been amended by hand.
[831] Queensland BDM registration No. 1911/C/6959 but the date of birth is specified as 17 December 1894 and the surname is spelt Pritchard.
[832] See for example, Family Notices (1924, July 18). *The Sydney Morning Herald* (NSW: 1842-1954), p. 8. Retrieved May 25, 2023, from http://nla.gov.au/nla.news-article16134722 . No birth record can be found on either the NSW or Queensland BDM registries for Arvan's sister.

his family where he commenced work as an engineer. The family lived at *Wyee*, 17 Havelock Street, Drummoyne.[833]

Arvan was 18 years old at the time of his enlistment on 19 April 1915, only a few days before ANZAC forces landed at Gallipoli. The day before his enlistment, his parents signed a letter permitting their young son to join the 'Australian Imperial Expeditionary Forces in the Army Medical Corps only'.[834] As will become apparent, his parents' caveat to their consent was ignored.

At the time of his enlistment, like other recruits, Arvan was given a medical examination. The certificate of examination signed by the examining medical officer recorded that although considered fit for active service, he had defective eyesight and was designated as 'suitable for AMC' or the Army Medical Corp.[835] While this may well be true, it may also have been a means by which the examining officer could give effect to the wishes of Arvan's parents. Notwithstanding this, Arvan was assigned to D Company of 20th Battalion in the 5th Infantry Brigade.

On 26 June 1915, he embarked from Sydney on HMAT *Berrima* bound for Egypt. His ship arrived in Alexandria on 26 July 1915 whereupon his unit disembarked and boarded troop trains, eventually marching into the Australian camp at Heliopolis. Between 27 July and 14 August 1915, the unit was occupied with training in 'Musketry, Protection, Entrenching & Attack'.[836] On 14 August, orders were received from 5th Brigade to join the MEF. On 16 August, the 20th Battalion, along with the 19th and one company from the 18th Battalion, boarded a transport ship in Alexandria, bound for the island of Lemnos. On 20 August, they departed Lemnos on a troopship, and headed for the beaches of ANZAC Cove.

---

[833] The house is recorded in the General Index 1914-1916 as being occupied by William G Pritchard.
[834] War Service Records for Arvan James Prichard accessible at http://recordsearch.naa.gov.au/scripts/Imagine.asp?B=8020529, page 52.
[835] War Service Records - http://recordsearch.naa.gov.au/scripts/Imagine.asp?B=8020529, page 3.
[836] 20th Infantry Battalion Unit Diary July-August 1915 - (https://www.awm.gov.au/collection/C1356708?image=2

Arvan landed at Gallipoli on 20 August 1915, only a few weeks after the Allies' major August offensive which included attacks by Australian forces on Lone Pine and the Nek. The arrival of the 20th Battalion on ANZAC is described in the unit diary as confusing, with units mixed up and delays experienced before all troops had arrived.[837] Eventually, orders were received to march to Reserve Gully on the way to Beauchop's Hill. The battalion had 27 officers and 972 other ranks, including Arvan Prichard, on landing at ANZAC.[838]

Almost immediately on arrival, the battalion started to take casualties. On 23 August alone, the battalion suffered six casualties with another three being taken to hospital sick. This was before the unit had reached the front-line proper. On 26 August, the battalion relieved the 8th, 9th and 10th Light Horse at Russell's Top but was already down to 927 other ranks.[839] From 26 August until 9 November 1915, the 20th Battalion was in continuous occupation of the front-line trenches at Russell's Top. During that time, the unit diary noted the daily loss of men not just to enemy shell fire, stick grenades and snipers, but also illness, with significant numbers evacuated to hospital.[840]

Pulled out of the front line, the battalion took up quarters in Fatigue Gully, and received reinforcements. The procession of men to and from the hospital continued, possibly exacerbated by the first snow fall, recorded in the unit diary on 27 November 1915. On 30 November, the diary recorded that seven men were evacuated to hospital.[841]

---

[837] 20th Infantry Battalion Unit Diary July-August 1915 - https://www.awm.gov.au/collection/C1356708?image=5

[838] 20th Infantry Battalion Unit Diary July-August 1915 - https://www.awm.gov.au/collection/C1356708?image=5

[839] 20th Infantry Battalion Unit Diary July-August 1915 - https://www.awm.gov.au/collection/C1356708?image=7

[840] 20th Infantry Battalion Unit Diary, August, September, October and November 1915 - https://www.awm.gov.au/collection/C1356708?image=8 ; https://www.awm.gov.au/collection/C1343442?image=1; https://www.awm.gov.au/collection/C1343451; and https://www.awm.gov.au/collection/C1343953

[841] 20th Infantry Battalion Unit Diary November 1915 - https://www.awm.gov.au/collection/C1343953?image=6

Arvan Prichard was one of the seven taken to ANZAC beach that day, said to be suffering from jaundice, later to be diagnosed as hepatitis. He was evacuated to the hospital ship HS *Dongola* on 1 December 1915, arriving in Cairo on 3 December 1915 where he was admitted to hospital. A week later he was transferred to Mena House Convalescent Hospital.

While absent sick, the battalion returned to Russell's Top, taking up positions on 12 December. Between 13 and 19 December, the battalion was heavily and consistently shelled, suffering numerous casualties. On 17 December, the battalion received instructions for the evacuation of Gallipoli, which commenced on 18 December and was completed during the night of 19–20 December, with the unit arriving back in Mudros Harbour, Lemnos.

Arvan had sufficiently recovered by 19 January 1916 that he could return to his unit, which at the time was stationed near Giza in Egypt. As part of the 5th Brigade, his unit was moved east to assist in guarding the Suez Canal from an anticipated Turkish attack. For the next two months, the battalion trained and took on reinforcements, while there continued a constant stream of men to and from hospital. In March 1916, the 5th Brigade was replaced at the front by the units from the New Zealand Rifle Brigade and Auckland Mounted Rifles. On 9 March, the brigade received 16 Lewis machine guns, and on 12 March was addressed by the commander of ANZAC forces, General Birdwood, 'on matters of discipline and behaviour in France'.[842] At that time, Arvan was one of 34 other ranks transferred to the newly established 5th Machine Gun Company of the 5th Brigade before his unit departed Alexandria for Marseilles, France, on 19 March 1916.

The 5th Machine Gun Company travelled north by train from Marseilles, and eventually made camp at Boesegham, in the vicinity of Hazebrouck in northern France. After a period of training, including a demonstration of 'liquid fire'[843] (presumably a reference to the newly

---

[842] 5th Infantry Brigade Unit Diary March 1916 - https://www.awm.gov.au/collection/C1343071?image=6
[843] 5th Infantry Brigade Unit Diary April 1916 - https://www.awm.gov.au/collection/C1347031?image=2

invented flame thrower), the 5th Brigade broke camp and made its way to take up positions in the front line at La Rolanderie near Erquinghem. On the way there, the brigade was reviewed by French Supreme Commander, Marshall Joffre. The units of the brigade spent April, May and June acclimatising to life in the trenches, including patrols of no man's land, enemy shelling and attacks by aeroplanes. The brigade was relieved by the 4th Infantry Brigade at the end of June 1916.

After a brief period as divisional reserve, the brigade including the 5th Machine Gun Company, was moved to a place the unit diary describes 'near Posiere?' [sic].[844] The brigade and the whole 1st, 2nd and 4th Australian Divisions would come to know Pozières very well over the next two months. The number of lives lost at Pozières in six weeks would be as many as the entire eight months of the Gallipoli campaign.[845] The attack on Pozières had commenced on 1 July 1916 as part of the broader Somme offensive, but initial attempts to capture it by British troops had been unsuccessful.

The 1st Australian Division was brought in to renew the attack on the German strongpoint, which commenced on 23 July and succeeded in capturing the remnants of the village. The 2nd Australian Division including the 5th Brigade moved forward to relieve the 1st Division on 25 July and commenced their attack to broaden the front on 26 July. The 5th Brigade diary noted that the Germans detected the advance as soon as it began and 'very heavy casualties resulted as the hostile artillery and machine gun fire grew very intense'.[846] The Germans counter-attacked over the next few weeks. The period was marked by heavy close quarter hand-to-hand fighting and bombing with grenades, and frequent gas attacks. Unable to retake the village, the Germans then launched one of the heaviest artillery bombardments of the war. The brigade was relieved on 5 August and was

---

[844] 5th Infantry Brigade Unit Diary July 1916 - https://www.awm.gov.au/collection/C1354955?image=4
[845] McLachlan, *Walking with the ANZACs*, p. 135.
[846] 5th Infantry Brigade Unit Diary July 1916 - https://www.awm.gov.au/collection/C1354955?image=5

addressed the next day by the Army Corps Commander to thank it for their work during recent operations.[847] By 21 August, the unit was back in Pozières, experiencing continued artillery bombardment, and enemy counter-attacks. Often, trenches ceased to exist with isolated units fighting in and holding onto shell craters. Relieved by the 4th Australian Division, the 5th Brigade and other units of the 2nd Division moved into reserve on 27 August.

In September, the brigade moved to the Ypres sector but returned to the Somme sector in early October 1916 to take part in attacks around Flers. During that time, the unit, along with the other elements of the Australian forces, experienced some of the worst conditions on the Western Front with rain and mud making roads impassable, and trenches unliveable. It was recorded as one of the harshest winters in decades.

In November 1916, Arvan was promoted to temporary lance corporal following the wounding of Corporal Lyons, and on 1 January 1917 received two promotions on the one day: first to temporary corporal following the promotion of Corporal Fraser, and immediately to temporary sergeant with the promotion of Sergeant Glover. While holding the rank of corporal, Arvan wrote a letter to his father reporting on his exciting encounter with a German Fokker aeroplane while serving on the Somme, which letter was published in the *Sydney Mail* in February 1917[848]:

> WRITING to his father (Mr. W. G. Prichard, of Drummoyne), Corp. Arvan Prichard, of the — Machine Gun Section, says: — I am sending you another interesting souvenir. It is a speedometer dial and pointer of a Fritz Fokker, which was brought down by one of our aviators on November 29, just behind the front line on the Flers front on the Somme.

---

[847] 5th Infantry Brigade Unit Diary August 1916 - https://www.awm.gov.au/collection/C1347419?image=4
[848] THE RAILWAYMEN: APPEAL FOR REINFORCEMENTS. (1917, February 14). *Sydney Mail* (NSW: 1912-1938), p. 14. Retrieved May 25, 2023, from http://nla.gov.au/nla.news-article160387739

At the time I was firing one of our guns at the Fokker, but do not claim to have had any hand in bringing it down.

It was rather a cloudy day, and the German did not notice our 'plane above him until too late. Our airman dived at the Fokker, firing his gun whilst doing so. They were about 3000ft up at the time, and the Fokker just tilted up and dived at the earth, landing within 100yds or so of me. Naturally, I was amongst the first on the scene. The 'plane was smashed to pulp, also the aviator. It was one of Fritz's latest, having been made in Sept., 1916; 863 was the number. I have seen many 'planes brought down, but that was the best sight so far.

A picture of the speedometer dial was published with the letter.

Image that appeared in the Sydney Mail on 14 February 1917 of the speedometer Arvan retrieved from the crashed German Fokker aeroplane, which bears the inscription 'A German Souvenir. The speedometer dial of a Fokker brought down by one of our airmen at Flers.

On 9 February 1917, Arvan was transferred to the Machine Gun Training Depot at Grantham, England, and noted for promotion to second lieutenant, which news quickly made it into newspapers back home.[849] On the same date he was transferred to the 22nd Machine Gun Company. In a confidential note, a report from the training school states[850]:

> This officer is quite satisfactory. He is keen efficient but as yet a little lacking in confidence.

Photo of officers and men at the Australian Machine Gun Training School, Grantham, Lincolnshire. They are firing a Vickers Machine Gun. Date made: 11 April 1917. AWM ID No. P02670.003.

---

[849] MILITARY PROMOTION. (1917, March 15). *The Sydney Morning Herald* (NSW: 1842 1954), p. 6. Retrieved May 25, 2023, from http://nla.gov.au/nla.news-article15725801
[850] War service records - http://recordsearch.naa.gov.au/scripts/Imagine.asp?B=8020529, page 57.

In March 1917, the newly formed 22nd Machine Gun Company departed Southampton for Le Havre. By the end of April 1917, it was providing support to the attack on Bullecourt as part of an assault on the German Hindenburg Line. By May 1917, Arvan was noted to be promoted to lieutenant, but after a brief period back with the 22nd Machine Gun Company, in July 1917, he was transferred along with three NCOs to the Machine Gun Training Depot in England, presumably as an instructor.

Outdoor group portrait of Lieutenants (Lts) C Cowle, Imperial Machine Gun Company; Arvan James Prichard, 22nd Machine Gun Company (later 2nd Battalion, Machine Gun Corps, died 18 July 1918); Duncan, 6th Machine Gun Company; C M Bartell, 6th Machine Gun Company; T C Davies, Machine Gun Company; R M Watson, Machine Gun Company; Reginald Clive Callister MC, 6th Machine Gun Company. The reverse is inscribed: 'Dear Mother, more beastly Anzacs' with their names. Photo c 1916-1918. AWM ID No. P10189.001.

Arvan stayed with the Training Depot until 28 February 1918 when he briefly rejoined his unit in France on 2 March 1918[851] before being posted to undertake a course at the Australian Gas Training School on 10 March 1918. By 26 March, the unit diary noted that all schools had been cancelled,[852] presumably owing to the major German offensive, whereupon Lt Prichard rejoined the 22nd Machine Gun Company. The company was ordered to the area around Amiens to assist in the defence of that city.

In early July 1918, the 22nd Machine Gun Company took up positions on the Villers-Bretonneux front for the purpose of supporting the 21st and 23rd Battalions of the 2nd Australian Division in their attack along with other battalions drawn from the 3rd and 4th Australian Divisions. On 4 July, the Battle of Hamel commenced with the unit diary describing in uncharacteristic, effusive language the quick success of the attack, the efficiency with which the guns in the unit were able to get quickly into position to prevent any counter-attack developing, and the close cooperation with tanks and aeroplanes in resupplying the guns with ammunition.[853]

The unit diary recorded that on the night of 17–18 July, Lt Prichard with two guns advanced in cooperation with the 26th Battalion in an attack on enemy positions east of Monument Wood, the objective being gained.[854] This was part of a general attack by Australian forces east of Villers-Bretonneux, during which heavy German machine gun and artillery fire was experienced. The diary noted[855]:

---

[851] 22nd Machine Gun Company Unit Diary March 1918 - https://www.awm.gov.au/collection/C1344596?image=3
[852] 22nd Machine Gun Company Unit Diary March 1918 - https://www.awm.gov.au/collection/C1344596?image=5
[853] 22nd Machine Gun Company Unit Diary July 1918 - https://www.awm.gov.au/collection/C1344582?image=3
[854] 22nd Machine Gun Company Unit Diary July 1918 - https://www.awm.gov.au/collection/C1344582?image=5
[855] 22nd Machine Gun Company Unit Diary July 1918 - https://www.awm.gov.au/collection/C1344582?image=5

At 9.pm. the enemy put down a heavy barrage and counter-attacked the position taken from him last night. During the bombardment prior to enemy counter-attack, Lt. Prichard and 3. O.R's were killed and 3 O.R's were wounded.

Arvan was only 20 years old. It is noted that 'he was buried by members of his unit and a cross with his name and Battalion erected on the grave'.[856] A personal notice was published in August 1918 in *The Sydney Morning Herald*[857]:

PRICHARD. — July 20, France, Lieut. Arvan (Jim) Prichard (an Anzac), 22nd Machine Gun Corps. By his sincere friend, Dorothy Thomas Drummoyne, and comrade, Sgt. Cyd. Thomas, O.A.S.

Further family notices were published on the anniversary of Arvan's death including the following[858]:

PRICHARD. - In memory of our precious son and brother, Lieut. Arvan Prichard (Jimmy), aged 20 years killed in action. Villers Bretonneux, July 18, 1918. Inserted by his mother, father, and sister.

---

[856] War Service Records - http://recordsearch.naa.gov.au/scripts/Imagine.asp?B=8020529 , page 40.
[857] Family Notices, *The Sydney Morning Herald* (NSW: 1842-1954) 10 August 1918: 12. Web. 25 May 2023 http://nla.gov.au/nla.news-article15797493
[858] Family Notices (1922, July 18). *The Sydney Morning Herald* (NSW: 1842-1954), p. 8. Retrieved May 25, 2023, from http://nla.gov.au/nla.news-article16013857 . Similar notices were published in 1919, 1923 and 1924 – see respectively Family Notices (1919, July 18). *The Sydney Morning Herald* (NSW: 1842-1954), p. 8. Retrieved May 25, 2023, from http://nla.gov.au/nla.news-article15857945 , Family Notices (1923, July 18). *The Sydney Morning Herald* (NSW: 1842-1954), p. 12. Retrieved May 25, 2023, from http://nla.gov.au/nla.news-article16081457 and Family Notices (1924, July 18). *The Sydney Morning Herald* (NSW: 1842-1954), p. 8. Retrieved May 25, 2023, from http://nla.gov.au/nla.news-article16134722

Arvan's photograph also appeared in the *Sydney Mail* on 28 August 1918 in an article recording a letter from a French family thanking Australia for its sacrifice in the recent fighting in France.[859]

Photograph of Arvan Prichard. Source - FRANCE'S GRATITUDE. (1918, August 28). *Sydney Mail* (NSW: 1912-1938), p. 21. Retrieved May 25, 2023, from http://nla.gov.au/nla.news-article160627352

---

[859] FRANCE'S GRATITUDE. (1918, August 28). *Sydney Mail* (NSW: 1912-1938), p. 21. Retrieved May 25, 2023, from http://nla.gov.au/nla.news-article160627352

Statements obtained by the Red Cross over the course of September and October 1918, confirmed the circumstances surrounding Lt Prichard's death. Private Scott in a statement in October 1918 said[860]:

> I saw him killed at Villers-Bretonneux when he was killed instantly. A shell landed about his feet and killed 4 others with him, he was badly hit on body. Casualty happened in the early morning, at which time he was putting a gun into position. He was a very popular Officer and was well liked by everyone. ... I did not see his grave, but he was buried at place of casualty and grave was marked.

Lt Prichard's batman, Gunner Chas Prater, corroborated this statement. Corporal R Dillaway confirmed the location where he had buried Lt Prichard and the cross erected on the grave. Corporal PN Wallace states that thought was given to retrieving Lt Prichard's body but it was too difficult, so they decided to bury him where he fell. He reflected 'he was well-liked by all the boys.'[861] Although not present, Lieutenant Kershaw reported that Lt Prichard was[862]:

> 'in charge of two machine guns, having to take them forward in support of the infantry. Having reached his objective about 1,000 yards east by south of Villers-Bretenneux [sic], he was killed by a shell which burst very close to him. Death was instantaneous.'

Notwithstanding the evidence relating to the location of the grave, the remains of Lt Prichard were never located to enable them to be reinterred as cemeteries were being consolidated after the war. In September 1919, Kathleen Prichard wrote to the OIC to request a photograph of the grave of her son. She was advised that action was

---

[860] Australian Red Cross Wounded and Missing Files - https://www.awm.gov.au/people/rolls/R1501838/
[861] Australian Red Cross Wounded and Missing Files - https://www.awm.gov.au/people/rolls/R1501838/
[862] Australian Red Cross Wounded and Missing Files - https://www.awm.gov.au/people/rolls/R1501838/

being taken and a photograph would be forwarded when available. On 15 January 1920, William Prichard was advised by letter that his son was buried in Adelaide British Cemetery, two and a half miles south of the town of Corbie.[863]

A photograph of the grave is contained in the AWM collection, with the description that it is the 'original gravesite' of Lt Arvan Prichard. It is not clear if this photo was ever provided to Arvan's parents as requested. However, subsequent correspondence raises doubts as to whether it was the original gravesite or where the cross erected by Lt Prichard's comrades might have been relocated to at the end of the war.

The original gravesite of 504 Private Henry Bridge and Lieutenant Arvan James Prichard, both of the 22nd Machine Gun Battalion. Photo AWM ID No. H15568.

---

[863] War service records - http://recordsearch.naa.gov.au/scripts/Imagine.asp?B=8020529, page 47.

In about 1921, William Prichard, now resident at *Dunbury*, Woolwich Road, Hunters Hill, wrote to the OIC requesting the addresses of the next of kin of Pte H Bridge and Lt R Shelley.[864] The photograph of the cross said to have been erected on the grave of Lt Prichard also refers to Private Bridge.[865] Lt Shelley is likely to have been Lt Roland Shelley who was also in the 22nd Machine Gun Company, and who was killed on 4 July 1918 by a sniper while doing a patrol between his guns.[866] He may have been a friend mentioned by Arvan in letters to his parents.

Four years later, however, the OIC advised Mr Prichard by letter that reports of Lt Prichard's burial in the Adelaide British Cemetery were incorrect. The letter states[867]:

> I regret having to inform you that the Imperial War Graves Commission have been unable to satisfactorily identify the late officer's resting place. The former report of internment was based on the finding of a cross erected in the above named cemetery bearing the regimental particulars of Lt Prichard, but as a result of recent investigations it has definitely been ascertained that the cross was of a memorial nature only, and not marking an actual grave site.

---

[864] War service records - http://recordsearch.naa.gov.au/scripts/Imagine.asp?B=8020529, page 42.
[865] War service records for Private Henry Bridge accessible at http://recordsearch.naa.gov.au/scripts/Imagine.asp?B=3120187. According to additional information recorded against AWM ID No. H15568, Henry Bridge was formerly a footman to the Governor of Victoria.
[866] War service records for Roland Shelley accessible at http://recordsearch.naa.gov.au/scripts/Imagine.asp?B=8081621; 22nd Machine Gun Company Unit Diary July 1918 - https://www.awm.gov.au/collection/C1344582?image=4
[867] War service records - http://recordsearch.naa.gov.au/scripts/Imagine.asp?B=8020529, page 39.

Steps however are now being taken to suitably perpetuate the memory of your son by name of special permanent headstone which will be erected in the Memorial Plot of the Adelaide British Cemetery, and upon which will be engraved the full regimental description and date of death of the late officer, preceded by the words 'Believed to be buried in this cemetery, actual grave unknown', together with the personal inscription previously furnished in this connexion [sic].

Assuring you of the Department's sympathy at the distressing circumstances arising.

No permanent headstone commemorating Lt Prichard appears to have been made and no such gravestone was erected in the Adelaide British Cemetery where Lt Prichard was thought to have been buried. Arvan Prichard is commemorated at the Australian National Memorial, Villers-Bretonneux as one of the more than 10,000 Australian who were killed in action in France and who have no known grave.

Inscription of the name of Arvan Prichard on the 2nd Division panel at the Australian National Memorial, Villers-Bretonneux (author, 2018).

Colin Godfrey Wilson

Private, No. 1303

33rd Battalion, 9th Infantry Brigade, 3rd Australian Division

Killed in action 28 July 1918, Sailly Laurette, France

Buried Villers-Bretonneux Military Cemetery,
Villers-Bretonneux, France

Have Mercy Upon Him Lord and Let Perpetual Light Shine Upon Him

Colin Godfrey Wilson was born in Brisbane, Queensland on 24 May 1896 the son of Colin Porteous Wilson and Georgina Josephine Wilson (nee Mant).[868] He was one of four children, his siblings being William Robert,[869] Amy[870] and Keith.[871] As Amy was born in NSW a year before Colin, it would appear that the family returned to NSW shortly after Colin's birth as he attended school at Moree Superior Public School and Christian Brothers, Paddington, with his younger brother Keith born in Woollahra in 1904.[872] His father, Colin senior, died in Sydney in 1904[873] and his mother Georgina married Charles Hubbard in the district of Newton in about 1913.[874] Charles Hubbard is recorded as living at *Turon*, 16 Therry Street, Drummoyne.[875]

According to his war service records[876] Colin enlisted in the AIF at the age of 19 years and seven months in Narrabri, NSW, on 4 February 1916. He described his occupation as a 'porter' and gave his current address as care of the Imperial Hotel, Moree. Information in a personal notice published in a local Moree newspaper indicates that he was employed by Dehlsen Bros. laundry at the time.[877] As he was under 21 years of age at the time of enlistment, he obtained the approval of his mother to join up.

After a brief period with B Company, Depot Battalion at Armidale, he was posted to serve with the 33rd Battalion. The battalion had been established in January 1916 in Armidale and was dubbed 'New England's Own' as its recruits were largely drawn from that region. His records describe his military occupation as company bugler.

---

[868] Queensland BDM Registration No. 1896/B/58475.
[869] Queensland BDM Registration No. 1890/C/7963. William enlisted in the AIF in 1917.
[870] NSW BDM Registration No. 13769/1895.
[871] NSW BDM Registration No. 8718/1904.
[872] Colin's name also appears on the Moree Superior Public School WW1 Roll of Honour which lists ex-pupils who enlisted in the First World War.
[873] NSW BDM Registration No. 7895/1904.
[874] NSW BDM Registration No. 5012/1913.
[875] General Index 1914-1916.
[876] War service records for Colin Godfrey Wilson accessible at http://www.naa.gov.au/collection/explore/defence/service-records/army-wwi.aspx
[877] Personal. (1918, September 3). *Moree Gwydir Examiner and General Advertiser* (NSW: 1901-1940), p. 2. Retrieved May 26, 2023, from http://nla.gov.au/nla.news-article115768806

The 33rd Battalion embarked from Sydney on the troopship HMAT A74 *Marathon* in May 1916 bound for Southampton, England. The battalion trained for four months in England. It was during this time that Colin had his first run in with his commanding officer, Lt Col Leslie Morshead,[878] in September 1916 when he was charged with being absent without leave from 23–25 September. He was awarded '7 days FP No. 2' (field punishment with hard labour), and forfeiture of 10 days' pay.

The 33rd Battalion formed part of the 9th Brigade of the 3rd Australian Division, which proceeded to France in November 1916. The 33rd Battalion was initially posted to the front line in the Somme sector at La Chapelle-d'Armentières where it learned the routine of trench warfare and experienced the terrible winter of 1916–17. During one field march in April 1917, Lt Col Morshead noted in the rather dour unit diary the poor state of the men's boots after having been exposed to the wet and mud of the Somme during winter.

After periods in and out of the line, the 33rd Battalion was moved to the Ypres sector in Belgium where it saw action in the Battle of Messines near Ypres that commenced on 7 June 1917. It was in this action that Colin suffered his first injury, a gunshot wound to the face, with his name appearing in casualty lists published in June and July 1917.[879] He was moved from a field ambulance unit to a CCS at Boulogne, before finally being sent to a rest camp. Private Wilson did not rejoin his unit until October 1917, four months later, which suggests that his injury had been a serious one.

While Colin Wilson's war service records do not indicate what happened between him rejoining his unit and the close of 1917, the battalion's war diaries confirm that it continued to see action in Flanders during the Third Battle of Ypres including the bloody battles at

---

[878] Lt Col Leslie Morshead would achieve fame as the commander of the 9th Australian Division in the Second World War defending Tobruk during its siege by German and Italian forces in North Africa in 1941.

[879] NEW SOUTH WALES. (1917, June 28). *The Sydney Morning Herald* (NSW: 1842-1954), p. 8. Retrieved May 26, 2023, from http://nla.gov.au/nla.news-article15757782 and Australian Casualties. (1917, July 4). *Australian Town and Country Journal* (Sydney, NSW: 1870-1919), p. 15. Retrieved May 26, 2023, from http://nla.gov.au/nla.news-article263769981

Broodseinde Ridge and Passchendaele in October and November 1917.

In January 1918, the 33rd Battalion was posted to England for leave with it due to catch the leave train from Victoria Station, London, on 28 January 1918, to return to the front. Colin had his second run in with his commanding officer when he failed to report to 'a place of parade appointed by his Superior Officer'.[880] He was admonished by Lt Col Morshead and docked one day's pay.

On returning to France, the 33rd Battalion was posted to the Somme region. In March 1918, the Germans launched their spring offensive. Initially very successful, the Allies were in retreat, fighting desperate rearguard actions to try to stop the German offensive. The 33rd Battalion, like many Australian units, was thrown into action in an effort to stop the Germans capturing Amiens. It was in one of those actions outside of Amiens that Private Wilson was wounded for a second time on 31 March 1918 with gunshot wounds to his left thigh.

Colin was evacuated to England in early April 1918 for treatment, firstly at the Northamptonshire War Hospital at Duston, then to Harefield, before recuperating at a training brigade based at Deverill. His second wounding was reported in casualty lists published in April and May 1918.[881]

Between April and July 1918, Australian units had succeeded in stopping the German offensive, recapturing Villers-Bretonneux on 24–25 April, and then in slowly pushing back the German army, including the successful attack on Hamel in July 1918. Having crossed the Somme Canal at Sailly Laurette, the Australian Corps began preparing for the Allied August offensive, which would involve an attack

---

[880] War service records - http://www.naa.gov.au/collection/explore/defence/service-records/army-wwi.aspx
[881] 394th CASUALTY LIST. (1918, April 27). *The Sydney Morning Herald* (NSW: 1842-1954), p. 15. Retrieved May 26, 2023, from http://nla.gov.au/nla.news-article15769200 and Australian Casualties. (1918, May 1). *Australian Town and Country Journal* (Sydney, NSW: 1870-1919), p. 16. Retrieved May 26, 2023, from http://nla.gov.au/nla.news-article263624337

on the German Hindenburg Line, including strong points at Mont St Quentin and Péronne.

On 20 July 1918, Private Wilson rejoined his unit, which at the time was serving around Sailly Laurette, near the Somme Canal. While serving with the 13th Platoon, D Company of the 33rd Battalion, Private Wilson was on duty manning a Lewis gun in a front-line trench somewhere between Sailly Laurette and Sailly-le-Sec, north of the Somme Canal on 28 July 1918. Although there are a number of conflicting reports regarding when the trench came under attack from a German *minenwerfer*, or trench mortar, it appears that early in the morning Private Wilson was killed instantaneously by a shell explosion with injuries to his head and chest. Also killed by the explosion was his friend Private Ryan, and another Private WJC Wilson was injured.

Colin was buried nearby at Vaux Communal Cemetery near Vaux-sur-Somme on 30 July 1918 with Rev. S Bower in attendance. Men from his unit erected a cross on the grave. Memorial notices were published by family and relatives in August 1918[882]:

WILSON. — Killed in action in France, July 28, 1918, Private C. G. (Col.) Wilson, 33rd Batt., aged 22 years.
O France, thou holdest one of Australia's noblest.
Inserted by his ever-loving friend, M. Emerton.

---

[882] Family Notices (1918, August 29). *The Sydney Morning Herald* (NSW: 1842-1954), p. 6. Retrieved May 26, 2023, from http://nla.gov.au/nla.news-article15800292 and Family Notices (1918, August 17). *The Sydney Morning Herald* (NSW: 1842-1954), p. 12. Retrieved May 26, 2023, from http://nla.gov.au/nla.news-article15798616

> WILSON. - My dear son, Colin Godfrey Wilson (Col.), 33rd Battalion, killed in action, July 28, 1918. Inserted by his loving mother, Mrs. G. Hubbard,
> (N.Z. papers please copy.)

> WILSON. - Killed in action, July 28, 1918, Colin Godfrey Wilson, second son of the late Colin Wilson (New Zealand), age 22 years, brother of Keith, Amy, William (on active service), nephew of Gunner Mant (on active service).
> His life on the battlefield was spent,
> And Australia raises the monument,
> A soldier and a man he died,
> Honoured by all, his country's pride.

Official reporting of Colin's death occurred on 27 August 1918 when his name appeared in the 425th casualty list.[883] News of Colin's death was also reported in the local Moree newspaper in September 1918[884]:

> Rev. Father Lloyd received the sad news on Saturday that Private Colin Wilson had been killed in action in France. Private Wilson, whose parents, we understand, reside at Drummoyne, Sydney, enlisted in Moree about two years ago. He was formerly employed at Dehlsen Bros.' laundry.

Statements obtained by the Red Cross[885] in late 1918 and early 1919 from men who were also serving with the 33rd Battalion at the time Colin was killed confirm that he had been hit in many places by shell fragments, including a large fragment that penetrated his steel helmet. Many men described him as a good mate with one describing him as

---

[883] 425th CASUALTY LIST. NEW SOUTH WALES. (1918, August 27). *The Sydney Morning Herald* (NSW: 1842-1954), p. 8. Retrieved May 26, 2023, from http://nla.gov.au/nla.news-article15799975

[884] Personal. (1918, September 3). *Moree Gwydir Examiner and General Advertiser* (NSW: 1901-1940), p. 2. Retrieved May 26, 2023, from http://nla.gov.au/nla.news-article115768806

[885] Australian Red Cross Wounded and Missing Files - https://www.awm.gov.au/collection/R1473351

'a little bugler, everybody liked him'. It is unclear if this was a misspelling or a reference to his occasional company role.

Initially, Mrs Hubbard was advised of her son having been killed in action with no further details. The war service records indicate that Private Wilson's sister, Amy Wilson, wrote to Victoria Barracks in August 1918 seeking further particulars of her brother's death.

Colin's brother William had been serving with the 4th Sanitation Section since late 1918. In December 1918, William wrote a letter seeking information on the whereabouts of his brother's grave so that he might visit it before he returned to Australia. The Red Cross records indicate that there was some uncertainty about Colin's initial burial site. It was not until February 1919 that his grave was officially recorded as being at the communal cemetery at Vaux-sur-Somme.

On 22 May 1919, some nine months after his death, Mrs Hubbard was officially advised of the circumstances in which her son was killed and the location of his then grave. The letter from the OIC states[886]:

> I am now in receipt of advice which shows that he was killed in action on 28 July 1918, by an enemy high velocity shell which landed in the trench in which he was standing. He was hit by fragments and death was instantaneous. He was buried in the Vaux Communal Cemetery, France, the Rev. S Bower officiating. A cross was erected over his grave.

A family notice was published on the anniversary of Colin's death in July 1919[887]:

---

[886] War service records - http://www.naa.gov.au/collection/explore/defence/service-records/army-wwi.aspx
[887] Family Notices (1919, July 28). *The Sydney Morning Herald* (NSW: 1842-1954), p. 8. Retrieved May 26, 2023, from http://nla.gov.au/nla.news-article15854120

WILSON. - In sad and loving memory of my dear son and our brother, Colin G. Wilson, 33rd Battalion. Of Drummoyne, aged 22 years, killed in action on July 28, 1918, at Vaux-sur-Somme.

No more we listen to his kindly voice.
That never failed to make our hearts rejoice.
No more we look upon his manly face.
Nor clasp his hand, nor share his fond embrace.

Inserted by his fond mother, G. Hubbard, and his sister and brothers, Amy, Bill (O.A.S.), and Keith.

As was common after the Armistice in November 1918, war graves located throughout the battlefields were consolidated, resulting in large numbers of bodies being exhumed and reburied at cemeteries that were being enlarged throughout the course of 1919 and 1920. In or about September 1919, Private Colin Godfrey Wilson was officially reburied at Villers-Bretonneux Military Cemetery, becoming one of the 779 Australians and one of the 2141 buried at this cemetery, which also is the location of the Australian National Memorial. It was not until April 1920 that Mrs Hubbard was advised that her son's remains had been reburied at Villers-Bretonneux Military Cemetery.

Colin is also commemorated on the Moree ANZAC Centenary Memorial and Moree Superior Public School WW1 Roll of Honour. Erected in March 1921, the school memorial includes the names of 202 ex-pupils of Moree Superior Public School who enlisted in the First World War.[888]

---

[888] https://www.warmemorialsregister.nsw.gov.au/memorials/moree-superior-public-school-first-world-war-roll-honour

Photograph of the grave of Colin Wilson, Villers-Bretonneux Military Cemetery (author, 2009).

The 100 Days 1918

The Allied Supreme Commanders were already planning for fighting into 1919 when they launched the offensive on the Somme on 8 August 1918. The Somme offensive was pictured as the beginning of a series of limited Allied offensives, not the final effort. Little did the Allied leaders appreciate that in just over three months, or 100 days of fighting, an armistice would be signed to come into effect at 11 a.m. on 11 November 1918, bringing an end to hostilities.

A weakness was sensed in the German positions opposite the Australian divisions on the Somme sector of the front, considered to be a consequence of the success of the 'peaceful penetration' tactic deployed by the Australian infantry. This harried and prevented the Germans from constructing proper defensive lines,[889] as well as the favourable terrain offered by the Villers-Bretonneux plateau for the deployment of tanks, so the Supreme Allied Commander, Marshall Foch, and BEF Commander-in-Chief, Field Marshall Haig, determined to strike at this point. The 1st Australian Division was transferred from Belgian Flanders to join the other divisions of the Australian Corps, and in a surprise move, the Canadian Corps was transferred from Arras to behind the positions of the 4th Australian

---

[889] Bean, *ANZAC to Amiens*, p. 465.

Division. Some 430 tanks[890] were assembled for the attack along with all three British Cavalry Divisions.

The Fourth British Army, under General Rawlinson, comprising the Australian, Canadian and III British Corps, would launch the first stroke from the direction of Villers-Bretonneux heading southeast, followed by a second stroke by the French First Army further to the south heading north. The British decided to forego the preliminary artillery bombardment, relying instead on aeroplanes to drown the noise of the advancing tanks, with artillery only joining in once the attack commenced. The method of operation of the attacking British forces was largely modelled on that developed by General Monash in the successful attack on Hamel on 4 July 1918, who would be knighted in the field by King George a few days after the opening of the offensive.

At 4.20 a.m. on 8 August 1918, the attack commenced in a dense fog. Known as the Battle of Amiens and regarded as a true turning point in the war, within a matter of hours the German front was completely broken with most of the enemy's field artillery overrun and captured. The 2nd and 3rd Australian Divisions, leading the attack on the Australian Corps sector, secured the first objective by 7.30 a.m. The 4th and 5th Australian Divisions took up the advance at 8 a.m., with the 4th on the left rushing to seize Morcourt and with it many German prisoners and stores. The second and third objectives were quickly secured, sweeping away some fifteen miles of the German front south of the Somme River. Complete surprise had been achieved with the British Fourth Army alone capturing some 13,000 prisoners and 200 guns[891] in one day of fighting. German General Erich Ludendorff recorded in his memoirs[892]:

---

[890] Bean, *ANZAC to Amiens*, p. 467; Sheffield cites that the number of tanks was 552 – *Forgotten Victory*, p. 240.
[891] Bean, *ANZAC to Amiens*, p. 473. Sheffield cites that the Germans lost 27,000 men, including 12,000 prisoners, and 450 guns – *Forgotten Victory*, p. 237.
[892] Bean, *ANZAC to Amiens*, p. 473.

... the blow of the 8th of August fell upon me ... August 8th was the black day of the German Army in this war .... The 8th of August put the decline of the [German] fighting power beyond all doubt ... The war must be ended.

The Allied attacks continued over the next few days but encountered increasing German resistance as they reached the trenches of the old Somme 1916 battlefields, and as the infantry got beyond the support of their artillery and dwindling number of tanks. After a brief respite to allow for the reorganisation of forces, the effort was renewed, this time by the British Third Army on 21 August further north, before the British Fourth Army rejoined the offensive on 22 August with the 3rd Australian Division seizing its objective north of the village of Bray. It was then the turn of the 1st Australian Division to join the attack on 23 August, which captured some 2,000 prisoners and a large naval gun. It was through this combination of successive actions, rapidly switching the point of attack from one sector to another, that the German Army was placed under continuous pressure without any chance to recover.

Field Marshall Haig began to appreciate that there was now an opportunity to inflict a significant defeat on the Germans and perhaps bring an end to the war in 1918, rather than 1919.[893] Haig and Foch agreed on a general plan to engage the Germans with all Allied armies on a very wide front so that the enemy would not be in a position to mount any major counter-attack.[894]

---

[893] Haig, *War Diaries*, 21 August 1918, p. 448; 10 September 1918, p. 458.
[894] Haig, *War Diaries*, 30 August 1918, p. 451.

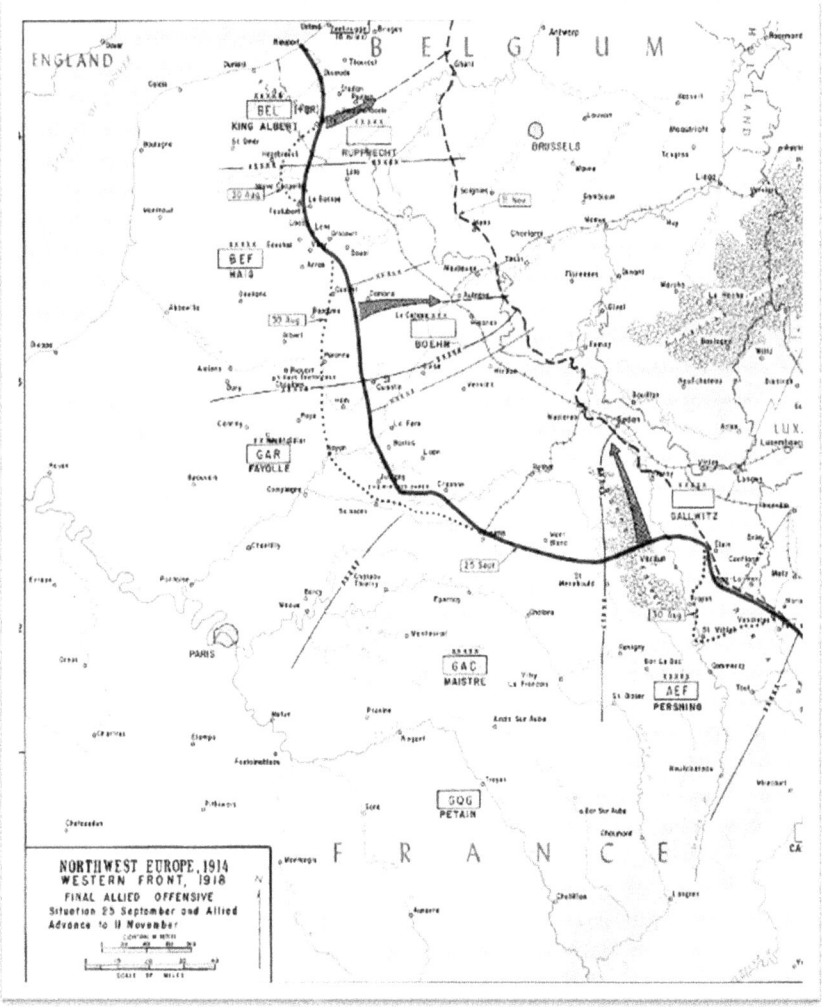

Plan of what would be the final Allied offensive on the First World War (source Wikipedia).

Taking full advantage of the broad strategy advocated by Foch and Haig, General Monash now pursued an aggressive policy of enhanced 'peaceful penetration', intending to force the Germans back from the old Somme battlefields. In a brilliantly impressive action, and without tanks or support from a creeping barrage, the 5th Brigade of the 2nd Australian Division in a surprise attack forced its way across the

Somme River and secured the formidable heights of Mont St Quentin above the town of Peronne on 31 August, with the 14th Brigade of the 5th Australian Division entering the town itself. By 2 September, the 15th Brigade seized the rest of Peronne. Combined with other successful attacks by British and French forces, General Ludendorff ordered a retreat to the Hindenburg Line.

Sensing further opportunity to test German Army morale and organisation, an attack was launched on 18 September in thick fog on the German outpost lines in front of the Hindenburg Line. Described by Charles Bean as overwhelmingly successful,[895] and only assisted by some detached field guns, the 1st and 4th Australian Divisions secured their objectives and succeeded in cutting off and capturing some 4,300 enemy troops and 76 guns. In the 50 days since the beginning of the Battle of Amiens, the BEF had advanced some 25 miles across a 40-mile front.

Spurred by the success, Foch and Haig authorised the undertaking of what would be called the 'Grand Offensive'. It would again involve a series of alternating attacks across the entire front with the toughest job being given to the British Fourth Army. This would involve an attack on the Hindenburg Line near St Quentin which would commence on 29 September with the Australian Corps leading the main attack.

The Australian divisions had by this stage been engaged in almost continual fighting since March 1918, and many battalions now had a fighting strength of only about 300 men or one third their normal complement. An order was given to disband certain battalions, which led to a minor mutiny in the Corps, resulting in a decision not to proceed with the proposed amalgamation of battalions. Australian Prime Minister Billy Hughes was deeply concerned about the use of the Australian divisions as shock troops in the recent fighting, and the risk that further offensive action would only further deplete the five divisions, threatening their Corps status and with it Australia's role in any

---

[895] Bean, *ANZAC to Amiens*, p. 485.

post-war settlement. He demanded that the Australian Corps be withdrawn for rest no later than 15 October 1918.

The Australian Corps was considered much too weak for the formidable task of breaking through the Hindenburg Line. Monash was offered and readily accepted the commitment of two new American divisions and organized for a cadre of experienced Australian officers and men from the 1st and 4th Australian Divisions to be attached to the American units to assist them.

Devising what is said to be the most elaborate plan of his career,[896] Monash arranged for the American divisions to lead the attack. The 3rd and 5th Australian Divisions would then pass through them, without the protection of a creeping barrage, to capture the remaining lines of the German defences. Tanks and smoke would be used to protect the attacking troops to enable them to fan out and seize the St Quentin canal to the north and south. Despite difficulties being encountered by the American divisions, chiefly through inexperience, the 5th Australian Division succeeded in crossing the canal. The 2nd Division relieved the 3rd and 5th Divisions on 3 October and broke through the third part of the Hindenburg Line, before Monash committed the 6th Brigade to capture Montbrehain, described by Charles Bean as a most brilliant but expensive action, resulting in the loss of 30 officers and 400 men including many experienced leaders.[897]

After the capture of Montbrehain on 5 October 1918, the Australian infantry divisions were withdrawn for rest and refitting in anticipation of rejoining the fighting later in the year and indeed into 1919. As it would transpire, Montbrehain would be the last action fought by the Australian infantry in the First World War as in just over a month's time, the fighting would come to an end with the Armistice. In the fighting since 8 August, the Australian Corps suffered casualties of 1,317 officers and 22,845 other ranks.[898]

---

[896] The plan was also criticised as being too complex particularly given the involvement of the inexperienced American divisions – see for example Sheffield, *Forgotten Victory*, p. 250.
[897] Bean, *ANZAC to Amiens*, p. 493; Bean, *Official History*, Vol. VI, p. 1043.
[898] Bean, *Official History*, Vol. VI, p. 1044.

John Michael Joseph Wills

Private, No. 7099

13th Battalion, 4th Infantry Brigade, 4th Australian Division

Killed in action 8 August 1918, Morcourt, France

Buried Heath Cemetery, Harbonnières, France

He Gave His Life for King & Country His Loving Wife

John Michael Joseph Wills was born in Balmain in about 1889,[899] the eldest of four children of James and Jessie Wills.[900] John was educated at the Sacred Heart School, Darlinghurst and St Mary's High School. John married Opal Roslyn Wills (née Wynyard) in about 1910[901] and they had three children,[902] their youngest, Tom, being baptised at St Mark's Catholic Church, Drummoyne on 4 June 1916 by Father Klein, the then Parish Priest.[903]

John worked for the Postmaster–General as a postman or 'letter carrier'. The address given at time of enlistment was c/- Mrs Violet Norman of *Takapuna*, Park Avenue, Drummoyne.[904] Subsequent correspondence in John's war service records show that John's last recorded address was 24 Roseby Street, Drummoyne and that his father, James Wills, a retired policeman, lived at 177 Trafalgar Street, Annandale.

According to his war service records,[905] John Wills enlisted in the AIF at the Royal Agricultural Showground at Moore Park on 19 September 1916. His brother, Norbert, enlisted a month later, eventually serving as a driver with the 2nd Field Artillery Brigade.[906] John had three years' experience with the GPS Cadets and a further three years' with the City of Sydney Scottish Rifles 25th Infantry Regiment with which he was still serving at the time of enlistment.[907] Family notices

---

[899] NSW BDM Registration No. 4478/1889.
[900] The other children were James (37941/1892), Norbert (36010/1895) and Bertha (24716/1897).
[901] NSW BDM Registration No. 11960/1910.
[902] The three children are Ian A (14409/1916), George J (26954/1913) and Marion R (1444/1911).
[903] This is presumably a reference to Ian Wills who was born in 1916.
[904] Correspondence with the Public Trustee in 1918 from the OIC on the war service records indicates that the address of John Wills prior to enlistment was 24 Roseby Street, Drummoyne. The General Index published in 1914-1916 records George H Wynyard as living at *Takapuna*, 39 Park Avenue who may have been a relative of Opal Wills.
[905] War service records for John Michael Joseph Wills accessible at http://www.naa.gov.au/collection/explore/defence/service-records/army-wwi.aspx.
[906] https://aif.adfa.edu.au/showPerson?pid=326984. Norbert returned to Australia in June 1919.
[907] The Honour Roll Circular completed by Opal Wills states that John had six years' military experience with the Scottish Rifles – see https://www.awm.gov.au/collection/R1667601. This is possibly a reference to the 25th

indicate that John held the rank of Lieutenant with the CMF which may account for the fact that two days after enlistment, John was sent to the depot school for non-commissioned officers. A month later John passed out of the NCO school with the rank of corporal. John's rank during his service would appear to involve some element of controversy with references to several promotions including possibly to lieutenant, but also to a court martial. What we do know is that according to official records he had reverted to the rank of private by the time he joined the 13th Battalion in France.

John was initially allocated to the 23rd Reinforcements to the 13th Battalion and embarked at Sydney on HMAT A72 *Beltana* on 25 November 1916. During the voyage John received an escort duty promotion (EDP) to the rank of Quarter Master Sergeant. John arrived with the 23rd Reinforcements at Devonport in England on 29 January 1917 whereupon he was assigned to the 4th Training Battalion at Codford, reverting to private before again receiving an EDP, this time of corporal. John appears to have remained with the 4th Training Battalion from February 1917 to November 1917, when he was transferred to the 12th Training Battalion of Codford and promoted to the rank of acting Sergeant.

On 29 October 1917, just prior to him being assigned to the 12th Training Battalion, John appears to have been subject to a court martial. The offence with which he was charged is not disclosed. The record of the proceedings of the court martial in John's war service records has the initials 'NG' marked in the space provided for the sentence to be entered. As there is no other information regarding any punishment or description of the offence, it is likely that John was found not guilty of the offence with which he was charged.

In late November 1917, John was transferred for temporary duty with the Australian Provost Corps, or military police, with the rank of temporary provost sergeant. He was then assigned to the Assistant Provost Marshall with AIF Headquarters in London where he served

---

Infantry Regiment (City of Sydney, Scottish Rifles). Family notices published after his death indicate that he held the rank of Lieutenant with the CMF.

until 4 March 1918 when he returned to the 12th Training Battalion.[908] His time back in Codford with the 12th Training Battalion was brief as he was returned to the rank of private and departed on 16 April 1918 for France to finally join the 13th Battalion.

It was shortly after John proceeded overseas for active service in France that his father wrote to the OIC. On 2 May 1918, James Wills wrote:

> I shall deem it a great favour if you will be good enough to inform me, direct, in the event of anything occurring to my son, John Michael Wills (Sergeant) No. 7099, 23rd Reinforcements, 13th Battalion, AIF who sailed for the front on the 25-11-1916. His wife has removed and I cannot get into communication with her. It would be much more satisfactory if you will kindly accede to this request.

In a letter dated 10 May 1918, the OIC responded to Mr Wills' letter advising that it was not possible to individually notify him as well as the next of kin but provided him with Opal's then current address being *Rendezvous*, Brighton Boulevard, Bondi, so that he might be able to contact John's wife.

Prior to John Wills joining the 13th Battalion in France, it had seen action around Hébuterne, assisting to stop the German attack towards Amiens. The battalion had been pulled out of the front line and was resting and recuperating in the billets at Coigneux. The unit diary records the arrival of 130 reinforcements on 17 April 1918, describing them as 'men of fair-average physique and training, generally smart in appearance, and of an average age of 27'. The next day, the reinforcements were sent for range practice with the results noted as 'not yet

---

[908] A notice published in January 1918 recounts that Sgt J Wills had been promoted to Lieutenant in the field in France – 'Sergeant J. Wills, one of the burly 'Scotties,' and an ex-attendant at Lidcombe State Hospital, has received his promotion on the fields of France as first lieutenant.' See OF "THE BOYS" (1918, January 19). *The Cumberland Argus and Fruitgrowers Advocate* (Parramatta, NSW: 1888 - 1950), p. 11. Retrieved May 29, 2023, from http://nla.gov.au/nla.news-article86205096. There is nothing on John's service records which suggest a promotion to lieutenant, even if only temporary.

up to battalion standard, but keenness shown'. Considerable time was also spent on training men including the reinforcements on the use of the Lewis machine gun, and it would appear that John Wills was one of those nominated to form part of a Lewis gun crew.

Australian soldiers training with Lewis guns. September 1917. AWM ID No. E00683.

Between April and July 1918, the 13th Battalion alternated between time in reserve and training, and time on the front line on the Somme sector to the east of Villers-Bretonneux. The battalion had participated in the successful attack on Hamel in early July 1918 and was being prepared for the next major Allied attack. On 8 August, the battalion, along with other elements of the 4th Australian Division, participated in an attack in the vicinity of Morcourt, with the unit diary noting that by 10.00 a.m., the objective of the 'red line' had been secured, and was being consolidated by members of B Company. It also notes that the vicinity of the red line was the only spot where opposition was met by the battalion, resulting in 57 casualties, the majority from German artillery.

Statements taken by the Red Cross[909] from members of John Wills' unit indicate that on 8 August 1918, he was serving with B Company in front of the village of Corbie, as part of a Lewis gun team with Private EJ Quinn.[910] They were involved in the 'hop-over' which started what would be the final big offensive of the war. The battalion had secured its objective early in the morning of the attack and was digging in. At about midday, the Germans opened up with artillery and a shell landed where Ptes Wills and Quinn were manning their Lewis gun position. Both were killed instantly, and another two men wounded. Ptes Wills and Quinn were carried to the rear of the trench and buried there, with crosses erected over their graves.

News of John's death reached his family before the end of August 1918 with the following notice published in *The Hillston Spectator and Lachlan River Advertiser* relaying the news received by John's brother James[911]:

> Mr. J. Wills, of the staff of the local Post Office, received the sad news this week that his eldest brother, Quarter-master Sergeant John Michael Wills, was killed in action in France on 8th inst. The deceased soldier, prior to enlistment about 2 years ago, was employed at the G.P.O., Sydney, and also held the rank of Lieutenant in the 23rd Infantry Home Forces. Quartermaster Sergeant Wills, who was 28 years of age, leaves a widow and young family of three children, the eldest of whom is 6 years. A younger brother of deceased is also serving with the A.I.F.

---

[909] Australian Red Cross Wounded and Missing Files for John Michael Joseph Wills - https://www.awm.gov.au/people/rolls/R1478262/.
[910] Although the statements given to the Red Cross state that EJ Quinn was a private, accordingly to the records of the Commonwealth War Graves Commission, he held the rank of Lance Corporal.
[911] Local and General News. (1918, August 31). *The Hillston Spectator and Lachlan River Advertiser* (NSW: 1898 - 1952), p. 4. Retrieved May 29, 2023, from http://nla.gov.au/nla.news-article131033620

A family notice was subsequently published on 16 September 1918 in *The Sydney Morning Herald*[912]:

WILLS. - Killed in action in France August 8, 1918, Q.M.S. John Michael Wills of 13th Batt., beloved son of James and Jessie Wills, and beloved brother of Bertha Wills, Annandale, Norbert Wills, A.I.F., and James and Millie Wills, Hillston. Sweet Jesus, have mercy on his soul.

A few days later, the following notice appeared in *The Catholic Press*[913]:

Quartermaster-Sergeant John Michael Wills, who was killed in action in France on August 8, was 28 years of age, and was born in Balmain. He was educated by the Marist Brothers at the Sacred Heart School, Darlinghurst, and at St. Mary's High School. For some years he was employed as attendant at the Reception House, Darlinghurst, at the Balmain, Rydalmere, and Rookwood Asylums. About six years ago he entered the Postal Department as a letter-carrier, which position he held when he enlisted about two years ago. The deceased soldier was a fine, big, typical Australian, being over 6ft. high and weighing over 16 stone. He had belonged to the Scottish rifles from boyhood, and was a lieutenant in the home forces when he sailed abroad. He was a fine, jolly, manly fellow, a splendid Catholic, and leaves a widow and three young children to mourn their loss. His father, ex-Constable James Wills, now resides at Annandale. — R.I.P.

On 30 August 1918, the Postmaster-General's (PMG) Department wrote to the OIC seeking confirmation of the report of John's death

---

[912] Family Notices (1918, September 16). *The Sydney Morning Herald* (NSW: 1842 - 1954), p. 6. Retrieved May 29, 2023, from http://nla.gov.au/nla.news-article15802795
[913] All About People: Tittle Tattle (1918, September 19). *The Catholic Press* (Sydney, NSW: 1895 - 1942), p. 22. Retrieved May 29, 2023, from http://nla.gov.au/nla.news-article105963426

and requesting the address of his next of kin. The OIC replied on 16 September 1918 confirming that John had been killed on 8 August and providing contact details for John's wife.

On 4 September 1918, James Wills wrote to the OIC as follows:

> My Daughter in law received Official advice that her husband, John Michael Joseph Wills, was killed in action on the Western Front on the 8-8-18. Now I would deem it a great favour if you could ascertain and forward any particulars as to how he met his death etc. And also proof of his death, which is required to recover insurance money and allowance from Odd Fellows Lodge.
>
> This is a very sad case as he leaves a widow & three children, the eldest being only 7 years.

On the same date as the OIC responded to the letter from the PMG Department, the OIC responded to James Wills' letter advising that to date the only available information was contained in a brief cable message that John had been killed in action.

On 9 October 1918, Opal Wills wrote to the OIC requesting a copy of the certificate of John's death, which was provided by the OIC under cover of a letter dated 8 November 1918. Opal was at the time living at 70 Birrell Street, Waverley. This was one of a number of addresses recorded on the war service records for Opal Wills.

In April 1919, the Public Trustee acknowledged receipt of a parcel containing the personal effects of John Wills, being a wallet, a purse, photos and some coins. A number of family notices were published on the anniversary of John's death in 1919[914]:

---

[914] Family Notices (1919, August 8). *The Sydney Morning Herald* (NSW: 1842 - 1954), p. 6. Retrieved May 29, 2023, from http://nla.gov.au/nla.news-article15847373

WILLS - In loving memory of Sergeant J. M. Wills. 13th Battalion, killed in action, France. August 8. 1918. Long shall his memory ever dwell in our sorrowing hearts. Inserted by his parents, sister, and brothers.

WILLS - In loving memory of our dear friend, Q.M S. John Michael Wills, killed in action, August 8, 1918. His friends, Mr. and Mrs. Proctor and family, Edgecliff.

On 20 March 1920, while living at Freshwater, Manly, Opal Wills was officially advised that John was buried in Heath Cemetery, Harbonnières, France. In September the following year, Opal received a photograph of the grave, and subsequently received the memorial scroll and plaque in respect of John's service.[915]

In about 1926, Opal was residing at *Roslyn*, Shepherd Street, Ryde, and wrote to the OIC inquiring about the cancellation of the war pension following her re-marriage.[916] The inquiry appears to have been referred to the Repatriation Commission with a note that Opal's present husband appears to be identical to No. 5488 Private Arthur Lewis 13th Battalion 'who originally served as No. 619 Private Arthur Diver-Tuck, 7th Light Horse Regiment'.[917]

In 1943, Opal was still corresponding with the OIC, this time in relation to obtaining a replacement Nearest Female Relative badge. In a statutory declaration made on 15 October 1943, Opal declared that she had married Arthur L Diver-Tuck in January 1926 and had lost her badge on ANZAC Day, 25 April 1938 in Sydney when on the

---

[915] In 1922, Opal was again living at *Takapuna*, Park Avenue, Drummoyne.
[916] Opal remarried in about 1925 to Arthur L Diver-Tuck – NSW BDM Registration No. 313/1925.
[917] The embarkation records show that Arthur Lewis was 30 years old and a cook at the time he embarked, and enlisted on 6 November 1915. His date of embarkation was 9 April 1916 as part of an earlier reinforcement to the 13th Battalion. He gave as his address and that of his mother Mrs S Diver-Tuck as 13 Kenilworth Street, Waverley which may account for Opal's subsequent addresses in and around that suburb. AWM Embarkation Records accessible at https://www.awm.gov.au/people/rolls/R1825347/?query=arthur+lewis&section%5B0%5D=people&op=Search&filter%5Brelated_conflicts%5D=First+World+War%2C+1914-1918&filter%5Brank%5D=Private.

train coming home, presumably from the march, when she was living at 33 Valerie Street, Toongabbie. A subsequent document indicates that her son, Gunner Wills, was serving with the 19th Field Regiment in the 2nd AIF. The witness signature on the document appears to be T Wills, possibly Tom Wills who was baptised at St Mark's in June 1916.

The graves register and the graves inscription records held by the CWGC for John's grave include the following:

> WILLS, Pte. John Michael Joseph, 7099. 13th Bn. Australian Inf. Killed in action 8th Aug., 1918. Age 28. Son of Jessie and the late Mr. Wills; husband of Mrs. O. R. Wills, of 29, Tasmain St., Bondi, New South Wales. INDEX No. Fr. 52(HEATH CEM. HARBONNIERES I. G. 19.

Based on the graves register information provided by Opal, it would appear that James Wills died sometime after he received confirmation of the death of his son in September 1918. The age of John Wills at the date of his death stated on these records does not reconcile with the birth records or the age given on his attestation papers at the time of enlistment as 27 years and 10 months. John was aged 29 years at the time he was killed in action.

Heath Cemetery is located near the village of Harbonnières which was captured by French troops in the summer of 1916. It was retaken by the Germans on 27 April 1918 and regained by the Australian Corps on 8 August 1918. Heath Cemetery was established after the Armistice. Graves were brought into it from the battlefields between Bray and Harbonnières and from other burial grounds in the area. The remains of John Wills and L/Cpl EJ Quinn were exhumed after the war from the grave dug by their comrades and reinterred at Heath Cemetery. The records of the CWGC confirm that the bodies of each were identified by a cross over the grave.

Photograph of the grave of John Wills at Heath Cemetery, Harbonnières (author, 2018).

John Donald Edwards

Private, No. 3093

53rd Battalion, 14th Infantry Brigade, 5th Australian Division

Killed in action 31 August 1918, Peronne, France

Buried Herbecourt British Cemetery, France

Tread softly by our hearts are here with our beloved Jack

John (Jack) Donald Edwards was underage when he applied to enlist in the AIF on 25 May 1916. One of possibly four children of Thomas Norris Edwards and Mary Ann Edwards of *Dervin* 5 Broughton Street, Drummoyne, John was born at Millers Point in about 1899.[918] Educated at Drummoyne Superior Public School, John must have not been long working in the Hunter Valley when he decided to enlist at West Maitland. With his father's written consent and putting his age up by one year so as to declare his age as 18 years and two months,[919] John was accepted into the AIF and initially assigned to the 7th Reinforcements to the 1st Pioneer Battalion.

John embarked from Sydney on HMAT A30 *Borda* on 17 October 1916, arriving in Plymouth, England on 9 January 1917. During the voyage, John committed a youthful indiscretion, and was charged with disobeying the lawful command of an NCO in being late to parade and was punished with 24 hours' detention. John never fell foul of the authorities again.

In March 1917, John was with the Pioneer training battalion in England, but by April was temporarily assigned to No. 7 Reserve Squadron of the Royal Flying Corps based at Netheravon, Wiltshire. In May 1917, John made his will, where he left the whole of his estate to his brother William Robert Edwards (6314). William was even younger than John and had enlisted two months after him.[920]

In July 1917, he was again temporarily detached, this time to the 7th Training Squadron of the Australian Flying Corps, but shortly thereafter was transferred to the 14th Training Battalion to the 53rd Battalion on 11 July 1917. On 12 October 1917, along with other reinforcements, John proceeded overseas to France via Southampton,

---

[918] NSW BDM Registration No. 8993/1899. The other children are possibly Ivy M (27646/1896), Amy E (1332/1894) and William (19303/1901).
[919] The Honour Roll Circular completed by his mother stated that he enlisted at the age of 17 years and 2 months. This reconciles with Jack's date of birth.
[920] William Robert Edwards was born in about 1901 and enlisted in July 1916 and served with the 20th Battalion, returning to Australia on 31 July 1918 - https://aif.adfa.edu.au/showPerson?pid=89482. According to William's enlistment papers, he claimed to be 18 years on his enlistment, but this is crossed out and the age of 15 years has been inserted. He was discharged from the Army in October 1918 on account of being underage.

arriving at Le Harve the next day. John joined his battalion on 26 October 1917 while it was serving in the Ypres salient near Zillebeke.[921] The 53rd Battalion's immediate previous major engagement had been the attack on Polygon Wood.

Not long after joining his battalion, John was attached to the 14th Light Trench Mortar Battery, but he returned to his battalion on Christmas eve, 1917. Again, his attachment to his battalion was short lived as in February 1918, he was assigned for duty with the 177th Tunnelling Company but this too was short lived, lasting less than a fortnight. This time, John's reassignment to the 53rd Battalion would be permanent.

In February 1918, the 53rd Battalion was still seeing active service in Flanders in the Ypres salient, occupying German positions captured after the Third Battle of Ypres. The battalion experienced periodic patrolling and counter-patrols in the sector throughout February and March.

On 23 March the battalion received word that it was to be relieved, which the battalion diary noted was probably because the division would be going south to help stem the German advance. On 21 March 1918, the Germans had launched Operation Michael as part of a final attempt to achieve a breakthrough before the arrival of large numbers of American forces. Sure enough, by the end of March 1918, the battalion had made its way to the Somme sector and on the evening of 5-6 April 1918 was relieving the 17th Lancers in the front line at Villers-Bretonneux. Finding that no defences had been prepared, the battalion spent the remainder of the night hastily digging in, in anticipation of a German attack in the morning. The battalion diary notes that all ranks 'stood to' and confidently waited for the onslaught.[922] The attack did not eventuate on the battalion's sector of the front line, but the battalion remained on edge and eventually came under

---

[921] 53rd Battalion Unit Diary, October 1917 - https://www.awm.gov.au/images/collection/bundled/RCDIG1006764.pdf
[922] 53rd Battalion Unit Diary April 1918 - https://www.awm.gov.au/images/collection/bundled/RCDIG1006867.pdf

sustained and intense artillery and gas attack on 17 April, suffering gas casualties of nine officers and 155 other ranks.

By August 1918, the battalion was moving forward to new bivouacs near Querrieu to commence preparations for a new offensive and received instruction and practical training in working with tanks in attack. The battalion diary notes on 6 August 1918 how for the first time in AIF history all five Australian divisions would be involved in the forthcoming offensive[923]:

> All ranks are eagerly looking forward to the next few days, and the air of absolute confidence and grim determination bodes ill for the Bosche who may happen to be opposing us.

The offensive was scheduled to commence at 4:20 a.m. on the morning of 8 August. The battalion's diary notes on 7 August the displeasure that the 14th Brigade had been assigned as reserve brigade and may not get too involved in any of the fighting. Although not involved in the fighting the battalion was cheered by the reports of success of the offensive and the stream of prisoners which had been pouring back all day.

By late August, the battalion was continuing to move forward, covering old ground that had been fought over during the Somme offensive of 1916. The battalion diary notes that on 31 August, it had received orders to cross the Somme River at Omiecourt in preparation for an attack on the town of Peronne. After reconnoitring the ground, it was determined by the battalion CO that it was impractical to cross the river at that point due to enemy shelling. It was decided to cross by pontoon bridge further west along the canal bank at Bussecourt. The battalion diary notes that the crossing was carried out quickly with the only casualties being two other ranks killed and three wounded while on the canal bank prior to the crossing.

It is likely that one of those casualties was John Edwards as it was while the battalion was moving into position outside Peronne on 31

---

[923] 53rd Battalion Unit Diary August 1918 - https://www.awm.gov.au/images/collection/bundled/RCDIG1006871.pdf

August 1918, that John's company come under artillery fire. John was hit by shrapnel in the pelvis, and left thigh and knee. Evacuated by stretcher bearers, John had his leg amputated at a CCS, but died of his wounds while at the 15th Australian Field Ambulance.

Red Cross records[924] contain a witness statement from Private Claude Harris (3396) given in October 1918. He stated that John was in 5th Platoon of B Company in the battalion, and while advancing in 'Fritz's country' on 31 August, at about 4 p.m., John was hit by a shell which carried away one leg. Private Harris assisted to stop the bleeding until he was carried away by stretcher bearers while still conscious and cheerful. Cpl William Edwards (2357) corroborated the statement of Pte Harris, noting that the unit was moving towards its jump off point of the attack which was to commence the next day. The Officer Commanding the 15th Australian Field Ambulance reported that Private Edwards arrived at the Field Ambulance unconscious, dying later the same day of his wounds and being buried in Herbecourt Military Cemetery.

News of John's death was reported in *The Sydney Morning Herald* but not until 24 December 1918.[925] A number of family notices were published prior to this date[926] since John's name appeared in the 436th casualty list published on 22 October 1918 as having died of wounds.[927] Personal notices also appeared on the anniversary of John's death in 1919 and 1920 from family and a friend[928]:

---

[924] Australian Red Cross Wounded and Missing Files - https://www.awm.gov.au/collection/R1486110
[925] WAR CASUALTIES. (1918, December 24). *The Sydney Morning Herald* (NSW: 1842 - 1954), p. 8. Retrieved May 29, 2023, from http://nla.gov.au/nla.news-article15817059
[926] Family Notices (1918, October 26). *The Sydney Morning Herald* (NSW: 1842 - 1954), p. 13. Retrieved May 29, 2023, from http://nla.gov.au/nla.news-article15808273 and Family Notices (1918, November 2). *The Sydney Morning Herald* (NSW: 1842 - 1954), p. 12. Retrieved May 29, 2023, from http://nla.gov.au/nla.news-article15809409
[927] 436th CASUALTY LIST. NEW SOUTH WALES. (1918, October 22). *The Sydney Morning Herald* (NSW: 1842 - 1954), p. 8. Retrieved May 29, 2023, from http://nla.gov.au/nla.news-article15807619
[928] Family Notices (1919, August 30). *The Sydney Morning Herald* (NSW: 1842 - 1954), p. 16. Retrieved May 29, 2023, from http://nla.gov.au/nla.news-article28096854 and Family Notices (1920, August 31). *The Sydney Morning Herald* (NSW: 1842 - 1954), p. 6. Retrieved May 29, 2023, from http://nla.gov.au/nla.news-article15904751

EDWARDS. — In loving memory of our dear nephew cousin, Pte. John Donald Edwards, killed in action at Peronne, August 31, 1918. Sadly missed by all who loved him. Inserted by R. and A. Cairns and family.

EDWARDS. - In loving memory of my dear chum, 3093 Pte. J. D. Edwards, 53rd Batt, who died of wounds received near Peronne, August 31. 1918.
This day brings back to memory fresh,
A dear chum gone to rest;
And those who miss him most of all,
Are those who loved him best.
Inserted by his chum, Andy Young (returned).

EDWARDS. - In loving memory of our dear son and brother, Private John Donald Edwards, who died of wounds received at Peronne, August 31, 1918.
A beautiful memory left behind, and a duty nobly done.
Inserted by his loving mother, Amy, Ivy, and Will.

EDWARDS. - In loving memory of our dear nephew Pte. J. D. Edwards, killed at Peronne, August 31. 1918. J. and M. Smyth.

John's personal effects were returned to his brother William via his father at Broughton Street, Drummoyne in April 1919. On 13 June 1919, the OIC wrote to William Edwards confirming that John had been wounded on 31 August 1918 and died of his wounds on the same date at the 15th Australian Field Ambulance, before being buried at Herbecourt Communal Cemetery Extension about 4 ½ miles west of Peronne. However, in May 1921, Mrs Edwards[929] was advised that John's remains had been exhumed and reinterred at Peronne Communal Cemetery Extension. We can only imagine the angst that Mrs Edward's experienced when twelve months later she was advised that

---

[929] John's service records indicate that in or about 1920, William Edwards had died.

this was an error and that her son was indeed buried at his original resting place at Herbecourt Communal Cemetery Extension. John is one of 60 war casualties buried in this cemetery from the First World War.[930]

Photograph of the grave of John Edwards at Herbecourt British Cemetery, France (author, 2018).

---

[930] http://www.cwgc.org/find-a-cemetery/cemetery/32103/HERBECOURT%20BRITISH%20CEMETERY

Albert Bates

Sergeant, No. 3004
55th Battalion, 14th Infantry Brigade, 5th Australian Division
Killed in action 2 September 1918, Peronne, France
Buried Heilly Station Cemetery, Mericourt-L'Abbe, France

Albert Bates was born in Drummoyne sometime about 1896,[931] one of five children of James Henry and Mary Jane Bates.[932] Although a medical report on his service file[933] suggests that he was 27 at the time of his enlistment and a farm driver by occupation based in Singleton, the Honour Roll completed by his mother after the war records that he was 19 years old at the time of his enlistment on 7 August 1915 and a store packer.[934]

Albert was initially assigned as a private to the 10th Reinforcements to the 3rd Battalion and embarked on HMAT A69 *Warilda* on 8 October 1915 bound for Egypt. Along with the other reinforcements, Albert was destined to arrive in Egypt, just as the Australian forces were being evacuated from the Gallipoli peninsula. Albert was initially taken on strength with the 3rd Battalion on 5 February 1916, but as the Australian forces were being doubled in size, the 3rd Battalion was split with half of it to form the basis of the newly established 55th Battalion. Half of the 3rd Battalion and all of the 9th and some of the 10th and 11th Reinforcements formed the basis of the new battalion under the command of Major DM McConaghy.[935] Albert joined the 55th Battalion on 13 February. In March, the battalion left Tel-el-Kebir for Ferry Post to commence garrison duties.[936] The battalion continued training on the outer line of canal defences until June 1916, albeit with a break on 25 April 1916 to mark 'ANZAC Day' with a day of sports. On 19 June, the battalion received orders to entrain at Moascar for Alexandria.[937]

---

[931] NSW BDM Registration No. 21135/1896.
[932] His siblings were George R (12632/1890), Ruby (12194/1892), Hector (11800/1894) and Pearl (2870/1900).
[933] War service records accessible at https://recordsearch.naa.gov.au/SearchNRetrieve/Interface/ViewImage.aspx?B=3056631
[934] https://s3-ap-southeast-2.amazonaws.com/awm-media/collection/RCDIG1068852/document/5550569.PDF
[935] 55th Battalion Unit Diary February 1916 - https://www.awm.gov.au/collection/C1345988?image=2
[936] 55th Battalion Unit Diary March 1916 - https://www.awm.gov.au/collection/C1355912?image=4
[937] 55th Battalion Unit Diary June 1916 - https://www.awm.gov.au/collection/C1344288?image=5

On 22 June 1916, the battalion departed Alexandria on board HMT *Caledonian* to join the BEF in France, arriving in Marseilles later that month. The battalion immediately entrained and headed north, arriving at the town of Thiennes on the early morning of 3 July.[938] Almost immediately, the battalion commenced training on aspects of trench warfare on the Western Front including defensive measures in the event of gas attacks, with many route marches through the countryside. The battalion eventually took over its first section of front-line trenches on 12 July from the 45th Battalion near Bac St Maur. Two days previously, Albert Bates had received his first promotion to lance corporal. By 13 July, the battalion had taken its first casualty to enemy action, and on the 15th had experienced its first gas attack.

On 19 July, after less than a fortnight at the front, the battalion as part of the 14th Brigade, 5th Australian Division, received orders to participate in its first attack on the German fortified trenches near the town of Fromelles.[939]

The unit diary describes the attack as a complete success with the German trenches taken, but under heavy counterattack and enemy shelling, some 'refinement' of the line was required. On the 20th the unit diary notes:

> The losses were heavy, but the Battalion, four-fifths or more of whom were strangers to battle, acquitted itself honourably in its first engagement, and returned with 40 German prisoners.

The battle, which was in fact intended to be a diversionary attack, was a disaster, resulting in heavy casualties across the division without any territory being gained. It has been variously described as the worst night and worst twenty-four hours in Australian military history.[940]

---

[938] 55th Battalion Unit Diary July 1916 - https://www.awm.gov.au/collection/C1344289?image=2
[939] 55th Battalion Unit History - https://www.awm.gov.au/unit/U51495/ and Battle of Fromelles, AWM - https://www.awm.gov.au/military-event/E159/
[940] Ross McMullin, *Wartime* Issue 36 - Disaster at Fromelles - https://www.awm.gov.au/wartime/36/article/ ;
https://www.awm.gov.au/blog/2008/07/18/the-worst-night-in-australian-military-history-fromelles/

Although in reserve, the 55th Battalion was quickly committed to the attack and eventually played a critical role, forming the rear guard for the 14th Brigade's withdrawal.[941]

Accounting for the cost of the first engagement was completed on 20 July; two officers and 35 other ranks reported killed, five other ranks dead from wounds, five officers and 149 other ranks wounded, and four officers and 139 other ranks missing.[942] This was almost half the battalion's strength in an engagement lasting less than 24 hours. As we now know, many other battalions in the 5th Australian Division fared much worse. Owing to the heavy losses, on 23 July, A and B Companies were temporarily combined as one company, as were C and D Companies.[943]

That Albert managed to survive his first action which also happened to be one of the AIF's worst disasters is perhaps nothing short of miraculous. Five other men, Walter Williamson, Downie Dodd, Edward Boyle, John Wall and Michael Hawley who are also commemorated on the Drummoyne War Memorial were not as fortunate.

During early August 1916, the battalion worked at repairing the trenches at Fromelles, and began to replace the losses from the battle, with reinforcements arriving such that by 16 August, the battalion's complement was at 23 officers and 754 other ranks.[944] On 22 August Albert was promoted to the rank of Corporal and by early September 1916, Albert spent a week at the bomb school of instruction.

The 55th Battalion continued to serve in and out of the front lines around Fromelles for the rest of August and September 1916, engaging in continuous artillery and patrolling engagements with the Germans. The unit diary notes on 15 September that the number of 'dud' shells was becoming noticeable, which itself had been one of the

---

[941] 55th Battalion Unit History AWM - https://www.awm.gov.au/unit/U51495/
[942] 55th Battalion Unit Diary July 1916 - https://www.awm.gov.au/collection/C1344289?image=5. Those reported missing the diary admitted would eventually be determined to have been killed.
[943] 55th Battalion Unit Diary July 1916 - https://www.awm.gov.au/collection/C1344289?image=6
[944] 55th Battalion Unit Diary August 1916 - https://www.awm.gov.au/collection/C1344290?image=4

failings of the Somme offensive.[945] The same routine continued during the first half of October, but under deteriorating weather conditions as autumn broke, and with it increasing heavy rain. The battalion finally left the Fromelles sector in mid-October, making its way to the Dernacourt and Fricourt sector of the Somme front. Under increasing rain, the battalion was sent in to take over a sector of the frontline to prepare for a forthcoming attack by British XVth Corps.[946] The weather caused the attack to be delayed several days with the unit diary noting:

> The conditions under which the men were now living are the worst yet experienced by them and 4 or 5 men are daily being evacuated to hospital.

Rain continued to delay the proposed attack, but the men now found great difficulty in actually getting to the front line because of the mud. On 2 November the unit diary describes the conditions as most trying with 60 men sent to hospital.[947] Eventually, the battalion was withdrawn from the frontline with the planned attack cancelled. The battalion moved to new billets at a training camp at Rainneville, 10 kms north of Amiens, and was inspected by the BEF Commander, General Sir Douglas Haig on 11 November 1916.

In early December 1916, the battalion moved back into the frontlines, this time around the village of Flers including in Switch Trench and Delville Wood, and with what the unit diary describes as 'a fair quantity of duck boards'.[948] The unit remained there until 19 December when they returned to billets near Buire and enjoyed some rest up to and including Christmas day before training recommenced in

---

[945] It is estimated that 30% of the 1.7 million British shells fired during the Somme offensive did not explode
https://nationalarchives.gov.uk/education/greatwar/g4/cs3/background.htm
[946] 55th Battalion Unit Diary October 1916 - https://www.awm.gov.au/collection/C1344292?image=8
[947] 55th Battalion Unit Diary November 1916 - https://www.awm.gov.au/collection/C1356948?image=2
[948] 55th Battalion Unit Diary December 1916 - https://www.awm.gov.au/collection/C1345989?image=3

earnest. The battalion's rest came to an end when it returned to intermediate lines around Flers at the end of January 1917.[949] The water and mud previously experienced by the battalion was now frozen hard, with trench foot being a major concern for the men in the trenches.

The battalion's routine continued in February and March 1917 with periods in the line followed by brief periods in reserve. On 17 February the unit diary notes a change in the weather with the ground thawing but with more rain making conditions difficult for the men.[950] For Albert, the routine was broken by a week's instruction at the Fifth Army's musketry school in early March. Shortly after re-joining the battalion, Albert was promoted to the rank of Sergeant.

In mid-March, the battalion's diary notes that the Germans were evacuating their positions and retiring.[951] The battalion cautiously moved forward occupying the former German trenches in the vicinity of Beaulencourt, before continuing to advance over the areas evacuated by the Germans. The battalion would ultimately come to appreciate that the German withdrawal was part of a plan by the Germans to shorten their defensive line and occupy newly constructed fortified defences and villages called the Hindenburg Line. The battalion diary noted that the men's spirits had improved due to the new surroundings and being on higher ground.[952]

In early April, the battalion attacked and captured the village of Doignies. The day of 25 April was devoted to a sports meeting to mark the second anniversary of the landing of the Australians at Gallipoli.[953] On 8-9 May, the battalion moved into the frontlines outside of Noreuil, where it supported the 54th and 56th Battalions repulse a

---

[949] 55th Battalion Unit Diary January 1917 - https://www.awm.gov.au/collection/C1355910?image=7
[950] 55th Battalion Unit Diary February 1917 - https://www.awm.gov.au/collection/C1345990?image=6
[951] 55th Battalion Unit Diary March 1917 - https://www.awm.gov.au/collection/C1345991?image=6
[952] 55th Battalion Unit Diary March 1917 - https://www.awm.gov.au/collection/C1345991?image=9
[953] 55th Battalion Unit Diary April 1917 - https://www.awm.gov.au/collection/C1345992?image=10

German attack, ultimately relieving the 56th Battalion on 17 May. By mid-June, the battalion was in Millencourt for rest. The battalion diary notes[954]:

> The period spent in billets at Millencourt since 15th June has been most beneficial for all ranks. In addition to the training – cricket and other sports have been indulged in after parade hours. 10% leave to AMIENS has been granted daily. The rest in billets has been more appreciated on account of the Battalion not having been out in back area billets since January.

The battalion spent all of July and August 1917 in training and on route marches between billets,[955] culminating in an inspection by now Field Marshall Sir Douglas Haig on 29 August.[956] Albert however missed the opportunity for a second inspection by the Commanding Officer of the BEF, as on 2 August 1917, he had been posted to the 14th Training Battalion at the AIF Headquarters based at Tidworth in England. Albert was eventually appointed to that unit's cadre on a permanent basis.

In November 1917, Albert attended the 51st course of instruction at the Southern Command Bombing School, Lyndhurst where he qualified as an instructor. The school specialised in training in grenade use[957] and it is likely that on completion of the course, Albert returned to Tidworth to train men in the use of grenades. He would have also

---

[954] 55th Battalion Unit Diary June 1917 - https://www.awm.gov.au/collection/C1355911?image=7
[955] https://www.awm.gov.au/images/collection/bundled/RCDIG1007416.pdf 55th Battalion Unit Diary July 1917;
https://www.awm.gov.au/images/collection/bundled/RCDIG1007417.pdf 55th Battalion Unit Diary August 1917
[956] 55th Battalion Unit Diary August 1917 - https://www.awm.gov.au/collection/C1345995?image=4
[957] http://www.newforestheritage.org/southern-command-school-of-bombing/ Southern Command School of Bombing. Students sent from across the British Empire would spend a few weeks learning every aspect of grenade use, their mechanisms, tactics, including attacking and clearing trench systems. Students were expected to be familiar with every type of grenade they may encounter including enemy types and be able to use them proficiently. Those who passed were entitled to wear a red grenade badge on their right arm.

been wearing the British Trench Bombers Proficiency Badge on his right arm.

WWI British Trench Bombers Proficiency Badge. http://www.newforestheritage.org/southern-command-school-of-bombing/

Tidworth, England. Changing the guard outside Administrative Headquarters of the AIF Depots in the United Kingdom at Bhurtpore Barracks. At right is a chalked drawing of a kangaroo, map of Australia and emu in front of the flag. Photo taken 12 June 1919. AWM ID No. P10688.011.002

Australian soldiers receiving instruction in grenade throwing, at the Rollestone training camp live bombing range. United Kingdom: England, Leicestershire, Rollestone. Photo taken September 1916. AWM ID No. P10688.011.002.

Albert's time in the UK ended in early 1918 when he rejoined his battalion on 17 February 1918. While he had been absent, the battalion had seen action Belgian Flanders, outside of Ypres near Polygon Wood, as part of the Third Battle of Ypres in September 1917, including on the area around the Butte fortified with concrete pill boxes.[958] The battalion continued to see action on the Flanders front during October and November around Westhoek and Wytschaete. After a period out of the line, the battalion returned to Wytschaete at the end of January 1918.

---

[958] 55th Battalion Unit Diary September 1917 - https://www.awm.gov.au/collection/C1345996?image=4. The 5th Australian Division Memorial is now constructed on the Butte at Polygon Wood.

Looking towards Wytschaete, from Prince Rupert's Dugouts. Wytschaete was occupied by the 55th Battalion at this time. Belgium: Flanders, West-Vlaanderen, Heuvelland, Wytschaete. 11 February 1918. AWM ID No. E04555.

It was at Wytschaete that Albert rejoined his unit, just as preparations for a raid on a series of enemy strong points called 'Whiz Farm' were commencing. On 27 February four NCOs and 17 other ranks volunteered to be in the raiding party to be led by Lieutenant S Colless DCM. Although we do not know whether Albert was one of the NCOs in the raiding party, it is possible that having freshly arrived from the UK, he may have wanted to get back into action. On the night of 2-3 March, the raid was carried put, with the battalion diary recording that the most striking feature of the raid was the enemy's unusually strong determination to resist[959]:

---

[959] 55th Battalion Unit Diary March 1918 - https://www.awm.gov.au/collection/C1344273?image=3

It was a hard fight from start to finish, but the superiority of our lads over the Germans in hand-to-hand fighting won the fight for us. 18 of the enemy killed and one .. brought in as prisoner, whilst our party sustained only two casualties .. .

The battalion diary remarks on both 8 and 10 March that the German attitude was becoming increasingly aggressive, and troops holding the enemy trenches were imbued with a more offensive spirit.[960] The diary also describes a dummy or 'Chinese' raid undertaken on the night of 13 March whereby men placed figures in trenches and no-man's land simulating an attack, with the intention of drawing German attention.[961] It was successful in attracting considerable enemy machine gun and trench mortar fire. One figure became jammed and continued to attract heavy German fire until the early morning. On 21 March the diary records a minor German operation which had been effectively dealt with, but which was simultaneous with the opening of the long threatened German offensive further south. The battalion was relieved the next day and moved from the Ypres front south to form part of a reserve at Louvencourt. On 5 April, the battalion received orders to move to Aubigny, from whence it advanced to Villers-Bretonneux in heavy rain to relieve the 3rd Dragoon Guards on 6 April.[962]

The battalion was pushing its line forward around Villers-Bretonneux on 8 April 1918 to establish jumping off trenches for an attack on the German lines when Albert was wounded.[963] He suffered a gunshot wound to the back and was admitted to the 10th General Hospital at Rouen with his wounding reported in casualty lists

---

[960] 55th Battalion Unit Diary March 1918 - https://www.awm.gov.au/collection/C1344273?image=7
[961] 55th Battalion Unit Diary March 1918 - https://www.awm.gov.au/collection/C1344273?image=9
[962] 55th Battalion Unit Diary April 1918 - https://www.awm.gov.au/collection/C1344274?image=4
[963] 55th Battalion Unit Diary April 1918 - https://www.awm.gov.au/collection/C1344274?image=6

published in May 1918.[964] In Albert's absence, the battalion continued to be heavily involved in the defence of Villers-Bretonneux, withstanding heavy artillery and gas attacks. The unit also observed increased aerial activity including on 20 April a large aerial engagement with the diary recording that the German squadron involved was believed to be under the leadership of Baron von Richthofen, 'the celebrated German airman'. The battalion was relieved and returned to Aubigny, and on 21 April the unit diary records[965]:

> During the day an enemy plane was brought down, [and] it was later ascertained that the famous German airman BARON VON RICHTOFEN had been brought down by the 53rd (Aust) Battery.

While billeted in Aubigny, the battalion was subjected to heavy shell fire and gas attack on 23 April, suffering 90 casualties. This was a prelude to a heavy German attack on 24 April. While the 54th Battalion held the line north of Villers-Bretonneux, the British troops defending the village itself were thrown back. The 13th and 15th Australian Brigades counterattacked, retaking the village on 25 April.

After a period in the 2nd Convalescent Depot, Albert rejoined the battalion on 28 May 1918 when it was still in the front line near Villers-Bretonneux, about to relieve the 53rd Battalion in the forward trenches.[966] In July, the battalion found itself in trenches north of Sailly-Le-Sec, undertaking a diversionary attack including a 'Chinese' or dummy attack in support of the main attack on German lines at Hamel by units of the 4th Australian Division.[967]

In August 1918, the battalion was taken out of the line to billets north-west of Amiens where it prepared to renew the offensive on

---

[964] DOUBLE CASUALTY LIST. (1918, May 9). *The Sydney Morning Herald* (NSW: 1842 - 1954), p. 8. Retrieved May 29, 2023, from http://nla.gov.au/nla.news-article15774210
[965] 55th Battalion Unit Diary April 1918 - https://www.awm.gov.au/collection/C1344274?image=12
[966] 55th Battalion Unit Diary May 1918 - https://www.awm.gov.au/collection/C1344275?image=14
[967] 55th Battalion Unit Diary July 1918 - https://www.awm.gov.au/collection/C1344277?image=3

the German lines, with 8 August being 'Z' day. The diary notes that all men were 'keyed up to concert pitch'.[968] The offensive was a resounding success but the 55th Battalion was not directly involved. On 10 August, the diary notes the frustration of the men in the battalion who were eagerly awaiting a share of the opportunity for 'biffing of the Hun'.[969] They were disappointed to receive orders to return to billets at Villers-Bretonneux. Later that month, as the 3rd Division was involved in an attack north of the Somme River, the men in the battalion were again very disappointed to be missing out on the 'stunt'.[970]

The battalion would soon have its chance with an attack on the town of Peronne which commenced on 1 September 1918. The new attack was a success and was renewed the following day with an artillery barrage commencing at 5.30 a.m. The unit diary notes that an enemy barrage occurred at almost the same time in expectation of an attack, but with greater intensity than the previous day.[971] Two companies of the battalion suffered twelve casualties just prior to zero hour as a result of the counter barrage. Albert was likely to have been one of those casualties, and one of 46 other ranks in the battalion killed during the capture of Peronne.

Albert suffered a shell wound to the face and was evacuated to the 6th Field Ambulance before being transferred to the 20th Casualty Clearing Station. It was here that Albert succumbed to his wounds and died. He was 22 years old. Albert's name appeared in the 436th casualty list published in October 1918 as having died of wounds.[972] The service records note that Albert was buried at Heilly Station Cemetery with Reverend J Williamsin in attendance. Albert's death

---

[968] 55th Battalion Unit Diary August 1918 - https://www.awm.gov.au/collection/C1344279?image=4
[969] 55th Battalion Unit Diary August 1918 - https://www.awm.gov.au/collection/C1344279?image=5
[970] 55th Battalion Unit Diary August 1918 - https://www.awm.gov.au/collection/C1344279?image=5
[971] 55th Battalion Unit Diary September 1918 - https://www.awm.gov.au/collection/C1344280?image=10
[972] 436th CASUALTY LIST. NEW SOUTH WALES. (1918, October 22). *The Sydney Morning Herald* (NSW: 1842 - 1954), p. 8. Retrieved May 29, 2023, from http://nla.gov.au/nla.news-article15807619

occurred a little more than a month before all Australian forces would be withdrawn for rest, and two months before the Armistice on 11 November 1918.

It was not until March 1919, that the OIC was able to formally confirm the details of Albert's death to his parents. In May 1919, Mary Jane Bates requested a certificate of death from the OIC so that she could apply for administration of Albert's estate, with Letters of Administration being granted by the Supreme Court of NSW over Albert's estate to his mother on 27 May.

Personal notices from family and friends were published on the anniversary of Albert's death in 1919[973] and again in 1920[974]:

> BATES - In loving memory of my dear son and our brother, Sergeant Albert Bates, died of wounds France, September 2, 1918. A young life nobly ended. Inserted by his loving mother, brothers, and sisters. George, Hector, Ruby, Pearl.

> BATES. - In loving memory of my dear friend, Sgt A. Bates, died of wounds in France, September 2, 1918. Inserted by his sincere friend, T. Anderson.

> BATES. — In fond memory of my "Cobber." 3004, Sgt. A. ("Biddy") Bates, 55th Battalion, died of wounds, Peronne, September 2nd, 1918. Inserted by Sgt. Jack McGovern, 55th Batt.

In December 1919, Albert's mother received photographs of his grave, at Heilly Station Cemetery, Mericourt-L'Abbe, France. Albert would also be remembered on the gravestone of his father erected in the Field of Mars, Ryde.[975]

---

[973] Family Notices (1919, September 2). *The Sydney Morning Herald* (NSW: 1842 - 1954), p. 8. Retrieved May 29, 2023, from http://nla.gov.au/nla.news-article15860171
[974] Family Notices (1920, September 2). *The Daily Telegraph* (Sydney, NSW: 1883 - 1930), p. 4. Retrieved May 29, 2023, from http://nla.gov.au/nla.news-article239700514
[975] https://aif.adfa.edu.au/showPerson?pid=16092

Photograph of the grave of Albert Bates, Heilly Station Cemetery, Mericourt-L'Abbe, France (author, 2018).

Harold Kingsley Percival

Flight Cadet, No. 137709

Royal Air Force

Killed by accident 23 September 1918, Montrose, Scotland

Buried Sleepyhillock Cemetery, Montrose, Scotland

Photograph of Harold Kingsley Percival. Source - University of Sydney http://beyond1914.sydney.edu.au/profile/3808/harold-kingsley-percival

Harold Kingsley Percival was the eldest of seven children of Rev. George Charles Percival and Emily McCoy. Married in March 1889 in Hurstville, George and Emily were living in Bulli when their first child, Harold, was born on 7 January 1890.[976] Another son, Cecil Humphrey, was born a year later also in Bulli,[977] with Marjorie (1892)

---

[976] Some records including those of the University of Sydney record Harold's place of birth as Woonona.
[977] NSW BDM Registration No. 38980/1891.

in Milton,⁹⁷⁸ Norman Arnold (1894)⁹⁷⁹ and Dorothy (1895)⁹⁸⁰ in Albury, and Madeline (1898)⁹⁸¹ and Marion (1900)⁹⁸² in Taree.

A Methodist Minister, George Percival held various postings including during the war at Drummoyne Methodist Church where they resided at *Chalfort* on Collingwood Street, Drummoyne. Harold was educated at Sydney Boys High before attending Teacher's Training College. On completion of his training, he was on the staff of the Technical High School at Ultimo, Sydney. He also attended the University of Sydney for two and a half years as an evening student where he was enrolled in an Arts degree.

Said to be suffering from a rheumatic disability which prevented his enlistment in the AIF, he joined the YMCA and spent several months at military camps in and around Sydney providing services to the enlisted men. His younger brother, Cecil, had enlisted in the AIF in October 1915 at the age of 24 years and was assigned as a motor transport driver in the Army Service Corps. Cecil embarked from Sydney on 4 May 1916 on board HMAT A74 *Marathon*.⁹⁸³

It was on the eve of Harold's final examination in his Arts course at Sydney University that he was said to have received 'the call of conscience and duty'.⁹⁸⁴ In July 1916, Harold was accepted for a YMCA military field secretary position at the front⁹⁸⁵ and, not long after Cecil's departure, Harold would himself be sailing to England. In the same month an incident occurred on a tram when Harold was with

---

⁹⁷⁸ NSW BDM Registration No. 22595/1892.
⁹⁷⁹ NSW BDM Registration No. 3684/1894.
⁹⁸⁰ NSW BDM Registration No. 29637/1895.
⁹⁸¹ NSW BDM Registration No. 35009/1898.
⁹⁸² NSW BDM Registration No. 7761/1900.
⁹⁸³ Cecil survived the war and returned to Australia, when he was finally discharged in March 1920. See AIF Project (https://aif.adfa.edu.au/showPerson?pid=238470) and NAA Service Records - https://recordsearch.naa.gov.au/SearchNRetrieve/Interface/DetailsReports/ItemDetail.aspx?Barcode=8010834&isAv=N
⁹⁸⁴ AN AUSTRALIAN AIRMAN KILLED. (1918, September 26). *Camden News* (NSW: 1895 - 1954), p. 1. Retrieved May 29, 2023, from http://nla.gov.au/nla.news-article136791389
⁹⁸⁵ BRIEF MENTION (1916, July 8). *The Methodist* (Sydney, NSW: 1892 - 1954), p. 7. Retrieved May 29, 2023, from http://nla.gov.au/nla.news-article155433129

his sisters which inspired Harold to send a letter to the editor of *The Sydney Morning Herald*[986]:

LOAFERS AND GIRLS.

TO THE EDITOR OF THE HERALD.

Sir - On Saturday night I was returning home by a late tram with my sisters, who, as usual in these times, were busy knitting. A fellow of about 25, a little the worse for drink, joined the car and immediately began to amuse himself at their expense. 'See now I'm perling; now I drop one on the heel and turn. Are you decreasing?. I am. There, I've got sixteen stitches on the front needle, and twenty-four on the back, what's next?' This to ladies who had not spoken a word; and his half-dozen male companions laughed at the joke. I interfered, and at once the loyalty of his soul was roused, and he told me I ought to be at the war. I am at present in camp, wearing plain clothes, and will shortly be going to the front as a Y M C A field secretary; my brother is in Salisbury Plains Camp now, as a motor-driver. It must not be thought that I am writing this to support conscription. It would be quite unfair. It would be undemocratic to get such men to do their share in the war.

Their liberty must not be tampered with. Before that happens the lesson of suffering insult in their own city must be patiently learned by lonely girls who knit socks in public places for the lads doing their duty abroad.

---

[986] LOAFERS AND GIRLS. (1916, July 19). *The Sydney Morning Herald* (NSW: 1842 - 1954), p. 8. Retrieved May 29, 2023, from http://nla.gov.au/nla.news-article15695227

The presence of these characters at home is necessary for the crowding of hotels and stadiums. But the lads in camp and at the front have an immovable faith in the real men and women of Australia to see that the noble-minded girls they leave behind are properly respected and taken care of in their absence.

Thanking you Sir, for making it possible for me to reach such men and women, I am, etc,

July 17. H K PERCIVAL

On 30 September 1916 Harold departed Australia on board the *Aeneas*, bound for the AIF depot at Westham, England, where he was put in charge of YMCA services.[987] While in England with the YMCA, Harold found time to write an article for *The Methodist* newspaper[988]:

WHEN STRONG MEN PRAY.

Y.M.C.A. BATTLE FRONT SERVICES.

Writing from France, Mr. H. K. Percival, a military secretary of the Y.M.C.A. with Australian troops, says:

'Our Australian men do appreciate sacred music of the best kind, and, what is more, they will always stop and listen to a Gospel address; they will respond to it, too. On one Sunday evening recently I gave an opportunity after the address, and seventeen men signed the war roll cards. It is a treat to be at some of these meetings. God moves in them.

---

[987] http://beyond1914.sydney.edu.au/profile/3808/harold-kingsley-percival
[988] WHEN STRONG MEN PRAY. (1917, September 1). *The Methodist* (Sydney, NSW: 1892 - 1954), p. 8. Retrieved May 29, 2023, from http://nla.gov.au/nla.news-article155428260

Only last night His presence was felt especially – a weeknight service. I ran the singing and let a soldier speak – one of God's soldiers, and no mistake; a man who has been to France, and has suffered with them, and who has led many men to Christ. He gave the simple Gospel invitation, gave it in the strength given him by God, and I never experienced a more powerful appeal. It is great to hear these strong men pray; aye, strong because they have suffered and kept hold in Christ. We have all sorts of men in our circle from time to time. One of the most devout is a former 'pugilist.'

Harold remained at the AIF Depot at Westham for a period of 18 months. It was said that the English climate was more agreeable to Harold and he benefitted considerably from his time there, such that he was successful in enlisting in the Royal Air Force (RAF) in March 1918.[989] His father noted in a subsequent tribute that Harold was too old to join the Australian Flying Corps which is why he chose to join the RAF. Harold took a course of training at Hastings and then at the No. 1 School of Aeronautics at Reading, before moving to Montrose Aerodrome in Scotland to complete his training through flight practice. All going well, Harold expected to have gone to France in November 1918 on active service.

It was during what was said to be his final practice flight on 23 September 1918 at Montrose Aerodrome that a mishap occurred[990] with Harold's aeroplane crashing, killing him instantly. A Court of Inquiry was held which determined that the cause of the accident was due to an error on Harold's part in that he attempted to turn back to the aerodrome allowing his machine to get into a spin, and had not sufficient height to counteract it.[991]

---

[989] AN AUSTRALIAN AIRMAN KILLED. (1918, September 26). *Camden News* (NSW: 1895 - 1954), p. 1. Retrieved May 29, 2023, from http://nla.gov.au/nla.news-article136791389
[990] http://beyond1914.sydney.edu.au/profile/3808/harold-kingsley-percival
[991] https://ww1austburialsuk.weebly.com/uploads/4/9/7/8/4978039/percival__harold_kingsley.pdf

News of Harold's death quickly appeared in local newspapers[992] with a detailed article also appearing in the *Camden News* on 26 September 1918[993]:

AN AUSTRALIAN AIRMAN KILLED.

FLIGHT-CADET H. K. PERCIVAL.

Rev. G. C. Percival of Camden, received a cabled message from the office of the Royal Air Force, England, on Tuesday last, September 24th, informing him that his eldest son, Flight-Cadet Harold Kingsley Percival, had on the previous day been killed by an aeroplane accident during flight practice, at the Montrose Aerodrome, Scotland. Flight Cadet Percival was up to the time of his entrance on war work, a member of the staff of the Technical High School, Ultimo, Sydney. ….. He was an apt student, and was on the eve of his final examination for the arts course at the Sydney University, when he answered the call of conscience and duty. The study involved in his preparation for a commission in the Royal Air Force appealed strongly to him.

---

[992] PERSONAL. (1918, October 2). *The Sydney Morning Herald* (NSW: 1842 - 1954), p. 10. Retrieved May 29, 2023, from http://nla.gov.au/nla.news-article28099569; HAROLD PERCIVAL. (1918, September 28). *The Cumberland Argus and Fruitgrowers Advocate* (Parramatta, NSW: 1888 - 1950), p. 6. Retrieved May 29, 2023, from http://nla.gov.au/nla.news-article86214422 . See also CAMDEN. (1918, October 2). *Australian Town and Country Journal* (Sydney, NSW: 1870 - 1919), p. 17. Retrieved May 29, 2023, from http://nla.gov.au/nla.news-article263629019 ; BRIEF MENTION (1918, September 28). *The Methodist* (Sydney, NSW: 1892 - 1954), p. 7. Retrieved May 29, 2023, from http://nla.gov.au/nla.news-article155265121 ; Family Notices (1918, September 28). *The Daily Telegraph* (Sydney, NSW: 1883 - 1930), p. 8. Retrieved May 29, 2023, from http://nla.gov.au/nla.news-article239361560 ; Advertising (1918, October 3). *Goulburn Evening Penny Post* (NSW: 1881 - 1940), p. 1 (EVENING). Retrieved May 29, 2023, from http://nla.gov.au/nla.news-article99029547
[993] AN AUSTRALIAN AIRMAN KILLED. (1918, September 26). *Camden News* (NSW: 1895 - 1954), p. 1. Retrieved May 29, 2023, from http://nla.gov.au/nla.news-article136791389

In two out of the seven subjects he secured the maximum number of 100 marks, and in all but one of the remaining ones, he was well in the nineties. As a student of history, he was profoundly interested in the places he was privileged to visit in the Old Land during leave, and as a man he made many friends. His career gave promise of great usefulness. He would have been 29 years of age in January next.

A moving tribute from his father, George, appeared in the publication *The Methodist* on 26 October 1918[994]:

OUR SON.

BY HIS FATHER.

I heard his first cry, and a little later saw his puzzled glance round, as if to say, 'What kind of place is this, that I have come into?' That was when he came to us, our first-born, in the happy long ago. With a cry of another kind — of victory and unqualified joy— though with something, probably, of the same puzzled glance round, he entered upon the life of the better and brighter world, on Monday, September 23rd, 1918, stepping from his aeroplane from the one world to the other. The same keen interest in life, the same, mood of mental alertness and enquiry, and the same spiritual earnestness, that characterised him here, is with him there, only in richer degree and vastly ennobled form. He loved study, and save for the time spent in England as a military secretary of the Y.M.C.A., he was a student all his life. But he loved men more; and studied only to qualify himself to serve them better.

---

[994] OUR SON. (1918, October 26). *The Methodist* (Sydney, NSW: 1892 - 1954), p. 3. Retrieved May 29, 2023, from http://nla.gov.au/nla.news-article155263473

He was an earnest Christian, his religion being of a robust, manly type, intensely practical. He never knew a spiritual crisis. He could not remember the time and circumstances of his conversion; which obviated his having to remember any previous time and circumstances associated with an unconverted state. He never had any other notion than that of being a follower of Jesus Christ. His name was placed on the membership roll of the church at his birth, and throughout his life ever after, though by no means free from faults and failings, he justified the confidence.

Had he remained in Australia two or three months longer, he would have completed his arts course at the Sydney University. At least, he would have faced his final examination in the course — and he had not failed in any previous one. On account of rheumatic tendencies, following upon a severe attack of the disorder in boyhood, he was unable to enlist; so he chose the service of the Y.M.C.A. Leaving with a transport of the A.I.F. on September 30th, 1916, he was appointed to Westham Camp, England. The English climate proving beneficial, he decided to enter upon air work. Being past the age for the Australian air service — had he remained with us till January 7th, 1919, he would have been 29 years old — he was accepted by the Royal Air Service (British); and studied first at Hastings, then at Reading, and finally passed on to Montrose Aerodrome, Scotland, to confirm his commission by flight-practice. He expected to go to France about November.

As a reader of history, the Old Land opened its great heart to him; and his numerous letters, and a literal load of post-cards and books of illustrations, tell of his delight in the listening. But far outstripping all, was his interest in men; and both in his Y.M.C.A. work and later at the aviation schools, he revelled in personal contacts, and rendered help and influence to those less fortunate than himself. He was a devoted, lover of his home; and his letters to his mother breathe a passionate tenderness of affection.

Speaking of the great purpose that had decided him to enter the air force, he wrote, 'I have always done my best work when I have harnessed my will to a great task.' Later he wrote, 'It may be that the Lord will bring me through the war; though I do not make any silly statement. But I am far more concerned that the Lord shall make me 'more than conqueror.' Though not a local preacher, he occasionally conducted services when requested, both before his departure for England, and in the churches of more than one denomination at Weymouth and other English towns. As occasion offered, he was privileged to make many friends, whose expressions of appreciation have been a source of comfort to his dear ones. The Rev. C. W. Andrews, of the British Wesleyan Methodist Conference, writes, some time before his final departure from us, 'To know him was not only to love him, but to admire and respect his high ideals of life.'

Mr. W. Gillanders, General Secretary of the Y.M.C.A., Sydney, writes, 'I have rarely known a young man who combined so perfectly strength and gentleness.' The Hon, Secretary to the staff of the Teachers' College, New South Wales Department of Education— of the High School staff of which he was a member — writes that 'the teaching service, the College, and the State have suffered a great loss by his death'.

The letter to his mother, in which he told of his decision to enter the air service — a decision put into force some time before the letter arrived — he concluded with the words, 'Don't worry, I shall not do silly things; and remember, mother, "Underneath are the everlasting arm"'s.' It was a fitting airman's text. - Those 'everlasting arms' were true to their commission. They did not suffer him to fall. No: they caught the jewel, released from its broken casket only, and bore it on to light and life eternal.

Thus lived, briefly, but effectively and not unworthily, and so passed on to larger life, our son, Flight-Cadet Harold Kingsley Percival.

According to a notice published in the *Camden News* on 21 November 1918, Harold's parents had received letters from his flight instructor and fellow officers at Montrose Aerodrome providing further particulars of the accident which had caused Harold's death.[995] These letters provided quite a different explanation for the cause of the crash than that determined by the Court of Inquiry. The notice went on to report:

---

[995] THE LATE FLIGHT-CADET H. K. PERCIVAL. (1918, November 21). *Camden News* (NSW: 1895 - 1954), p. 1. Retrieved May 29, 2023, from http://nla.gov.au/nla.news-article136788136n. A similar report appeared in *The Methodist*– see THE LATE FLIGHT-CADET H. K. PERCIVAL (1918, November 23). *The Methodist* (Sydney, NSW: 1892 - 1954), p. 11. Retrieved May 29, 2023, from http://nla.gov.au/nla.news-article155267472

It appears he had become quite expert at flying, having several times looped the loop and performed other necessary manoeuvres and flown at an altitude of 10,000 feet. At the time of his fatal accident, his machine was coming to land over the aerodrome, when a fault developed in the engine, causing the machine to "stall" – or fall perpendicularly – and spin.

Being less than 100 feet from the ground, there was no room for matters to be righted. Death was judged to have been instantaneous.

His instructor speaks in highest terms of his keenness and ability as an airman, and looked forward to his doing exceptionally good work in France, whither he expected to go almost immediately.

The funeral took place on September 25th, at Montrose Cemetery, with full military honours.

Harold was 28 years old at the date of his death, and his parents were living at Peat's Ferry Road, Hornsby when they received word that Harold had been killed in the accident.

Harold is buried at Sleepyhillock Cemetery, Montrose, Angus, Scotland.[996] His name was added to the Camden Methodist Roll of Honour in 1919.[997]

---

[996] According to records maintained by the CWGC, Harold's gravestone was replaced in 1993 - https://www.cwgc.org/find-war-dead/casualty/327484/percival,-harold-kingsley/
[997] CAMDEN METHODIST ROLL OF HONOUR. (1919, March 20). *Camden News* (NSW: 1895 - 1954), p. 1. Retrieved May 29, 2023, from http://nla.gov.au/nla.news-article136646737

Drummoyne's Great War Volume 3

Photograph of the grave of Harold Percival, Sleepyhillock Cemetery, Montrose, Angus, Scotland. Source - https://ww1austburialsuk.weebly.com (reproduced with permission).

John Walker

Gunner, No. 35672

4th Field Artillery Brigade, 2nd Australian Division

Killed in action 5 October 1918, Montbrehain, France

Buried Roisel Communal Cemetery Extension, Roisel, France

John Walker was born in Manbeen, North Elgin, Scotland in 1884,[998] the son of Mr & Mrs James Walker. John attended Miltonbrae School near Elgin and worked as a tailor's cutter with D Falconer in Elgin for four years. During that time, he also served as a volunteer with the Seaforth Highlanders before leaving Scotland for Australia at about the age of 30.

After a brief period in Australia where he also volunteered for home service in NSW, John enlisted in the AIF on 12 January 1917[999] at the age of 32, giving as his address, *Partree*, Lyons Road, Drummoyne.[1000] John nominated his father James as his next of kin, and gave his address as 206 High Street, Elgin, Scotland.

John was assigned to the May reinforcements to the Field Artillery Brigades and sailed from Sydney on HMAT A28 *Militiades* on 2 August 1917. He disembarked in Glasgow on 2 October 1917 and marched into the Australian training base at Lark Hill on the Salisbury Plain the next day.

On 29 November 1917, John proceeded overseas to France via Southampton, arriving at the Australian General Base Depot at Rouelles the next day. John marched out to the join the artillery of the 2nd Australian Division where he was taken on strength with the 4th Australian Field Artillery Brigade and assigned to the 11th Field Battery on 7 December 1917. John was among 88 men taken on strength by the brigade during December.[1001]

John would have joined his unit when it was based at Steenwerck in French Flanders where the 4th AFA Brigade was resting after intensive involvement over a four-month period in the Third Battle of Ypres.[1002] The day after his arrival, the first snow of the season fell. On 21 December, the artillery of the 2nd Australian Division including

---

[998] Registration no. 135/ 152.
[999] War service records accessible at https://recordsearch.naa.gov.au/SearchNRetrieve/Interface/ViewImage.aspx?B=3004928
[1000] Located on the south side of Lyons Road between Gipps Street and Thompson Street.
[1001] Headquarters, 4th Australian Field Artillery Brigade Unit Diary December 1917 - https://www.awm.gov.au/collection/C1353126?image=7
[1002] Headquarters, 4th Australian Field Artillery Brigade Unit Diary December 1917 - https://www.awm.gov.au/collection/C1353126?image=2

the 4th AFA Brigade moved to the Ploegsteert area to relieve the artillery units of the 3rd Australian Division.[1003] John would have experienced the routine of static trench warfare with the artillery undertaking a program of harassing fire of enemy positions, weather permitting. John would also have celebrated Christmas day in the line which was no different to any other day other than that the officers made sure that an extra good dinner was made for the men which was regarded as the best 'Xmas sport' since the brigade left Australia in 1915.[1004]

At the end of January 1918, the brigade was relieved by the 8th AFA Brigade and during its time in the line the brigade suffered only five casualties, with the morale of the men much improved on account of light railways being used to bring up ammunition supplies, relieving them of the physical labour of doing so in the wintery conditions. February saw the men given liberal amounts of leave to Boulogne, St Omer and elsewhere, except the men of bad character.[1005]

The brigade was back in French Flanders in March 1918 where it remained until the end of the month. In all, the unit diary records that the brigade had been very fortunate in that sector.[1006] The following month saw the brigade move to the Somme sector to assist in meeting the German spring offensive then threatening Amiens, arriving in that city on 8 April 1918 and being brought into action in the early hours of 10 April.[1007] The brigade's diary notes that John's battery, the 11th, had a forward gun in one position for three days, and then transferred to another forward position for two days during which time it inflicted great damage on the enemy.[1008]

[1003] Headquarters, 4th Australian Field Artillery Brigade Unit Diary December 1917 - https://www.awm.gov.au/collection/C1353126?image=5
[1004] Headquarters, 4th Australian Field Artillery Brigade Unit Diary December 1917 - https://www.awm.gov.au/collection/C1353126?image=6
[1005] Instructions were also issued to stop the shooting of game animals with service rifles.
[1006] Headquarters, 4th Australian Field Artillery Brigade Unit Diary March 1918 - https://www.awm.gov.au/collection/C1353128?image=7
[1007] Headquarters, 4th Australian Field Artillery Brigade Unit Diary April 1918 - https://www.awm.gov.au/collection/C1353129?image=4
[1008] Headquarters, 4th Australian Field Artillery Brigade Unit Diary April 1918 - https://www.awm.gov.au/collection/C1353129?image=7

The brigade continued providing artillery support into May with the brigade's diary summing up its activity at the end of that month as follows[1009]:

> During this period the Brigade had been on a front that had been threatened by enemy attack. At the beginning of the month we were in strongly built positions made by ourselves, and on the 6th we were withdrawn to Army Reserve in anticipation of an attack on the 10th. This did not eventuate and we were put back into the line of the 14th, taking over positions upon which very little work had been done. .. The Battery positions have never been heavily shelled although a lot of shelling has gone on around them.

June 1918 saw the brigade provide support to a number of local infantry raids, as the front lines were gradually pushed forward. This required the batteries of the brigade to construct new forward battery positions to continue to provide effective support.[1010] At the same time the brigade was also fighting an outbreak of 'Spanish Fever' which put a drain on the resources of the brigade's batteries with as many as 100 cases down at a time.[1011] The effect of the infection continued into July, compounded by bouts of diarrhoea when the brigade moved to the Villers-Bretonneux area.[1012] Although the brigade found the enemy around Villers-Bretonneux more antagonistic, with more active artillery and enterprising infantry, the brigade was successful in harassing the enemy positions and supporting infantry raids.[1013]

[1009] Headquarters, 4th Australian Field Artillery Brigade Unit Diary May 1918 - https://www.awm.gov.au/collection/C1353131?image=9
[1010] Headquarters, 4th Australian Field Artillery Brigade Unit Diary June 1918 - https://www.awm.gov.au/collection/C1354028?image=9
[1011] Headquarters, 4th Australian Field Artillery Brigade Unit Diary June 1918 - https://www.awm.gov.au/collection/C1354028?image=10
[1012] Headquarters, 4th Australian Field Artillery Brigade Unit Diary July 1918 - https://www.awm.gov.au/collection/C1354031?image=15
[1013] Headquarters, 4th Australian Field Artillery Brigade Unit Diary July 1918 - https://www.awm.gov.au/collection/C1354031?image=15

August 1918 saw the brigade fully engaged in the opening of the Battle of Amiens, the major Allied offensive on the Somme sector. The brigade's diary summarised its involvement as follows[1014]:

> The month of August has been to this Brigade one of the most eventful in its history. It has been a month of movement and successful fighting and has provided plenty of excitement and opportunities for the Brigade to prove its mettle.

The heavy workload continued into September, with the brigade involved in supporting the capture of Mont St Quentin by Australian infantry, acclaimed by the French as one of the most marvellous feats of arms of the war.[1015] After a brief rest, the brigade was again in the thick of the fighting, commencing a series of forward pushes which took in their stride sections of the much-vaunted Hindenburg Line. Although the brigade's casualties had grown commensurately, having regard to the dangerous type of work at Mont St Quentin and the sweeping nature of the enemy's fire, the brigade considered itself lucky.[1016]

Early October 1918 had the brigade located near Bellicourt preparing for the next stage of the offensive which commenced in the early hours of 3 October. On 5 October, the brigade was outside Montbrehain, with John's battery, the 11th Field Battery, providing cover to the attacking Australian infantry, and firing on German positions. The unit diary summarised the day's fighting as constant with exceedingly good work done by observation post officers, with a good watch being kept on enemy positions with constant harassing fire.

It was during the fighting near Montbrehain on 5 October 1918 that John was killed in action,[1017] one of only four from the brigade

---

[1014] Headquarters, 4th Australian Field Artillery Brigade Unit Diary August 1918 - https://www.awm.gov.au/collection/C1354136?image=19
[1015] Headquarters, 4th Australian Field Artillery Brigade Unit Diary September 1918 - https://www.awm.gov.au/collection/C1354142?image=4
[1016] Headquarters, 4th Australian Field Artillery Brigade Unit Diary September 1918 - https://www.awm.gov.au/collection/C1354142?image=4
[1017] According to some of the CWGC records, John's date of death was 4 October 1918 - https://www.cwgc.org/find-records/find-war-dead/casualty-details/299789/john-walker/

killed in action in the whole of October.[1018] John would be the last of those commemorated on the Drummoyne War Memorial killed in action in the First World War, and is recorded to have been 33 years old at the time of his death.[1019] Although the brigade would continue to provide artillery support to the offensive, the capture of Montbrehain on this day would mark the last significant involvement of Australian infantry units in the First World War.

John's name was included in the 448th casualty list published on 30 November 1918, some weeks after the Armistice.[1020] There is no information concerning how John was killed or the circumstances surrounding his burial, but in about 1924-25 John's remains were exhumed by the then Imperial War Graves Commission and reburied in Roisel Communal Cemetery Extension north-east of the town of Peronne.[1021]

[1018] Headquarters, 4th Australian Field Artillery Brigade Unit Diary October 1918 - https://www.awm.gov.au/collection/C1354146?image=14
[1019] The AIF Project and Australian War Memorial record his age at the date of death as 37.
[1020] NEARER THE END (1918, November 30). *The Sun* (Sydney, NSW: 1910 - 1954), p. 3. Retrieved May 30, 2023, from http://nla.gov.au/nla.news-article221424902
[1021] https://www.cwgc.org/find-records/find-war-dead/casualty-details/299789/john-walker/#&gid=2&pid=2

Photograph of the grave of John Walker, Roisel Communal Cemetery Extension (author, 2018)

Mervyn Willoughby Thornton

Private, No 10088

14th Australian Field Ambulance, 5th Australian Division

Died of illness 30 October 1918, Harewood, United Kingdom

Buried Harefield (St Mary) Churchyard, Middlesex

When God Saw His Work Below Was Done He Gently Called Him "My Son"

Mervyn Willoughby Thornton was one of two sons of Sydney James and Sarah Ellen Thornton. Mervyn was the eldest born in about 1894[1022] in Redfern, with Charles born in 1895.[1023] It appears that there was another brother, Allan W born in 1898[1024] and a sister, Alma E born in 1901,[1025] but each would die within a year of their birth. Sydney and Sarah lived for a period at *Uki*, Bridge Road, Drummoyne[1026] with Mervyn attending Drummoyne Public School and Charles Cleveland Street Public School. Both Mervyn and his brother Charles had been members of the Senior Cadets.

Mervyn was the first of the brothers to enlist on 20 July 1915 at the age of 21 years and four months and was at the time a student wool-classer.[1027] Charles applied to enlist the following month on 13 August 1915. The fact that Mervyn and Charles have sequential regimental numbers suggests that they applied to enlist on the same day but that Charles was initially rejected as unfit until he had his medical matters attended to.

Both Charles and Mervyn were assigned to the 5th Reinforcements to the 8th Field Ambulance as part of the Australian Army Medical Corps and embarked from Sydney on HMAT A71 *Nestor* on 9 April 1916. The brothers travelled to Egypt before embarking again this time from Alexandria on 28 May 1916 on the *Corsican*. After a period of training in England, the brothers embarked for France on 16 July 1916, marching into the 5th Australian Division Base Depot at Etaples on 19 July 1916.

On 31 July 1916 the brothers marched out from the base camp, having been transferred to the 14th Field Ambulance. The brothers

---

[1022] NSW BDM Registration No. 28876/1894. According to one source, his actual date of birth was 27 March 1894 - https://rslvirtualwarmemorial.org.au/explore/people/288753 (accessed 11 September 2018). On Mervyn's birth registration details, his father's first name is spelt Sidney whereas it is spelt Sydney on his brothers' records.
[1023] See account of Charles Leslie Thornton.
[1024] NSW BDM Registration Nos. 34031/1898 and 3080/1899.
[1025] NSW BDM Registration Nos. 29509/1901 and 606/1902.
[1026] Renamed Victoria Road and Sydney Thornton is noted as living in the house located between Seymour Street and Drummoyne Avenue according to the Sands Directory
[1027] https://recordsearch.naa.gov.au/SearchNRetrieve/Interface/ViewImage.aspx?B=8390457

were among fourteen reinforcements to join the unit from Rouen.[1028] At the end of July 1916, the 14th Field Ambulance was stationed near Sailly in French Flanders serving with the 5th Australian Division, which division had been badly mauled following the catastrophic failed attack on Fromelles.

The 14th Field Ambulance served in the lines around Outtersteene in French Flanders before being withdrawn to Bellancourt in mid-October 1916 where it participated in the first conscription referendum and received word that it was to proceed to the Somme sector.[1029] On arrival near Albert in late October, the unit found its positions in poor condition due to recent rains, making the work of the stretcher bearers difficult. This resulted in a number of bearers breaking down from the strain and stress of the work and weather.[1030] This coincides with Mervyn being admitted to a rest station on 25 October where he remained until the end of the month.

The conditions through November 1916 continued to deteriorate, as did the state of the men in the unit with cases of influenza, diarrhoea and trench foot becoming prevalent.[1031] The 14th Field Ambulance endured the harsh winter of 1916-17 in and out of the line, and by March 1917 were based at the 1st ANZAC Collection Station at Becordel, just east of Albert on the Somme.[1032] It was at about this time that Mervyn was admitted to hospital sick on 17 March 1917 where he remained until 7 April 1917. Mervyn re-joined the unit when it was fulfilling the role of the Corps' scabies section at Chateau Aveluy near Albert.[1033]

[1028] 14th Field Ambulance Unit Diary July 1916 - https://www.awm.gov.au/collection/C1353548?image=8
[1029] 14th Field Ambulance Unit Diary October 1916 - https://www.awm.gov.au/collection/C1353551?image=4
[1030] 14th Field Ambulance Unit Diary October 1916 - https://www.awm.gov.au/collection/C1353551?image=6
[1031] 14th Field Ambulance Unit Diary November 1916 - https://www.awm.gov.au/collection/C1352965?image=2
[1032] 14th Field Ambulance Unit Diary March 1917 - https://www.awm.gov.au/collection/C1354680?image=2
[1033] 14th Field Ambulance Unit Diary April 1917 - https://www.awm.gov.au/collection/C1352969?image=3

The 14th Field Ambulance was detached in May and provided support to the second battle of Bullecourt in May 1917, where it processed a large number of casualties over the course of the fighting, and its stretcher bearers were placed under significant strain as well as suffering extensive losses. According to Charles Bean, on no one were the conditions more severely experienced than by the bearers of the Field Ambulances who were required to carry wounded for over a mile and a half entirely in the open.[1034] By June, the unit returned to duty at the scabies section[1035] before moving to the Divisional Rest Station near Warloy where it took stock of its losses from the fighting at Bullecourt and refitted.[1036]

At the end of July 1917, the unit began moving north to French Flanders[1037] and it was while there that on 13 August 1917, Mervyn was charged with the offence of 'neglect to the prejudice of good order and military discipline in that when ordered to attend a parade at 10 am on 11/8/17 he failed to do so'. Mervyn was awarded two days' Field Punishment No. 2.

On 17 September 1917 the 14th Field Ambulance moved to Steenvorde with the 14th Brigade of the 5th Division. On 20 September, sections of the unit were attached to the 1st and 2nd Australian Divisions for duty in the Ypres salient. The move would be a fateful one for Charles as on the next day, he was reported as being killed in action during the fighting at Polygon Wood[1038] while acting as a stretcher bearer.[1039]

[1034] Bean, *Official History*, Vol 4, p. 474.
[1035] 14th Field Ambulance Unit Diary June 1917 - https://www.awm.gov.au/collection/C1352971?image=2
[1036] 14th Field Ambulance Unit Diary June 1917 - https://www.awm.gov.au/collection/C1352971?image=3
[1037] 14th Field Ambulance Unit Diary July 1917 - https://www.awm.gov.au/collection/C1354681?image=5
[1038] As noted in the Honour Roll Circular completed by Charles' father after the war.
[1039] The Memorial Notice published in *The Sydney Morning Herald* on the anniversary of Charles' death on 21 September 1918 by his brother noted that he had been killed while stretcher bearing.

On 4 October 1917, along with Captains Jose and McGlashan and 16 other ranks,[1040] Mervyn was detached to the 3rd Canadian Casualty Clearing Station, during which time he was admitted to hospital suffering from 'NYD Pyrexia'[1041] or trench fever. Mervyn remained in hospital until 1 November 1917 when he re-joined to 3rd Canadian CCS before taking leave to the UK from 10-27 November 1917. Mervyn finally reunited with his old unit at the end of November 1917 and in the process missed the final stage of the Third Battle of Ypres, the attack on Passchendaele ridge. During the fighting at Ypres, the 14th Field Ambulance is reported to have borne a higher percentage of casualties compared to any other medical unit in the AIF.[1042]

The 14th Field Ambulance spent the remainder of 1917 and early 1918 based at Cormont south of Boulogne recuperating before it returned to front line service at the end of January 1918 near Kemmel in Belgium.[1043] The unit replaced the 2nd Australian Field Ambulance in taking care of the sick and evacuating the wounded from the 5th Australian Division, where it remained until the end of February 1918.

The unit was relieved in early March 1918 where it took over responsibility for the scabies section based at Dranoutre south-west of Ypres near the French border, and on 18 March the unit celebrated its second anniversary dinner. The unit moved to Daours just east of Amiens on the Somme, most likely in response to the German Spring Offensive, and in early April 1918 found itself near Villers-Bretonneux, which was being heavily shelled by German artillery, preventing the evacuation of wounded through the town.[1044]

[1040] 14th Field Ambulance Unit Diary October 1917 - https://www.awm.gov.au/collection/C1353429?image=3 . The unit diary records the date as 5 October 1917 whereas Mervyn's service records has the date as 4 October.
[1041] Defined as fever of 'not yet defined' origin - https://euro-pepmc.org/backend/ptpmcrender.fcgi?accid=PMC2354964&blobtype=pdf
[1042] 14th Field Ambulance Unit Diary November 1917 - https://www.awm.gov.au/collection/C1353433?image=18
[1043] 14th Field Ambulance Unit Diary January 1918 - https://www.awm.gov.au/collection/C1353431?image=6
[1044] 14th Field Ambulance Unit Diary April 1918 - https://www.awm.gov.au/collection/C1353532?image=8

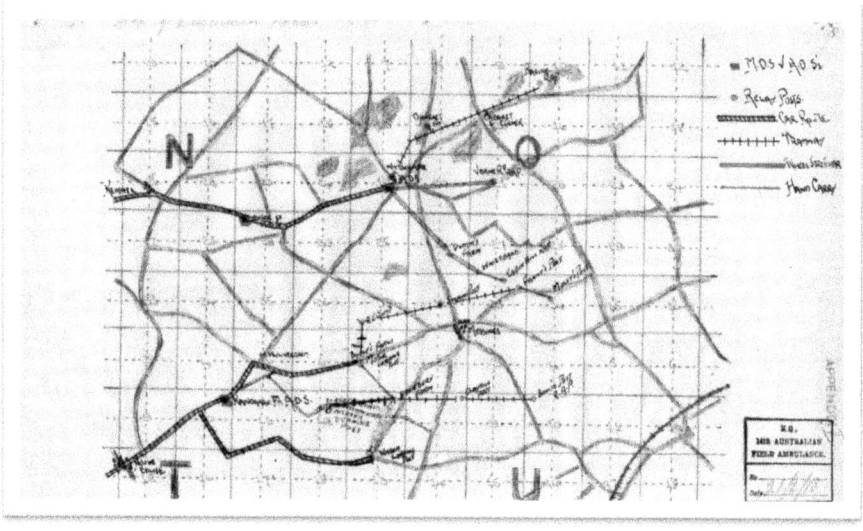

Disposition of 14th Field Ambulance at Ypres Salient January-February 1918. Source - 14th Field Ambulance Unit Diary February 1918 - https://www.awm.gov.au/collection/C1353432?image=7

The unit treated a large number of gas cases on 17 April but had insufficient replacement uniforms to change the wounded out of their gas contaminated clothing.[1045] Included among the gassed were a number of stretcher bearers who found it difficult to wear their gas masks and do their work.[1046]

On 23 April 1918, the 14th Field Ambulance was warned of an expected German attack on the village of Villers-Bretonneux and to be ready to supply bearers at a moment's notice.[1047] Wounded and gas cases arrived in a steady stream overnight at the unit's base at Daours, with the town itself coming under shelling. On the evening of 24 April, the 14th Field Ambulance was warned of a counter-attack to be

---

[1045] 14th Field Ambulance Unit Diary April 1918 - https://www.awm.gov.au/collection/C1353532?image=20
[1046] 14th Field Ambulance Unit Diary April 1918 - https://www.awm.gov.au/collection/C1353532?image=24 and https://www.awm.gov.au/collection/C1353532?image=47
[1047] 14th Field Ambulance Unit Diary April 1918 - https://www.awm.gov.au/collection/C1353532?image=29

made to retake Villers-Bretonneux[1048] with the stream of wounded from midnight much increased as a result of that counter-attack. In all, the 14th Field Ambulance treated 1,062 casualties between 23 April until noon 27 April 1918.[1049]

Despite the success of the counter-attack on Villers-Bretonneux, the situation on the front remained precarious as throughout May 1918, the unit's base at Daours continued to be subjected to heavy enemy shelling,[1050] resulting in the decision being made to evacuate the main dressing station.[1051]

On 1 June 1918, Mervyn was charged for a second time with 'conduct to the prejudice of good order and military discipline' in that contrary to orders he interfered with a pile of clothes which was contaminated with gas for which he was awarded one day's Field Punishment No. 2.

Illustration 14th Field Ambulance Advanced Dressing Station near Franvilliers-Bonnay July 1918 - https://www.awm.gov.au/collection/C1353537?image=26

[1048] 14th Field Ambulance Unit Diary April 1918 - https://www.awm.gov.au/collection/C1353532?image=30
[1049] 14th Field Ambulance Unit Diary April 1918 - https://www.awm.gov.au/collection/C1353532?image=61
[1050] 14th Field Ambulance Unit Diary May 1918 - https://www.awm.gov.au/collection/C1353533?image=5
[1051] 14th Field Ambulance Unit Diary May 1918 - https://www.awm.gov.au/collection/C1353533?image=22

In early August 1918, the 14th Field Ambulance received warning that the Australian Corp was to go on the offensive with the Assistant Director of Medical Services (ADMS) advising to be ready to move into action at short notice. Two days later the ADMS provided more details of the forthcoming major offensive.[1052] The offensive started on 8 August 1918 with the ADMS to the 5th Australian Division, which included the 14th Field Ambulance, initially assigned to be responsible for the evacuation of wounded from the red line to the green line.[1053] All bearer divisions were placed under the command of the 15th Field Ambulance to evacuate the wounded from the regimental aid posts.

In early September 1918, the unit had moved further east along the south bank of the Somme river, following the Allied advance. The unit was based near Cappy continuing to support the Australian advance which had succeeded in capturing Peronne and the village of Mont St Quentin. At the end of the month, the unit was receiving instructions regarding the next major attack, this time on the St Quentin Canal which formed part of the Hindenburg line near Bellicourt.[1054]

On the first anniversary of Charles' death, Mervyn along with his parents and relatives posted memorial notices in *The Sydney Morning Herald*. Mervyn wrote[1055]:

[1052] 14th Field Ambulance Unit Diary August 1918 - https://www.awm.gov.au/collection/C1353538?image=3
[1053] 14th Field Ambulance Unit Diary August 1918 - https://www.awm.gov.au/collection/C1353538?image=24
[1054] 14th Field Ambulance Unit Diary September 1918 - https://www.awm.gov.au/collection/C1353539?image=6
[1055] Family Notices (1918, September 21). *The Sydney Morning Herald* (NSW: 1842 - 1954), p. 11. Retrieved September 8, 2024, from http://nla.gov.au/nla.news-article15803682

In fond memory of my dearly-loved and only brother, Pte C Leslie Thornton, killed in action while stretcher-bearing, September 21, 1917.

Greater love hath no man than this

Inserted by his loving brother, Mervyn (on active service AIF)

In early October 1918, the Australian forces were relieved after having been fighting continuously since March. On 7 October the 14th Field Ambulance was relieved and entrained at Peronne en-route to Cisemont, west of Amiens.[1056]

On 10 October 1918, a month before the Armistice and two weeks after the anniversary of Charles' death, Mervyn was granted furlough to the UK. He was among a percentage of men from the 14th Field Ambulance granted leave to the UK or who were being granted furlough to Australia.[1057] While Mervyn was on leave he was admitted to the 1st Australian Auxiliary Hospital at Harefield on 23 October suffering from influenza. He would not return to France as on 30 October at 4:45 p.m. Mervyn died from influenza, broncho-pneumonia and syncope.[1058] He was 24 years old. Mervyn was buried in the Harefield Parish Churchyard on 6 November 1918 with his funeral officiated by Chaplain Rev. T Terry. The report of the funeral records that a wreath was supplied by Mr C Billyard & Leake of Harefield, with the headquarters' firing party and bugler in attendance and Captain JFS Murray MC the officer in charge. A small number of hospital staff and patients also attended the funeral.

Family notices were published on 8 and 9 November 1918 in *The Daily Telegraph* and *The Sydney Morning Herald*[1059]:

[1056] 14th Field Ambulance Unit Diary October 1918 - https://www.awm.gov.au/collection/C1353540?image=3
[1057] 14th Field Ambulance Unit Diary October 1918 - https://www.awm.gov.au/collection/C1353540?image=4
[1058] Temporary loss of consciousness caused by a fall in blood pressure.
[1059] Family Notices (1918, November 8). *The Daily Telegraph* (Sydney, NSW: 1883 - 1930), p. 4. Retrieved May 30, 2023, from http://nla.gov.au/nla.news-article239578149 ; Family Notices (1918, November 8). *The Sydney Morning Herald* (NSW: 1842 - 1954), p. 6. Retrieved

THORNTON. - Died of pneumonia, Mervyn Willoughby Thornton, late 14th Field Ambulance, dearly loved eldest son of Sid. and Nellie Thornton, "Glenwood," Queenscliffe Road, Manly after three years' active service.

THORNTON. - Oct. 30, 1918, Pvte. Mervyn Willoughby Thornton, 14th F.A., died of pneumonia, dearly-loved nephew of Mr. and Mrs. S. Hanlin, David-st, Croydon.

A second notice appeared on 24 December 1918 in *The Sydney Morning Herald*[1060]:

Private Mervyn W. Thornton, eldest son of Mr. and Mrs. Sydney J. Thornton, of Glenwood, Queenscliff-road, Queenscliff, Manly, has died from pneumonia. He was 24 years of age. His only brother, Leslie Thornton, was killed at Polygon Wood.

Further family notices were published on the anniversary of Charles and Meryn's death in 1919[1061] and 1920[1062]:

THORNTON. — In loving memory of our dearly – loved sons, Pte. C. Leslie Thornton, killed in action 21st Sept., 1917, and his only brother, Pte. Mervyn W. Thornton, died, pneumonia, while on leave, 31st October, 1918. Both late 14th Field Amb. Inserted by their loving mother and dad, Glenwood, Queenscliff Road, Manly.

May 30, 2023, from http://nla.gov.au/nla.news-article15810180 ; Family Notices (1918, November 9). *The Sydney Morning Herald* (NSW: 1842 - 1954), p. 12. Retrieved June 1, 2023, from http://nla.gov.au/nla.news-article28099849

[1060] WAR CASUALTIES. (1918, December 24). *The Sydney Morning Herald* (NSW: 1842 - 1954), p. 8. Retrieved May 30, 2023, from http://nla.gov.au/nla.news-article15817059

[1061] Family Notices (1919, September 20). *The Daily Telegraph* (Sydney, NSW: 1883 - 1930), p. 10. Retrieved June 1, 2023, from http://nla.gov.au/nla.news-article239640467

[1062] Family Notices (1920, September 21). *The Sydney Morning Herald* (NSW: 1842 - 1954), p. 8. Retrieved May 30, 2023, from http://nla.gov.au/nla.news-article16867064 . Additional notices were published in 1923 – see Family Notices (1923, September 22). *The Sydney Morning Herald* (NSW: 1842 - 1954), p. 14. Retrieved June 1, 2023, from http://nla.gov.au/nla.news-article16095160

THORNTON. — In loving memory of our dearly loved son, C. Lester Thornton, 14th Field Ambulance, killed in action, Polygon Wood, September 21, 1917; also his dearly loved only brother, Mervyn Thornton, 14th Field Ambulance, died influenza, Harefield, England, October 30, 1918, while on leave.
So deeply mourned, so sadly missed.
Inserted by sorrowing father, mother, and adopted brother, Fred.

THORNTON. — In loving memory of our dear nephews, Leslie and Mervyn Thornton, of 14th Field Ambulance, who died on active service, September 21, 1917, and October 31, 1918. M. and P. Taylor, Oatley.

THORNTON. - Oct. 30, 1918, Pvte. Mervyn Willoughby Thornton, 14th F.A., died of pneumonia, dearly-loved nephew of Mr. and Mrs. S. Hanlin, David-st, Croydon.

Charles is buried in Hooge Crater Cemetery, Zillebeke, Belgium, and Mervyn is buried at Harefield (St Mary) Churchyard, Middlesex.

Photograph of the grave of Mervyn Thornton. Source - https://ww1austburialsuk.weebly.com/o---w.html (reproduced with permission).

Harold Yabbicom Mortimore

Driver, No. 7240

4th Motor Transport Company, Australian Army Service Corps

Died of illness 26 November 1918

Buried Ste Marie Cemetery, Le Harve, France

And when the trumpet calls hold fast my hand my son

Harold Mortimore was the only child of Hugh and Elizabeth Frances Mortimore[1063] and was born in about 1893 at Burwood, NSW.[1064] Harold was educated at Kogarah Public School and Sydney High School before attending the Sydney Technical College. A qualified mechanical engineer, Harold was working at the Invincible Motor Co., Woolwich, before enlisting in the AIF.

Harold applied to enlist on 8 June 1915 at the age of 22 with one year's experience in the senior cadets in 1910 before undertaking compulsory militia training.[1065] He nominated his special qualifications as engineer and rifle shot, and gave his address as *Nerimbah*, 131 St Georges Crescent, Drummoyne. Harold nominated his mother Elizabeth also living at the Drummoyne address as his next of kin.

Harold undertook and passed various motor tests, receiving 1st class results in the technical and workshop tests, and a 3rd class in his driver's test. Appointed as a Motor Driver in the 9th Reinforcements to the Divisional Ammunition Park, Australian Army Service Corps in July 1915, Harold embarked from Sydney on 30 September 1915 on HMAT A8 *Argyllshire*. The day before, his parents had moved home to *Cambewarra*, Trelawney Road, Eastwood.

The 9th Reinforcements arrived in Egypt and Harold was attached to the Motor Transport Depot at the Levant Base, Mustapha in Alexandria, but was immediately admitted to hospital suffering from fever and soft sores. Harold was finally discharged for duty from a convalescent camp on 13 January 1916 and remained in Alexandria until late March when he was transferred to Tel-el-Kebir. In less than a month, Harold was heading back to Alexandria, this time to board the transport *Orsova* to re-join his unit which by this time had moved to England.

[1063] Hugh Mortimore was employed at the Comptroller Railway Stores, Wilson Street, Newtown.
[1064] NSW BDM Registration No. 9492/1893. There is another child, Hugh F born in about 1888 (5721/1888) but he died in about 1907 (9382/1907).
[1065] War service records accessible at https://recordsearch.naa.gov.au/SearchNRetrieve/Interface/ViewImage.aspx?B=7987279

After a brief period training in England, on 6 May 1916 Harold embarked on the *Copenhagen* at Southampton to re-join his unit, arriving at Rouen in France the next day. A week later, Harold was taken on strength by the 2nd Australian Divisional Ammunition Sub-Park (DASP) from the 1st Base Mechanical Transport Depot and appointed a Motor Transport Driver.

The role of the DASP was to transport ammunition and other supplies to the infantry of the division serving in the front lines. Invariably, their role extended to transporting troops and repairing the roads necessary to reach the front lines from their base depots.

No diaries exist for his unit until July 1917 which would give an insight into Harold's experience serving with the DASP during 1916. Having regard to the service of the 2nd Division, it is probable that Harold was involved in supplying troops in the battles of Pozieres and Mouquet Farm during July-August 1916. After a brief period in Flanders, the division returned to the Somme towards November where it served near Flers and experienced the harsh winter of 1916-1917. In February 1917, Harold may have been involved in moving forces and supplies forward as the 2nd Division engaged the German rearguard during its withdrawal to the Hindenburg Line.

In April 1917, the 2nd Division was in support during the First Battle of Bullecourt. According to his service records, on 7 April 1917 Harold was appointed Artificer, or skilled mechanic, a position which he retained until the end of September 1917. In May, the division was directly engaged in the Second Battle of Bullecourt where it suffered heavy losses.

In July 1917, the 2nd DASP was based near Bapaume, France but between 6 to 16 July 1917, Harold was on leave to UK. On 16 July, just as Harold's leave was ending, the 2nd DASP moved to Steenvoorde in Belgian Flanders to form part of British Fifth Army.[1066] Harold re-joined the unit from leave on 21 July just as the unit began to be involved in the retrieval of abandoned lorries near Zillebeke

---

[1066] 2nd Australian Ammunition Sub-park Unit Diary, July 1917 - https://www.awm.gov.au/collection/C1340560?image=4

while under heavy enemy fire. With the onset of rain in August 1917, the lorries of the unit battled the muddy conditions of the churned-up battlefield and roads, exposed to enemy shelling.[1067] The work of ferrying troops and ammunition, and materials to repair roads, continued throughout August 1917 in the preparation for the attack on the Menin Road ridge due in September 1917.

The 2nd DASP worked tirelessly throughout September and October 1917 carrying men and materiel to the front lines and keeping roads in repair, all the time exposed to shellfire and bombing by enemy airplanes. During this period of service, Harold reverted to the position of Motor Transport Driver. On 23 November, the unit received orders to strike camp and proceed to a site near Bailleul, France where it saw out the remainder of 1917.

After a period of leave in Paris during late 1917 and early 1918, Harold returned to his unit as it carried out its routine work of road repairs, ferrying supplies and transporting loads and materials. In March 1918, Aust. Corps Motor Transport was re-organised to form a headquarters and six motor transport companies, formed from the supply column and ammunition sub-park allotted to each of the five divisions.[1068] The 4th Australian Motor Transport Company (4th AMTC) was formed by the 4th Australian Divisional Supply Column and 2nd Australian Divisional Ammunition Sub-Park. These mechanical transport companies replaced the supply columns and ammunition sub parks in order to effect a more efficient utilisation of the available mechanical (as opposed to horse) transport by pooling it under corps control.[1069] As a consequence of this reorganisation, on 12 March 1918, Harold was taken on strength by the 4th AMTC.

[1067] 2nd Australian Ammunition Sub-park Unit Diary, August 1917 - https://www.awm.gov.au/collection/C1340561?image=3
[1068] http://www.diggerhistory.info/pages-badges/patches/mg.htm
[1069] http://newsarch.rootsweb.com/th/read/AUS-MILITARY/2005-03/1111869484

Photo of a Thornycroft lorry, serial number 51898, of the 4th Australian Motor Transport Company. A kookaburra (probably a company emblem) is also painted on the side on the truck. c 1918. AWM ID No. P08409.001.

April 1918 saw the newly formed unit based at Villers Bocage. Although the next few months would involve some of the fiercest fighting with the German spring offensive and the eventual successful counterattack by Allied forces, the unit diary provides little insight into the events of the last months of the war. The monotonous routine of moving supplies and men over difficult roads, under enemy fire and at times in atrocious weather continued for the 4th AMTC.

In late August, Harold received some respite when he was granted a fortnight's leave to UK, before he returned to France to join his unit in providing support to the breakthrough being effected by Allied forces across much of the Western Front. It is likely shortly before the Armistice came into effect on 11 November 1918 that Harold began to experience the symptoms of influenza which the unit diary noted was prevalent throughout the unit.[1070]

[1070] 4th Divisional Motor Transport Company Unit Diary November 1918 - https://www.awm.gov.au/collection/C1339348?image=3

Harold was admitted to hospital on 16 November 1918 suffering from what is described as debility,[1071] and was transferred to the 50th CCS the following day. On 20 November 1918 Harold was moved to the 2nd General Hospital at Harve where he was said to be suffering debility and acute myelitis. Harold's condition worsened such that on 21 November he was classified as dangerously ill and suffering from transverse myelitis.[1072] On 26 November 1918, Harold succumbed to his illnesses, and died in hospital at 7:35 a.m. from influenza transverse myelitis.[1073]

As so often occurred, events moved faster than communication as on 30 November 1918, some four days after Harold's death, a cablegram was sent by OIC to Harold's parents advising that he had been admitted to 2nd General Hospital on 25 November with transverse mylelitis. On same day a further telegram was sent advising that Harold was now dangerously ill. Although it is not clear from the records, at some point over the next two weeks, news of Harold's death finally reached his parents as on 10 December 1918, with an Roll of Honour notice was published in *The Sydney Morning Herald*[1074]:

> MORTIMORE - Died of Influenza, at No. 2 General Hospital, Havre France, on November 26, 1918, Driver Harold Y. Mortimore, only son of H. and E. F. Mortimore. Epping, New South Wales. Enlisted May, 1915, and served with 4th Australian Mechanical Transport Co., aged 25 years.

It would be almost twelve months before final news of the circumstances of Harold's death would be communicated to his parents as

---

[1071] Physical weakness often as a consequence of sickness - https://medical-dictionary.thefreedictionary.com/debility

[1072] Inflammation of the spinal cord. This neurological disorder often damages the insulating material covering nerve cell fibres (myelin). Transverse myelitis interrupts the messages that the spinal cord nerves send throughout the body - https://www.mayoclinic.org/diseases-conditions/transverse-myelitis/symptoms-causes/syc-20354726

[1073] Australian Red Cross Wounded and Missing Files - https://www.awm.gov.au/collection/R1492407

[1074] Family Notices (1918, December 10). *The Sydney Morning Herald* (NSW: 1842 - 1954), p. 6. Retrieved June 1, 2023, from http://nla.gov.au/nla.news-article15814855

on 28 October 1919. In a letter from the OIC to Elizabeth Mortimore then living at *Elaine*, Hillside Crescent, Epping, the OIC advised:

> With reference to the report of the regrettable loss of your son ... I am now in receipt of advice that he was evacuated to hospital on 16th November, 1918 and admitted to the 50th Casualty Clearing Station on 17th November, 1918, suffering with debility; transferred to No.35 Ambulance Train on 19th November, 1918, thence to 2nd General Hospital Harve on 20th November, 1918, suffering from debility and acute myelitis; pronounced dangerously ill on 21st November 1918, and died on 26th November, 1918.

Elizabeth Mortimore responded on 17 November 1919:

> I should have acknowledged the official report about our beloved son's illness and death sooner, but was away, now home after my husband's annual holiday when the letter came.
>
> ...
>
> The report of course was heartbreaking reading to me. Such a sad ending to a clever boy ... he was a motor engineer with a future full of promise.
>
> The details today write what I had already heard, save the dates.
>
> Many thanks for all the trouble. In course of time I may feel less bitter at the loss of our only child.

Family notices were published on the anniversary of Harold's death in 1919[1075]:

[1075] Family Notices (1919, November 26). *The Sydney Morning Herald* (NSW: 1842 - 1954), p. 10. Retrieved June 1, 2023, from http://nla.gov.au/nla.news-article15872434

MORTIMORE - In loving memory of Harold Y. Mortimore, driver 4th Mechanical Transport Co A. I. F, only son of H. and E. F. Mortimore, Epping, who died at Havre, France on November 26, 1918.
They laid our hero down to rest,
In the flag with a Southern Cross.
And we mourn for him as one of the best,
For his death was Australia's loss.

MORTIMORE - In affectionate remembrance of cousin Harold who died from influenza whilst on active service in France, November 1918. Mr and Mr Heath, Kate and George Edmonton, London, England.

MORTIMORE - In fond memory of my dear cousin Harold who died from influenza whilst on active service at Le Havre France November 26, 1918. Always remembered, Maude Edmonton, London, England.

Harold is buried at the Ste Marie Cemetery, Le Harve, France. As Le Harve was a major base during the war, eventually accommodating five hospitals and four convalescent depots, the cemetery continued to expand during its course.[1076] Harold was buried in division 62 of the cemetery along with more than 2,000 other servicemen and civilians.

[1076] CWGC - https://www.cwgc.org/find-a-cemetery/cemetery/2008000/ste.-marie-cemetery,-le-havre/

Photograph of the grave of Harold Mortimore, Ste Marie Cemetery, Le Harve, France. The War Graves Project, CWGC. Reproduced with permission.

Brendan Bateman

Photograph of Ste Marie Cemetery, Le Harve, France. The War Graves Project, CWGC. Reproduced with permission.

Frederick Jordan

Private, No. 11832

2nd Battalion Sherwood Foresters (Notts and Derby Regiment), 18th Brigade, British 6th Division

Died of illness, 22 February 1919

Buried Nottingham Road Cemetery, Derby, Derbyshire

He Fought the Good Fight

Frederick (Fred) Jordan was born in 1895 in Bradley, Derbyshire,[1077] the son of Herbert and Sarah Jane Jordan.[1078] According to 1911 UK Census, his father Herbert was an assistant domestic gardener and the family was then living at King Street, Duffield, Derbyshire.[1079]

Frederick enlisted in 1914 as a private and joined the 2nd Battalion Sherwood Foresters (Notts and Derby Regiment), a regular unit of the British Army.[1080] According to the Drummoyne War Service Record, Fred Jordan enlisted in August 1914, attained the rank of corporal and was part of the 'Reserve' unit. It is likely that Frederick was a former member of the British regular army prior to 1914 and at the time of the declaration of war, was a member of the Territorial reserve. The Territorials were mobilised in early August 1914 and many went to fill up the ranks of the regular army units to their war establishment.[1081]

This is as much as we know about Frederick as his service records do not survive. About 60% of the service records of British soldiers in First World War were destroyed or badly damaged as a result of enemy bombing in 1940 during the Second World War.[1082]

In August 1914, the 2nd Battalion was stationed at Sheffield as part of the 18th Brigade of the 6th Division when on 4 August it received orders to start mobilisation.[1083] Three hundred and fifty reservists

---

[1077] https://derbyshirewarmemorials.wikispaces.com/FREDERICK%20JORDAN. According to the graves registration details held by the CWGC his forename is sometimes spelt Frederic. The headstone on his grave records his surname as Jordon but this does not reconcile with the CWGC information. What exists of his service records have his name as Frederick Jordan.

[1078] https://www.cwgc.org/find-records/find-war-dead/casualty-details/351475/frederic-jordan/

[1079] https://derbyshirewarmemorials.wikispaces.com/FREDERICK%20JORDAN

[1080] The Regiment was officially formed in 1881 when the 45th and 95th Regiments of Foot were amalgamated as part of the Childers Reforms which restructured the British army infantry Regiments into a network of multi-battalion Regiments of two regular and two militia battalions, to form the Sherwood Foresters (Nottinghamshire and Derbyshire Regiment) - https://www.forces-war-records.co.uk/units/319/sherwood-foresters-nottinghamshire-and-derbyshire-regiment

[1081] http://www.longlongtrail.co.uk/soldiers/a-soldiers-life-1914-1918/enlisting-into-the-army/british-army-reserves-and-reservists/

[1082] https://greatwar.co.uk

[1083] 2nd Battalion Sherwood Foresters War Diary August-September 1914 - http://discovery.nationalarchives.gov.uk (National Archives UK accessed 10 June 2018).

arrived on 6 August and this is likely to have included Frederick. The battalion comprised 30 officers and 929 other ranks when it first moved to Edinburgh before travelling to Cambridge where it remained until 7 September. The battalion embarked for France on 8 September 1914 on SS *Georgian*, landing at St Nazaire in France on 11 September 1914.

Moving north-east, the battalion crossed the Aisne River on 19 September at Bourg, where it temporarily took over an entrenchment from another old British Army regiment, the Black Watch, before itself being relieved by the Gloucester Regiment whereupon it moved to relieve the Kings Royal Rifles at Troyon. The 18th Brigade formed part of the extreme right of the BEF, in touch with the French army. On 20 September, the battalion was under attack from a German column, and although ultimately successful in retaking captured trenches, the battalion suffered heavy casualties. In the confusion of battle, the companies of the battalion became mixed up and no clear idea of casualties could be gained. Some four officers and 40 other ranks were thought to have been killed, with about another 150 officers and men wounded.

Over the next few days, the battalion's position was heavily shelled by German artillery until it was relieved by the East Yorks Regiment on 22 September, whereupon it retired to the reserve trenches closer to Troyon. It was only then that the battalion could take a proper account of its losses in its first action of the war – five officers and 44 other ranks killed, and eight officers and 165 other ranks wounded.

On 10 October, the battalion was ordered to move to the north-west closer to Hazebrouck as part of a general move by the BEF from the Aisne to Flanders in an attempt to outflank German forces in the 'race to the sea'. A week later, the battalion was acting as the brigade's rear guard as it withdrew towards Bois Grenier and Fleurbaix. The battalion relieved the Durham Light Infantry in the front lines on 18 October near the village of Ennetieres. On that night the battalion's position came under heavy rifle and shell fire until 1 a.m. the next morning. It remained in the same position the next day and at daybreak on 20 October, the Germans commenced to shell the position heavily, destroying the battalion's headquarters. At 7:10 a.m. reports were received that a considerable number of Germans had got around the right flank of the battalion's position. Despite committing the battalion's reserve as well as some units from the Durham Light Infantry, the German advance was rapid, and the British forces heavily outnumbered. The Germans managed to cut off the British forces in the village who were unable to fall back quickly enough. The catastrophe of the fighting for the battalion was recorded in the unit's diary - some 710 NCOs and men were reported missing.

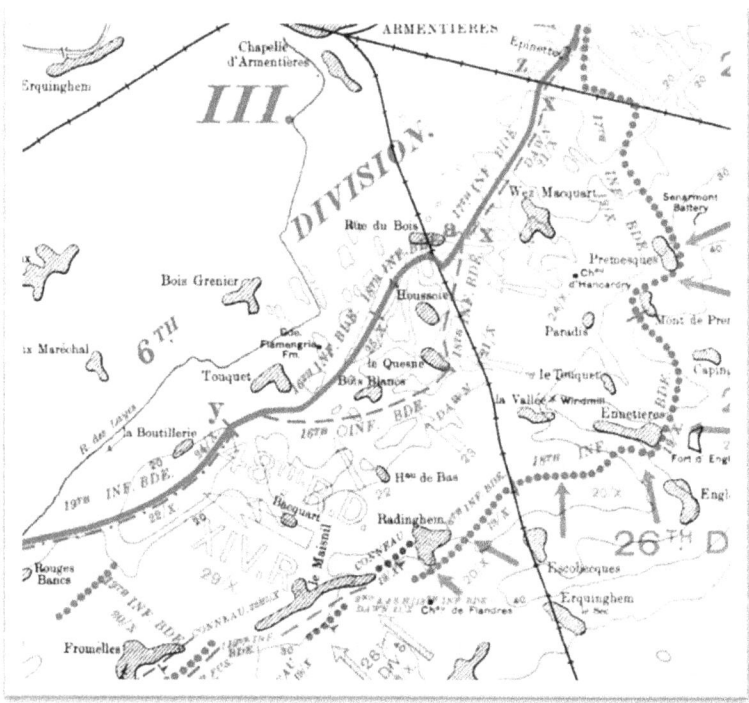

Part of map showing disposition of Frederick's 18th Infantry Brigade as part of the British 6th Division in October 1914 around the village of Ennetieres. British Official History of Military Operations, France and Flanders, 1914 volume II. copyright. Reproduced in http://www.longlongtrail.co.uk/battles/battles-of-the-western-front-in-france-and-flanders/the-battles-of-la-bassee-armentieres-and-messines-1914/

A report from the commander of D Company included in the unit's diary records how the company became surrounded on 20-21

October and subjected to enfilade fire from three sides. At 5:15 a.m. on 21 October, the commander of the company surrendered with about 50 men. The commander of the battalion, Major PL Gower, reported that 'the loss of the position was entirely due to the flank attack, that was overpowering in numbers, there being no adequate reserve to meet it'. Another report also forming part of the unit's diary simply says:

> They were surprised, surrounded and overpowered by the strong German force … our men were tired out, disorganised and what they took to be reinforcements turned out suddenly to be German.

Frederick's service medal card is inscribed with the initials 'P of W'. That Frederick was a prisoner of war is confirmed by a search of the records of the International Red Cross which details that Frederick was captured near Lille in northern France on 20 October 1914. At the time that he became a prisoner of war, Frederick held the rank of Lance Corporal.[1084]

Frederick Jordan's War Service Medals Records. Source - http://discovery.nationalarchives.gov.uk/details/r/D3174221

[1084] International Committee of the Red Cross
https://grandeguerre.icrc.org/en/File/Search/#/3/2/224/0/British%20and%20Commonwealth/Military/jordan

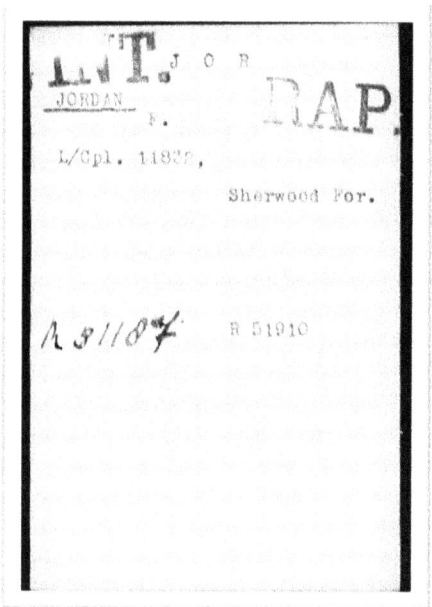

International Red Cross card for Frederick Jordan. Source - https://grandeguerre.icrc.org/en/File/Search/#/3/2/224/0/British%20and%20Commonwealth/Military/jordan

Frederick is recorded as being held as a prisoner at a camp in Hameln, Germany as at 4 March 1918. Hameln was one of the larger German prisoner of war camps, estimated to house approximately 20,000 prisoners. During the period of his confinement, Frederick is likely to have been employed in a working unit.[1085] It was fortunate that Frederick had been imprisoned in Germany rather than being assigned to a POW labour company closer to the front lines, where these prisoners were often mistreated and generally endured worse working and living conditions.[1086]

A photograph of the POW camp at Hameln, taken by camp director Richard Bochalli. This image is from the Europeana collection submitted by Dr. Ulrich Siegers und Rudolf Siegers and is reproduced under Creative Commons Licence.

It is probable that Frederick's health suffered during the period that he was a prisoner, affected by the deprivations of the naval blockade of Germany which resulted in famine in the later stages of the war. During 1918, there is also recorded an outbreak of Spanish

---

[1085] It is estimated that 90% of all prisoners held in German prisoner of war camps were employed outside the camp in a labour unit - https://encyclopedia.1914-1918-online.net/article/prisoners_of_war_germany .
[1086] https://encyclopedia.1914-1918-online.net/article/prisoners_of_war_germany

Influenza in German camps, which affected much of Europe in the immediate aftermath of the war. Frederick was repatriated from Germany relatively shortly after the Armistice, on 18 November 1918, on SS *Abbroarth* via Hull in England.

List of repatriated prisoners which includes Frederick Jordan. Source - https://grandeguerre.icrc.org/en/List/5712826/699/51910/

Despite his repatriation, Frederick died of illness on 22 February 1919 at his home district of Derby at the age of 24.[1087] The Drummoyne War Service Record also notes that Frederick died of

---

[1087] https://www.cwgc.org/find-war-dead/casualty/351475/jordan,-frederic/ . Prince Edward Road is first listed in the Sands Directory in 1922, with Herbert Jordan recorded in 1923 as residing at Prince Edward Road, Gladesville -
http://cdn.cityofsydney.nsw.gov.au/learn/history/archives/sands/1920-1924/1923-part4.pdf . The name is changed in the 1926 directory to Prince Edward Street and the house is referred to for the first time as *Sherwood* -
http://cdn.cityofsydney.nsw.gov.au/learn/history/archives/sands/1925-1929/1926-part4.pdf . Herbert is still recorded as residing there in 1932-33.
http://cdn.cityofsydney.nsw.gov.au/learn/history/archives/sands/1930-1933/1932-1933-part5.pdf .

illness but records the date as February 1917, most likely a typographical error.

After the war, Frederick's parents moved to Australia and lived at *Sherwood*, Prince Edward Street, Gladesville.[1088] Frederick is buried in Nottingham Road Cemetery, Derby, Derbyshire and his name is recorded on the Drummoyne War Memorial and several memorials in Duffield, Derbyshire.[1089]

Photograph of the grave of Frederick Jordan, Nottingham Road Cemetery, Derby, Derbyshire. Note the spelling of the surname. The War Graves Project, CWGC. Reproduced with permission.

[1088] https://www.cwgc.org/find-war-dead/casualty/351475/jordan,-frederic/ According to NSW BDM, there is a Sarah Jane Jordan who died in 1937 in Balmain (Registration No. 11044/1937).
[1089] https://www.derbyshirewarmemorials.com/amber/55411/55411-pic01.html , https://www.derbyshirewarmemorials.com/amber/14511/14511-pic01.html#secondrow and https://www.derbyshirewarmemorials.com/amber/55398/55398.html (accessed 1 June 2023).

Photograph of Nottingham Road Cemetery, Derby, Derbyshire. The War Graves Project, CWGC. Reproduced with permission.

Commemoration and Remembrance

Much in the same way that the experiences of the men commemorated on the Drummoyne War Memorial reflected Australia's experience during the First World War, so too would it be for the Drummoyne Community in the lead up to the war's end and in its aftermath.

Even before the end of the war, initiatives were taken by local Australian communities to recognise the service of those men who had volunteered to serve from their community and to honour those who had died in the cause. The community of Drummoyne was no exception. The Drummoyne Progress Association at its meeting in early March 1916 considered the erection of a memorial to those from the district who had enlisted but without immediate resolution[1090]:

[1090] DRUMMOYNE SOLDIERS' MEMORIAL. (1916, March 3). *The Daily Telegraph* (Sydney, NSW: 1883 - 1930), p. 3. Retrieved June 8, 2023, from http://nla.gov.au/nla.news-article238791220

DRUMMOYNE SOLDIERS' MEMORIAL.

The Drummoyne Progress Association discussed the question at Wednesday night's meeting of erecting a memorial to the soldiers who enlisted from the Drummoyne district. It was stated by Mr. Knight that over 300 men had enlisted from the locality, and he considered that a structure worthy of the district should be erected as a memorial. He did not think there would be any difficulty in raising between £2000 and £3000 for the object, as the Drummoyne district was both progressive and rich. After discussion the question was deferred.

The Drummoyne Soldiers, Sailors & Dependents Welfare Association was subsequently established on 23 March 1916.[1091] The objects of the Association were[1092]:

> Registration of all men serving at the Front whose homes and families are in Drummoyne proper; ensure the families and dependents of such Soldiers and Sailors being efficiently looked after by the Authorities and supplement the aid received where necessary; also welcome back all Local men on their return from the Front, supply temporary assistance where required, help in obtaining their dues from the Authorities and endeavour to place them in earning a livelihood suitable to their capacity.

The Association was very successful in raising funds to meet the needs of the soldiers and their families. In less than four months it had already achieved a surplus of funds.[1093] In January 1917, the

---

[1091] DRUMMOYNE WAR WORKERS. (1917, August 13). *The Sydney Morning Herald* (NSW: 1842 - 1954), p. 5. Retrieved June 8, 2023, from http://nla.gov.au/nla.news-article15743000
[1092] Drummoyne War Service Record, held by the Local Studies Section of Canada Bay City Library.
[1093] DRUMMOYNE WAR WORKERS. (1917, August 13). *The Sydney Morning Herald* (NSW: 1842 - 1954), p. 5. Retrieved June 8, 2023, from http://nla.gov.au/nla.news-article15743000

Association requested approval to erect a temporary honour board in front of the Council chambers at the corner of Lyons Road and Marlborough Street, Drummoyne. The request was approved by the Council at its meeting on 30 January 1917 subject to the proviso that the names of all those who had enlisted from the then municipality of Drummoyne being written on the board.[1094] The honour board was erected on the Lyons Road frontage of the Council chambers on the second anniversary of Anzac Day on 25 April 1917.

Local residents applied to the Association to have names included on the Honour Memorial. The names recorded on the Honour Memorial, however, far exceed the number of the names on the memorials that would eventually replace it. Whereas the Association estimated there would be 600 men from the Drummoyne area who had volunteered, more than 3,600 names were eventually listed on the Honour Memorial.[1095]

With the end of the war the focus shifted from recognising those who had volunteered, to the repatriation of returning servicemen and commemoration of those who would not return. Indeed, as early as June 1918, some five months before the end of the war, the Association foreshadowed its merger with the Repatriation Committee.[1096]

The jubilation and relief that greeted the Armistice in November 1918 was not universal. For many families, the mourning for their loved ones who had been reported killed or missing continued. The Armistice brought no relief for those families, only the faint hope in the case of the missing that the end of the war would permit answers to be found. For some this was the forlorn hope that their loved one would be returned as prisoner of war but in most cases, it would be the desire that the remains of their father, husband, son or relative would be found and given a decent burial. The Armistice marked a new phase in the story of the dead and the missing. While the fighting

---

[1094] Council Meeting Minutes, 30 January 1917, page 333.
[1095] https://canadabayheritage.asn.au/drummoyne-remembers/ (accessed 7 October 2023).
[1096] DRUMMOYNE SOLDIERS. (1918, June 27). *The Daily Telegraph* (Sydney, NSW: 1883 - 1930), p. 6. Retrieved June 3, 2023, from http://nla.gov.au/nla.news-article239258221. The Association would formally dissolve on 13 October 1920.

and dying may have ended, the searching, commemorating and remembering for tens of thousands of families had just begun.

Photograph of the temporary Drummoyne Honour Memorial. Source - Canada Bay Library (reproduced with permission).

Concern about the improvised care of war graves and the fate of the missing had grown during the war. As the conflict grew in intensity and the scale of the casualties mounted, the inadequate preparations to manage the remains on those killed or find the missing were cruelly exposed. On the Western Front, responsibility was initially assumed by the British Red Cross, but its resources were quickly overwhelmed. The British War Office agreed to establish the Graves Registration Commission in March 1915 under the leadership of Sir Fabian Ware to address the issue of recording and managing war graves. However, the demands on the British Army from inquiries of bereaved families reached a critical point with the British Somme offensive in 1916. The remit of the Graves Registration Commission was expanded to handle enquiries from bereaved relatives and was renamed the Directorate of Graves Registration and Enquiries. Its overstretched resources meant that the Red Cross Wounded and Missing Enquiry Department continued to provide a valuable and entirely voluntary service to trace the fate of the dead and missing as evident from the many statements on the files of Drummoyne's war dead.

The Imperial War Graves Commission,[1097] also conceived by Sir Fabian Ware, was established in May 1917 and was made responsible for planning the construction and long-term care of cemeteries and memorials. Its work began in earnest after the cessation of hostilities, taking over the work of the Directorate of Graves Registration and Enquiries. Graves Registration Units scoured the battlefields to locate isolated graves and the remains of the missing. Australia contributed such a unit on the Western Front and Gallipoli battlefields. There was also a need to consolidate the number of cemeteries, especially in France and Belgium, to minimize the amount of land alienated for war graves, which resulted in the exhumation of thousands of dead from isolated war graves or smaller cemeteries, known as the process of 'concentration'.

The task of the Graves Registration Units was an immense one. Of the 12,000 Allied soldiers reported as killed at ANZAC Cove on the Gallipoli peninsula, some 4,000 lay in cemeteries or makeshift graves, while nearly 6,0000 (or half) remained unburied, scattered about the ridges. Although the fighting on the Gallipoli peninsula had largely ceased at the end of 1915, the graves and remains of those killed had been left unattended for several years, exposed to the elements.

The numbers for the Western Front were of a substantially greater magnitude. For Australia alone among the combatants on the Western Front, of the 40,000 Australians reported as killed in that theatre of the war, only half (some 21,000) had registered graves. Of the other

---

[1097] Renamed Commonwealth War Graves Commission on 28 March 1960.

half, 11,000 were reported as having been buried but without adequate details to enable their graves to be registered, with the remaining 8,000 having no known grave.

The active recovery work commenced at the end of 1918 until brought to an end in 1921, perhaps prematurely, as the earth continued to reveal the remains of the missing over the ensuing decades. Indeed, bodies continue to be recovered more than one hundred years later. The final statistics would reveal that of the approximately 62,000 Australians reported as killed in action during the First World War, about a third have no known grave. Regrettably, the percentage is higher for those men commemorated on the Drummoyne War Memorial – of the ninety-five men listed on the memorial who served and died in the First World War, thirty-eight of them or 40% are recorded as having no final resting place.

The Drummoyne War Service Record 1914-1918 was designed, engrossed and decorated in 1921 by H. J. A. Baron, the father of Harley Baron who was killed in action in September 1916. The book was compiled from the records of the Drummoyne Soldiers, Sailors and Dependents' Welfare Association and intended to be a comprehensive list of those who enlisted and of those 'who made the supreme sacrifice.' It records a total of 658 enlistments and 94 dead.[1098] The notable omission from the list of those killed is Robert Henderson, with his name mistakenly included among those who returned from service.

Perhaps owing to its source, or perhaps the broad criteria defining who had a connection with the Drummoyne locality, the Drummoyne War Service Record includes among the names of the dead many who have an uncertain connection to Drummoyne. The Drummoyne War Service Record would serve as the basis for the names eventually inscribed on the Drummoyne War Memorial and indeed a copy would be placed within the memorial itself when it was unveiled in 1928.

[1098] The original number of those who volunteered was 657 but a supplementary list added one more.

A Drummoyne War Memorial Committee was established in 1923 and a campaign launched to raise the funds to construct the memorial, the cost of which was estimated at £1,500.[1099] A competition was conducted by the Public Monuments Advisory Board to secure a design for the Drummoyne war memorial which resulted in first place being awarded in 1923 to Mr. B. Toykander, care of Messrs. Robertson and Marks, 14 Martin Place, Sydney[1100] and a tender price of £1,200 eventually accepted for the building costs.[1101]

On Armistice Day in 1927, the foundation stone for the memorial was laid within the grounds of the Town Hall, Lyons Road by Major-General Sir Charles Rosenthal, the former commander of the 2nd Australian Division. General Rosenthal said on the occasion[1102]:

> It seems to me peculiarly fitting that this memorial should stand within civic grounds, as the men who served came from all the churches, and some from no church at all.

The memorial was officially unveiled on ANZAC Day 1928 with *The Sydney Morning Herald* publishing a report of the event[1103]:

[1099] Advertising (1923, July 7). *The Sydney Morning Herald* (NSW: 1842 - 1954), p. 7. Retrieved June 8, 2023, from http://nla.gov.au/nla.news-article16078809
[1100] 1923 Design competition award - DRUMMOYNE WAR MEMORIAL. (1923, September 11). *The Sydney Morning Herald* (NSW: 1842 - 1954), p. 8. Retrieved December 6, 2022, from http://nla.gov.au/nla.news-article16092633
[1101] HERE AND THERE (1927, September 14). *The Sun* (Sydney, NSW: 1910 - 1954), p. 11 (FINAL EXTRA). Retrieved June 8, 2023, from http://nla.gov.au/nla.news-article222424610
[1102] FOR ALL WHO SERVED (1927, November 14). *The Daily Telegraph* (Sydney, NSW: 1883 - 1930), p. 18. Retrieved June 4, 2023, from http://nla.gov.au/nla.news-article246397595. See also AT DRUMMOYNE. (1927, November 14). *The Sydney Morning Herald* (NSW: 1842 - 1954), p. 10. Retrieved June 4, 2023, from http://nla.gov.au/nla.news-article16418817 and ROSENTHAL ON PREPAREDNESS. (1927, November 14). *Lithgow Mercury* (NSW: 1898 - 1954), p. 1. Retrieved June 8, 2023, from http://nla.gov.au/nla.news-article219661173
[1103] 1928 Unveiling– WAR MEMORIAL. (1928, April 26). *The Sydney Morning Herald* (NSW: 1842 - 1954), p. 12. Retrieved December 6, 2022, from http://nla.gov.au/nla.news-article16459989

WAR MEMORIAL.

UNVEILED AT DRUMMOYNE.

The unveiling in the grounds of the Drummoyne Town Hall of the new, war memorial attracted one of the largest gatherings ever seen in the district. The Mayor, Ald. W. Udall, presided.

The unveiling ceremony was performed by Brigadier-General T. H. Dodds, District Base Commandant, who said it was most appropriate that the foundation-stone should have been laid last Armistice Day, and that the memorial should be ready for unveiling on Anzac Day. They were all proud of the heroic men whom they honoured that day, and of, those mothers, wives and sisters who cheerfully sacrificed themselves year in and year out during the war. (Hear, hear.) As time passed the personal element would disappear, and history alone would record the deeds of the men who came from the Southern Seas. It was the purpose of that memorial to perpetuate.

During the past few months, General Dodds said, he had spent many weeks in camps of annual training. At the time of the landing at Gallipoli 13 years ago, those trainees were boys of six, seven, and eight years of age, but from what he had seen of them in camp he felt sure they were worthy descendants of the Anzacs. They had the true Anzac spirit. The Mayor, on behalf of the council and municipality, accepted the memorial as a sacred trust, and said he could assure General Dodds that the council would never betray that trust. He emphasised the point that 656 men enlisted from Drummoyne, 95 of them being killed.

Sir Thomas Henley, M.L.A., placed in a receptacle in the memorial a steel shell containing the Drummoyne war record.

In proposing a vote of thanks to General Dodds, the Minister for Trade and Customs (Mr. Pratton) said it was a pleasure and privilege for each and all to be present to see the consummation of the effort of the public spirited citizens of Drummoyne for the recognition of their local heroes.

Commendation of the activities of the memorial committee was, expressed by the Minister for Justice (Mr. Lee). The ceremony concluded with the sounding of the 'Last Post' and the 'Reveille.'

The memorial, which was designed by Mr. A. J. Osborne, is constructed of trachyte, and designed on the circular principle supported by six columns surmounted on a base with three steps. In a column in the centre of the memorial is a mausoleum or chamber in which the records have been placed. Bronze tablets bearing the names of those killed have yet to be placed in position.

Such was the success of fundraising to meet the costs of constructing the memorial that there was a surplus of funds which the Drummoyne War Memorial Committee resolved to disburse to other charitable causes.[1104]

Notwithstanding the sentiments expressed by General Rosenthal at the laying of the foundation stone regarding the secular location of the memorial, its tabernacle style design evokes an evident sacral quality as to be almost a shrine. This was likely intentional – to provide those persons mourning loss the opportunity to make their own pilgrimage, in circumstances where they could not visit the grave or memorial to their loved one overseas. The memorial design also

---

[1104] DRUMMOYNE WAR MEMORIAL FUND. (1929, March 20). *The Sydney Morning Herald* (NSW: 1842 - 1954), p. 11. Retrieved June 8, 2023, from http://nla.gov.au/nla.news-article16539580

embodies cemetery iconography, representing a public symbol of mourning and remembrance for all the dead of the Drummoyne community. The fact that a copy of the Drummoyne War Service Record which lists the names of those who had served and died would be placed or 'entombed' in the memorial itself, reinforces its role as a public centre for mourning, providing a visible connection for each mourner with their dead.

Much like the memorials at Lone Pine, Fromelles, Villers-Bretonneux and the Menin Gate at Ypres, the Drummoyne War Memorial fulfilled a need in the immediate aftermath of the war for those mourning the loss of a loved one. After a century, the mourning of those loved ones may have abated. However, the fact that it is now more than one hundred years since the end of the First World War should not diminish our acknowledgement of the service of the men commemorated on the memorial, their suffering and their loss.

The Drummoyne War Memorial continues to serve as a poignant reminder of the men associated with Drummoyne who answered a call, volunteered to fight in a war far from Australia, and paid the ultimate sacrifice in that Great War.

Cover of the Drummoyne War Service Record which lists the names of those who volunteered to serve and those who died in service. A copy of the war service record would be placed within the Drummoyne War Memorial in 1928 (courtesy Canada Bay Heritage).

The Drummoyne War Memorial (author, 2024).

Drummoyne War Memorial watercolour by Ann-Marie Bateman

Acknowledgements

I would like to acknowledge the support of the Five Dock RSL Sub-branch and its Drummoyne chapter to the publication of this work, including its financial support. I also would like to thank the Local Studies section of Canada Bay Council Library in providing suggestions for inquiry and research, and for the contributions from the relatives of the Adam, Baron, Clegg and Englert families whom I have connected with through my research.

Heartfelt thanks must also go to Dr Juliette Lachemeier, managing editor at The Erudite Pen, for her patient guidance and thoughtful professionalism. Undaunted by the scale of the challenge, Juliette has made this dream a reality.

Finally, I must acknowledge the loving support of my family who have indulged me in my passion. I am grateful to my brother David for accompanying me while I visited graves and memorials in 2018. I maintain that we would have been the first Australians at the opening of the Sir John Monash Centre if you had not stopped to check your bag! To my wife, Ann-Marie, in addition to a creative contribution, her constant support and encouragement is a priceless gift for which I am eternally indebted.

ABOUT THE AUTHOR

Brendan Bateman was born in Sydney, Australia. A lifelong history enthusiast, Brendan studied both ancient and modern history at the University of Sydney. Acknowledging the truism that 'there is no future in history', he also pursued a law degree and has practised as a lawyer with a leading Australian law firm for over thirty years. However, his passion for history never waned.

In 2009, he scratched that itch which eventually led to him self-publishing *I am the First and the Last: The Fallen World War One ANZACs of St Mark's Drummoyne* in 2015. This work paved the way for his latest three volumes, *Drummoyne's Great War*, which chronicle the lives of the ninety-five men commemorated on the Drummoyne War Memorial who served and died in the First World War. Brendan is married with three children, all of whom have avoided both law and history, and shudder whenever he enters a bookshop.

Select Bibliography

Primary Sources

1914-1918 Prisoners of the First World War. ICRC historical archives. Retrieved from https://grandeguerre.icrc.org/en/

2nd Battalion Sherwood Foresters War Diary. (October 1914). The National Archives. Retrieved from http://discovery.nationalarchives.gov.uk

Adam, W. R., (n.d.). Personal documents and photographs courtesy of John Adam.

ANZAC Book. Inscribed by William Russell Barton Kirkwood. Port Macquarie Museum Object number B70. Retrieved from https://ehive.com/collections/3977/objects/927073/the-anzac-book

Australian Imperial Force unit war diaries, 1914-18 War. Unit and Commander's War Diaries (various dates and units). Retrieved from https://www.awm.gov.au/collection/C1338583

Australian Red Cross Wounded and Missing Enquiry Bureau (various). Retrieved from https://www.awm.gov.au/collection/C1414585

Baron, H., (n.d.). Personal correspondence courtesy of Harley Tarrant.

Baron H. J. (1921, August 23). *Drummoyne War Service Record of the men who enlisted for the defence of the Empire & civilization in the Great War, 1914-1918*. Local Studies Section of Canada Bay City Library. Retrieved from https://www.flickr.com/photos/canadabayconnections/albums/72157646904221674/

Births, deaths and marriages Victoria. Retrieved from https://www.bdm.vic.gov.au/

Clegg, T. A., (n.d.). Personal documents and photographs courtesy of Ian Rowles and extended Clegg family.

Commonwealth War Graves Commission. Grave registration records (various dates). Retrieved from https://www.cwgc.org

Council Meeting Minutes of Drummoyne Municipal Council. (30 January 1917). Canada Bay Council.

Englert, B., Personal correspondence and photographs courtesy of Greg Englert and Jason Smith.

General Register Office. Retrieved from https://www.gov.uk/general-register-office

Henderson, R. J., (various dates). Collection of photographs, certificates, documents, postcards and personal letters. Retrieved from https://www.awm.gov.au/collection/C92650

Louch, T. S. (1970). *Biography World War I*. Unpublished memoirs, Brigadier T S Louch MC QC.

National Archives. Retrieved from http://discovery.nationalarchives.gov.uk

National Archives of Australia. Retrieved from http://nla.gov.au

National Records of Scotland. Retrieved from https://www.nrscotland.gov.uk/contact-us/

Nominal roll of Australian Imperial Force who left Australia for service abroad. Retrieved from https://www.awm.gov.au/collection/C1380321

Nominal roll of Australian Naval and Military Expeditionary Force to New Guinea, 1914-18 War. Retrieved from https://www.awm.gov.au/collection/C1425491

Registry of births, deaths and marriages, New South Wales. Retrieved from https://www.nsw.gov.au/family-and-relationships/family-history-search/registry-records

Registry of births, deaths and marriages, Queensland. Retrieved from https://www.qld.gov.au/law/rbdm

Roll of Honour cards, 1914-1918 War, Army. Retrieved from https://www.awm.gov.au/advanced-search/people?roll=Roll%20of%20Honour

Sands General Index and Postal Directory (various dates). John Sands Ltd. Retrieved from https://archives.cityofsydney.nsw.gov.au/nodes/view/495003

Unit embarkation nominal rolls, 1914-18 War. (AWM8). Retrieved from https://www.awm.gov.au/collection/C1378317

Newspapers and gazettes

https://trove.nla.gov.au/help/categories/newspapers-and-gazettes-category

Books and articles

Bean, C. E. (1946). *Frontline Gallipoli: CEW Bean's diaries from the trenches*. Ed. Fewster, K. North Sydney. Allen & Unwin.

Bean, C. E. (2018). *The Western Front Diaries*. Ed. Burness, P. Sydney. NewSouth Publishing.

Colley-Priest, L. W. (1919). *The 8th Australian Field Ambulance on active service: a brief account of its history and services from 4th August 1915 to the 5th March 1919.*

Sydney. D. D. Ford. Retrieved December 15, 2024, from http://nla.gov.au/nla.obj-37956543

Haig, D. (2005). *War Diaries and Letters 1914-1918*. Ed. Sheffield, G and Bourne, J. London. Weidenfeld & Nicholson.

Henley, T. (1917). *After the war, Christendom and the coming peace: from an Australian point of view, the Christian Church's opportunity*. Retrieved December 15, 2024, from http://nla.gov.au/nla.obj-48793767

Secondary sources

Books

Andrews, E. M. (1993). *The ANZAC Illusion: Anglo-Australian relations during World War I*. Melbourne. Cambridge University Press.

Barton, P. (2014). *The Lost Legions of Fromelles*. London. Allen & Unwin.

Bean, C. E., (various). *Official History of Australia in the War 1914-1918*. Vols. I-VI. Sydney. Angus & Robertson.

Bean, C. E. (1968). *ANZAC to Amiens*. Fifth Edition. Sydney. Halstead Press.

Bennett, S. (2018). *The Nameless Names: Recovering the missing Anzacs*. Brunswick, Vic. Scribe.

Burness, P. (1996). *The Nek*. Kenthurst, N.S.W. Kangaroo Press.

Byrnes, P. (2019). *The Lost Boys*. South Melbourne. Affirm Press.

Carlyon, L. (2006). *The Great War*. Sydney. Pan McMillan.

Carlyon, L. (2007). *Gallipoli*. Sydney. Pan McMillan.

Coultart, R. (2014). *Charles Bean*. Sydney. Harper Collins.

Dolan, H (2010). *36 Days*. Sydney. Pan McMillan.

Gullett, H. S. (1936). *Official History of Australia in the War 1914-18*. Vol. VII. 3rd Edition. Sydney. Angus & Robertson.

Jordan, L. (2017). *Stealth Raiders: A few daring men in 1918*. North Sydney. Penguin Random House.

King, J. (2003). *Gallipoli Diaries*. Pymble, N.S.W. Kangaroo Press.

King, J. (2008). *The Western Front Diaries*. Pymble, N.S.W. Simon & Schuster Australia Pty Ltd.

Lindsay, P. (2007). *Fromelles*. Prahan, Vic. Hardie Grant Books.

McLachlan, M. (2007). *Walking with the ANZACS*. Sydney. Hachette Australia.

Perry, R. (2007). *Monash: The outsider who won a war*. Sydney. Random House Australia.

Rogers, J. (2009). *To Give and Not to Count the Cost: Riverview and the Great War*. Lane Cove, N.S.W. St Ignatius College Riverview.

Sackville-West, R. (2021). *The Searchers: The quest for the lost of the First World War.* London. Bloomsbury.
Sheffield, G. (2002). *Forgotten Victory.* London. Headline Book Publishing.
Warner, P. (1988). *Passchendaele.* London. Sidgwick & Jackson.
Warner, P. (1991). *Field Marshall Earl Haig.* London. Cassell & Co.
Winter, D (1979). *Death's Men: Soldiers of the Great War.* London. Penguin Books.
Ziino, B. (2007). *A Distant Grief: Australians, war graves and the Great War.* Crawley, W.A.. University of Western Australia Press.

Articles

McMullin, R. (2006, September 2). Disaster at Fromelles. *Wartime*, issue 36. Retrieved from https://www.awm.gov.au/wartime/36/article/

Great War 1914-1918. The National Archives. Retrieved 15 December, 2024 from https://www.nationalarchives.gov.uk/education/resources/great-war-1914-1918/

Jones, H., Hinz, U. (2014, October 8). Prisoners of War (Germany). *International Encyclopedia of the First World War.* Ed. Daniel U., Gatrell, P., Janz, O., Jones, H., Keene, J., Kramer, A. and Nasson, B. Freie Universität Berlin, Berlin 2014-10-08. DOI: 10.15463/ie1418.10387. Retrieved 2024, December 15 from https://encyclopedia.1914-1918-online.net/article/prisoners-of-war-germany/

Websites

AIF Project. Retrieved from https://aif.adfa.edu.au/
ANZAC Memorial, Sydney. Retrieved from https://www.anzacmemorial.nsw.gov.au
Beyond 1914 — The University of Sydney and the Great War. Retrieved from http://beyond1914.sydney.edu.au/
City of Canada Bay Heritage Society. Retrieved from https://canadabayheritage.asn.au
Digger History - Unofficial history of the Australian & New Zealand Armed Services. Retrieved from http://www.diggerhistory.info/
Derbyshire War Memorials. Retrieved from https://www.derbyshirewarmemorials.com
Discovering Anzacs. Retrieved from https://discoveringanzacs.naa.gov.au/browse/person/138695 (since decommissioned by the National Archives of Australia)
Europeana 1914-1918 – untold stories & official histories of WW1. Retrieved from http://www.europeana1914-1918.eu/

Forces War Records by Ancestry. Retrieved from https://www.forces-war-records.co.uk
Fromelles Association of Australia. Retrieved from https://fromelles.info
International Encyclopedia of the First World War. Retrieved from https://encyclopedia.1914-1918-online.net
Lemnos Gallipoli Commemorative Committee. Retrieved from https://lemnosgallipolicc.blogspot.com/2017/08/
Lijssenthoek Military Cemetery. Retrieved from http://www.lijssenthoek.be/en
Mayo Clinic. Retrieved from https://www.mayoclinic.org/diseases-conditions/
New Forest Heritage. Retrieved from http://www.newforestheritage.org/
New Zealand Ministry for Culture and Heritage. Retrieved from https://nzhistory.govt.nz/
NSW War Memorials Register. Retrieved from https://www.warmemorialsregister.nsw.gov.au/
NSW Railways Remembers. Retrieved from https://nswrailwaysremember.com.au/honour-boards.php#gallery1-44
RSL Virtual Memorial. Retrieved from https://rslvirtualwarmemorial.org.au/
Scottish Military Articles. Retrieved from http://www.scottishmilitaryarticles.org.uk
The Long, Long Trail - Researching soldiers of the British Army in the Great War of 1914-1918. Retrieved from http://www.longlongtrail.co.uk
The Sir John Monash Centre. Retrieved from http://sjmc.gov.au
WWI Australian Soldiers and Nurses Who Rest in the United Kingdom. Retrieved from https://ww1austburialsuk.weebly.com/

Index

A

Adelaide British Cemetery – 371, 372, 373
Allonville – 351, 352-354
Allonville Communal Cemetery – 355
Allsop, William G – 116
Amiens – 248, 251, 269, 294, 378, 396
Amiens, battle of – see August Offensive
Amman – 232, 240
ANZAC Cove – 190, 307 (evacuation)
ANZAC Day – 107, 195, 206, 210, 251, 310-311, 401, 414, 417
Armentieres – 20, 35, 52, 66, 134, 169
Armistice – 385, 390, 485
August Offensive, 1918 – 378, 385-390, 447
Australian Army Corps – 248 (establishment), 253, 385, 386, 389, 390, 458
   Australian Corps Motor Transport - 466
Australian Army Service Corps - 464
Australian Corps Motor Transport - 466
Australian Imperial Forces (AIF)
   Artillery – 115 (re-organisation), 116-117 (operational plans for Messines and Third Battle of Ypres), 155-156
   Australian Army Medical Corp (AAMC) – 133, 206 (organisation), 359
   Australian Flying Corps – 406, 434
   "Chinese" raids – 423, 424
   Doubling of battalions – 44, 107, 179, 192, 205, 309, 414
   Enlistment standards – 65, 258
   Manpower shortage – 248, 389
   Peaceful penetration – 251, 253, 385, 387
   Sickness – 101, 134, 135, 360, 467
   1st Division – 74, 77, 78, 96, 102, 108, 117, 125, 126, 210, 222, 224, 251, 362, 385, 387, 389, 390
      1st Brigade – 126, 222, 223
         1st Battalion – 124, 193, 221, 225 (losses)
         2nd Battalion – 221, 266
         3rd Battalion – 133, 222, 414
      1st Field Artillery Brigade – 147
      2nd Brigade – 224, 281
         6th Battalion – 107
         8th Battalion – 280
      3rd Brigade – 224
         9th Battalion – 267
   1st Pioneer Battalion – 87, 406
   2nd Division – 74, 77, 78, 79, 95, 96, 102, 107, 108, 125, 126, 147, 148, 222, 224, 250, 291, 362, 363, 367, 386, 388, 390, 465
      5th Brigade – 95, 96, 148, 182, 295, 359, 361, 362, 363, 388
         17th Battalion – 291
         18th Battalion – 94, 95, 96, 125, 146, 359
         19th Battalion – 295, 395
         20th Battalion – 96, 147, 220, 295, 359
      6th Brigade – 126, 390
         21st Battalion – 367
         23rd Battalion – 260, 367
         24th Battalion - 148
      7th Brigade – 156
         26th Battalion – 94, 367
      4th Field Artillery Brigade – 444
      2nd Machine Gun Battalion – 294
         5th Machine Gun Company – 291, 361, 362
         22nd Machine Gun Company – 365, 366, 367
      2nd Divisional Ammunition Sub-Park - 465
   3rd Division – 11-12 (Messines), 77, 80, 125, 126, 147, 161, 169, 182, 198, 249, 250, 367, 377, 386, 387, 390, 425, 445
      9th Brigade – 52, 67, 161, 169, 198, 199, 250, 377
         33rd Battalion – 20, 67, 178, 376
         34th Battalion – 19, 20, 35, 67, 169, 172
         35th Battalion – 67, 160, 163 (casualties), 172

36th Battalion – 65, 67, 168
10th Brigade – 52, 198
37th Battalion - 51
40th Battalion – 53
11th Brigade
41st Battalion – 53
44th Battalion – 53
9th Field Ambulance – 133
11th Field Ambulance - 135
8th Field Artillery Brigade – 115, 445
23rd Field Artillery Brigade - 115
4th Division – 11, 14, 44, 74, 76, 80, 109, 118, 125, 126, 224, 248, 249 (proposed breakup), 252-243 (Hamel), 351, 362, 363, 367, 385, 386, 389, 390, 397, 424
    4th Brigade – 42, 44, 181, 189, 249, 307, 330, 334, 350, 351, 362
        13th Battalion – 42, 178, 181, 259, 304, 334, 335, 350, 395
        14th Battalion – 42, 334, 335, 345, 350
        15th Battalion – 42, 189, 259, 315, 334, 350
        16th Battalion – 42, 315, 319, 334, 350
        12th Field Company Engineers -
    12th Brigade – 44, 53, 179, 182, 192, 198, 250
        45th Battalion – 44, 179, 415
        46th Battalion – 194, 197, 336, 350
        47th Battalion – 182, 192, 194, 198, 337
        48th Battalion – 181, 182, 193, 194, 198
        12th Machine Gun Company –
    13th Brigade – 44, 181, 250, 251, 424
        50th Battalion – 315
        51st Battalion – 315
        52nd Battalion - 225
    10th Field Artillery Brigade – 45, 155
    11th Field Artillery Brigade -
5th Division – 45, 74, 76, 102, 109, 118, 126, 205, 224, 331, 386, 389, 390, 415, 416, 452, 458
    8th Brigade – 205
    8th Field Ambulance – 100, 204, 452
    14th Brigade – 389, 408
        53rd Battalion – 193, 406, 424
        54th Battalion – 283, 417, 424
        55th Battalion – 126, 414
        56th Battalion – 109, 417, 418
        14th Field Ambulance – 101, 452
    15th Brigade – 4, 251, 389, 424
        58th Battalion – 106
        59th Battalion - 336
    15th Field Ambulance – 208, 409, 458
6th Division – 248
1st Cyclist Battalion – 146
Light Horse Brigades – 229
    2nd Light Horse Brigade – 239, 240
    1st ALH – 44
    2nd ALH – 233
    4th ALH – 231
    6th ALH – 239, 240
    8th ALH – 360
    8th ALH – 360
    9th ALH – 360
    12th ALH - 231
Military Police (Provost Corp) - 395
Australian and New Zealand Army (ANZAC) Corps
    I ANZAC Corp – 74, 77, 88, 117, 118, 137, 147, 223
    II ANZAC Corp – 11, 77, 125, 135, 169
ANZAC Mounted Division – 229, 230, 232, 233
Camel Brigade – 233, 240
New Zealand and Australian Division – 43, 189
Australian National Memorial, Villers-Bretonneux – 263, 373, 382
Australian Naval and Military Expeditionary Force (ANMEF) – 124

B

Balmain District Cricket Club – 303, 339
Balmain Public School - 258
Baron, Harley James – 488
Bates, Albert - **413**
Bavaria House (Ypres) – 136, 137, 138, 139
Beersheba – 231-232
Bellewaarde– 95, 118
Bethleem Farm – 53
Birdwood, Sir William – 147, 179, 248, 259, 323, 361
Boer War – 50, 55
Bois Grenier – 315, 475

Boyle, Edward Francis - 416
British Expeditionary Force (BEF)
  'bite and hold' tactic – 10, 67, 281
  Second Army – 11, 73, 74, 179
  Third Army – 248, 249, 387
  Fourth Army – 386, 387, 389
  Fifth Army – 73, 74, 248, 252, 465
    III Corps – 386
    XVth Corps - 417
    7th Division – 222
    6th Division – 474
      18th Brigade – 474, 475
        2nd Battalion Sherwood Foresters – 474
    8th Division – 351
    25th Division - 11
    3rd Dragoon Guards – 423
    4th Guards Brigade – 284
    7th London Regiment – 223
    16th Manchester Regiment – 260
British Red Cross – 486
Brown, George – **159**
Bullecourt – 46, 107, 125, 281, 326, 366
  First battle – 180, 194-195, 465
  Second battle – 102, 147, 210, 222, 454, 465

C

Camden Methodist Roll of Honour – 440
Canadian Corps – 80, 385, 386
  4th Canadian Division - 45
Carmichael's Thousand – 65, 168
Chauvel, Sir Henry George (Harry) – 229, 230, 231
Christian Brothers High School, Paddington – 376
Citizens Military Forces (CMF) –
  18th Infantry – 100
  22nd Infantry – 124
  25th (City of Sydney Scottish Rifles) Infantry - 394
  26th Infantry – 18
  29th Infantry – 146
  31st Infantry – 154
  60th (Brunswick-Carlton) Infantry - 114
  Victorian Mounted Rifles - 50
Cleveland Street Public School – 100, 452
Colley, Sidney Harold – **33**
Colley, Louis – 38
Colley-Priest, Langford W – 206, 208
Connell, Joseph Ignatius – **203**

Conscription – 101, 453
Coolahan, Arthur Francis – 290, 298
Coolahan, John Stephen – **289**
Crudine Public School – 266
Cummings, Edward James – 141

D

Deceased Soldiers Estate Act 1918 – 215, 273, 285
Directorate of Graves Registration and Enquiries – 487
Dodd, Downie - 416
Dodds, Thomas Henry – 490
Drummoyne Honour Memorial – 485, 486
Drummoyne Methodist Church Honour Roll - 66
Drummoyne Presbyterian Church – 30, 39
Drummoyne Progress Association – 483
Drummoyne Public School – 18, 19, 94, 100, 406, 452
Drummoyne School of Arts – 87
Drummoyne Soldiers, Sailors & Dependents Welfare Association – 484, 485, 488
Drummoyne Tennis Club – 140, 141
Drummoyne War Memorial Committee – 489, 491
Drummoyne War Service Record – 488, 489, 491, 492
Duntroon Officer Training College – 290

E

Edwards, John Donald – **405**
Edwards, William Robert – 406, 410
Englert, Bertie George – **343**
Englert, Eldred – 344, 345, 346
Etaples Military Cemetery – 338, 340, 341
Evans, Gainsford Wilton – **257**

F

Field of Mars Cemetery, Ryde – 287, 426
Fitzgerald, Jack Hammond – **113**
Fitzgerald, Robert Edwin – 114, 120
Flers – 46, 208, 221, 363, 417, 418
Foch, Ferdinand – 250, 385, 387, 388, 389
Fort Street Public School – 132, 142, 303
French army
  First Army – 73, 386

Mutinies - 9
Fromelles – 45, 207, 415

G

Gallipoli
  August offensive – 191, 360
  Baby 700 – 43
  Beauchop's Hill – 191, 360
  Durrant's Post – 307
  Hill 971 – 191
  Monash Valley – 43, 190
  Pope's Hill – 43, 190
  Quinn's Post – 43, 190
  Reserve Gully – 360
  Russell's Top – 360, 361
Gaza – 230, 232
Gear, George Campbell – **237**
Gladstone Park Public School, Balmain – 146
Godley, Sir Alexander – 80, 169, 329
Gough, Sir Hubert – 73
Grave concentration – 487
Graves Registration Commission – 486
Graves Services Unit (GSU) (also Graves Registration Units) – 486, 487

H

Haig, Sir Douglas – 9, 14 (Messines), 74, 79, 95, 162, 179, 248, 249, 250, 252, 253, 385, 387, 388, 389, 417, 419
Hamel (battle) – 252, 367, 378, 386, 397
Hangard Wood – 295
Harefield (St Mary) Churchyard, Middlesex – 461
Harrison, Stephen John – **123**
Harrison, Richard Seth – 124, 125
Harwood, John Michael – 178
Harwood, Joseph Marcus – **177**
Hawley, Michael - 416
Hazebrouck – 250, 251, 283, 475
Heath Cemetery, Harbonnieres – 401, 402
Hebuterne – 250, 251, 261, 334, 396
Heilly Station Cemetery – 425, 426
Henderson, Leonard – 303, 305, 307, 309, 325, 337
Henderson, Robert James – **301**, 488
Henley, Harold Leslie – 304, 307, 308, 317, 321
Henley, Sir Thomas – 491
Herbecourt Communal Cemetery Extension – 410, 411
Hill 60 (Ypres) – 225
Hindenburg Line – 108, 366, 379, 389, 390, 418, 447

German withdrawal – 95, 107, 210, 221, 281, 418
  Fortified villages – 107, 221
HMAT A17 *Afric* – 106
HMAT A8 *Argyllshire* – 133, 464
HMAT A11 *Ascanius* – 205
HMAT A70 *Ballarat* – 178, 347, 348-349 (sinking)
HMAT A43 *Barunga* – (sinking) 142, 263, 270, 285
HMAT A24 *Benalla* – 65, 146, 155
HMAT A72 *Beltana* – 169, 259, 395
HMAT A35 *Berrima* – 359
HMAT A30 *Borda* – 406
HMAT A73 *Commonwealth* – 239
HMAT A20 *Hororata* – 19, 35
HMAT A74 *Marathon* – 377, 431
HMAT A7 *Medic* – 115
HMAT A28 *Militiades* – 444
HMAT A71 *Nestor* – 100, 452
HMAT A67 *Orsova* – 220
HMAT A16 *Port Sydney* – 160
HMAT A9 *Shropshire* – 51, 304
HMAT A49 *Seang Choon* – 189
HMAT A38 *Ulysses* – 43
HMAT A69 *Warilda* – 414
HMAT A18 *Wiltshire* – 87, 94
Holmes, Sir William – 14
Hooge – 118, 120
Hooge Crater Cemetery, Zillebeke – 98, 102, 461
Hooge Tunnel – 88
Hughes, Sir William Morris – 389
Huts Cemetery, the - 120

I

Imperial War Graves Commission (IWGC) – 128, 487
Inverell District Great War Honour Roll – 38
Inverell Methodist Church Honour Roll – 38
Inverell War Memorial and Cenotaph – 38
Invincible Motor Co., Woolwich - 464

J

Jacka, Albert – 350
Jarvis, Russell Thompson Sydney -**131**
Jericho – 232, 239
Jerusalem – 232, 239
Jerusalem War Cemetery – 243, 246
Joffre, Joseph – 362
Jordan, Frederick – **473**
Jordan Valley - 232

K

Kandahar Farm Cemetery - 70
Kilgour, James – 86-87
Kilgour, John – **85**
Kirkwood, William Russell Barton – 304
Kirkwood, Phillip Barton – 304
Kirkwood, Noel Edmund – 304
Kirkwood, John Barton – 304
Kogarah Public School – 464

L

Lagnicourt – 107
Lawrence, T E – 232
Lemnos – 43, 141, 189, 191, 305, 359, 361
Lewis gun – 107, 108, 109, 284, 361, 379, 397, 398
Lijssenthoek Military Cemetery – 90, 217
Lone Pine Cemetery and Memorial – 492
Long Plain Soldier's Memorial Hall – 39
Ludendorff, Erich – 248, 386-387, 389
Lyndhurst Bombing School – 20

M

McQuat, Hugh – **219**
Maguire, Frederick A – 133, 134, 135, 138
Mediterranean Expeditionary Force (MEF) – 43
    60th Infantry Division – 232
    Desert Mounted Corps - 230
Menin Gate Memorial, Ypres - 492
Messines – 9-14, 21 (attack on Messines Ridge), 47, 52, 67, 116-117, 125, 135, 161-162, 170, 181, 196-197, 250, 327, 328, 377
Miller, Frederick – **145**
Miller, Emily – 147, 149, 150
Mining – 10-11, 13
Missing, search for – 487-488
Monash, Sir John – 11-12, 386, 388, 390
    4th Brigade – 42, 189, 350
    3rd Division – 169
    Australian Army Corps - 252, 253
Mont St Quentin – 379, 389, 447
Montbrehain – 390, 447, 448
Morchies – 107
Moree ANZAC Centenary Memorial – 382
Moree Superior Public School – 376, 382 (Honour Roll)
Morshead, Leslie – 377, 378
Mortimore, Harold, Yabbicom – **463**
Mouquet Farm – 193, 315-317, 319
Murray, Sir Archibald – 229, 230
Murray, Harry – 316, 317, 319-320, 327, 330

N

Namps-au-Val British Cemetery – 276
New Zealand and Australian Division – see Australian and New Zealand Army Corps (ANZAC)
New Zealand Expeditionary Forces
    Auckland Mounted Rifles – 361
    New Zealand Mounted Brigade – 233, 240
    New Zealand Rifle Brigade – 361
    New Zealand Division – 11, 13, 77, 80, 126
    Otago Battalion - 68
NSW Teachers Honour Roll – 30
Nieppe-Bois (Rue-Du-Bois) British Cemetery, Vieux-Berquin – 287
Noreuil – 46, 180, 418
Nottingham Road Cemetery, Derby, Derbyshire – 481, 482

O

Oban War Memorial, Scotland – 90
Outtersteene Communal Cemetery Extension, Bailleul – 226
Oxley School, Wangaratta - 50

P

Palestine – 229-233
Passchendaele – see Ypres, Third Battle
Pearce, Senator George Foster – 149
Percival, Harold Kingsley – **429**
Percival, Cecil – 431
Perham Downs – 326
Peronne – 379, 389, 408, 425
Pierpoint, Claude Edward – **279**
Ploegsteert – 13, 21, 24, 52, 155, 445
Plumer, Sir Herbert – 9, 73, 179, 259
Poison gas – 73n, 74, 116, 225, 332, 456
Potiphar, Alfred William – **63**
Pozieres – 180, 193, 362-363
Price, Thomas Charles – **93**
Prichard, Arvan James – **357**
Princes Hill State School, North Carlton – 114
Prisoners of war – 296, 477-480

Q

Querrieu British Cemetery - 120

R

Railway Dugouts Burisal Ground (Transport Farm), Zillebeke – 151
Rawlinson, Sir Henry – 386
Red Cross Wounded and Missing Enquiry Department – 487
Richthofen, Manfred von - 424
RMS *Osterley* – 266
Roisel Communal Cemetery Extension, Perone – 448
Rosenthal, Sir Charles – 489, 491
Perone – 389, 408, 425, 458, 459
Romani – 229, 230
Royal Air Force – 434
Rozelle Public School – 178
Ruffley, William – **187**
Russian Revolution – 9, 247
Ryng, George Columbus - **41**

S

St Bede's Anglican Church, Drummoyne – 50
St Benedict's Christian Brothers – 204
St Johns Church of England, Balmain – 152
St Mark's Catholic Church, Drummoyne – 394, 402
St Mary's High School – 394
St Quentin – 389
Ste Marie Cemetery, Le Harve – 470, 472
Sacred Heart School, Darlinghurst – 394
Selig, Oscar Moritz – 149
Shannon, Ernest – **17**
Silvertown Munitions Factory explosion – 324
Simpson, Bert Arthur – **167**
Sinclair Public School and Long Plain First World War Honour Roll – 38
Sleepyhillock Cemetery, Montrose – 440
Smith, Robert Alexander – **265**
Somme offensive – 362, 417
Spanish Influenza – 446, 479-480
Spring, William - 65
Spring Offensive 1918 (German) – 247-253, 269, 283, 334, 367, 378, 407, 445, 455
SS Port Napier – 280
SS Port Nicholson – 124, 290
Strand Military Cemetery, Ploegsteert – 30
Sydney Boys High – 431
Sydney Grammar School – 154, 303
Sydney Teachers Training College – 18, 431

Sydney Technical College – 464

T

Tanks – 116, 194, 252, 385, 386, 387, 390, 408
Technical High School, Ultimo – 431
The Huts Cemetery – 120
Thompson, Clive Townsend – **153**
Thornton, Charles Leslie – **99**, 452, 454
Thornton, Mervyn Willoughby – **451**
Townsville 9th Field Ambulance Honour Roll – 142
Tyne Cot Cemetery – 81-82, 128, 174, 185

U

Underage enlistment – 406
University of Sydney – 18, 25 and 30 (book of remembrance), 29, 132, 431

V

V.C. Corner Cemetery and Memorial, Fromelles – 492
Valenciennes Communal Cemetery – 299, 300
Vaux Communal Cemetery – 379
Venereal disease – 46, 192, 194, 197
Villers-Bretonneux – 250, 251, 294, 334, 335, 336, 351, 367, 378, 385, 386, 407, 423, 424, 446, 455, 456-457
Villers-Bretonneux Military Cemetery – 382
Vincent, Arthur James – **49**
Vincent, George – 51

W

Wagga Wagga High School – 18, 28
Walker, John – 443
Wall, John Douglass - 416
Wallabies recruitment march – 34
Ware, Sir Fabian – 486, 487
West Marrickville Public School – 168
Westhoek – 81, 89, 95, 126, 147, 148, 181, 182, 212, 241, 267, 291, 421
White, Sir Cyril Brudenell – 248
Whitney, George – 132, 140
Wilder, Herbert John – **105**
Williamson, Walter Burt - 416
Wills, John Michael Joseph – **393**
Wilson, Colin Godfrey – **375**
Wilson, William Robert – 376, 381

Y

Ypres – 9, 136, 211, 250, 260

Third Battle of Ypres – 9, 73-82, 108, 182, 260, 267, 281, 291, 407, 421, 455
   Broodseinde Ridge – 76-78, 126, 137, 156, 171, 224, 332, 378
   Menin Road Ridge – 74-75, 88, 95, 102, 108, 117, 125, 147, 156, 198, 223, 281
   Passchendaele Ridge – 79-80, 162, 171-172, 181, 198, 378, 455
   Polygon Wood – 76, 109, 110, 111, 118, 126, 212, 224, 331, 407, 421
Ypres (Menin Gate) Memorial – 37, 48, 61, 111, 165, 200, 492
Ypres Reservoir Cemetery – 142
Ypres Town Cemetery Extension - 157

Z
Zeppelins – 321, 324
Zillebeke – 88, 407, 465
Zonnebeke – 109, 148, 162, 198, 260, 267, 293

Enjoyed the book? You can follow Brendan Bateman at:

Facebook: Brendan Bateman - Author
https://www.facebook.com/profile.php?id=61566235882471

Email: Ww1drummoyne@gmail.com

Instagram: @WW1Drummoyne

If you liked the book, please leave a review on Amazon, Goodreads or with the author directly. Reviews are invaluable in supporting an author's hard work and are greatly appreciated.

www.ingramcontent.com/pod-product-compliance
Lightning Source LLC
Chambersburg PA
CBHW040748020526
44118CB00041B/2729